Hispanics / Latinos in the United States

Hispanics / Latinos in the United States

Ethnicity, Race, and Rights

Edited by
Jorge J. E. Gracia
& Pablo De Greiff

Routledge
A Member of the Taylor & Francis Group
New York and London

Published in 2000 by
Routledge
29 West 35th Street
New York, NY 10001

Published in Great Britain by
Routledge
11 New Fetter Lane
London EC4P 4EE

A Member of the Taylor & Francis Group

Printed in the United States of America on acid-free paper.
Design: Jack Donner

Library of Congress Cataloging-in-Publication Data

Hispanics / Latinos in the United States : ethnicity, race, and rights / edited by Jorge J. E. Gracia and Pablo De Greiff.

p. cm.

Includes bibliographical references (p.) and indexes.

ISBN 0–415–92619–X (acid-free paper) — ISBN 0–415–92620–3 (pbk. : acid-free paper)

1. Hispanic Americans—Ethnic identity. 2. Hispanic Americans—Race identity. 3. Hispanic Americans—Civil rights. 4. United States—Ethnic relations. 5. United States—Race relations. I. Gracia, Jorge J. E. II. De Greiff, Pablo.

E184.S75 H627 2000

305.8'68073—dc21 99–048696

Contents

Hispanic/Latino Ethnicity, Race, and Rights 1
An Introduction

PART 1: HISPANIC/LATINO IDENTITY, ETHNICITY, AND RACE

1. Is Latina/o Identity a Racial Identity? 23
Linda Martín Alcoff

2. The Making of New Peoples 45
Hispanizing Race
Eduardo Mendieta

3. Negotiating Latina Identities 61
Ofelia Schutte

4. Cultural Particularity versus Universal Humanity 77
The Value of Being *Asimilao*
Paula M. L. Moya

5. The Larger Picture 99
Hispanics / Latinos (and Latino Studies) in the Colonial Horizon of Modernity
Walter D. Mignolo

6. "It Must Be a Fake!" 125
Racial Ideologies, Identities, and the Question of Rights
Suzanne Oboler

PART 2: HISPANIC/LATINO IDENTITY, POLITICS, AND RIGHTS

7. Structure, Difference, and Hispanic / Latino Claims of Justice 147
Iris Marion Young

8. Universalism, Particularism, and Group Rights 167
The Case of Hispanics
Leonardo Zaibert and Elizabeth Millán-Zaibert

9. Accommodation Rights for Hispanics in the United States 181
Thomas W. Pogge

10. Affirmative Action for Hispanics? Yes and No 201
Jorge J. E. Gracia

11. Latino Identity and Affirmative Action 223
J. Angelo Corlett

12. Deliberation and Hispanic Representation 235
Pablo De Greiff

Bibliography 253

Contributors 269

Subject Index 273

Name Index 277

Hispanic/Latino Ethnicity, Race, and Rights

An Introduction

The purpose of this volume is to address some fundamental issues that concern Hispanics/Latinos in American society today. The number of Hispanics/Latinos is increasing at a fast pace. According to recent figures, we already constitute the largest minority group in the country. By the year 2050, it is expected that our numbers will be greater than those of all other minority groups combined. This means that our presence and impact on American society cannot be ignored. Our values, views, and rights must be taken into account by the American population at large. But Hispanics/Latinos do not appear to be homogeneous. We differ in terms of origin, race, language, religion, political affiliation, customs, social altitudes, physical appearance, economic status, education, class, and taste, among other things. This raises questions about both our identity and our rights. Do we really constitute a group? Do we have rights as a group or just as individuals?

The essays collected in this volume represent the efforts of a varied and interdisciplinary group of scholars to come to grips with some of these pressing issues. Although the government generally defines Hispanics/Latinos in ethnic terms, the category is often used racially. One of the central unifying threads in this volume, then, is the relationship between Hispanic/Latino identity, on the one hand, and ethnicity and race, on the other.

The questions arising from this first concern have major political implications not just for Hispanics/Latinos but also for all citizens. Hence, the second major unifying thread in the collection is the relationship between different concepts of the Hispanic/Latino identity and other social and political issues, especially those concerning rights.

Needless to say, there is no hard-and-fast separation between the themes explored by the essays in the two parts of the collection. Indeed, these essays share a significant area of overlap, namely, the discussion of identity. But they are also related in many other ways, for they are the fruit not only of common concerns, but of intense discussion. Of course, any principle of organization emphasizes some issues and neglects others. At least two other principles of organization could have been easily used: the relevance of history for the understanding of the condition of Hispanics/Latinos in the United States, and the importance of relational accounts of identity in conceptualizing who we are.

After providing a sketch of the contents of the two parts of this volume, this introduction will discuss briefly some of the underlying tensions between the positions defended by these authors, and will attempt to locate their discussions in the broader context of contemporary social and political philosophy.

Part 1: Hispanic / Latino Identity, Ethnicity, and Race

One of the unifying threads of this collection is the question of the status of the Hispanic/Latino category. Is it an ethnic category, a racial category, neither, or both? In the first part of this volume six papers make the question of the relationships between Hispanic/Latino identity, ethnicity, and race their central concern.

In the opening essay of Part I, Linda Alcoff considers three alternative ways of dealing with the question of identity in relationship to the racial categories dominant in the United States. One possibility is to assimilate to the individualistic ideology pervasive in some circles in the United States and to reject the salience of group identities. This strategy, according to Alcoff, is the one that dominant groups in particular prefer, alleging that the "obsession" with group identity is a result of the benefit-seeking generated by welfare programs. But this, for Alcoff, gets the history backward. She points out that in emphasizing group identity, ethnic and racial groups are merely giving value to categories that were originally imposed on them, and trying to have a hand in the construction of their own identities. Alcoff also provides an illuminating explanation of the sensitivity of dominant groups to the affirmation of group identity on the part of non-Europeans: whereas some European ethnic groups can claim redress for discrimination, the claim raised by non-Europeans in the United States is often much more radical, targeting the country's legitimizing narratives. After all, these identities remind dominant groups of acts of brutalizing slavery, of the violent appropriation of land, and of the forced extinction of whole cultures and traditional ways of life.

Another strategy for conceptualizing the Hispanic/Latino identity consists of rejecting racialized designations and insisting that "Hispanic/Latino" is an ethnic label. This attractive strategy can be supported by attending to both metaphysical and political considerations. As to the former, it appears that "Hispanic/Latino" is a category that encompasses not just many nationalities, but many races as well. An ethnic understanding of the category seems to capture what ties the members of the group together, namely, some combination of common language, a shared history, a common ancestry, or different historical and cultural factors. Politically, insisting on an ethnic understanding of the "Hispanic/Latino" category obeys the same rationale that motivates the corresponding move in favor of the ethnic label "African American" in the case of blacks. This move is defended by arguing that it constitutes a rejection of essentialistic racialization in favor of the use of a label that, in being connected to culture, confers agency on those who identify themselves in this manner. Both the denial of essentialistic racialization and the affirmation of agency are said to offer the possibility of reducing racism.

The problem with this alternative, according to Alcoff, is that the category "Hispanic/Latino" in fact often functions as a racial category: "People may talk culture, but they continue to think race." So realism would seem to dictate at least considering a third alternative, namely, accepting that Hispanics/Latinos have become a racialized population. Alcoff's point is not that we should give in to essentialistic racialization, but rather that we should pin our hopes on the possibility of transforming the meaning of the category "race." In fact, other ethnic groups who were formerly racialized have succeeded in transforming race designators into cultural ones. Prominent among these groups are Italians, Irish, and Jews. Although surely there are important differences between these groups and Hispanics/Latinos, Alcoff insists that understanding our category in terms of ethnorace would lead to an appropriately complex analysis of our identity. This analysis would heed the normative possibility of transforming race from an insulting category to a cultural one, and at the same time capture the facticity of the racialization of Hispanics/Latinos by others.

Eduardo Mendieta agrees with Alcoff in thinking that, as a matter of fact, the term *Hispanic* has been racialized in the United States. But, contrary to Alcoff, who is willing to make partial concessions to the category of race in her defense of ethnorace, Mendieta thinks that Hispanics/Latinos should resist this racialization. Four reasons justify, in his mind, such resistance. First, the history of the category is a disastrous one, which we would do well to overcome. Second, race has polarized political discourse in this country, creating the impression that there are (just) two camps to any debate, black and white, blinding the country to other colors. Third, it would be odd for Hispanics to accept their racialization just when race is being questioned as a category by other groups, such as African Americans. And, finally, accepting the racialization of Hispanics involves imposing a relationship with race that is foreign to our self-identity, for racial categories are construed differently in the cultures of origin of most Hispanics in the United States.

Concentrating on this last reason for rejecting the racialization of Hispanics, Mendieta provides a challenging sketch of the diverging histories of racial categorization in the United States and in Latin America. Without denying the historical significance of race in Latin America, Mendieta counts himself among those who think that in that context class, not race, has traditionally been the central social category. He traces the ambiguities of racial categorization in Latin America to the confusion that Spaniards experienced in facing the new peoples of the continent armed only with the two categories of "infidel" and "traitor," with which Muslims and Jews, respectively, were conceptualized around 1492. Given that Amerindians did not fit either category, they were initially thought of as lost souls in need of salvation. This set off a pattern of social classification that differed markedly from the way in which racial categories were used in Anglo-Saxon America, where, for reasons that Mendieta briefly reviews, race was from the beginning not only an administrative category, but a mark of (diminished) moral status.

The point of Mendieta's historical sketch is to illustrate the relevance of historical considerations not only for policy making, but even for philosophical reflection. The history of racial categories constitutes an important part of their meaning, and both enables and constrains their possible uses. The differences in the experience with racial categories in the United States and in Latin America leads Mendieta to argue that, rather than accepting the racialization of Hispanics/Latinos, what we should defend is the Hispanizing of race in the United States. This would involve increased awareness not only of the historicity of race, but also of the ways in which the dialectical relationship between recognition and identity opens up the possibility that increased recognition of Hispanics/Latinos—who as a people do not fit neatly into the existing racial categories—will lead to a significant change in the identity of all citizens of the United States.

Ofelia Schutte shares Mendieta's interest in the way in which identities have to be constructed by means of categories and within institutions that are not entirely under our control. In a globalized economy, which functions according to a homogenizing imperative, even institutions (such as affirmative action) meant to foster and promote the identity of disfavored groups become double-edged swords. While these institutions might improve the prospects of a number of minorities, at the same time they obey a logic of assimilation that rewards integration into the mainstream over solidarity with particular identities. The same general lack of control obtains with the general categories with which we are supposed to construct a sense of who we are. "Latino," "Cuban-American," "Puerto Rican," "Colombian," and so on are designations that locate us within a social structure in positions that have been to some extent prearranged by others.

Schutte's point, however, is not merely to remind us of the many ways in which we cannot control how we are identified by others, but rather, after recognizing the relevant constraints, to insist—with Mendieta and Moya—upon the importance of the possibilities that remain. Taking a cue from Gloria Anzaldúa's work, and engaging in a revealing autobiographical reflection, she exemplifies the way in which individuals can use preexisting categories in order to articulate a new sense of identity. The crucial move in this articulation of identity is the idea that cultures are understood or adopted not as unified wholes but piecemeal. This complex process of identification is neither wholly voluntary nor wholly involuntary, but rather a process in which both individuals, through their personal choices, and groups, through socially constructed general categories, play a role. Its end result is, therefore, a hybrid identity.

Latinos, who as a rule have at their disposal various identity markers, are, according to Schutte, in a good position to negotiate and integrate novel identities. In her own case, she recounts how "*Latina*" is a signifier of the demand for inclusion, while "*cubana*" is a signifier of the demand for freedom. To identify herself as a "Latina" allows Schutte to address the difficulties that a Cuban American encounters in her efforts to have normal relations with the island. The category enables Schutte to explore the broader set of links with Hispanic culture that she has as a Latina. On the other hand, to identify herself as Cuban enables Schutte not merely to raise the general claim to inclusion that all Latinos, as minorities, raise in the United States, but also to particularize this claim as the claim raised by one who is a member of a freedom-loving people. The general point, then, is that although any designation we might use is one that marks us in specific ways, Latinos are in a position to demonstrate how a plurality of identity categories increases the possibility of recovering some control in the process of constructing our identity.

In her essay, Paula Moya returns to one of the alternative ways of responding to Hispanic difference briefly mentioned by Linda Alcoff, namely, assimilation. Moya focuses specifically on the arguments in favor of assimilation proposed by contemporary neoconservative minority-identity critics such as Stephen Carter, Linda Chávez, Richard Rodríguez, or Shelby Steele. These critics coincide in their insistence on the importance of emphasizing commonalities rather than differences among persons and, particularly, among groups. Moya's aim is threefold: first, to disclose the unacknowledged particularity that lurks behind what is offered as universal by the neoconservative critics; second, to dispute the way in which they set collective identity in opposition to individual identity; and third, to offer an alternative to assimilation.

According to Moya, the ideal of universality espoused by defenders of assimilation is in reality the ideal of the white middle-class European American. Defenders of assimilation speak about integrating minorities into a mainstream that, although white, affluent, and largely male-dominated, is not perceived as a racialized, class-structured, gendered, concrete, and particular cultural location. Moya is willing to acknowledge circumstances in which a shared culture might be indispensable for the achievement of certain aims—just as a shared language is necessary for a certain type of communication. But she argues that commonalities need not be organized around what tries to pass as deracinated, ungendered, unsexed, and postcultural. Rather, the central commonality can be taken to be a universal capacity to reason and to evaluate contextually.

In response to the assimilationists' tendency to oppose collective and individual identity, Moya offers a relational account of identity, reminding us that just as there is no collectivity that is not made out of individuals, there can be no sense of identity in isolation from cultural collectivities. Indeed, for Moya, it is because individuals belong to (a plurality of) groups that they can construct unique personal identities. It is by virtue of the differential expression of group attachments that we distinguish ourselves from others. Other authors in this volume, including Schutte, Young, and Gracia, also give relational accounts of group identity.

Finally, Moya offers as an alternative to assimilation—which in her case means the forced, unidirectional, cultural change to a white middle-class norm—a process of multidirectional cross-cultural acculturation through which all of us could become "*asimilaos.*" Here Moya is concerned, as are all the other authors in this part of the collection, with exploring the possibilities of cultural transformation inherent in processes of collective identity formation. The core of Moya's idea is a defense of multiculturalism that is interested in diversity not out of sentimentalism, but rather because it perceives diversity as an epistemic resource. Undergirding this defense is a view of cultures as both repositories of and laboratories for behavioral and moral knowledge. From this perspective, the sort of assimilation defended by neoconservative critics appears as a strategy for impoverishment, while multiculturalism appears as a form of epistemic cooperation.

In addition to providing a challenge to the disciplinary boundary that separates Latino studies from Latin American studies (and which subordinates the former to the latter), Walter Mignolo's essay provides a broad historical account of the racial-ethnic character of the label "Hispanic." His paper constitutes another explicit defense of the relevance of history to discussions about the situation of Hispanics/Latinos. Mignolo uses a modified version of Immanuel Wallerstein's world-system analysis as the point of departure for his account of the meaning of Hispanicity. Central to this analysis is the concept of the coloniality of power, which in turn is constructed around two axes: the claim that the modern/colonial world system has an ethnoracial foundation, and the claim that modernity/colonialism rests upon and expresses the subalternation of knowledges. That is, although modernity made possible the study of other (non-European) belief systems, it always had difficulties in taking these as alternative, sustainable knowledge systems as well, ranking them by order of deficiency when compared to the "neutral" standard of European science.

For Mignolo, 1898 is the crucial date for the constitution of the place of Hispanics in a subordinate position that we still occupy today. In the Spanish-American War, Spain not only lost a war, but also finally surrendered a place in the classification of races that it had been losing since its power had crested in the sixteenth century and which had been in serious danger since the Napoleonic invasion. From then on, a distinction between Anglo-Saxon white and Spanish-Christian white became significant. Cuba and Puerto Rico, then, and by extension the rest of Latin America, were twice demoted—first because of their connection with Spain and second, because of their *mestizaje* with Amerindians and African Americans.

The year 1898 is also crucial for Mignolo with respect to the second axis of the coloniality of power. By then, Spanish had already lost most of the power it had had as a language of scholarship, as had happened before to Latin, Italian, and Portuguese, which together with Spanish constituted the four languages of the Renaissance. By 1898 these languages had been replaced by English, French, and German. The change was not merely linguistic, but disciplinary as well: in the study of culture, the primacy of the humanities was replaced by the primacy of the social sciences.

Knowledge was subalternated along a division of labor that stood in place until the end of the cold war. Sociology and economy were the disciplines whose domain of study was the First World; the Second World was mainly the domain attributed to political science; and the Third World became mainly the domain of anthropology. Even within the last domain, subalternation took place, for knowledge produced in Latin America was subordinated to that produced by American and European scholars.

The crucial question for Mignolo is how to come to grips with the coloniality of power in whatever domain it manifests itself. In the personal life of Hispanics, there are, according to Mignolo, three alternatives: assimilation, with its consequent losses; resistance, with its attending marginality; and "critical assimilation." Mignolo compares the last of these with the attitude of Moya's *asimilaos*, an attitude that requires acute awareness both of similarities and of difference, and which manifests itself "in the right to be different because we are all equal." In the academic sphere, the alternatives seem also to be three: first, the continuation of the collaboration between Latin American studies, or more generally area studies, and the ethnoracial and subalternating perspective of modernity/colonialism; second, a looser, bottom-up, more essayistic caricature of Latino studies unfairly offered by its critics; and third, a position that becomes aware of the colonial difference and tries to think about the epistemic limits of Latin American studies from the perspective of Latino studies. Mignolo favors the third alternative, which he translates into a relentless claim for justice for subaltern groups, a claim stemming from incessant engagement with those groups.

The last paper in Part I of this collection sets the stage for the discussions in Part II. Like the other authors in the first part of the volume, Suzanne Oboler makes the racialization of Hispanics and other minorities the focus of her work. From Oboler's standpoint, discussions about the insignificance of race are premature given the persistence of racism, on the one hand, and the lack of clear alternatives to programs that seek to promote the interests of minorities, on the other. For Oboler, what is urgently needed is an understanding of the context in which discussions about race are taking place. This is a context that makes the achievement of a society of equals extremely unlikely.

To say that it is premature to talk about the decreasing significance of race is not to say that racist structures have not changed. According to Oboler, a new ideology of race is emerging, one that replaces the old biological racism with a social racism that creates a rigid racialized hierarchy of ethnic groups. This new ideology, which resembles Latin American racism in the way in which it silently assigns a place to everyone, differs from its Latin American counterparts not only in being state-sanctioned, but also in having significant distributive consequences. The United States, after all, not only classifies its people according to the five ethnic labels adopted by the Office of Budget and Management in 1977—white, Asian or Pacific Islander, black, American Indian or Alaskan Native, and Hispanic—but also uses these categories for policy-making purposes.

Some of the various ways in which the racialization of the population that these categories encourage thwarts the project of creating a society of equals are revealed by examining the consequences of using the label "Hispanic." For Oboler, the label homogenizes people with different ethnic, racial, historical, religious, and linguistic backgrounds. While the label allows us to keep track of the social and economic indicators of the members of the group, the classification has not helped to improve the situation of Hispanics in any significant way. The pervasive use of ethnic labels has also created the sort of social fractures that redistribute not only resources but responsibilities. Today, the burdens and the responsibilities associated with the protection of the human and citizenship rights of individuals lies primarily with the particular ethnic group to which an individual ostensibly belongs. Finally, according to Oboler, it is important to keep in mind that some of the ways in which ethnic labeling becomes an obstacle to equality are associated with processes of globalization. These processes, insofar as economic integration has thus far outstripped political integration, have led to the demise of the political arena: many areas of decision making that previously were open to political deliberation are now surrendered to the logic of the market. Frequently, Oboler points out, this has led to the dedemocratization of different spheres of activity, to increased economic inequality, to social polarization, and to a worsening inability on the part of states to guarantee the rights of their own population. For Oboler, as for the other authors who have contributed to Part I of this collection, discussions about rights that are not informed about the manifold ways in which racism permeates even discussions about ethnic identity are at best disingenuous.

Part 2: Hispanic / Latino Identity, Politics, and Rights

Whereas most of the authors in the second part of this volume continue the discussion about the nature of Hispanic/Latino identity, their main focus is not so much its significance or history, but rather the conceptual alternatives that could be deployed in order to understand that identity and the social institutions to which it is related. This part begins with an illuminating argument by Iris Young about the structural aspects of disadvantage that justifies redress in different domains of civic life. In contrast, Leonardo Zaibert and Elizabeth Millán-Zaibert explore in the next essay the distinction between collective and individual rights, and argue on individualist grounds against group rights. Each of the succeeding papers deals with related justificatory issues: Jorge Gracia and Angelo Corlett focus on affirmative action programs for Hispanics/Latinos; Thomas Pogge concentrates on accommodation rights in general and linguistic rights in particular; and Pablo De Greiff addresses rights to political representation.

One of the initial aims of Iris Young's paper is to locate the claims raised by Hispanics/Latinos within broader political debates in the United States. Identity politics have of late come under criticism not only from the political right, but also, more surprisingly, from various streams within democratic theory. Neorepublican, nationalist, and socialist strains in recent democratic theory converge on the assertion that certain claims arising from cultural particularity can be divisive, fragmenting, or distracting. Partially conceding the criticisms of identity politics, Young nevertheless wants to argue that the claims raised by Hispanics/Latinos can be seen as a type of a more defensible politics of difference, one that concentrates on claims of justice. Moreover, she insists that justice is best served by acknowledging the cultural and structural differences that distinguish social groups.

Central to this effort to interpret the claims of Hispanics as claims to justice is establishing that these claims are grounded not so much on the cultural particularity of Hispanics as a group, but rather on the structural disadvantages under which most Hispanics live. Earlier attempts to conceptualize group identities have encountered familiar difficulties. Essential attributes always seem to leave out of the group people who lack those attributes, but who nevertheless identify themselves or are identified by others with the group. Conversely, some members of the group who possess the required attributes deny that group membership is significant for their identity. The definition of group identity through essential attributes also risks different forms of homogenization. This includes the attribution of uniform political interests and views to all members of a given group, and worse, the abstraction from all other differentiating factors such as race, class, religion, gender, age, national background, and so on.

Instead of engaging in one more doomed attempt at finding the necessary and sufficient conditions for counting as a Hispanic/Latino, Young, like Gracia and Moya, offers a relational account of group identity. A group is constituted not only when all members share the same characteristics with one another, but also when the members stand in a particular relationship to nonmembers. In the case of Hispanics, what this means is that the defining characteristics of the group are not merely those that Latinos allegedly share with one another, whether ethnicity, race, language, historical experience, or religion. The group is also defined by the relations that members of the group have with a community outside, namely an Anglo-European society.

Needless to say, a relational account of group identity leaves open questions about the status of the claims raised by particular groups. In order to complete the interpretation of the claims of Hispanic/Latino politics as claims to justice, Young takes a further, and crucial, step in her argument. She articulates a notion of structural inequality that connects those who suffer this condition with a justice claim that needs to be addressed. Social structures do not exist as reified entities or as states, but rather as processes in the rules and expectations according to which we act, and in the way in which the results of previous actions have intentionally and unintentionally shaped the physical and the social environment in which we now live. Nonetheless, these structures create social positions that condition the opportunities and lives of people. Each of the differentiating factors by which a group is constituted might on its own be inconsequential or neutral with respect to the distribution of opportunities for the members of the group. But together they can form a structure, a web of constraints, that puts the members at a significant disadvantage with respect to nonmembers. Structural inequality consists in "the relative constraints some people encounter in their freedom and material well-being as the cumulative effect of the possibilities of their social positions, as compared with others who in their social positions have more options or easier access to benefits."

A narrative of the structural disadvantages that afflict Hispanics/Latinos should include the way in which disadvantages concerning citizenship and inclusion, language use, and racism and stereotyping interact with one another to create the sort of patterned maldistribution of opportunities that often burdens Hispanics. For Young, the fact that Hispanics/Latinos are frequently positioned as foreigners, and that so many who are illegal or even legal residents do not enjoy the same rights as citizens, has determinate consequences for Latinos' economic, social, and political opportunities. The same occurs regarding disadvantages associated with language use. Many Hispanics, particularly those in the Southwest, are still suffering the diminished opportunities generated by a border that was drawn militarily and which implied a disabling language shift. More generally, though, equality of opportunities is put into question in a context in which so much hinges on linguistic competence, so few services are offered in languages other than English, and so little inexpensive English-language instruction is provided. Finally, racism and stereotyping constitute another plank that leads to systematic, structural disadvantage. To the extent that racism and stereotyping are pervasive features of social life, with manifestations in the workplace, housing, education, culture, entertainment, and so on, they help to shape an interlocking structure that conditions the quality of life of Hispanics/Latinos and their freedom to pursue their chosen goals. To this extent, claims for redressing these structural inequalities are claims of justice. They are different from the claims associated with the politics of identity in that they concern everyone. They are not self-regarding demands made by a particular group in order to foster its interests at the expense of others, but rather claims concerning the basic possibilities of living under conditions of fairness in a society such as ours.

In their contribution, Leonardo Zaibert and Elizabeth Millán-Zaibert raise doubts about group rights in general and their attribution to Hispanics in particular. To take the latter point first, the authors find the category "Hispanic" too unwieldy to form the basis of a rational distribution of political benefits. As it is presently used, they argue, the category not only covers people of diverse backgrounds and histories but, more to the point, includes individuals who do not deserve special treatment, because they have not been personally harmed.

But the real target of the essay is the notion of group rights in general, against which the authors argue as follows. First, they agree with the defenders of group rights that, all things considered, a political system is more rational if it tries to restrict the influence of chance. However, contrary to those who support group rights, the authors argue that rather than restricting the influence of chance, group rights entrench unchosen differences such as nationality, ethnicity, and race. In the second place, while agreeing that harms deserve restitution, they argue against the inference from the collective nature of certain harms—such as discrimination due to ethnic group membership—to the collective nature of the rights that guarantee redress. From their standpoint, it is wronged *individuals* who deserve restitution, and class remedies are questionable not only from a pragmatic standpoint but, worse, from a normative standpoint. This consideration is deployed both against group rights in general and against restitutive defenses of group rights.

Against representational arguments, the authors raise questions about the view according to which representation is best achieved by members of the same group. Furthermore, they argue that representational strategies encounter difficulties with boundaries, for these strategies introduce the notions of underrepresented groups and, conversely, overrepresented groups; this in turn invites even further complications.

Thomas Pogge is also concerned with articulating the general principles on the basis of which certain accommodation rights for Hispanics could be justified. In particular, he is interested in the type of language policy that considerations of fairness might require. After arguing that history is largely irrelevant for settling questions about the rights of present generations, Pogge examines the possibility of grounding linguistic rights on the basis of the general principle that in a liberal society persons should not be disadvantaged because of unchosen inequalities. Since it is patently true that most members of a linguistic minority have unequal access to the benefits of our common life, one could defend special rights on this ground. The problem with this argument, from Pogge's point of view, is that although this formulation of the liberal principle does justify the conclusion, it justifies as well so many other demands that it easily amounts to a reductio ad absurdum of the principle. Clearly, a liberal state cannot and should not compensate for all unchosen inequalities.

Accommodation rights have also been defended on the basis of broader considerations of equal treatment of different groups on the part of government. This is a version of the argument in favor of state neutrality. The reason why the state should be neutral with respect to different cultural or religious groups, say, is that if it favored a particular one, it would be meting out unequal treatment to the members of the other groups. Now, since there is no such thing as language neutrality—after all, the state needs some language(s) to conduct business—it is incumbent upon the state to rectify the unequal treatment inevitably suffered by some by providing special, and presumably compensatory, advantages. Such advantages might take the form of special language rights, so that, for instance, children of minority groups might be educated in publicly funded schools in a language of their own.

Pogge, however, thinks that the case is more complicated than it seems. After all, the claim just made can be interpreted in different ways. One interpretation says that it amounts to the claim that denying the members of disadvantaged minority groups access to publicly funded education in the majority language is justifiable by the purpose of protecting the cultural context of the minority community. But clearly, a liberal state cannot condone coercively pressing minority children into the service of perpetuating a cultural community irrespective of whether this benefits the children concerned or whether the children themselves or their parents support this purpose. A weaker interpretation of the claim is that members of minority cultures should have the right to send their children to a public school where their instruction is entirely in the minority language. This claim is usually defended, once again, on the basis of equal respect. For Pogge, however, this appeal to respect is problematic in this context, since what is at stake are decisions concerning children who might have interests independent of those of their parents.

Pogge's position on the question of language education is unabashedly children-centric. For him, naturally, liberal states are committed to the principle of equal treatment, but this is a duty to individual citizens and residents, and not to groups and cultures. For him, among the individual interests bearing on the question of how to design a public education system, the interests of those children are of paramount importance. These two commitments Pogge summarizes in a fundamental principle of public education, according to which "the fundamental duty of a just public education system is to promote the best interests of each child and to do so equally." The different options regarding language instruction should be judged by whether, and to what degree, they satisfy this duty.

Pogge's own position is a cautious defense of the justifiability of running a modified English-first educational system. He bases his defense on the claim that "the most important linguistic competence for children now growing up in the United States is the ability to communicate in English." Of course, he acknowledges that because the overriding concern is to promote the children's interests, empirical research on the most conducive way of making children competent in English should play a crucial role in the determination of language education. Similarly, Pogge distances his defense of English-first schemes from defenses of English-only initiatives. The former is compatible with the teaching of minority languages as academic subjects and with other measures that give children, minorities as well as others, the opportunity to develop full competence, at public expense, in languages of any minorities that are locally numerically significant. However, this concession should not obscure the main point: to the extent that a liberal state is committed to the promotion of the interests of individuals, and to the extent that the interests of children are tied to their ability to communicate well in English, the fundamental commitment of public education should be to the achievement of the latter aim.

Jorge Gracia's efforts center on an examination of whether Hispanics should be made beneficiaries of affirmative action programs. But before attempting to address this question, he joins the discussion about the nature of Hispanic identity. Here he puts Wittgenstein's notion of family resemblance to a novel use. In his view, Hispanics constitute an identifiable group not by virtue of sharing the same set of characteristics, whether racial, religious, ethnic, linguistic, or others, but by virtue of something akin to a family resemblance holding among them. Although there is no property or set of properties that characterizes all Hispanics at all times and in all places, Hispanics are nonetheless united by "a web of historical relations that also separates us from other groups in the way a family is separated from other families." In context, Hispanics can be identified and distinguished from others by language, or by religion, and so on. But this does not mean that any of these characteristics is a necessary condition for counting as a Hispanic (and that all Hispanics therefore share it), nor that there are no properties that can be used to pick out Hispanics in context.

Although the previous point is worthy of consideration in its own right, in the paper it is actually a way of clearing a first justificatory hurdle for affirmative action programs, for if Hispanics do not form an identifiable group, it makes no sense to talk about affirmative action for them. Having cleared this hurdle, however, is nothing more than a first step. After all, affirmative action programs can be defended as means to achieve three different aims, namely, ensuring equal opportunity, redressing past wrongs, and promoting the participation of underrepresented groups, and these aims can be further justified by appealing to considerations of justice or utility. It might turn out that some of these considerations support affirmative action for Hispanics, whereas some might not. Gracia wants to clarify these issues for us.

In the end, he argues that affirmative action for Hispanics cannot be justified by appealing to either equality of opportunity or redress, on the grounds that "(1) not all, not even most, Hispanics have suffered discrimination, (2) the degree of discrimination and abuse some have suffered never reached the levels suffered by African Americans or women, and (3) it is difficult to prove that the reason some Hispanics have suffered discrimination and abuse in the United States is because they are Hispanics."

By contrast, however, Gracia defends affirmative action for Hispanics on the basis of increasing their participation in the life of the nation. This aim may also be justified by appealing to either justice or utility. It is clear that in both the political and the general cultural arenas, Hispanics are underrepresented by large margins, with the consequent erosion of the claims that we live in a fair and free society. Increasing the participation of Hispanics in these spheres would go a long way toward shoring up these claims and toward accruing overall benefits to society. Gracia illustrates his position by describing both the underrepresentation of Hispanics in academic philosophy in the United States and the way in which his defense of affirmative action would serve to increase those numbers while avoiding some of the familiar difficulties associated with the arguments about equal opportunity or redress.

Angelo Corlett's paper raises questions about the usefulness for public policy purposes of Gracia's nonessentialist understanding of Hispanic/Latino identity. Corlett's worry is that the argument that there is no characteristic that can be used in all contexts and at all times to identify Latinos opens up the category to the charge of arbitrariness. According to Corlett, this understanding of Latino identity makes courts and administrative bodies responsible for choosing which traits are necessary for counting as a Hispanic, and to what degree the relevant traits should be exhibited or practiced. The point is that this sort of choice would be one for which Gracia's conception of identity will offer no guidance.

Corlett defends instead "a genetic kind of moderate essentialism," which takes a genetic tie to those who are Latino as the defining characteristic of Latino identity. The main advantage of this definition, according to Corlett, is that in defining the question of identity in terms of genetic ties, it provides a criterion of group membership that the law can easily verify or falsify. Additionally, this understanding of identity accords with the general desiderata that a theory of ethnic identity should pursue. First, not surprisingly, a theory of Latino identity should be able to pick out members of the group with as little ambiguity as possible. Second, it should identify Latinos according to standards that are used generally for the identification of members of other ethnic groups. Third, the theory should separate questions of identity from questions of moral worth. Fourth, the conditions for what counts as being Latino should not be overly politicized. Fifth, the theory should reflect an in-group perspective of what counts as being Latino. Sixth, the theory should be sensitive to the historicity of the category "Latino."

Corlett takes issue with the grounds on which Gracia denies the justifiability of affirmative action for Hispanics as a form of reparation or as means for promoting equal opportunity. In both instances Corlett's target is Gracia's assertion that Hispanics should not be made beneficiaries of affirmative action programs conceptualized in this manner, for Hispanics have not suffered the required degree of discrimination. Since this is an empirical issue, Corlett's paper joins at this point the discussion about the relevance of history for understanding and addressing the condition of Hispanics, a discussion that is one of the many unifying threads of this collection.

Finally, De Greiff's concern lies with the possibility of justifying guarantees to political representation for Hispanics/Latinos. Part of his paper seeks to clarify one approach to the justification of such guarantees that has attracted increased attention lately, an approach that takes as its starting point recent articulations of discourse theory. Discourse theory has appeared to many as an attractive basis for such an argument, for its account of legal legitimacy in terms of the rational acceptability of norms to all those who are affected by them is correctly perceived to obey an inclusive imperative. A general, discourse-theoretical argument on behalf of guaranteed group representation would take this account of legitimacy and patterns of systematic exclusion into consideration. It would aim to conclude that, under conditions of oppression and discrimination, the basic condition of the legitimacy of our laws would remain unsatisfied unless we guarantee the political participation of some groups.

This argument shares the intuitive attractiveness of the move that, in the sphere of morality, led theorists such as Apel and Habermas from a monological point of view to a dialogical one. Moreover, it restricts the range of arguments on behalf of guaranteed minority representation that can be constructed on the basis of discourse theory. In particular, De Greiff argues that although it is possible to construct on the basis of discourse theory an effective defense of guaranteed representation as a form of prevention and redress for discrimination, it is not possible to construct on the same basis an argument for guaranteed representation as a mechanism to foster diversity. One way of seeing the point is by examining a way in which such an argument is framed. It is commonly said that unless minority representation is guaranteed, the contribution that in this case Hispanics/Latinos could make to political deliberation would be lost. But from the standpoint of discourse theory, what sort of contribution could warrant guaranteed representation? It can be said that the differences that make groups into minorities give their members an epistemic advantage that deserves representation. However, there are two different accounts of such epistemic advantage, and only one of them leads to guarantees of political representation.

The first version of the argument says that unless minority representation is guaranteed, everyone would be deprived of the insight offered by those who have experience of aspects of institutional life in this country that the majority simply lacks. The contribution that Hispanics/Latinos could make, then, consists of reminders of the many ways in which the majority mistakenly thinks that its norms are fair. The second version of the argument seeks to generalize the first. Now the epistemic advantage of minorities is accounted for not in terms of our experience of the way our legal system (mal)distributes benefits and burdens—what Young calls structural disadvantages—but rather in terms of the fact that we, as minorities, have a different cultural perspective.

The problem with the second account of the epistemic advantage that minorities have is not that the claimed difference does not obtain. Rather, it is that, at least from the standpoint of discourse theory, it does not constitute the sort of claim that deserves a special guarantee. Guaranteeing political representation on the basis of cultural difference would require making substantive judgments about the distinctiveness of different contributions, and these are judgments that the proceduralism of discourse theory simply does not tell us how to make. So while the cultural diversity argument might be sufficient to justify certain corrective advantages in other domains (such as education), in the domain of politics what is important in the justification of guaranteed representation is not cultural diversity but rather the experience of structural discrimination.

Tensions and Fractures

Whereas the aims of the two previous sections of this introduction were to provide an overview of the contents of the volume and to extract some of the threads that run through the different essays, it is also important to highlight some of the many disagreements among their authors, and to at least mention a few perspectives that, although not explicitly represented in this volume, are relevant to general debates about Hispanic/Latino identity and politics.

The authors of the essays in this book disagree with one another on a range of topics, large and small. There is an important difference between Mendieta and Oboler concerning the interpretation of facts about racism in Latin America. Similarly, Gracia and Corlett differ about the nature and degree of discrimination against Hispanics in the United States.

Beyond questions of the evaluation of the meaning and significance of certain historical facts, there are broader disagreements concerning philosophical approaches to issues of identity. Most of the authors in this collection espouse nonessentialist, nonreductionist accounts of identity. With the exception of Corlett, who defends the primacy of genealogical links on the basis of their usefulness for legal-political purposes, most contributors do not think it is plausible or advisable to define simple necessary and sufficient conditions for counting as Hispanic/Latino. For example, Gracia puts Wittgenstein's notion of family resemblance to use in this domain in order to offer a pluralist account of Latino identity in which culture, ancestry, language, history, and many other identity markers can play a role in defining who is a Hispanic, without any of them necessarily being present in all members of the class. Other authors, especially Moya and Young, offer relational accounts of identity that differ both from Gracia's and from each other. While one might say that Gracia is concerned with understanding the identity of Hispanics/Latinos in terms of characteristics they share with one another (granted, in a highly complex structure resembling family relations), others approach identity by focusing on the dialectical relationship between insiders and outsiders, that is to say, they are interested in capturing the way in which any efforts to define the others defines oneself and vice versa. Some contributors, such as Alcoff, Mendieta, and Moya, not only take note of this fact, but are sanguine about the impact that the presence of Hispanics/Latinos can have on general race relations in the United States. Oboler, by contrast, worries that notwithstanding the dialectical relationship between the identities of different groups, solidarity among groups has eroded to the point that it seems increasingly the case that violations of rights and failures of respect are of concern to members of the victim's group alone.

Even those authors who do not offer a general account of the nature of group identity differ among themselves concerning which are the most salient factors in the formation of Hispanic identity. Some, such as Mendieta and Mignolo, emphasize the importance of history; some, including Young, De Greiff, and Pogge, highlight social structural factors; and some, specifically Alcoff and Schutte, include market and advertising forces in the constitution of the identity of Hispanics. Clearly, this is a complex issue, and the differences represented here are a reflection of that complexity.

Apart from the importance of the differences between the authors of these essays concerning issues of historical interpretation, historical relevance, and Hispanic/Latino identity, there are two related disagreements that are fundamental. In the first place, the contributions are divided by the general difference between supporters of postmodernism and those who espouse different but more traditional philosophical approaches. Although it is no longer possible to talk about postmodernism (or its "other") in the singular, it is clear that in the essays there is some tension between those who want to raise more ambitious claims on behalf of the universality and impartiality of reason, on the one hand, and those who defend a more contextualist, particularist position, on the other. Since none of the contributions deals with epistemological questions specifically, this disagreement is easier to see at the level of politics. Here the difference can be described in very broad terms as a disagreement between those who espouse a liberal-democratic framework and those who express different degrees of reservations. The political positions represented in these essays cover a broad spectrum. Zaibert and Millán-Zaibert, for instance, espouse the most classical liberal individualist position in the whole collection. Pogge frames his article on the basis of traditional liberal values of equal treatment and respect for individuals above groups. De Greiff espouses a form of deliberative democracy that is still liberal in thinking that individuals are the ultimate unit of moral-political concern, but which emphasizes the social nature of individual identity and the public nature of processes of legitimation. Young continues her long-standing defense of a politics of difference that conflicts with classical interpretations of the liberal principles of equal treatment and of impartiality. Moya and Schutte do not work out in detail the political presuppositions of their essays, but both express skepticism toward liberal claims to the neutrality of the state. Finally, Mignolo, adopting the most frankly postmodern position in the volume, epistemologically opposes all attempts at establishing hierarchies of knowledge and politically moves in the direction of a radical democracy. This proposal puts into question most liberal principles, including the priority of the individual, equal treatment, state neutrality, and the impartiality of law.

Finally, there is one more axis of difference worth making explicit in this introduction. There is no essay in this collection that explicitly assumes the sort of perspective articulated by Foucault: a perspective interested in the microanalysis of institutions and practices, one that emphasizes the way in which processes of governmentalization not only constrain the choices individuals make, but, indeed, help constitute their identity. Nevertheless, such a perspective is not completely absent from the present work. Whereas Corlett, De Greiff, Gracia, and Pogge, for instance, are interested in macroanalysis of social institutions, Schutte and Oboler, among others, make it a point to highlight the ways in which legal institutions are penetrated by power relations.

In short, while the present volume is organized around a set of converging lines of discussion, it also reflects the plurality and heterogeneity of Hispanic/Latino identity and of scholarship on Hispanic/Latino issues.*

* Most of the essays contained in this volume were presented at the I Samuel P. Capen Symposium in Philosophy, sponsored by the Samuel P. Capen chair. The symposium took place at the University at Buffalo, on October 1 and 2, 1998.

PART 1

HISPANIC / LATINO IDENTITY, ETHNICITY, AND RACE

Is Latina/o Identity a Racial Identity? 1

Linda Martín Alcoff

Is Latina/o identity a racial identity? Given the social basis of racializing categories and the dynamic nature of identities, there is no decontextual, final, or essential answer to this question. However, I would describe my concern in this paper as being in the realm of social ontology in the sense that I seek the truth about how Latina/o identity is configured as well as lived in the context of North America today. The question then can be formulated in the following way: What is the best, or most apt, account of Latina/o identity that makes the most sense of the current political and social realities within which we must negotiate our social environment? Although I am interested here in the politics of identity, that is, the political effects of various accounts of identity in and on popular consciousness, both among Latinas/os and among Anglos, my principal concern is at the level of experience, ideology, and meaning rather than the attendant political rights that may be associated with identity.

As will be seen, much of the debates over Latinas/os and race weave together strategic considerations (a concern with political effects) and metaphysical considerations (a concern with the most apt description). It is not clear to me that these concerns can, in fact, be disentangled. There are two reasons for this. One is that strategic proposals for the way a community should represent itself cannot work if there is no connection whatsoever to lived experience or to the common meanings that are prominent in the relevant discourses and practices. Thus, the strategic efficacy of political proposals are dependent on correct assessments of metaphysical realities. But, second, the question of what is the most apt description of those metaphysical realities is not as clear-cut as some philosophers might suppose. And this is because the concepts of "race," "Latina/o," and even "identity" admit of different meanings and have complicated histories, such that it is not possible to simply say, "This is *the* meaning." Thus, we must make a judgment about meaning, a judgment that will be underdetermined by usage, history, science, or phenomenological description of experience. And in making these judgments, we must look to the future and not just the past. In other words, given that we are participating in the *construction* of meanings in making such judgments, we must take responsibility for our actions, which will require carefully considering their likely real-world effects.

The question of Latina/o identity's relationship to the conventional categories of race that have been historically dominant in the United States is a particularly vexing one. To put it straightforwardly, we simply don't fit. Racialized identities in the United States have long connoted homogeneity, easily visible identifying features, and biological heredity, but none of these characteristics apply to Latinas/os in the United States, nor even to any one national subset, such as Cuban Americans or Puerto Ricans. We are not homogeneous by "race," we are often not identifiable by visible features or even by names, and such issues as disease heredity that are often cited as the biologically relevant sign of race are inapplicable to such a heterogeneous group.

Moreover, the corresponding practices of racialization in the United States—such as racial border control, legal sanctions on cross-racial marriage, and the multitudinous demands for racial self-identification on nearly every application form from day care to college admissions—are also relatively unfamiliar south of the border. Angel R. Oquendo recounts that before he could even take the SAT in Puerto Rico he was asked to identify himself racially. "I was caught off guard," he says. "I had never thought of myself in terms of race."[1] Fortunately, the SAT included "Puerto Rican" among the choices of "race," and Oquendo was spared what he called a "profound existential dilemma." Even while many Latinas/os consider color a relevant factor for marriage, and antiblack racism persists in Latin America along with a condescension toward indigenous peoples, the institutional and ideological forms that racism has taken in Latin America are generally not analogous to those in the North. And these differences are why many of us find our identity as well as our social status changing as we step off the plane or cross the river: race suddenly becomes an all-important aspect of our identity, and sometimes our racial identity dramatically changes in ways over which it feels as if we have no control.

In the face of this transcontinental experiential dissonance, there are at least three general options possible as a way of characterizing the relationship between Latina/o identity and race. One option is to refuse a racialized designation and use the concept of "ethnicity" instead. This would avoid the problem of racial diversity within Latina/o communities and yet recognize the cultural links among Latinas/os in the North. The concept of ethnicity builds on cultural practices, customs, language, sometimes religion, and so on. One might also be motivated toward this option as a way of resisting the imposition of a pan-Latina/o ethnicity, in order to insist that the only meaningful identities for Latinas/os are Cuban American, Puerto Rican, Mexican American, and so on.[2]

A second option would resist the ethnic paradigm on the grounds that, whatever the historical basis of Latina/o identity, living in the context of North America means that we have become a racialized population and need a self-understanding that will accurately assess our portrayal here. A third option, adopted by many neoconservatives, is to attempt to assimilate to the individualist ideology of the United States both in body and in mind, and reject the salience of group identities a priori.

None of these responses seems fully adequate, though some have more problems than others. It is hard to see how the diversity among Latinas/os could be fairly represented in any concept of race. And it is doubtful that many Latinas/os, especially those who are darker-skinned, will be able to succeed in presenting themselves as simply individuals: they will still be seen by many as instantiations of a group whose characteristics are considered both universally shared within the group and largely inferior, even if they do not see themselves this way. On the face of it, the first option—an account of Latina/o identity as an ethnic identity—seems to make the most sense, for a variety of reasons that I will explore in this paper. This option could recognize the salience of social identity, allow for more internal heterogeneity, and resist the racializing that so often mischaracterizes our own sense of self. However, I will ultimately argue that the "ethnic option" is not fully adequate to the contemporary social realities we face, and may inhibit the development of useful political strategies for our diverse communities. My argument in this paper primarily will take the form of a negative: that the ethnic option is not adequate. Developing a fully adequate alternative is beyond my scope or ambitions here, but the very failure of the ethnic option will establish some of the necessary criteria for such an alternative.

My argument will take the following steps. First, I will explain briefly the context of these debates over identity, which will go some way toward refuting the individualist option. Next, I will go over some of the relevant facts about our populations to provide the necessary cultural context. Then I will zero in on the ethnicity argument, assess its advantages and disadvantages, and conclude by posing the outline of an alternative.

Why Care about Identity?

If I may be permitted a gross overgeneralization, European Americans are afraid of strongly felt ethnic and racial identities. Not all, to be sure. The Irish and Italian communities, as well as some other European-American nationalities, have organized cultural events on the basis of their identities at least since the 1960s, with the cooperation of police and city councils across the country. The genealogy of this movement among the Irish and the Italians has been precisely motivated by their discrimination and vilification in U.S. history, a vilification that has sometimes taken racialized forms.

But there is a different attitude among whites in general toward "white ethnic" celebrations of identity and toward those of others, that is, those of nonwhites. And this is, I suspect, because it is one thing to say to the dominant culture, "You have been unfairly prejudiced against me," as southern European ethnicities might say, and quite another to say, "You have stolen my lands and enslaved my people and through these means created the wealth of your country," as African Americans, Latinas/os, and Native Americans might say. The latter message is harder to hear; it challenges the basic legitimizing narratives of this country's formation and global status, and it understandably elicits the worry, "What will be the full extent of their demands?" Of course, all of the cultural programs that celebrate African, indigenous, or Latina/o heritage do not make these explicit claims. But in a sense, the claims do not need to *be* explicit: any reference to slavery, indigenous peoples, or Chicano or Puerto Rican history implies challenges to the legitimizing narrative of the United States, and any expression of solidarity among such groups consciously or unconsciously elicits concern about the political and economic demands such groups may eventually make, even if they are not made now.

This is surely part of what is going on when European Americans express puzzlement about the importance attached to identity by non–European Americans, when young whites complain about African Americans sitting together in the cafeteria, or when both leftist and liberal political theorists, such as Todd Gitlin and Arthur Schlesinger, jump to the conclusion that a strong sense of group solidarity and its resultant "identity politics" among people of color in this country will fracture the body politic and disable our democracy.[3]

A prominent explanation given for these attachments to identity, attachments that are considered otherwise inexplicable, is that there is opportunism at work, among leaders if not among the rank and file, to secure government handouts and claim special rights. However, the demand for cultural recognition does not entail a demand for special political rights. The assumption in so much of contemporary political philosophy that a politics of recognition—or identity-based political movements—leads automatically to demands for special rights is grounded, I suspect, in the mystification some feel in regard to the politics of cultural identity in the first place. Given this mystification and feeling of amorphous threat, assumptions of opportunism and strategic reasoning become plausible.

Assumptions about the opportunism behind identity politics seem to work on the basis of the following understanding of the recent historical past: in the 1960s, some groups began to clamor for the recognition of their identities, began to resist and critique the cultural assimilationism of liberal politics, and argued that state institutions should give these identities public recognition. Thus, on this scenario, first we had identity politics asserting the political importance of these identities, and then we had (coerced) state recognition of them. But denigrated identity designations, particularly racial ones, have *originated* with and been enforced by the state in U.S. history, not vice versa. Obviously, it is the U.S. state and U.S. courts that initially insisted on the overwhelming salience of some racial and ethnic identities, to the exclusion of rights to suffrage, education, property, marrying whomever one wanted, and so on. Denigrated groups are trying to reverse this process; they are not the initiators of it. It seems to me that they have two aims: (1) to valorize previously derided identities, and (2) to have their own hand at constructing the representations of identities.

The U.S. pan-Latina/o identity is perhaps the newest and most important identity that has emerged in the recent period. The concept of a pan-Latina/o identity is not new in Latin America: Simón Bolívar called for it nearly two hundred years ago as a strategy for anticolonialism, but also because it provided a name for the "new peoples" that had emerged from the conquest. And influential leaders such as José Martí and Che Guevara also promoted Latin American solidarity. It is important to note that populations "on the ground" have not often resonated with these grand visions, and that national political and economic leaders continue to obstruct regional accords and trade agreements that might enhance solidarity. But the point remains that the invocation of a pan-Latina/o identity does not actually originate in the North.

Only much more recently is it the case that some Latina/o political groups in the North have organized on a pan-Latina/o basis, although most Latina/o politics here has been organized along national lines, for example, as Puerto Ricans or Chicanos. But what is especially new, and what is being largely foisted on us from the outside, is the representation of a pan-Latina/o identity in the dominant North American media, and it is this representation we want to have a hand in shaping. Marketing agencies have discovered/created a marketing niche for the "generic" Latina/o. And Latina/o-owned marketing agencies and advertising agencies are working on the construction of this identity as much as anyone, though of course in ways dominated by strategic interests or what Habermas calls purposive rationality. There are also more and more cultural representations of Latinas/os in the dominant media and in government productions such as the census. Thus, the concern that U.S. Latinas/os have with our identity is not spontaneous or originating entirely or even mostly from within our communities; neither is the ongoing representation of our identity something we can easily just ignore.[4]

What We Are Depends on *Where* We Are

Social identities, whether racial or ethnic, are dynamic. In Omi and Winant's study of what they call "racial formations" in the United States between the 1960s and the 1980s, they argued, "Racial categories and the meanings of race are given concrete expression by the specific social relations and historical context in which they are embedded."[5] Moreover, these categories are constantly facing forms of resistance and contestation that transform both their impact and their effective meaning. Clearly this is the case with ethnic as well as racial identities. As social constructions imposed on variable experiential facts, they exist with no stable referent or essential, non-negotiable core. And because such identities are often also the site of conflict over political power and economic resources, they are especially volatile. Any analysis of Latina/o identity, then, must chart historical trends and contextual influences, which themselves will vary across different parts of the country.

Since the passage of the 1965 immigration law that ended the quotas on immigration from South and Central America and the Caribbean, millions of Latinas/os have entered the United States from various countries, causing a great diversification of the previously dominant Chicano, Puerto Rican, and Cuban communities. Thus today, Dominicans are vying with Puerto Ricans in New York City to be the largest Latina/o population, and even Cubans no longer outnumber other Latinas/os in Miami. As the immigrant communities settle in, younger generations develop different identities than their parents, adapting to their cultural surroundings. Young people also tend to experience similar problems across the national divisions, such as Dominican and Puerto Rican, and this promotes a sense of common identity. So in one sense diversity has increased as new immigrations continue and new generations of younger Latinos depart from some aspects of their parents' cultural identity, such as being Spanish-dominant or being practicing Catholics, while in another sense diversity has decreased as

Latinas/os experience common forms of discrimination and chauvinism in the United States and an increasingly common cultural interpellation.

In the 1960s, U.S. state agencies began to disseminate the ethnic label "Hispanic" as the proper term for identifying all people of Latin American and even Spanish descent.[6] So today we have a population of thirty million or so "Hispanics" in the United States. The mass media, entertainment, and advertising industries have increasingly addressed this large population as if it were a coherent community.[7] As Suzanne Oboler's study reveals, this generic identity category feels especially socially constructed to many of the people named by it, given that it is not how they self-identified previously.[8] Oboler asks, somewhat rhetorically:

> Are marketers merely taking advantage of an existing "group" as a potentially lucrative target population? Or are their advertising strategies in fact helping to "design" the group, "invent" its traditions, and hence "create" this homogeneous ethnic group?[9]

One might well be concerned that adapting to any such pan-Latina/o identity as constructed by dominant institutions—whether economic or political ones—represents a capitulation or is simply the inevitable effect of what Foucault might call governmentality.

However, much of the debate over this interpellation among those named by it does not so much critique the fact of its social construction or even the fact that its genesis lies in government and marketing agencies, but focuses instead on its political implications and its coherence with lived experience, for example, the way in which it disallows multiplicity or the way in which it erases national allegiance. In this way, the debate shifts to a more productive set of concerns, it seems to me. I witnessed an interesting exchange on some of these points at the "Hispanics: Cultural Locations" conference held at the University of San Francisco, in 1997. Ofelia Schutte, a leading Latina philosopher, presented a paper arguing that a pan-U.S. Latina/o identity may be a means to disaffiliate us from our nations of birth or ancestry, nations that have been invaded or otherwise harmed by the U.S. government. Thus, thinking of ourselves primarily as U.S. Latinas/os rather than, say, Panamanians or Salvadorans may work to dislodge or weaken feelings of loyalty to countries outside the U.S. borders. In the discussion period after her paper, one member of the audience argued strongly that as a half-Spanish, half–Puerto Rican woman who grew up among Chicanos in California, she had found the emergence of a pan-Latina/o identity a welcome relief. Although she recognized the dangers that Schutte was describing, identifying herself simply as Latina allowed her to avoid having to make complicated choices between the various aspects of her identity, and it helpfully named her experience of connection with a multiplicity of Latina/o communities.[10]

Another political concern I have heard voiced against overhomogenizing Latina/o identities is that it could allow those members of the group who are themselves less disadvantaged to reap the benefits of affirmative action and other forms of economic redress that have mainly been created for (and often mainly fought for by) Chicanos and Puerto Ricans, that is, the more disadvantaged members. We are already seeing this happen because of the label "Hispanic." It is unclear how to effectively police this problem other than to rely on people's own moral conscience (which is not terribly effective). In some cases, targeted groups are designated with specificity as Mexican Americans or Puerto Ricans in order to avoid, for example, giving scholarships to Argentinians of recent European extraction. However, the problem here is that one cannot assume that no Argentinians in the United States have suffered discrimination, given their particular racialized identity, skin tone, the way their accent may be mediated by their class background, and so forth. Given the racial heterogeneity of every Latin American and Caribbean country, one cannot exclude an entire country from measures aimed at redressing discrimination without excluding many who are racially marked as inferior north of the border.

The resistance to a pan-Latina/o identity is most likely a losing battle, moreover, as both government and marketing agencies are increasingly winning hegemony in their public interpellations. Moreover, as both Arlene Davila and Daniel Mato have argued in separate studies, the marketing and advertising agencies are not simply forcing us to use labels that have no real purchase on our lives, but participating in a new subject construction that affects how Latinas/os think about and experience our identity and our interrelatedness to other Latinas/os with whom we may have felt little kinship before.[11] Mato points out that the television corporation Univisión, which is jointly owned by U.S. and Latin American companies, is exposing its viewers to a wide array of programming such that viewers are becoming familiar with a diversity of communities, in both the South and the North, and in this way "Univisión is participating in the social construction of an imagined community."[12] To say that an identity is socially constructed is to say not that it does not refer to anything in reality, but that what it refers to is a contingent product of social negotiations rather than a natural kind. And the exchange I described above at the "Hispanics: Cultural Locations" conference indicates that the pan-Latina/o identity does in fact correspond at least to some contemporary Latina/os' lived experience.

Latin America itself is probably the most diverse area in the world, producing extreme racial and ethnic diversity *within* Latina/o communities.

By U.S. categories, there are black, brown, white, Asian, and Native American Latinas/os. There are many Latinas/os from the Southern Cone whose families are of recent European origin, a large number of Latinas/os from the western coastal areas whose families came from Asia, and of course a large number of Latinas/os whose lineage is entirely indigenous to the Americas or entirely African. The majority of Latinas/os in North and South America are no doubt the product of a mix of two or more of these groups. And being mixed is true, as Jorge Gracia reminds us, even of the so-called Hispanics who are direct descendants of Spain and Portugal. And it is true as well of many or most of the people identified as black or *moreno*, as is the case in the United States. Latin Americans are thus generally categorized "racially" in the following way: white (which often involves a double deceit: a claim to pure Spanish descent, very rare, and a claim that pure Spanish descent is purely white or European, also very rare); black (meaning wholly or mostly of African descent, usually sub-Saharan); Indian (meaning being some or mostly of pre-Columbian or Amerindian descent); and mixed (which is sometimes divided into subcatgeories, mestizo, mulatto, *cholito*, and so on), with the mixed category always enjoying a majority. Asians are often entirely left off the list, even though their numbers in several countries are significant.

Different countries vary these main racial designations, however. During a recent weekend festival for Latino Heritage Month in Syracuse, Latinas/os of different nationalities provided information about their countries for passersby, information that included statistics, culled from government sources, on what in every case was called the country's "ethnic makeup." Racial categories of identity were given *within* this larger rubric of ethnic makeup, suggesting an equation between ethnicity and race. For example, in the Dominican Republic the ethnic makeup is said to consist of 73 percent "mixed people," 16 percent "white," 11 percent "black." In Ecuador the categories are listed as "mestizo," "Indian," "Spanish," "and "black." In Chile there is a single category called "European and mestizo," which makes up 95 percent of the population. In Cuba we get categories of "mulatto," which is 51 percent of the population, and we also get categories of "white," "black," and "Chinese." In Bolivia the breakdown is between "Quechua," "Aymara," "mestizo," and "white."

One is reminded of the encyclopedia invented by Borges, which divides dogs into such categories as "(a) belonging to the Emperor . . . (b) tame . . . (c) drawn with a very fine camel hair brush . . . and (d) having just broken the water pitcher."[13] There is no internally consistent or coherent theory of ethnic or racial identity underlying the diversity of categorizations. Under the rubric of ethnicity are included a mix of cultural, national, and racial groups, from Spanish to Quechua to white. The sole point that seems to be consistent throughout is that the category "black" is the only one that is invariably racialized, that is, presented as black or mulatto and never presented as "West Indian" or "African." Interestingly, the category "white" is also often racialized, though it is sometimes replaced with "European" or "Spanish." I would suggest that there is a strong relationship between these two facts. That is, it becomes important to use the category "white," and to self-identify as "white," when the category "black" is present, in order to establish one's clear demarcation, and out of concern that a category such as "mestizo" might be allowed to include black people. "White" is also used to distinguish oneself from "Indian," a category that bears racialized meanings in Latin America and negative associations similar to the associations with African Americans in the United States.

Blackness does, of course, signify differently in Latin America; thus it is not likely that a typical white American landing in Santo Domingo would look around and think only 11 percent of the population is black. However, it seems clear that the striking use of the category "black" for all people of African descent, rather than cultural and national markers, is an indication of antiblack racism. The people so designated are reduced to skin color as if this were their primary characteristic rather than some self-created marker such as nationality, language, or culture. One may have been born into a culture and language not of one's own choosing, but these are still more indicative of human agency than is any classification by phenotype. From this, one might argue that replacing "black" with another ethnicity category, such as "West Indian" or "African," might help equalize and dignify the identities.

The category "Indian," however, even though it might initially look to be more of an ethnicity than a race (since it is not merely the name of a color), has primarily a racial meaning, given that the term does not say anything about language, mode of life, religion, or specific origin. Also, in non-indigenous communities of discourse, the term often carries associations as negative as "black" does. Here one might argue that disaggregating the category "Indian" would be helpful. If the main meaning of "Indian" is a kind of racial meaning, then the use of "Quechua," "Aymara," and so on reduces the significance of the racialized connotations of the identity, subordinating those to the specificity of linguistic and cultural markers.

Despite all this variety and heterogeneity, when Latinas/os enter the United States, we are often homogenized into one overarching "Hispanic" identity. This generic Hispanicity is not, as Jorge Gracia reminds us, actually homogeneous. That is, in European-American eyes, "Hispanic" identity does not carry the same connotations in every part of the United States. Gracia explains:

> In Miami it means Cuban; in New York City it means Puerto Rican; and in the southwest it means Mexican. So in California I am supposed to have as my native food tacos, in New York City, *arroz con gandules*, and in Miami, *arroz con frijoles negros*![14]

I, too, cannot even count the times it has been assumed that I must naturally like hot and spicy food, even though the typical food in Panamá is extremely mild.

Still, there is one feature at least that persists across this variety of "generic" Hispanic identities, and that is that our identity in the United States, whether or not it is homogenized, is quite often presented as a racial identity. In a recent report in the *Chronicle of Higher Education*, just to give one example, differences in average SAT scores were reported in the following way:

> The average verbal scores *by race* were: white, 526; black, 434; Asian-American, 498; American Indian, 480; Mexican-American, 453; Puerto Rican, 452; and other Hispanic students, 461.[15]

So again, like Angel Oquendo, we find that "Puerto Rican" is a racial identity, and a different one at that from the "race" of Mexican Americans. Whereas in the categorizations I just analyzed from Latin America, racial categories are subsumed within an overall account of "ethnic makeup," in this example from the United States, ethnic categories are subsumed within an overall account of racial difference. But in both cases, race and ethnicity are all but equated.

The Ethnicity Paradigm

Latinas/os in the United States have responded to racialization in a variety of ways. One response, still ongoing, has been to deny vigorously any racial interpellation as other-than-white. Thus some Latinos have literally campaigned to be called white, apparently thinking that if they are going to have to be racialized, whiteness is the one they want. Anita Allen reported in 1994 that the largest petitioning group that had thus far requested changes to the year 2000 U.S. census was the Association of White Hispanics, who were agitating for that designation to be on the census form.[16] In the self-interested scramble for social status, this group perceived correctly where the advantages lay.

Another response, especially among groups of young people, has been to use the discourse of racialization as it exists in the United States to self-identify, but in positive rather than derogatory ways. Thus Chicanos in the August Twenty-Ninth Movement and in Mecha, as well as the primarily

Puertorriqueno Young Lords in the Northeast, at times adopted and adapted the concept of a brown racial identity, such as the "Brown Berets," as if Latinas/os in these communities shared a visible phenotype. One relevant causal factor for this among Puerto Ricans may be their long experiential history of U.S. colonization, which imposed racialization even before they ever entered the United States. Latinas/os from countries without this experience of intensive colonization are more surprised by being racially designated when they come here.[17]

But neither "white" nor "brown" works for a pan-Latina/o identity (or even for the specific nationalities they want to represent). What better unites Latinas/os both across and even within our specific national cultures is not race or phenotype but precisely those features associated with culture: language, religious traditions, cultural values, characteristics of comportment. Thus, another response to forced racialization that has existed for a long time among some Latina/o communities and which has enjoyed a recent resurgence is to deny that race applies in any way to Latinas/os and to argue for, and self-identify as, an ethnic group that encompasses different nationalities and races within it.[18] The U.S. census has adopted this approach at times, in having no Latina/o identity listed under possible racial categories and including it only under the list of ethnic categories. Let us look at the main arguments in favor of this approach, both the political as well as the metaphysical arguments.

1. There is powerful sentiment among Latinas/os toward resisting the imposition of U.S. racializations and U.S. categories of identity. It is not as if the system of racial classification here has benefited anyone except the white majority. As Jorge Klor de Alva provocatively put it to Cornel West in a conversation in *Harper's*, "What advantage has it been, Cornel, for blacks to identify as blacks?"[19] Oquendo argues against the use of such racial terms as "Black Hispanics" and "White Hispanics" on the grounds that these categories "project onto the Latino/a community a divisive racial dualism that, much as it may pervade U.S. society, is alien to that community."[20] Our identity is about culture and nationality, not race: for example, as Clara Rodriguez has shown, Puerto Ricans of all colors self-identify first as Puerto Rican.[21]

But in the United States, cultural, national, ethnic, religious and other forms of identification are constantly subordinated to race. So Afro-Cubans, English-speaking West Indians, and Afro-Brazilians are grouped as "black," in ways that often counter people's own felt sense of identity or primary group alliances. Race trumps culture, and culture is sometimes even seen as a simple outgrowth of race. Shouldn't this ridiculous biological essentialism be opposed and the use of race as an identity or as an all-important category of identity be diminished?

2. Within the United States itself, many African Americans have been opting out of racial categories ever since Jesse Jackson started pushing for the use of the term "African American" in the late 1980s. This was a self-conscious strategy to encourage analogies between African Americans and other hyphenated ethnic groups—to, in a sense, normalize African-American identity by no longer having it set apart from everyone else. Shouldn't Latinas/os unite with and support this trend?

3. The strategy of using ethnic terms rather than racial ones will have the effect of reducing racism or prejudice generally. This was clearly Jackson's thinking. A representation by ethnic terms rather than racial ones confers agency on a people; it invokes historical experience as well as cultural and linguistic practices, all of which are associations with human subjectivity, not objectivity. In contrast, race is often said to be something one has no control over, something one "can't help." This surely perpetuates the association between denigrated racial categories and victimhood, animal-driven natures, inherent inferiority and superiority, and so on. For whites, racial essentialism confers superiority whether or not they've done anything to deserve it; superior intelligence is just in their genes. These beliefs may be more unconscious than conscious, but given the historically sedimented and persistent layers of the ideology of race as an essential determinant, no matter what one intends by use of a word, its historical meanings will be brought into play when it is in use. Naomi Zack, Anthony Appiah, Klor de Alva, and many others today argue that any use of racial terms will be inevitably embedded with biological essentialism and historically persistent hierarchies of moral and cognitive competence.[22] Luis Angel Toro calls on us to "abandon the outdated racial ideology embodied in [the Office of Management and Budget's Statistical] Directive no. 15 and replace it with questions designed to determine an individual's membership in a socially constructed, cultural subgroup."[23] The goal here, of course, is not only to change whites' assumptions about racialized groups, but also to help alter the self-image of people in those groups themselves toward a more affirming identity, an identity in which one can take justifiable pride.

Some also point to the relative success of Jamaican immigrants in the United States as an example here. Grosfoguel and Georas write, "The Jamaican's community's strategy was to emphasize ethnic over racial identity. The fact that Jamaicans were not subsumed under the categorization 'African American' avoided offsetting the positive impact of their skilled background. Thus Jamaicans were successfully incorporated into the host labor market in well-paid public and private service jobs ... [and] are currently portrayed by the white establishment in New York as a model minority."[24]

These are strong arguments. To summarize them, the political arguments are that (1) the use of ethnicity will reduce racism because it refers to self-created features rather than merely physiological ones, and (2) this will also resist the imposition of U.S. forms of identifying people, thus disabusing North Americans of their tendency to naturalize and universalize the predominant categories used here in the United States. The metaphysical arguments are that (3) ethnicity more accurately identifies what really holds groups together and how they self-identify, and (4) ethnicity is simply closer to the truth of Latina/o identity, given its racial heterogeneity. All of these arguments are, in my view, good ones. But the problem is that there are other considerations, and once they are put on the table, the picture unfortunately becomes more complicated.

Racial Realities

Let us look at the case of Cuban Americans. By all measures, they have fared very well in this country in terms of both economic success and political power. They have largely run both politics and the press in Miami for some time, and presidential candidates neglect Cuban issues at their peril. Of course, one cannot argue, as some do in the case of Jamaicans, that Cubans' strong ethnic identification is the main reason for their success; most important has been their ability to play an ideological (and at times military) role for the United States in the cold war. The enormous government assistance provided to the Cubans who fled the Cuban revolution was simply unprecedented in U.S. immigration history: they received language training, educational and business loans, job placement assistance, and housing allocations, and their professional degrees from Cuban institutions were legally recognized to an extent other Third World immigrants still envy. In 1965, when President Johnson began his Great Society programs, the amount of assistance they received from the government actually increased.[25]

But one may legitimately wonder whether the Cubans' status as refugees from Communism was all that was at work here, or even the overriding factor. The Cubans who came in the 1960s were overwhelmingly white or light-skinned. They were generally from the top strata of Cuban society. It is an interesting question whether Haitians would ever have been treated the same way. The Cubans who left Cuba after 1980, known as the Marielitos, were from lower strata of Cuban society, and a large number were Afro-Cubans and mulattos.[26] These Cubans found a decidedly colder welcome. They were left penned in refugee camps for months on end, and those who were not sent back to Cuba were released into U.S. society with little or no assistance, joining the labor ranks at the level of Puerto Ricans and Dominicans.

There are no doubt many factors at work in these disparate experiences of Cuban immigration, having to do, for example, with the geopolitical climate. But surely one of these important factors is race, or racialized identity. Perceived racial identity often *does* trump ethnic or cultural identity.

Look again at the passage about Jamaicans quoted earlier from Grosfoguel and Georas, with certain words emphasized: "The Jamaican community's strategy was to emphasize *ethnic* over *racial* identity. The fact that *Jamaicans* were not subsumed under the categorization '*African American*' avoided offsetting the positive impact of their skilled background." Grosfoguel and Georas contrast the *ethnic* Jamaican identity with what they revealingly take to be a *racial* African American identity, even though the term "African American" was Jackson's attempt to replace race with ethnicity. This again suggests that the racialization of black Americans will overpower any ethnic or cultural marker. It may also be the case that the category "African" is overly inclusive, since under its umbrella huge cultural and linguistic differences would be subsumed, and thus it is incapable of signifying a unified ethnic identity. But that may be assuming more knowledge about Africa among white Americans or even among Latinas/os than one reasonably should. More likely is the fact that "African American" is still understood primarily as a racial designation, in a way that terms such as "German American" or "Irish American" never are. Thus it is questionable whether the strategy of using an ethnic term for a currently racialized group will have the effect of reducing racism if it continues to simply signify race.

And after all, the first meaning given for the word *ethnic* in *Webster's Unabridged Dictionary* is "heathen, pagan." The concept of ethnicity is closely associated with the concept of race, emerging at the same moment in global history, as this meaning indicates. The common usage of the category "white ethnic" indicates that unless otherwise identified, "ethnics" are assumed to be nonwhite and thus they are racialized. For many people in the United States, "ethnic" connotes not only nonwhite but also the typical negative associations of nonwhite racial identity. Meanings given for the word *heathen* in the same dictionary include "rude, illiterate, barbarous, and irreligious." In this list, it is striking that "irreligious" comes last.

Like "African American," the fact is that in the United States the category "Latina/o" often operates as a racialized category. Grosfoguel and Georas themselves argue that "no matter how 'blonde or blue-eyed' a person may be, and no matter how successfully he can 'pass' as white, the moment a person self-identifies as Puerto Rican, he enters the labyrinth of racial Otherness."[27] Virginia Dominguez even makes this case in regard not only to ethnicity but to cultural identity as well. She suggests that case studies from Canada to Brazil reveal that "people may speak culture but continue to think race.

Whether in the form of cultural pluralism or of the current idiom of multiculturalism, the concept of culture is used in ways that naturalize and essentialize difference."[28]

My suspicion is that this works for some Latina/o identities, such as Puerto Rican, Dominican, and Mexican, but not always for others, such as Chilean or Argentinian or perhaps South Americans in general, depending on their features. And as mentioned earlier, some of these groups—Puerto Ricans and Mexicans in particular—have a long history of seeing their identities interpellated through dominant U.S. schemas. In terms of the pan-Latina/o identity, this would mean that when Mexicans or Puerto Ricans are called "Latina/o," the latter category will connote racial meanings, whereas Argentinians who are called "Latina/o" in the North may escape these connotations. Identity terms, as Omi and Winant argue, gain their meaning from their context. Just as Gracia said "Latino" means tacos in California and *arroz con gandules* in New York, it will mean race in California, Texas, New York, and Florida, and perhaps ethnicity only in a few locations. Thus, moving from race to ethnicity is not necessarily moving away from race.

Surely, an optimist might want to interject here, the persistence of racial connotations evoked by ethnic categories is not insurmountable. After all, the Irish *did* transform in wide popular consciousness from a race to an ethnicity, and Jews are making the same transition, at least in the United States. Is it truly the case that only light-skinned people can enjoy this transformation, and that darker-skinned people will *never* be able to?

In order to answer this question, we need to ask another one: What *are* the obstacles to deracializing people of color in general?[29] Is it really the mere fact of skin tone?

I would make two suggestions. First, race, unlike ethnicity, has historically worked through visible markers on the body that trump dress, speech, and cultural practices. In Mississippi, a Jamaican is generally still a black person, no matter how skilled. Race demarcates groups visually, which is why racist institutions have been so upset about nonvisible members of "races" and why they have taken such trouble in these cases to enforce racial identifications. What I am suggesting is that in popular consciousness—in the implicit perceptual practices we use in everyday life to discern how to relate to each other—ethnicity does not "replace" race. When ethnic identities are used instead of racial ones, the perceptual practices of visual demarcation by which we slot people into racial categories continue to operate because ethnic categories offer no substituting perceptual practice. In other words, the fact that race and ethnicity do not map onto the same kinds of identifying practices will make race harder to dislodge. This was not the case for the Irish or for at least some Jewish people, who could blend into the European

American melting pot without noticeable distinctiveness. For them, ethnicity could replace race, because their racial identity as Irish and Jewish did not operate exclusively or primarily through visible markers on the body so much as through contextual factors such as neighborhood and accent. So their identity could shift to white race plus Jewish or Irish ethnicity without troubling the dominant perceptual practices of racial identification. However, for those who are visibly identified by such dominant practices as non-white, as "raced," the shift to a primary ethnic identity would require eradicating these practices. It is unlikely that the use of new terms alone will have that effect. At best, for people of color, ethnic identities will operate alongside racial ones in everyday interactions. At worst, ethnic identities, perhaps like "African American," will operate simply as a racial identity.

Although this is a fact about the visible features of the body, it is not an immutable fact: the meanings of the visible are of course subject to change. However, the phenomenology of perception is such that change will be neither quick nor easy, and that word usage will be nowhere near sufficient to make this change.[30] The transformation of perceptual habits will require a more active and a more practical intervention.

The second obstacle to the deracialization of (at least most) people of color has nothing to with perception or bodily features. This obstacle refers back to a claim I made at the beginning, that assertions of group solidarity among African Americans, Native Americans, and Latinas/os in the United States provoke resistance among many whites because they invoke the history of colonialism, slavery, and genocide. Thus, their acceptance as full players within U.S. society comes at much greater cost than the acceptance of previously vilified groups such as the Irish and Jews—groups that suffered terrible discrimination and violence including genocide but whose history is not a thorn in the side of "pilgrim's progress," "manifest destiny," "leader of the free world," and other such mythic narratives that legitimize U.S. world dominance and provide white Americans with a strong sense of pride. The Irish and Jews were (are) colonized peoples in Europe, and there they are reminders of colonization and genocide. But they do not play this role in the legitimizing narratives of the U.S. state. Thus, the line between European ethnicities and people of color is not merely or perhaps even primarily about skin tone but about history and power and the narratives by which currently existing power arrangements are justified.

So what are we to do? If the move from race to ethnicity is not as easy as some have thought, what is a more realistic strategy, one that will also resist being fatalistic about racialization? How can we avoid both fatalism and naïveté? Are we to accept, then, that Latina/o identity is a racial identity, despite all the facts I have reviewed about our heterogeneity and different methods of self-identification, and all the pernicious effects of racialized identity? In conclusion, I can only sketch the outlines of an answer.

Although racial ideology and practices of racialization seem to always carry within them some commitment to biological essentialism, perhaps the *meaning* of race is transformable. If race is going to be with us for some time to come, it might still be the case that race itself will alter in meaning, even before the perceptual practices of racialization can be done away with. It seems to me that this change in meaning is exactly what Paul Gilroy is attempting to chart, as well as to promote, in *The Black Atlantic*, as well as what some other African-American theorists are doing, such as Robert Gooding-Williams, bell hooks, Lewis Gordon, and Patricia Williams.[31] You will notice in their works an intentional use of the term *black* rather than *African American*; I think this is meant as a way to "be real" about the social reality we live in, and also as a way to suggest a linked fate between all black people across nationalities, at least in the diaspora. But in their works, blackness has been decidedly de-essentialized and given a meaning that consists of historical experience, collective memory, and forms of cultural expression. For Gilroy, there is a "blackness" that transcends and survives the differences of U.K. , Caribbean, and U.S. nationalities, a blackness that can be seen in culture and narrative focus. Blackness is social location, shared history, and a shared perception about the world. For Gooding-Williams, black identity requires a certain self-consciousness about creating the meaning of blackness. It requires, in other words, not only that one is treated as a black person, or that one is "objectively" black, but that one is "subjectively" black as well, and thus that one exercises some agency in regard to their identity. His argument is not simply that this is how we should begin to use the term *black,* but it is how the term is actually used in common parlance, as in "Is Clarence Thomas really black?"

Whether such an approach can be used for Latinas/os, I am not sure. There is probably even greater diversity among Latinas/os in relation to history, social location, and forms of cultural expression than there is among black people across the diaspora. And the question of where black Latinas/os "fit" is still unresolved, even when we make racial identity a matter of self-creation. This is a serious weakness in Gilroy's broad conceptualization of a "black Atlantic": Brazil, as large a country as it is, is nowhere to be found.

But I believe that we can take an important lesson from this body of work because it suggests that, even while we must remember the persistent power of racialization and the inability of ethnicity to easily take its place, the meanings of race are subject to some movement. Only a semantic essentialist could argue that race can mean nothing but biological essentialism; in reality, this is not the way meaning works. Let me be clear about my position here: I don't believe, à la some postmodernists, that signifiers are slippery items whose meanings and associations can be easily transformed. Like Michelle Moody-Adams, I would argue that some *can* be (as in "black is beautiful") and some *cannot* be (as in "spic").[32] Meaning works through iterability, that is, the invocation of prior meanings. When those prior meanings are centuries old and globally spread, they are going to be hard to dislodge. On the other hand, words do not simply pick out things that exist prior to their being picked out, and thus reference is mutable.

So the first point I am making is this: despite our hopes that the influx of Latinas/os on the North American continent, in all of our beautiful diversity, would transform and annhilate the binaries and purist racial ideologies prevalent in the United States, this is not likely, at least not very soon. Existing systems of meaning will absorb and transform our own self-identifying terms in ways that may not be immediately obvious but which we need to become aware of. However, although we may be stuck with racial categories for longer than some of us would wish, it may be easier to help "race" slowly evolve than to try to do away with it as a first step.

Latinas/os in the United States have without a doubt been racialized. And I would argue that the history, and even the contemporary socioeconomic situation, of Latinas/os in the United States simply cannot be understood using ethnicity categories alone; we have been shut out of the melting pot because we have been seen as racial and not merely cultural "others."

However, this has not been true to the same degree for all of us. It has been true of Mexicans, Puerto Ricans, and Dominicans most of all, much less so of some others. So what are we to do in the face of this diversity of historical experience and social location? Is race perhaps a way to understand some Latina/o identities but not all? For a pan-Latina/o moniker, shouldn't we refer to ethnicity?

My argument has been that given the way in which our ethnicity has been racialized, this is a doubtful solution. Moreover, we are in almost all cases racially different from Anglos, in the commonly used sense of race. That is—even for Spaniards, as Jorge Gracia is arguing—we are not "purely European," claims of white Hispanicity notwithstanding. In the very name of antiracism and solidarity with other racialized people of color, shouldn't we acknowledge this, and not go the route of those who would seek to better their social status by differentiating themselves from the vilified racial others? Perhaps we can help lift the meaning of race out of its status as an insult by uniting with the efforts of those such as Gilroy and Gooding-Williams, who seek to give it a cultural meaning.

Of course, it does not make sense to say simply that Latinas/os constitute *a* "race," either by the common-sense meaning or by more nuanced references to historical narrative and cultural production. I (still) believe that if the concept of "mestizo" enters into U.S. culture, it can have some good effects against the presumption of purity as having an intrinsic value. Still, the concept of mestizo when applied to Latinas/os in general, as if all Latinas/os or the essence of being Latina/o is to be mestizo, has the effect of subordinating all Latinas/os, both North and South, whose descendants are entirely African, Indian, or Asian. Mestizos then become the cornerstone of the culture, with others pushed off to the side. This is clearly intolerable.

A concept that might be helpful here has been coined by David Theo Goldberg: ethnorace. Unlike race, ethnorace does not imply a common descent, which is precisely what tends to embroil race in notions of biological determinism and natural and heritable characteristics. Ethnorace might have the advantage of bringing into play the elements of both human agency and subjectivity involved in ethnicity—that is, an identity that is the product of self-creation—at the same time that it acknowledges the uncontrolled racializing aspects associated with the visible body. And the term would remind us that there are at least two concepts, rather than one, that are vitally necessary to the understanding of Latina/o identity in the United States: ethnicity and race. Using only ethnicity belies the reality of most Latinas/os' everyday experiences, as well as obscures our own awareness about how ethnic identifications often do the work of race while seeming to be theoretically correct and politically advanced. Race dogs our steps; let us not run from it lest we cause it to increase its determination.

Notes

Jorge Gracia gave me substantive help with this paper at all stages, for which I am extremely grateful. I am also very grateful to Pablo De Greiff, Eduardo Mendieta, Paula Moya, Angelo Corlett, and an anonymous reviewer for their helpful comments.

1. See Angel R. Oquendo, "Re-imagining the Latino/a Race," Richard Delgado and Jean Stefancic, eds. , in *The Latino/a Condition: A Critical Reader* (New York: New York University Press, 1998), 61.
2. I do not mean to imply here that the recent marketing construction of a pan-Latina/o U.S. identity is the first or only time such an identity has been imagined. I will discuss this further on.
3. See Todd Gitlin, *The Twilight of Common Dreams: Why America Is Wracked by Culture Wars* (New York: Henry Holt, 1995), and Arthur M. Schlesinger Jr. , *The Disuniting of America: Reflections on a Multicultural Society* (New York: W. W. Norton, 1992). Also see Jennifer L. Hochschild, *Facing Up to the American Dream* (Princeton: Princeton University Press, 1996), and Jean Bethke Elshtain, *Democracy on Trial* (New York: HarperCollins, 1997).
4. See Daniel Mato, "Problems in the Making of Representations of All-Encompassing U.S. Latina/o—'Latin' American Transitional Identities," in *The Latino*

Review of Books 3, 1–2 (1997): 2–7; Arlene Davila, "Advertising and Latino Cultural Fictions," in Arlene Davila and Agustín Lao-Montes, *Mambo Montaje: The Latinization of New York* (New York: Columbia University Press, forthcoming); Juan Flores and George Yudice, "Buscando América: Languages of Latino Self-Formation," *Social Text* 24 (1990): 57–84.

5. Michael Omi and Howard Winant, *Racial Formations in the United States: From the 1960s to the 1980s* (New York: Routledge, 1986), 60.
6. Suzanne Oboler, *Ethnic Labels, Latino Lives: Identity and the Politics of (Re)Presentation in the United States* (Minneapolis: University of Minnesota Press, 1995), xiii.
7. Mato, "Problems in the Making of Representations," 2.
8. Oboler, *Ethnic Labels, Latino Lives*; see esp. ch. 1.
9. Ibid., 13.
10. As a Panamanian American who vividly remembers the 1989 U.S. invasion but who has lived most of my life in the United States, growing up especially around Cubans, I found both arguments persuasive.
11. See Davila, "Advertising and Latino Cultural Fictions"; Mato, "Problems in the Making of Representations."
12. Mato, "Problems in the Making of Representations," 2.
13. Cited in Michel Foucault, *The Order of Things: An Archaeology of the Human Sciences* (New York: Random House, 1970), xv.
14. Jorge Gracia, personal communication, December 1998.
15. "Disparities Grow in SAT Scores of Ethnic and Racial Groups," *Chronicle of Higher Education*, Sept. 11, 1998, A42. Emphasis added.
16. Anita Allen, "Recent Racial Constructions in the U.S. Census," paper presented at the "Race: Its Meaning and Significance" conference, Rutgers University, November 1994.
17. Ramón Grosfoguel and Chloé S. Georas, "The Racialization of Latino Caribbean Migrants in the New York Metropolitan Area," *CENTRO Journal of the Center for Puerto Rican Studies* 8, 1–2 (1996): 199.
18. See, for example, Jorge Klor de Alva's arguments (against Cornel West) on this point in "Our Next Race Question: The Uneasiness between Blacks and Latinos," *Harper's*, April 1996, 55–63.
19. Klor de Alva, "Our Next Race Question," 56.
20. Oquendo, "Re-imaging the Latino/a Race," 60.
21. Clara E. Rodríguez, *Puerto Ricans Born in the U.S.A.* (Boston: Unwin Hyman, 1989).
22. Anthony Appiah, *In My Father's House: Africa in the Philosophy of Culture* (New York: Oxford University Press, 1992); Naomi Zack, *Race and Mixed Race* (Philadelphia: Temple University Press, 1993).
23. Luis Angel Toro, "Race, Identity, and 'Box Checking': The Hispanic Classification in OMB Directive No. 15," in Richard Delgado and Jean Stefancic, eds., *The Latino/a Condition* (New York: New York University Press, 1998), 58. Emphasis in original.
24. Grosfoguel and Georas, "The Racialization of Latino Caribbean Migrants," 197.
25. Ibid, 198.
26. Ibid, 199.

27. Ibid, 195.
28. Virginia Domínguez, "Editor's Foreword: The Dialectics of Race and Culture," *Identities: Global Studies in Culture and Power* 1, 4 (1998): 297–300.
29. I am very aware of the paradoxical way this question is raised (since in a project of deracialization one shouldn't refer to people by their color), and of other paradoxes with the categories I've used at times in this paper (e.g. the use of the category "black" when I have argued that it is oppressive). It is impossible to avoid all such paradoxes while maintaining clarity about which groups one is trying to pick out. All I can hope to have done is to problematize all such categories, and increase our self-reflectiveness about them.
30. I make these arguments in more depth in my paper "The Phenomenology of Racial Embodiment," *Radical Philosophy* 95 (May/June 1999): 15–26.
31. See Paul Gilroy, *The Black Atlantic: Modernity and Double Consciousness* (Cambridge: Harvard University Press, 1993); Robert Gooding-Williams, "Race, Multiculturalism, and Justice," *Constellations* 5, 1 (1998): 18–41; Patricia Williams, *Seeing a Color Blind Future: The Paradox of Race* (New York: Farrar, Straus, and Giroux, 1997); Lewis Gordon, *Bad Faith and Antiblack Racism* (Atlantic Highlands, N.J.: Humanities Press, 1995).
32. Michele Moody-Adams, "Excitable Speech: A Politics of the Performative," *Women's Review of Books* 15, 1 (October 1997): 13–14. And I would suggest that even John Leguizamo's brilliant comic use of terms like "Spic-o-rama" plays off the negative connotations of the term rather than transforming it into a positive term.

2 The Making of New Peoples

Hispanizing Race

Eduardo Mendieta

When Gunnar Myrdal published in 1944 a thousand-page summary of his investigation into the reasons for the persistence of poverty and political marginalization among blacks under the title of *An American Dilemma*, he provided U.S. society with a vocabulary with which to speak about its race problem. This American dilemma consisted of the struggle for America's soul between two mutually exclusionary ideals: the noble quest for democratic inclusion, and the ignominous ideal of racial exclusion. Many of the great legal, political, social, and cultural gains in the twentieth century by African Americans and other minorities were the direct result of attempts to resolve this dilemma in favor of the noble quest for democratic inclusion. Today, however, a new American dilemma begins to dawn on the horizon. It is a dilemma that has roots in the racial history of the United States, but that at the same time points beyond race. Latinos, or Hispanics, are the people that embody this new American dilemma. In this new millennium Hispanics and Latinos will be the largest minority. They are also the poorest of the poor, as well as the most undereducated (lowest percentage of higher-education attainment), and the ones with the lowest rate of home ownership (always a measure of economic stability).[1] Yet Hispanics and Latinos are being born, growing up, and arriving in the United States at a time when the state has begun to turn its back on minorities, the disadvantaged, the underclass. Hispanics are most in need precisely at the moment when less and less is being allocated to alleviate and ameliorate the harsh consequences of growing economic inequality. The dilemma that Hispanics and Latinos represent to the United States continues to be about the quest for democratic inclusion, but now denied not on the basis of race but because of other factors: language, ethnicity, class, religion, and political marginalization. Roberto Suro captured eloquently and acutely the new dilemma that we Hispanics and Latinos represent to a new America:[2] "Latinos are rapidly becoming the nation's largest minority group at a time when that term is quickly losing its meaning. Latino immigration can prompt the creation of a new civil rights framework that distinguishes between two distinct tasks—redressing the effects of past discrimination and providing protection against new forms of bias—and undertakes both aggressively."[3]

In the following essay I will address only one aspect of the dilemma that Hispanics and Latinos present to the United States, namely, their relationship to race. In view of the United States' racial history, it might be tempting to revert to discourses of racialization in order to develop a vocabulary that will allow Hispanics and Latinos to make justice claims. This essay argues against this temptation. I will first discuss the artificial, and highly charged, character of the labels "Hispanic" and "Latino." Next, I will offer a historical overview of the divergent experiences that the United States and Latin America have had with race. This historical detour allows me to offer evidence for the larger claim: that attempts to racialize Hispanics and Latinos are both inimical to our historical experience and counterproductive to our political goals. I conclude with what is a corollary of the prior claim, namely, that Hispanics and Latinos are acting as a powerful agent of change in the United States. As people who resist racialization, even if they were products of racial practices, they are also ineluctably altering the grammar of U.S. political, social, racial, and even economic culture. To paraphrase Roberto Suro, Latinos are players in the old and unresolved dilemma of race in America, but because they do not fit any of the available colors, they are a force that is changing the terms of that dilemma.[4]

This work, in other words, is guided by the following methodological and conceptual considerations. First, since identities, be they racial, ethnic, sexual, or other, are fluid and relational, it seems reasonable to assume that U.S. notions of race will not remain unaltered by the influx of so many people whose own experiences with race have been so different. Conversely, the construction and development of new identities is partly a process of negotiation that includes acceptance and assimilation but also rejection and disavowal. Hispanics and Latinos, even as they are racialized, resist and accept some aspects of race while transforming the very nature of "race." Second, too much speculation about race, class, and gender, to name just a few of the many markers and conditions of agent formation, proceeds without reference to history, to the way these attempts to identifying, naming, placing human agents are results of accumulations, of socio-politico-economic formations. To neglect, even to be ignorant of, the historicity of racial formations—to use Winant and Omi's felicitous phrase—in the United States can lead us to globalize U.S. racial ideologies while inuring us to critiques of racism that have emerged from other contexts in which different racial formations have arisen.[5] Which means, third, that the historical narrative I present is merely propadeutic and heuristic. I offer one reconstruction. I am sure that there are other ways of reconstructing the contrasts and comparisons I am going to make between the United States and Latin America. The core of my argument, however, is not rooted in my historical reconstruction, but the latter does offer some warrants for the plausibility of the former. I am not a historian but a social philosopher who wants to keep history at the center of his philosophizing.

Labeling Others, Naming Ourselves

In the United States "Hispanic" and "Latino" are social markers that have acquired meaning within the context of this country's ethnic and racial apportionment of its political territory. They are used to refer to a heterogeneous collection of people who do not see or recognize themselves as a single group. To be a "Hispanic" or "Latino" is to be signified upon rather than to be the one who signifies. These are terms through which others refer to us, discounting the many other ways in which we refer to ourselves. To be a "Hispanic" or "Latino" is to be like a third in a conversation who serves as a relay and a translator. Rarely, however, do we "Hispanics" or "Latinos" in our daily life, in relations with others who share our supposed ethnicity, talk to each other as either "Hispanics" or "Latinos." We generally say something like "we Colombians" or Caribeños, Venezuelans, Mexicans, and so on. In fact, we are not Hispanic in the same way as blacks are African-American, that is, by race, and thus by fate. We become Hispanic. For us "Hispanic" and "Latino" are not fate but a quest, a choice, even an alternative. We certainly do not begin with these categories. We learn to think through them as we become part of the society and culture of the U.S. political structure. We learn to think of ourselves through these imposed categories. It is in this sense that Hispanics are a people in the process of becoming. One arrives a Guatemalan, Salvadorean, Colombian, Cuban, Venezuelan, Peruvian, Costa Rican, or Dominican, and slowly, after painful experiences of oppression, marginalization, and isolation, starts to learn to become a Latino and Hispanic.[6] But in the process of learning to become a Latino and Hispanic, what were originally artificial and imposed labels now take on a different character. These terms become ways for us to claim and build a place in the political culture of the United States.

There is another side to this process of making and becoming Hispanics and Latinos. Just as Venezuelans, Colombians, Peruvians, Chileans, and so on are remade into Hispanics, North Americans, Estadounidenses, Norteamericanos, are re-creating themselves. The making of other peoples, of other ethnicities, that accounts for the drawing of the internal lines of the political territory of the United States also signifies the remaking of the "American" people in general. This, unfortunately, is less evident than it should be. For the other side of recognition is identification; that is, to recognize another entails that I identify myself in relation to those whom I recognize. Whom I am willing to recognize, and how I recognize them, tells all about who I think I am. Conversely, how I identify myself determines the scope of my ability to recognize others. In concrete terms this means that we, and here I mean the "we" of the United States, will not remain untouched and untransformed by the ways in which this "we" decides to mark and categorize others, others who are becoming part of that changing "we." Hispanics and Latinos are a people who are coming into being, but so are the people of the United States in general. America, in short, is remaking itself as it names and marks peoples within and without itself.

Racializing Hispanics and Hispanizing Race

Race has so indelibly marked the identity of the United States that one may want to agree with Howard Winant: "U.S. society is so thoroughly racialized that to be without racial identity is to be in danger of having no identity."[7] This much is indisputable, even if we cannot agree on what race is. We certainly know that it determined the Pilgrims' relationships to Native Americans, whom they displaced and decimated, and African Americans, whom they enslaved and then consistently continued to marginalize even after they became free. Even some European immigrants during the eighteenth and nineteenth centuries were initially racialized because of their eastern or southern European origin. However, the Irish, Germans, and Italians were eventually assimilated to the extent that they were deracialized.[8]

We also know that the political and constitutional history of the United States has been partly a process of negotiation of racial labels, and partly an attempt to redress the onerous consequences of the history of exclusion and disenfranchisement that resulted from racialization.[9] The alternation between exclusion and inclusion on the basis of race gave rise to a particular dialectic in the history of the United States. The history of the interpretation of our Constitution, for instance, evidences the simultaneous processes of acknowledgment of racism and the attempt to remedy the deleterious consequences of that racism.[10] Claims to justice, that is, to participation in the political, economic, social, and cultural life of the nation, have had to be made in terms of race.[11] Thus within the United States citizenship acquired the ambiguous character of both a status and a set of entitlements and claims to rights. As a status, it became a privilege that was exclusionary and particularist; as a set of entitlements and rights, it became an institution of inclusion and universalization. Of course, the history of citizenship and justice struggles also includes claims made with reference to sex and gender, but these I have to bracket for now. The history of the interpretation and self-understanding of the United States, whether it be cultural, political, or legal, has had to contend with the centrality of race in that history.[12]

Hispanics have been created in this context, and partly in response to its legacy.[13] At the very moment of the inception of this category, however, the attempt to racialize Hispanics encountered a major stumbling block: Hispanics are not a race, they are an ethnicity. One can argue that they do not even constitute an ethnicity, for an ethnicity consists of a set of social practices that can be discerned and distinctly drawn out. Yet Hispanics span the gamut of social practices and institutions. There are Catholic Hispanics as well as Protestant, Jewish, Muslim, syncretist, and post-Christian Hispanics. At times, if we dismantle and disaggregate all of the elements that purportedly constitute either race or ethnicity with respect to Hispanics, all that we can retain is the Spanish language as a unifying point of reference. But even this last threatens to melt away, for Hispanics also speak English, French, Portuguese, Quechua, Guaraní, Toltec, Nahuatl. Jorge Gracia has eloquently and persuasively demonstrated why "Hispanic" is too amorphous a category to agglutinate the plurality of cultural, religious, linguistic, and even racial experiences that are supposed to be referred to by the term.[14]

Nonetheless, there is the imperative logic of the grammar of political culture in the United States, which would like to conceive Hispanics in terms of both race and ethnicity. I will argue that efforts to racialize Hispanics should be resisted for at least four reasons. First, race has been the driving force behind a disastrous history that we can never forget but that we, as Americans, must overcome. Although we Americans can never forget how race has configured us, we have to begin to think of ways of constructing and creating our identity in other than racial terms. Second, race, precisely because it has been so central to U.S. identity, has polarized the grammar of U.S. political culture into two extremes: white and black. The United States thinks of itself as two nations, or a nation divided between two camps: white and black. Indeed, it would seem that the U.S. perception of race includes only two colors, and this makes us blind to other hues.[15] As Peter Winn noted in his excellent work *Americas: The Changing Face of Latin America and the Caribbean,*

"Compared to Latin America and the Caribbean, the United States is not just racist, but color-blind: people are either black or white."[16] Or, more appropriately with reference to Hispanics and Latinos in the United States, as Suro notes: "In the United States, a glance is suppossed to reveal everything, and people who are not white are immediately assigned to a minority group. Seeing immigrants that way is a form of blindness. Latinos challenge their hosts to cure the malady."[17] Third, at the present historical juncture race itself is being challenged as a category of political and economic analysis. Many are even questioning the usefulness of race as a rubric under which to gather cultural, economic, political, and legal claims.[18] As we move into a new millennium and become a more hybrid and mestizo people—in short, as we are Hispanicized (what is called the browning of America[19]), it is becoming increasingly difficult to make social, political, and economic claims on the basis of race.[20] The space in this essay is too short to expand on this point. However, in the context of the United States during the last decades, we have to look at the crisis of "race pride movements," or racial identity movements, in tandem with the crisis of the welfare state. The unraveling of the class compromise that was achieved in the early part of the twentieth century, which is why the welfare state was one of the greatest achievements of that century, has also led to the challenge of race as valid category of political and economic redress. As the welfare system begins to be dismantled, the ways in which race claims could be addressed has also been dismantled. Furthermore, the crisis of the welfare state is also linked to the globalization of the American economy. Thus, my claims about the "declining significance of race" have nothing to do with a rejection of the importance of race, or the derision of its validity as a rubric and category of social analysis; instead, they are about the changing force field that repositions race along with other vectors of social significance. Fourth, to racialize Hispanics, or to think of Hispanics as a racial category, forces a group of people who have had a very different relationship to race to adopt a very questionable and onerous label. Instead of a racialized Hispanic/Latino, we should think in terms of a dialogical Hispanicity, to use Pedro Lange-Churión's term.[21] A dialogical Hispanicity is challenging as well as challenged. Try as we might, Hispanics will resist being racialized. Simultaneously, however, the attempt to racialize us, and the experience of U.S. biological and institutional racism, will challenge Hispanics to become aware of their own *racismo*.[22]

I would like to focus my next remarks on this last reason for rejecting the racialization of Hispanics, and I do this by offering a historical detour. Race has also been central to the constitutions of Latin Americans, but in a different way.[23] This must be taken into account if we are to understand why Hispanics resist and should continue to resist being racialized.

Racial Formations in the Americas

The year 1492 marked not just the so-called discovery of the New World, but also the culmination of the expulsion of the Muslims from the Iberian peninsula, as well as the ultimatum to the Jews to either leave the peninsula or convert.[24] The discovery and conquest of the New World was deeply influenced by the drive to establish both religious homogeneity and territorial unity in the Iberian peninsula. The worldview of the Spaniards was constituted by a confrontation with the infidel, or Muslim, and the traitor, or Jew. The Spanish Inquisition, purportedly established to ensure orthodoxy, was also an institution that sought to police racial purity.[25] When the Spaniards discovered the New World, they faced a choice: to see these new people as either infidels or betrayers. But the radical otherness of the Amerindians, the original impressions that they were primitive, even innocent, creatures, made it difficult to assimilate them to the established schemas. In fact, the so-called *indios* became a "conundrum," to use Peter Wade's term.[26]

Evidently the fact that Amerindians were neither infidels nor traitors was to the advantage of the Spanish as well as the Portuguese, who went on to develop ideologies of evangelization. "Indians," then, were not a people to be either expulsed or waged holy war upon (not at the beginning, at least). To this extent they were truly a new people, one that did not fit the cultural map of the medieval Christians.[27] This map had begun to be racialized as the struggles against Muslims had finally reached their zenith. In the end, the Amerindian was a lost soul to be saved, a child to be guided and educated. This was the putative goal of the *encomienda* and the *repartimientos.* True, the conquistadors were also driven by a quest for riches and for a way to climb the social ladder. The Amerindians were decimated both by an unforeseeable and devastating clash of previously isolated immunogenic systems and by the logic of the money and labor economies that the Spaniards imposed upon the Amerindian trade and barter economies.[28] While Amerindians did get conscripted forcefully into the service of the Spanish and Portuguese, the ideological justification held that this was beneficial to them. In fact, their work was a way to pay for their own education, to put it in Aesopian language. Amerindians were not, however, enslaved, corralled into auction blocks, or vilified because they were seen as threatening and contaminating.[29] One may argue, in contrast, that before *indio* became a term of racial opprobrium it was above all a specific administrative and fiscal category that built on and continued the tributary economic system of native cultures.[30]

So much for the discovery and the first encounters. But what about the conquest and the period of colonization? There is a popular Mexican saying that the conquest was carried out by Indians, and independence was achieved by *criollos.* There is great irony and truth in this refrain. Cortés and Pizarro never would have accomplished their feats of conquest had it not been for the aid of dissenting tribes of Amerindians who in fact were carrying out a civil war by aiding the Spaniards. This is an important and not sufficiently acknowledged historical fact. Furthermore, once the Spaniards imposed themselves as rulers, they did so by essentially taking over the Aztec and Inca hierarchies. A modus vivendi was established between the old hierarchies and the new rulers.[31] In Peru, Pizarro and his brothers were essentially allowed to rule because it was thought they would be temporary dictators. The Spaniards, in short, were so successful in their conquest because they knew how to work with the already existing structures of social and political control.[32] In fact, Spanish and Aztec as well as Inca cultures lived side by side. Churches were built on top of pyramids or adjacent to them. Universities were founded in which Latin and Nahuatl were used as lingua francas to teach the trivium and quadrivium. Today Mexico and central South America remain areas with large indigenous populations, and this betrays the fiction that the Amerindians were everywhere exterminated.

In addition, powerful discourses of *indigenismo* developed in the territories that contained the high pre-Columbian civilizations, and which today are countries with growing Amerindian populations, especially Mexico and Peru. The Mexican revolution of 1910, which signaled both political and economic watersheds in the country, was motivated and accomplished through the mobilization of the myth of the Mexican by appealing to his Amerindian roots.[33] It can be argued that the projects of nation-state building of the nineteenth and twentieth centuries in Latin America have been predicated on discourses of both *indigenismo* and *mestizaje.* Here one needs to recall the discourses of Rodó, Vasconcelos, Martí, and Ureña.[34] The same cannot be said of the younger nations of the southern part of South America, namely, Argentina, Uruguay, Paraguay, and Chile, where Amerindians were indeed systematically exterminated. In short, the Spanish and Portuguese succeeded in conquering the New World partly aided by the Amerindian. This complicity was acknowledged at the time, even if it has been forgotten.

But Latin Americans are not just *criollos* or mestizos. They are also mulattos and *negros.* Latin America's "race problem," to use the U.S. expression, is compounded by the mixing of Spanish, Portuguese, Amerindian, and African. To give a pointed description of this history, I will quote from Santamaria's *Diccionario de Mejicanismos,* which attempts to draw a complicated taxonomy or phenotypic phylogeny out of the different mixes that can be discerned.

Español con India—Mestizo
Mestizo con Española—Castizo
Castizo con Española—Español
Español con Negra—Mulato
Mulato con Española—Chino
Chino con India—Salta atrás [*skip backward*]
Salta atrás con Mulata—Lobo [*wolf*]
Lobo con China—Gibaro
Gibaro con Mulata—Albarazado
Albarazado con Negra—Cambujo
Cambujo con India—Zambaigo
Zambaigo con Loba—Calpamulato
Calpamulato con Cambuza—Tente en el aire [*flaps in the air*]
Tente en el aire con Mulata—No te entiendo
No te entiendo con India—Torna atrás
[*throwback, back to the beginning*][35]

This list seems to suggest that race is in the eye of the beholder, malleable and disposable for those with wealth, inescapable and intractable for the poor. This next list, gathered in Brazil, illustrates even more starkly the subjective character of race in Latin America: "*Branco, preto, sarará, moreno claro, moreno escuro, mulato, moreno, mulato claro, mulato escuro, negro, caboclo, escuro, côr de canela, preto claro, roxo claro, côr de cinza, vermelho, caboclo escuro, pardo, branco sarará, mambebe, branco cabocaldo, mulato sarará, gazula, côr de cinza clara, creolo, louro, moreno claro caboclado, mulato bem claro, branco mulato, roxo de cabelo bom, preto escuro, pelé.*"[36] It is thus not surprising that Brazil considers itself a multiethnic and multicultural nation, with a strong tradition of Afro-Hispanic resistance and thus of dignity and self-respect. Haiti, since its independence in 1804, has unequivocally defined itself as a black nation, without apologies and with great pride. The Dominican Republic, on the other hand, is a mulatto nation, where three out of every four people are of mixed European and African descent. In contrast to Haiti, however, Dominicans are less clear about their identity, which underwent serious manipulation and reconstruction in the middle of the twentieth century.

These seem very distant historical events, processes that refer to world-historical trends. They do not seem to have any relevance to our present problems. Yet these events determined the ways in which the peoples from the misnamed West Indies, New Spain, New Granada, and what we today call the Americas came to think of themselves not necessarily in racial terms, or at least not in the way that Anglo-Saxons conceptualize and manipulate race. For

Latin Americans, race has been more a question of skin pigmentation, nose shape, and height than of human dignity and thus exclusion from socio-economic and political power. Indeed, the central category in Latin America is class, not race.[37] This must be qualified, however, so that I do not misrepresent what I am trying to say. While there is racism, this has more to do with access to extremely scarce social resources than with questions of the purity and hybridization of peoples who have been in a continuous process of *mestizaje*.[38] The history of colonialism weighs heavily upon the Latin American countries, and part of that ballast is the way in which relative social harmony and interracial and ethnic tolerance were bought at the expense of social mobility and political transformation.[39]

Anglo-Saxons, on the other hand, who arrived in the New World in the seventeenth century, almost 150 years later than the Iberians, came with very different goals and a very different worldview. Germán Arciniegas has described the differences between Hispanic America and Anglo America in terms of four stages of encounter with the New World: discovery, conquest, colony, independence. Whereas Hispanic America began with the discovery, proceeded with the conquest and then the colony, and finally gained independence in the eighteenth and nineteenth centuries, Anglo America began with independence, proceeded to establish its colonies, then conquered the continent, and began only in the nineteenth and twentieth centuries to discover it.[40] This juxtaposition is certainly an extreme characterization, not to say caricature. Yet it is illustrative of the different points of departure for two different ways of encountering the New World.

The fact is that most of the Anglo-Saxons who established the first colonies on the northern part of the North American continent came after a rupture had already taken place with their world. They came to establish a new Jerusalem, but one that was certainly different from that of the Old World. To this extent, their relationship to Amerindians was determined by belligerence and conflict, animosity and resentment.[41] The fact that the Anglo-Saxons did not encounter great Amerindian civilizations, as Cortés and Pizarro did, also determined the ways in which the Anglo-Saxon colonizer would look upon the Amerindian. Another fundamental difference between Anglo American and Hispanic America is that by the seventeenth century a highly elaborate and detailed European discourse on race had already developed to legitimize the enslavement of Africans, the ghettoization of Jews, and the creation of imaginary nations based on racial purity and homogeneity.[42] We know, furthermore, that Anglo-Saxons moved as groups—whole towns, communities, and churches—to the New World. The new colonies in the North were entire families and networks of filial links transplanted from Europe. This evidently made it less likely that Anglo-Saxons would either want or even be tempted to mix with Amerindians. As the colonies grew, the economy expanded, and the Anglo-Saxon Americans populated the northeastern coast of the North American continent, a struggle against Indians, Spaniards, and Frenchmen began. In this struggle the ideological construct of the racial inferiority of both Indians and blacks became pivotal. There was no space for accommodation or mutual tolerance. Indians were unworthy of the continent they occupied and blacks were beasts of labor that had to obey their white masters. Eduardo Subirats has beautifully shown how the notion that America was an "empty continent" was a precondition for the conquest and colonization of the New World. In contrast to the Iberian conquistadors and missionaries, the Anglo-Saxon colonizers saw America as empty of peoples, cultures, and religions—what we today call life worlds—worthy of respect and awe, and thus perhaps meriting preservation and reverence.[43]

In the eighteenth and nineteenth centuries, race continued to gain a hold on the imaginary and sociopolitical culture of the new nation that became known as the United States of America. Racist ideologies were deployed against the Native American peoples of its midwestern and western prairies, the Mexican and Spanish peoples of the Southwest, and the Chinese who began migrating to San Francisco in the eighteenth century.

Race, in short, has been part of an ideology of conquest, subjugation, and subalternization, of destruction and decimation. To this day, we do not cease to be shocked by the cold, deliberate, and calculating way in which Anglo Americans attacked, willfully infected with disease, betrayed, and deceived not just Native Americans but also blacks and even Mexicans. This is certainly contrary to the image of a Spaniard reading a *declaración* to a gathering of Amerindians, seeking to convert them to Christianity, and whose rejection would give grounds for waging "just war." For Hispanic America, race was about one's skin color and hair type, but never about one's humanity. To this extent, it really never meant more than a series of self-canceling regulations, mythological narratives of origins and lineage. Race self-destructed in the Latin American context. For Anglo America, race was a means to dispossessing others of their humanity so that they then could become beasts of labor under the "peculiar institution." In Anglo America, race crystallized in objective institutions, legal regulations, political dispensations, and cultural prescriptions, thereby becoming a social fact that refused to acknowledge its fictional character. Race was read as a biological fact, and as such, it became nature: ineluctable, irreversible, uncircumventable. Race became fate.

This narrative, too brief and too skewed by the immediate tasks of the essay, can be synthesized into the following observation. In the Americas, specifically in Latin America and the United States, racial formations have coalesced around two different axes: in the United States around the axis of domination and exclusion, in Latin America around the axis of hegemony and inclusion.[44] Latin American racial formations are defined by *mestizaje*, multiracial group inclusion, and color differentiation. Racial hegemony is maintained through co-optive incorporation and reinterpretation. U.S. racial formations are defined by hypodescent, strict phenotypic differentiation that polarizes into unreal biracial categories. Racial domination is maintained through exclusion, marginalization, and repression. Today, however, due to processes of globalization, these differences in racial formations in the Americas are disappearing, even though they informed the dynamics of ethnic struggles over the last century.[45] Still, underscoring and foregrounding these differences should not be interpreted as condoning one while vilifying the other. In other words, the malignancy of one does not entail the alleged innocuousness of the other. The point is that being ignorant of these differences makes us vulnerable to new forms of racism, and deleteriously uncreative and cynical before older forms of racism.

To conclude, the historical detour I provided above should allow us to appreciate the ways in which Hispanics are mystified and disoriented by the American urge to racialize everyone and everything. When we are sent looking for a Hispanic, we do not know what we are looking for. This is certainly a problem for both Hispanics and Americans. It is a problem for Hispanics because it makes it hard for us to posit our claims for justice—claims for redistribution, as Nancy Fraser calls them—on the basis of recognition claims.[46] This is not to say that we do not need to, or cannot, make recognition claims. We certainly can and must. But these claims are and will be of a different sort than those we are accustomed to because of the polarized racial imaginary of American political culture. That one does not know—and really cannot know—what a Hispanic looks like from his or her purported visible identity is also a problem for Americans in general because here they are faced with a people who must be acknowledged, recognized, and granted certain rights.[47] These rights, however, cannot be granted on appeals and claims that have anything to do with the United States' history of slavery and its endemic sexist puritanism.[48] Let me conclude by suggesting that, just as Latin Americans dismantled race through five hundred years of *mestizaje* and miscegenation, they are poised to contribute to the remaking and reconfiguration of America by dismantling its racial edifice, which has been as much auction block as confessional and penitential church.

Notes

I want to thank Jorge Gracia and Pablo De Greiff for their detailed comments on earlier versions of this paper. I would also like to thank the anonymous readers for Routledge who read the manuscript of this entire book and commented with great perspicuity and at length.

1. For these statistics, see Mary Romero's introduction to Mary Romero, Pierre Hondagneu-Sotelo, and Vilma Ortiz, eds., *Challenging Fronteras: Structuring Latina and Latino Lives in the U.S.* (New York: Routledge, 1997), xiii–xix.
2. I will throughout this essay use "we" in an ambivalent, always shifting sense. On the one hand, and at a more inmmediate level, "we" will refer to this created group called "Hispanic/Latinos." On the other, in a subtler but no less important sense, "we" will refer to the United States that is emerging from the ethnogenesis brought on by changing demographics: more immigrants, more miscegenation, more *mestizaje,* and so on. In both cases, I speak as part of a "we" that is emergent and transformative.
3. Roberto Suro, *Strangers among Us: How Latino Immigration Is Transforming America* (New York: Alfred A. Knopf, 1998), 25.
4. Suro, *Strangers among Us,* 10.
5. Michael Omi and Howard Winant, *Racial Formation in the United States: From the 1960s to the 1980s* (New York: Routledge, 1986). See also Howard Winant, *Racial Conditions: Politics, Theory, Comparisons* (Minneapolis: University of Minnesota Press, 1994).
6. On the dialectic between ethnicities and the redefinition of the United States, see Joseph Tilden Rhea, *Race Pride and the American Identity* (Cambridge, Mass.: Harvard University Press, 1997).
7. Winant, *Racial Conditions,* 16.
8. See the indispensable work by Ronald T. Takaki, *A Different Mirror: A History of Multicultural America* (Boston: Little, Brown, 1993).
9. Rogers Smith, *Civic Ideals: Conflicting Visions of Citizenship in U.S. History* (New Haven: Yale University Press, 1997); see also Richard Delgado, "Citizenship," in Juan F. Perea, ed., *Immigrants Out! The New Nativism and the Anti-Immigrant Impulse in the United States* (New York: New York University Press, 1997), 318–23.
10. See Nathan Glazer, *Ethnic Dilemmas: 1964–1982* (Cambridge, Mass.: Harvard University Press, 1983).
11. See Paul Finkelman, ed., *Slavery and the Law* (Madison, Wisc.: Madison House, 1997).
12. Judith N. Shklar, *American Citizenship: The Quest for Inclusion* (Cambridge, Mass.: Harvard University Press, 1991).
13. See Rhea, *Race Pride and the American Identity,* ch. 3: "Latinos."
14. See Jorge J. E. Gracia, *Hispanic/Latino Identity: A Philosophical Perspective* (Oxford: Blackwell, 2000); see also "Affirmative Action for Hispanics? Yes and No," in this volume.
15. See Juan F. Perea, "The Black/White Paradigm of Race," and Richard Delgado, "The Black/White Binary: How Does It Work?" both in Richard Delgado and Jean Stefancic, eds., *The Latino/a Condition: A Critical Reader* (New York: New York University Press, 1998), 359–68 and 369–75, respectively.
16. Peter Winn, *Americas: The Changing Face of Latin America and the Caribbean* (New York: Pantheon, 1993), 277.

17. Suro, *Strangers among Us*, 61.
18. See the fascinating and insightful conversation between Jorge Klor de Alva, Earl Shorris, and Cornel West: "Our Next Race Question: The Uneasiness between Blacks and Latinos," in Antonia Darder and Rodolfo D. Torres, eds., *The Latino Studies Reader: Culture, Economy and Society* (Oxford: Blackwell, 1998), 180–89.
19. In fact, the browning of America can be read in a pejorative way. I deploy Hispanicizing to counter this tendency. In fact, the very subtitle of my contribution should get us thinking about Hispanics not as a threat, problem, ballast, and so on, but actually as a positive, ameliorative, beneficient element in American society.
20. See William J. Wilson, *The Declining Significance of Race: Blacks and Changing American Institutions* (Chicago: University of Chicago Press, 1978), and *When Work Disappears: The World of the New Urban Poor* (New York: Knopf, 1996). See also Dana Y. Takagi, *The Retreat from Race: Asian-American Admissions and Racial Politics* (New Brunswick, N.J.: Rutgers University Press, 1998 [1992]). This last book is a fascinating case study of the tensions between two types of minorities: ethnic and racial minorities.
21. Pedro Lange-Churión, "Una hispanidad dialógica y conflictiva," *Quimera* 1998: 58–64.
22. See Earl Shorris, *Latinos: Biography of the People* (New York: Avon, 1994 [1992]), 146 ff. Shorris's discussion of Latino *racismo* is sobering, and one must never discount it. However, Shorris conflates class and *racismo*, and does not see how the two mix so inextricably in the Latin American context, especially in the context of immigrants. Compare with Winn, *Americas*, 277 ff., and Marvin Harris, *Patterns of Race in the Americas* (New York: Walker and Company, 1964).
23. See Peter Wade, *Race and Ethnicity in Latin America* (London: Pluto Press, 1997), and Winn, *Americas*. The classic works of reference are Frank Tannenbaum, *Slave and Citizen: The Negro in the Americas* (New York: Vintage, 1946), Carl N. Degler, *Neither Black nor White: Slavery and Race Relations in Brazil and the United States* (New York: Macmillan, 1971), and the wonderful articles by Thomas Skidmore, "Toward a Comparative Analysis of Race Relations since Abolition in Brazil and the United States," *Journal of Latin American Studies* 4, 1 (1972): 1–28, and "Bi-racial U.S.A. vs. Multi-Racial Brazil: Is the Contrast Still Valid?" *Journal of Latin American Studies* 25 (1993): 373–86. See also Anthony W. Marx, *Making Race and Nation: A Comparison of South Africa, The United States, and Brazil* (Cambridge: Cambridge University Press, 1998). Wade's work, however, remains the most succinct introduction and overview to the literature and theoretical debates.
24. Bernard Lewis, *Cultures in Conflict: Christians, Muslims, and Jews in the Age of Discovery* (Oxford: Oxford University Press, 1995).
25. See B. Netanyahu, *The Origins of the Inquisition in Fifteenth Century Spain* (New York: Random House, 1992), 975–1004.
26. Wade, *Race and Ethnicity in Latin America*, 26.
27. See Peter Mason, *Deconstructing America: Representations of the Other* (London: Routledge, 1990); Peter Hulme, *Colonial Encounters: Europe and the Native Caribbean, 1492–1797* (London and New York: Routledge, 1992); Anthony Pagden, *European Encounters with the New World* (New Haven: Yale University Press, 1993).

28. See Darcy Ribeiro, *The Americas and Civilization*, trans. Linton Lomas Barrett and Marie McDavid Barrett (New York: E. P. Dutton, 1972), 111.
29. See Ivan Hannaford, *Race: The History of an Idea in the West* (Baltimore: Johns Hopkins University Press, 1996), 150.
30. See Peter Wade, *Race and Ethnicity in Latin America*, 28.
31. See Nathan Wachtel, "The Indian and the Spanish Conquest," in Leslie Bethell, ed., *The Cambridge History of Latin America*, vol. 1: *Colonial Latin America* (Cambridge: Cambridge University Press, 1984), 207–48.
32. See Edwin Williamson, "Indians and Iberians," in *The Penguin History of Latin America* (New York: Penguin Books, 1992), 77–115.
33. See the fascinating study by Alan Knight, "Racism, Revolution, and *Indigenismo*: Mexico, 1910–1940," in Richard Graham, ed., *The Idea of Race in Latin America, 1870–1940* (Austin: University of Texas Press, 1990), 71–113.
34. See Germán Arciniegas, *Latin America: A Cultural History*, trans. Joan MacLean (New York: Alfred A. Knopf, 1975).
35. Cited in Shorris, *Latinos*, 149–50.
36. Harris, *Patterns of Race in the Americas*, 58.
37. For support of this claim, see Helen I. Safa's introduction, and her excellent bibliography on the question, in the special issue on race of *Latin American Perspectives* (25, 3 [1998]: 3–20). See also the discussion on the literature and theoretical debates surrounding this vexing question in Wade, *Race and Ethnicity in Latin America*, 29–30.
38. See Harris, *Patterns of Race in the Americas*, 95–99.
39. Ibid., 98.
40. Arciniegas, *Latin America: A Cultural History*, xxiii.
41. See Reginald Horsman, *Race and Manifest Destiny: The Origins of American Racial Anglo-Saxonism* (Cambridge, Mass.: Harvard University Press, 1981); Anthony Pagden, *Lords of All the World: Ideologies of Empire in Spain, Britain and France c. 1500–1800* (New Haven: Yale University Press, 1995).
42. See Theodore W. Allen, *The Invention of the White Race*, vol. 1: *Racial Oppression and Social Control* (London: Verso, 1994); see also Hannaford, *Race*, especially part II, "The Racialization of the West," 187 ff.
43. Eduardo Subirats, *El continente vacío* (México: Siglo XXI Editores, 1994).
44. See Helen Safa, "Introduction," 6
45. See Skidmore, "Bi-Racial U.S.A. vs. Multi-Racial Brazil." See also George M. Fredrickson, "The Strange Death of Segregation," *New York Review of Books* 46, 8 (1999): 36–38.
46. See Nancy Fraser, *Justice Interruptus: Cultural Reflections on the "Postsocialist" Condition* (New York: Routledge, 1996), ch. 1: "From Redistribution to Recognition? Dilemmas of Justice in a 'Postsocialist' Age."
47. I owe this term to Linda Alcoff, although I think I am using it in an entirely different sense.
48. The issue of affirmative action for Hispanics exemplifies what I mean. Jorge Gracia has dealt with this issue in a very enlightening way, reaching conclusions that I share. See Jorge J. E. Gracia, "Affirmative Action for Hispanics? Yes and No," in this volume.

Negotiating Latina Identities 3

Ofelia Schutte

This paper first calls attention to the problem of representing individuals as members of groups, taking the construction of Latino identities as a social process not primarily directed by individuals themselves, and therefore making them respond to larger interests. In the second part and as a way of contrast, the individual as agent in the definition of her own identifications is highlighted, and the analysis moves to the subjective question of negotiating Latina identities in a complexly constructed multicultural world.[1]

The Individual and the Group

If we look at individuals from the standpoint of social relations, one could say that the "I" is always already a part of a "we." Even in cases of a type of socialization that leads to the exclusion of persons from the group, the excluded may be seen in relation to the group or groups that exclude them. Broadly speaking, the identification of individuals as members of a group may be self-derived or imposed by others, and the qualities associated with group membership may be either positive or negative. One question that emerges in the consideration of group rights is the metastructure providing an umbrella for understanding the activity of multiple groups and the interactions among them. For a normative model of the healthy interaction among groups one would probably need to turn to social psychology, ethics, or a theory of justice. This is not the aim of my paper. What concerns me is the dynamic between the individual and the group (or groups), the role of groups in the definition of personal identity, and the subjection of individuals to prejudice and discrimination due to their inclusion in some groups or exclusion from others.

The civil rights movement and the struggle against racism have shown the difference between being excluded from a group *as an individual* and being excluded *as a member of a specific group*. The Martinican writer Frantz Fanon conceptualized the difference well when he noted that racism did not mean that he was disliked by one of his relatives or by a couple of neighbors across the street—situations that approximate the concept of individual rejection—but that the rejection is *group-derived*: "Look, a Negro!" anyone would say as he walked by.[2] The rejection had nothing to do with his individual characteristics, that is, with traits pertaining to his individual person; it had everything to do with his being identified as a member of the black race. Group membership, in normal conditions, is something that brings people social recognition—such as to be a member of a guild, of a profession, of a civic group. For this reason it is important that group membership does not turn into a condition of adversity for some and privilege for others. This is why, at the level of policy making, our society needs to be concerned with the balance of group representation, and to make sure that leadership positions in civil society and the state are not only open to, but also filled by, members of "underrepresented groups."

Racial discrimination and prejudice, just like ethnic discrimination and prejudice, are group-related forms of discrimination. Individuals caught in the web of group discrimination have at least three ways to fight it: (1) try to disassociate as much as possible from the discriminated group, by adopting the values and norms of the dominant group, sometimes (though not necessarily) by marrying a member of the dominant group, or by assimilating "upward" into the dominant power; the cost of this option could be the separation from relatives and friends who remain trapped in the discriminated group, or the rejection of qualities in oneself that "mark" one as a member of the discriminated group; (2) migrate (translocate) to a more congenial environment, which could signify a more positive and less alienated form of assimilation; again, this is not always a possible option, and there may not be environments sufficiently free from prejudice to which one may migrate successfully; (3) work to change the group status and to reconstitute group rights along a model of fairness aimed at transforming the dominant society. The first two constitute individual solutions; the third involves a social solution.

The work of Hispanic intellectuals engaged in Latino/Latin American studies may constitute an intersection of (2) and (3). That is, we have become sufficiently assimilated to work in the U.S. academy and do so successfully. At the same time, we use our position, at least in part, to help sustain the recognition of Hispanic studies and, insofar as possible, support the inclusion of marginalized groups in various spheres of citizenship activities, including higher education. This is tricky conceptually, because even as we may refer to group rights or to the need for inclusion of members of underrepresented groups in higher education, for example, what we are actually doing is promoting conditions for the assimilation of members of the underrepresented groups into the mainstream. The main difference between today and yesteryear, however, is that in the past the conceptual framework marking the assimilation referred to persons gaining inclusion in terms of their individual merits, whereas today the framework is given, more often than not, by identifying persons as members of a group deserving special attention.

If I am not mistaken, we seem to be living in an era whose cultural-political profile is the assimilation of groups into one national and, ultimately, global agenda. The inclusion of multiple perspectives one hopes to promote by extending leadership positions to persons of differently constituted groups (by sex, race, or ethnicity) remains subordinate to the goals of an impersonal "system" whose task is continually to increase its performance through the incorporation of differences and the delivery of new products for ever more extensive markets of consumption. In other words, group segregation is giving way to group assimilation as capitalism expands throughout the world without opposition, while in the United States a percentage of individuals from economically marginalized minorities joins the middle class. What we may be learning, however, from the current global crisis in capitalist markets is that where assimilation fails, the phenomenon that describes the position of the nonassimilated is more one of "dropping off" than one of outright exclusion. Whole nations, we are told, will simply drop off the global network of investments if they cannot adjust to the requirements and constraints established by the International Monetary Fund. Charity toward the needy is being ruled out. I suspect that somehow, in an analogous vein, the extension of entitlements to minority populations is predicated on the assumption that these populations (or influential parts of them) will become a highly productive part of the current socioeconomic system and will indeed extend the market value of the system and its products to "developing" regions and populations.

Seen in this context, affirmative action initiatives are fundamentally strategies of economic and cultural integration wherein previously marginalized or alienated populations (or segments thereof) are brought into the mainstream of socioeconomic mores, work habits, and productive activities. Affirmative action should be neither romanticized as the happy path to fame and fortune for women and minorities, nor vilified as the tool of special interests. One might look at it as a process of adjustment and balancing for stimulating a nation's economic indicators, much like what happens when the Federal Reserve raises or lowers interest rates by a fraction of a percent. Affirmative action involves the bet that the individuals recruited by the system—a fraction of its minority populations—will stimulate its growth and act as catalysts for the stability of the system. It is a process that accommodates some cultural and political interests that may otherwise be excluded and marginalized, in exchange for the revitalization and increased efficacy of an excessively homogeneous system dominated by whites, males, and the upper class. Of course, one has to believe one wants a diversified cultural elite (by gender, race, economic background, and ethnicity) in order for affirmative action programs to work. In a racist and masculine-dominant environment, affirmative action will not be taken seriously, and the leaders chosen will all look, think, and dress more or less alike.

If we follow the logic that the goal of affirmative action is the integration of the marginalized into the mainstream, then looking further into the future, it may be posited that in the long run this may lead to an indifference toward the preservation of diversity as constituted by ethnic or racial group membership. This is due to the fact that as groups become more assimilated into the global system, what will become more valued is the mobility of members across groups rather than their permanence or settlement within them. This is why territorial enclaves with a large predominance of (homogeneously defined) group members, who form part of a nation's racial and ethnic minorities, are vulnerable to being targeted for disfavor by the dominant economic establishment. The displacement of community populations from old-time neighborhoods, for example, shows that even the social structures of old barrios can be disbanded as upwardly mobile property owners move in, rezone a neighborhood, and expel the previous occupants toward ever more marginalized urban peripheries.

In the transitional phase in which we are living, a challenge for Hispanics is how to negotiate the tensions in our identities, taking into account our drive to succeed in the midst of adverse conditions, our interest in maintaining a meaningful degree of identification and solidarity with other Hispanics and with Hispanic communities even as we are assimilated into positions previously unoccupied by members of our ethnic group, and the knowledge that full assimilation calls for the erasure, abolition, and/or further marginalization and displacement of our groups. For example, in much popular (antidiversity) political rhetoric today, it is argued that it is *against* (not *for*) the benefit of Latino children to have Spanish taught in the schools, or that it is *against* (not *for*) the interest of minorities to have programs of affirmative action. In other words, one sees the trend today, except in enclaves where ethnic or racial minority status is politically and economically quite strong, as in south Florida, towards the erosion of minority group rights in the name of national unity and global citizenship.

My view is that, contrary to these indicators, it is in the best interest of Hispanics to retain our ethnic/cultural identifications and insist on some form of political representation based on group classifications. I say this, however, with some important reservations, for, like technology, which can either heal or kill, group classifications may be used for the good, but also for great evil—as in holocausts, genocides, ethnic cleansing, and massive discrimination. The classification of individuals into groups for purposes of social policy control is subject to a number of significant objections, including the fact that group identifications are vulnerable to manipulation, are subject to easy stereotyping, and in fact can do violence to individuals who differ substantially from the mainstream members of their groups. A different kind of objection with which I sympathize is that if one classifies people according to their membership in groups, in a racist society this will result in dividing people racially. There may be nothing more abusive than to classify individuals according to their racial features, especially if such features have had a long history of being used to privilege some and oppress others.

In view of these qualifications and objections, I think the argument for group rights should be derived from a broader principle of social justice, and not from an appeal to the intrinsic property of groups. I say this tentatively. But clearly, my tendency is to fortify not the concept of group properties as such, but a different and broader principle that looks at cultures in a broad scope, and then defends the concept of having a substrate of differentiating elements in cultures, such as the plurality of languages, the affirmation of historical-cultural precedents for individuals' current identifications, the extension of leadership positions to new constituencies that challenge the narrow-mindedness of patterns of behavior inherited from the past, and so on. In other words, the argument for "group rights" would not be derived (at least principally) from (1) the existence of groups or (2) the duty to preserve them (as, say, conservationists defend the preservation of endangered species—an approach that, in the case of biological groups, or species rights, I take to be fully justified). Rather, the argument would be derived from a conception guided by the principles of a culturally pluralist, democratic society. Such a conception recognizes that to deprive human beings of favorable conditions by which they can be recognized for their specific linguistic and historical-cultural achievements and contributions is to inflict a degree of violence on them. From an aesthetic-political standpoint, I tend to look at group differences as products of a vital way of affirming the plurality of cultures, rather than as a conservative apparatus used to demarcate, discipline, and police the boundaries and identities of groups. This is an important distinction, some of whose constitutive elements will be illustrated in the remaining part of this paper.

From Biculturality to Hybrid Identities

When my family moved to this country over thirty-five years ago, the term used to refer to the successful integration of immigrants into U.S. society was *bicultural.* Times have changed. The speed at which the mobility across and the interaction among cultures, so as to reach multiple sites of intersection among them, is taking place today has led to a paradigm change from the concept of biculturality to that of hybrid identities. The objective is no longer to master one, two, or more cultures as wholes, or totalities, that one must integrate or else juxtapose to each other in a neat, symmetrical fashion. The model is no longer to become a specimen of a cultural kind, which is conceived as an integral whole, but rather to "shop around" and become individuated by selecting from various aspects of cultural practices and options we can participate in, as citizens of a dynamic and changing multicultural society. This paradigm change from a bicultural identity to a hybrid one, however, may not be universally applicable to the experiences of each and every Hispanic because of the vast differences in the U.S. Latino population. This population includes, among others, recently arrived immigrants, older immigrants (now U.S. citizens), U.S.-born children of immigrants, descendants of residents of Hispanic territories occupied by the United States in the Southwest/Pacific area and Puerto Rico, children of unions between Latinos and other Americans of various races and ethnicities, and so on. The U.S. Latino today is situated in a cultural space apt for the negotiation of identities. These identities, as I classify them initially and somewhat freely, are: the assimilationist identity, the culture-of-origin identity (whether applied to the primary site of Hispanic identification within the United States—such as Miami or New Jersey for Cuban Americans—or to the country of origin), and the Latino identity. Clearly, it could be argued that at this point in history the Latino identity might function as a mediator of the other two. This is its power but also its weakness, since the Latino identity is doubly marginal: in one respect, it is marginal vis-à-vis the community/country/culture of origin, be it Cuba or "Little Havana" in Miami, for example; nevertheless, it is also marginal vis-à-vis the mainstream identity of the Anglo-American U.S. citizen.

The construction of identity is so problematic that even as one attempts to articulate and defend something one cares deeply about, one is simultaneously "written," or scripted, as something one is not—in the sense of the limits and borders placed on identities, the media representations that codify and distribute such identities, the consumer/marketing demands that reproduce and expand them in the economic sector, and the political platforms and interest groups organized to "represent" them. The result is the construction of blocks of political and economic interests that are no longer defined by individuals, but that rather define and limit the identities the "Latino" may represent.

For this reason some Hispanics are genuinely skeptical that the promotion of Hispanic "identity" does them any good, given the vulnerability these "identities" have to being manipulated by big business, politicians, and the corporate media. They see the commercialization of the term *Hispanic* in the same way I might see the commercialization of the term *woman*, realizing that under this label the markets are trying to sell me something—a hairdo, an outfit, a way of life—that does not necessarily fit my personal taste. I undertand what this view is pointing to, which is definitely a part of our reality in the contemporary world. But the fact that the words *woman* and *Hispanic* may be politicized or commercialized well beyond my taste, and even contrary to it, does not lead me to stop describing myself with these terms. It does not lead me to reject these categories even though I know that their stereotypes can offend me or that I can feel very differently from what poses as the norm for each. What it leads me to do is to adopt the principle of *recognizing the internal differences* among women, Hispanics, Cuban Americans, or what have you. This principle allows one to identify as a member of a group without being coerced into compliance with the group's image of its normative type. For example, in some sectors of Hispanic culture one is expected to approve of bullfights and cockfights, to enjoy eating the entrails of animals, or not to use birth control. I deplore bullfights and cockfights, I follow a semivegetarian diet, and as a feminist, I believe a woman has a right to the full control of her body in sexual and reproductive matters. Do my views make me less of a Hispanic? I don't think so. I share a cultural history with many other Hispanic people, even if we may disagree about some particular opinions. It is the sharing of the cultural history and my investment in continuing the narrative of that cultural history, adding my own modifications to it, that makes me a Hispanic. And yet I agree that since the first time I filled out a form and marked the little box saying "Hispanic," and even prior to checking that box, the signifier "Hispanic" and its mainstream representations have been marking me, no doubt. Where this leaves me politically is with the awareness that with respect to ethnicity, as with respect to gender or national origin, I must constantly negotiate my identifications (my identity) in relation to the representation and the political forces that mark me. In the concluding part of the paper I offer a description of some of the tensions this negotiation entails.

Identities in Tension

In her now-classic work *Borderlands/La Frontera*, Gloria Anzaldúa provides an illustration of the multifaceted identity of a Chicana feminist. Anzaldúa reflects on growing up in south Texas, where the legacies of different cultures intersect. She mentions how easy it is to be torn apart by the variable and sometimes conflicting demands of a multicultural background composed of Indian, Mexican, and North American elements. "Like all people," she says, "we perceive the version of reality that our culture communicates. Like others having or living in more than one culture, we get multiple, even opposing messages."[3] There is, above all, the pain of realizing that some of these elements have been oppressors of others: the Mexican has oppressed the Indian, and the North American has oppressed the other two. It is important for her to overcome the anger and the resentment that can build up when she sees the ways Chicanos are discriminated against. Anzaldúa realizes one must be strong to fight and overcome the effects of discrimination on one's people and on one's self. In her own self, however, she has to bring together her complex identifications, and not let one or more of them exploit another. She has to create a healing relationship between the Indian, the Chicana, and the North American aspects of her self. I think that, apart from her psychological attitude of inclusiveness and respect for all the different elements that make up her self, she succeeds in creating this balance through the use of language, alternating between English and Spanish in much of her prose, from time to time using indigenous imagery to ground her thoughts. In other words, in her writing and choice of how to define the topics she writes about, she is able to bring together creatively the different elements of her self. "The possibilities are numerous," she writes, "once we decide to act and not to react."[4] Yet she adds a warning in a mixed tongue: "*Pero es difícil* differentiating between *lo heredado, lo adquirido, lo impuesto*" (yet it is difficult to differentiate between what is inherited, what is acquired, and what is imposed).[5]

Anzaldúa's example shows one creative way to approach the heterogeneity and mixture of elements in a person's multicultural background. In fact, she describes her consciousness as one that speaks up for "la nueva mestiza" (the new mestiza), where the word *mestiza* already indicates the concept of mixture. In referring to her position as that of "la *nueva mestiza*" (emphasis added), a new cultural horizon is opened—one that allows us to move to a larger category than "Chicana/Tejana." The concept of "mestiza" is transferable to the category "Latina," which, like "mestiza," encompasses far more than a reference to Chicana feminists. Since the 1980s "Latina" has been used increasingly to describe women of all Hispanic-American backgrounds residing in the United States. It allows Hispanic-American women the use of a common designator, surpassing the more specific designators of "Chicana," *"puertoriqueña," "cubana-americana,"* and so on. One question I raise regarding this new identity category in terms of which we are often asked to speak and write as members of the designated group is: What are we gaining and losing with the use of the ethnic terms? What difference does it make, for example, if I speak as a Cuban American or as a Latina in various contexts?

The answer to this question is not a simple one. To start the discussion, let me raise another question: Is it the case that "Latina" references our identity in terms of a minority population in the United States (that is, taking the United States as a national entity), whereas a category such as "*Chicana*," "*puertoriqueña*," or "*Cubana-Americana*" references us in terms of our home region or homeland (whether inside or outside the official United States)? For example, is it the case that "*puertoriqueña*" would reference one with respect to the island culture or its diaspora, whereas "Latina," used to refer to the same person, would mark her as a minority of Latin origin in the United States? And what are the connotations of meaning taken by these signifiers of difference (since both signify a difference vis-à-vis the Anglo Americans in the United States)? What are the social expectations accompanying one term or another? In my own case, as a Cuban American, I ask: Is it the case that "Latina" functions as a mark of difference with respect to the dominant sectors of North American society, whereas "*cubana*" functions as something that gives me historical roots and the mark of a freedom-loving people? As these terms apply to my life, "Latina" is a signifier of the demand for inclusion; "*cubana*" is a signifier of the demand for freedom. As the representation of these two ethnic identities intersect in my life, sometimes they are in agreement, yet they can also be in conflict, for it is easy to see that the demand for inclusion could lead to a loss of freedom, and the demand for freedom to a loss of inclusion. In this context, one may note that both the socialist and the anti-Communist Cubans (despite their disparate objectives) have preferred to take the consequences of exclusion rather than accept inclusion into a dominant order where they do not feel free. Cubans in the island and those "in exile" have responded, however differently, to the political heritage of José Martí, whose vision of culture was essentially linked to the exercise of freedom.[6] Martí believed that a people should be educated for the practice of freedom. One could push this thought to the limit, raising this question: If the order of representation into which one is likely to be included does not permit one's freedom (or one's freedom as grounded in citizen participation in a sovereign nation, as Martí believed), what sense does it make to demand inclusion in it?

The conflict or tension between one's homeland heritage and one's "minority" condition in the translocated environment does not end here for Hispanic women. As in the case of all women living in masculine-dominant societies, whether these be of Hispanic or some other cultural heritage, the body of woman is overdetermined by a masculine orientation in social symbolism. For example, the *cubana*'s body is free but it is also a symbol of service to the *patria*, the fatherland. When subordinated to North American values, in contrast, the Latina's body is represented as undergoing liberation through assimilation in North American culture and its more individualistic values, yet it is also represented as a racialized (nonwhite) body, as an exotically sexual body, or as an impoverished, health-risk body in need of special assistance from the public health services. As Latina women, we have to negotiate our identity constantly in the midst of a complex of stereotypes that include masculine-dominant expectations (both Hispanic and non-Hispanic) as to what a woman should do with her body, in addition to undertaking another whole set of negotiations with respect to what a woman will do with her mind and how she will apply her intelligence.

In the imagined and existential horizons of Latino as well as Anglo-American moral expectations, ethical concepts such as freedom and justice can easily acquire one standard meaning for males, another for females. The moral virtues, such as prudence, love, and fairness, are engendered in their social codification, just as their social meaning also reflects a class stratification. Patriarchal gender ideology has understood sexual difference primarily through the symbolism of gender complementarity. The masculine and the feminine are viewed essentially as complementary, just as the feminine is essentially tied to the maternal. These views reinforce the view that heterosexuality and the woman's body as destined for motherhood are necessary requirements for a woman to be in good standing before the cultural community. It isn't until a culture provides alternative ways of constructing personal identity and gender identities—usually by introducing another principle of legitimization women can appeal to in order to justify new gender behaviors—that the old-fashioned gender requirements begin to get broken. This means that alternative gender cultures must be built and established that will break the hegemony, at the national or local level, of the body of woman serving to illustrate the unspoken myths of the nation or the community.[7] The body of woman needs to be disconnected from its instrumental role in the pursuit of national or ethnic objectives and given back to the women themselves. Thus the positions of reproductive choice, the right to pursue a person's sexual orientation, the rights to divorce, remarriage, and so on, constitute important developments in democratic culture, for a free person cannot exist without the right to regulate freely the affairs of her own sexuality and her own body. The traditionalists' appeal to culture in order to counter a woman's right to these freedoms is just as inappropriate as the appeal to culture to limit a subaltern race from receiving rights to full personhood.

Latinas and Race

With respect to the body of the Latina, some feminist writers have reported a racialized objectification of their bodies and persons.[8] As a partial answer to this problem, feminists in the United States have set forth the category "women of color" as a positive, empowering term to designate women whose backgrounds are Asian, African, Indo-American, and Hispanic.

The degree to which the category "women of color" has been embraced by a large number of Latinas in the United States appears to indicate that this category works well for many people. Still, for Latinas who are white, this category may represent a problem, at least initially. Much more clarification and discussion are needed to determine what meaning those of us who are directly affected by the use of these terms want to give this category. Here I address two concerns. The first is to recommend that the category "women of color" be used critically. It should not rest on a binary opposition between white and nonwhite, wherein it is assumed that unless a woman is white, she is a woman of color. To maintain this binary, where white is also hierarchized over nonwhite, is to reproduce the ideology that white is the norm and brown, yellow, red, black, and mixed race are the marks of difference. This way of thinking, which reproduces the vestiges of racism, limits the Latina's voice to the repeated demand for inclusion in an order of representation marking her as "other." Instead, the meaning of "women of color" needs to assume a political significance, as it generally does in feminist theory, with respect to the agency of women in racially and ethnically marginalized groups who actively oppose racism, sexism, cultural imperialism, heterosexism, and so on.[9]

The second concern is addressed to the tendency to reduce "women of color" to "nonwhite women," the result of which is to identify Latinas as nonwhite. Unless it is stipulated by definition that all Latinas are nonwhite, it will be observed that some Latinas are white. Why is this so? "Latina," which signifies one's cultural heritage, refers to people of a great many racial configurations and mixtures. The caution here would be not to collapse all ethnic or cultural categories into racial categories (as when a cultural category, "Latina," is collapsed into the racial category "nonwhite"). Moreover, it is important to keep in mind that features associated with groups are not necessarily distributed evenly among individuals pertaining to such groups. This principle applies when making generalizations about culture, race, and geography. For instance, just as it would be inappropriate to say that New Yorkers (as individuals) are not white because the group "New Yorkers" contains people of many different races, so it is inappropriate to say that Latin Americans (as individuals) are not white, because the group "Latin Americans" is multiracial. We need to be cautious about generalizations that fail to take into account the internal differences within groups, just as we need to be watchful regarding how various groups in different parts of the world exercise and reproduce their own forms of racism against vulnerable populations.

But what if "Latina" (in the United States) should come to be understood only in the sense of "woman of color?" Could "color" refer to a certain way of relating to people and to a culture, without a direct correlation to the "color" of one's skin? Should white Latinas in the United States be excluded from the category "Latina"? I do not think so, because we come from a mestizo culture, and this culture is profoundly infectious (in the positive sense), that is, it is deep in our psyches. At least those of us who are committed to celebrating the inclusion of indigenous, Afro-Latin, and mestizo elements of Latino cultures will continue speaking from the Latina position. In my case, I cannot pretend to speak as a nonwhite person because I have not suffered in my body the kind of racialized discrimination routinely affecting many other Hispanics. Still, I know what it is to feel ethnic discrimination in terms of my cultural differences and particularly as an immigrant. There is a part of me that would like to say I am nonwhite in solidarity with all the Hispanics—as well as women, men, and children of other ethnic, national, and racial groups—who have definitely suffered the profound effects of racial discrimination. Yet I stop myself from going so far because I write from my own lived experience, and with respect to race I have a relative privilege many others have not enjoyed. Each one of us has a different history of assimilation and discrimination. If we follow the recognition of internal differences I mentioned earlier, this principle will allow us to speak as Latinas and Latinos, though not all our experiences are identical. The differences among us are important in the degree to which they make us strong. The consciousness of the differences in the way we have been discriminated against—by class, color, gender, sexual orientation, accent, migration status, national origin, and so on—make us stronger as a collective when it comes to denouncing injustice than if we limited the Latino identity only to those who were most down-and-out, primarily the poverty-stricken, non-English-speaking population. In fact, it is a strategy of hegemonic power to try to limit the acceptable categories of what counts as discrimination to the minimum of instances and to the most extreme and dire cases of need, precisely so that the multiple forms of discrimination currently existing in our daily lives, and not fitting the extreme category of the supra-oppressed, remain unredressed and invisible.

Reconciling Differences

Finally, and speaking about the heterogeneity of Latino voices, as a Cuban-American individual I confess I have spent a good part of the last fifteen years of my life simply negotiating the meaning of this small hyphen that stands between my Cuban and U.S. identities. I have often thought of the political/ideological relation between these two terms (Cuba and the United States) as the greatest binary, something constructed as a hard political opposition where a person must choose one or the other but not both. In the eyes of the self-identified "exile," even a family visit to a relative in Cuba or a visit to the island for personal reasons may qualify as collaboration with "Communism" and the island's political regime. This interpretation of Cuban Americans' reality, however, denies the differences existing both within the Cuban-American population and within the population of Cubans living in Cuba.[10] It represents a construct projecting an inflexible reading on the meaning of individuals' variously motivated activities and desires, including the desire to travel to hard-to-reach places and see things firsthand, in terms of one's on-site, concrete, embodied experience.[11] These activities and desires have a personal meaning for each individual and cannot be legislated for individuals by a political group.

My views on Cuba resemble the mainstream views of Canadians, Mexicans, and Europeans (to choose only some examples). It should be up to individuals themselves whether or not they choose to travel to Cuba, including how often they want to travel. The control of information on Cuba for propaganda purposes is much more likely to take place when travel is restricted than when travel is open and free. I want to have a normal relationship to my country of birth and to the people who live there, which also includes some family members. One of the hardest elements in the negotiation of my Latina identity was getting my relatives in Miami to accept the fact that I was going to travel to Cuba, visit relatives, revisit the sites of my childhood, and participate in international conferences there (all acceptable though not necessarily recommended activities as far as the U.S. government is concerned). In this context, I have found the Hispanic-Latina identity very comforting, because it allows me to speak as a Latina in terms of a broader group whose political views are not homogeneous and whose conception of culture recognizes the diversity of Latino/a experiences.[12] The Latina identification encourages me to recover my early childhood roots in my culture of origin, without forcing me, as a Cuban American, to split my cultural legacy, in terms of national origin, into two irreconcilable political halves. In this case, the Latina identity has provided me with a freedom and an opportunity that the political pressures on the expression of my Cuban-American identity made very difficult, if not impossible.

Conclusion

The concept of negotiating identities is one that feminists have employed in discussions of the politics of location. Insofar as movements such as identity politics have become part of the political discourse in the United States, so have feminists' efforts to maintain a healthy distance from what I could call "essentialized locations." We have learned to look at identities through the lenses of historical, cultural, economic, and other characteristics. Thanks to women of different sexual orientations, to women of different racial and ethnic backgrounds, to young and aging women, we have learned to look at the differences within groups and not just at the external differences among groups. If identities are products of history and culture and if one is not born with an essential identity written up in heaven and destined to be carried out for the term of one's life, then, given the right historical circumstances, a person can negotiate her way through the different pressures, conflicts, and tensions that bear on her concept of self as well as on her ongoing understanding of her social and political identity. Opportunities for transformative experiences where one fights one's way through the many trappings of ideology are needed if there is to be personal growth. In particular, I have tried to argue that it is important to resist the pressure to fit into collective identities already predefined for us and where we are thought to belong by virtue of our race, gender, ethnicity, class, nation, or religion. Without losing sight of the role of these variables and, in the case of Hispanics, while retaining our commitment to the defense of our cultural history and the continued relevance of the Spanish language in a multicultural, multiethnic, and multiracial society, the critique of essentialism has taught us to be suspicious of orthodoxy and to consider the full political implications—as well as opportunities for personal fulfillment—associated with the identities-in-the-making we ascribe to ourselves.

Notes

1. In this essay, *Latino* and *Hispanic* have been used interchangeably. Throughout the paper, I am taking *identity* in the sense of the specificity of a person's self-image and values, rather than in a metaphysical sense of a oneness that exists in the midst of change and variations. The types of identities that are the focus of this paper are in fact identities in tension, unresolved identities. It is only because a human being occupies multiple social roles and because there can be an imperfect fit between these roles or between the individual and the roles she is forced to occupy that the question arises, how do I negotiate my way through these different expectations? Moreover, how does one establish priorities among potentially conflicting expectations and roles?
2. Frantz Fanon, *Black Skin, White Masks* (New York: Grove, 1967), 111–14.
3. Gloria Anzaldúa, *Borderlands/La Frontera* (San Francisco: Aunt Lute, 1987), 78.
4. Ibid., 79.
5. Ibid., 82.
6. Martí's political speeches and articles were often very pedagogical, insofar as he held that if others, including and especially North Americans, learned about the Cuban people's love of freedom, they would support and respect the Cubans' struggle against colonialism. For example, see the letter to the *New York Herald*

dated May 2, 1895, signed by José Martí and Máximo Gómez, in their respective roles as the delegate of the Cuban Revolutionary Party and the chief of the Liberatory Army in the Cuban war of independence against Spain. José Martí, *Política de Nuestra América* (México: Siglo XXI, 1979), 284–92.

7. Cf. Norma Alarcón, "Traddutora, Traditora: A Paradigmatic Figure of Chicana Feminism," in Inderpal Grewal and Caren Kaplan, eds. *Scattered Hegemonies* (Minneapolis: University of Minnesota Press, 1994), 110–33.
8. See particularly María Lugones and Elizabeth V. Spelman, "Have We Got a Theory for You! Feminist Theory, Cultural Imperialism and the Demand for 'the Woman's Voice,'" *Women's Studies International Forum* 6, 6 (1983): 573–81; María Lugones, "Playfulness, 'World-Travelling,' and Loving Perception," *Hypatia: A Journal of Feminist Philosophy* 2, 2 (1987): 3–19.
9. The oppositional sense is used by Lugones in the article coauthored with Spelman. But note that even here the Hispana's chief or primary concern is the "complaint of exclusion" (Lugones and Spelman, "Have We Got a Theory for You!" 575). Thus the Latina voice comes to symbolize what I note both here and above as the demand for inclusion (with recognition of specific differences). The oppositional sense of "woman of color" can also be extended further to signify opposition to a racist "heteropatriarchy." This latter meaning can elicit the cooperation of politically progressive people across racial categories and sexual orientations. Nevertheless, it may alienate members of minority groups who do not identify primarily as feminist, queer, gay, or lesbian.
10. For an example of the diversification of points of view among Cubans and Cuban Americans, see Ruth Behar, ed., *Bridges to Cuba/Puentes a Cuba* (Ann Arbor: University of Michigan Press, 1995).
11. It is insufficient to relate to a place of origin relying only on personal memories, photographs, videos and movies, radio reports, newsprint, or narratives of others who recently have lived in that place, though this is not to say that the former are not helpful. As long as human beings are embodied beings, full contact with a geographical site involves the ability to visit it at least on occasion.
12. There are in fact many internal differences among Cuban Americans, though on the issue of U.S. policy toward Cuba the predominant view is conservative.

Cultural Particularity versus Universal Humanity

4

The Value of Being *Asimilao*

Paula M. L. Moya

assimilated? qué assimilated,
brother, yo soy asimilao

—Tato Laviera

In this essay, I would like to consider the possibility that in trying to escape what they experience as the dehumanizing strictures of collective (especially racial) identity, neoconservative minorities such as Richard Rodríguez, Shelby Steele, Stephen Carter, and Linda Chávez raise a valid concern about the relationship between the culturally particular and the universally human.[1] Because neoconservative minorities view collective racial identities (that is, black or Chicana/o) as culturally particular, my inquiry will address directly the centerpiece of neoconservative minority identity politics—the insistence that members of culturally nondominant groups should be required to assimilate into mainstream American society.[2] In the process of examining the value of assimilation, I will unmask the false universality behind the ideal of assimilation defended by neoconservative minorities and argue against the way in which they oppose individual to collective identity. I will then propose and defend an alternative, postpositivist, realist conception of universal humanity that supports a workable alternative to the ideal of assimilation proposed by neoconservative minorities. After arguing that the value of assimilation resides in a legitimate need for productive human interaction, I will suggest that all of us—members of culturally non-dominant groups as well as members of culturally dominant ones—can benefit from engaging in a process of multidirectional cross-cultural acculturation (thus becoming *"asimilao"*). I will then posit one way in which progressive intellectuals interested in working toward a better society might go about fostering the conditions conducive to this goal. Working from within a postpositivist realist framework, I will claim that when we pay the right kind of attention to our own and others' particularity, we position ourselves to develop a more productive understanding of our universal humanity.[3]

Neoconservative Minorities and the Refusal of Racial Identity

The value, necessity, and/or inevitability of assimilation continues to be one of the most hotly contested political issues in the United States. This is because social policy decisions with significant material consequences are made on the basis of whether or not policy makers believe that cultural and racial minorities have an obligation to assimilate to mainstream American culture. If, like Shelby Steele, an educational policy maker supports the goal of assimilation, she is unlikely to support multicultural educational initiatives and bilingual education; if she agrees with Richard Rodríguez that the purpose of education is to indoctrinate children into mainstream American society—to provide them with a set of common cultural assumptions—she will actively oppose curricular reform efforts to make the curriculum representative of different cultural experiences.[4] If, like Linda Chávez, our policy maker equates "Americans" with white middle-class people, she will ensure that the educational system she influences will function to assimilate minority children; only by becoming more "American," she will insist, can minorities "move ahead" in our society. Her decisions will have a profound effect on the lives not only of the minorities affected by her policies, but of all Americans who fail to learn about the histories and experiences of people unlike themselves. At stake, then, is the question of the value of assimilation: What price—if any—should Americans (and especially minorities) be required to pay in order to foster a common American culture?

The obvious question to ask ourselves when considering the value of assimilation is this: Are members of minority groups who assimilate to white middle-class American culture in fact happier, healthier, and better off than those who do not? In asking this question, we might want to consider the possibility that Richard Rodríguez has a point when he says that highly educated Chicana/os who "scorn the value and necessity of assimilation" in effect "toy with the confusion of those Americans who cannot speak standard English as well as they can."[5] While Rodríguez is both unkind and inaccurate in his attribution of motives, it is apparent that those of us who "make it" do so, in part, by assimilating to dominant (that is, "white") American culture. We become skilled at negotiating the white man's way; we master his language and learn his social codes. Moreover, it is evident that the recipients of affirmative action fellowships have often been those who come from the most assimilated, least disadvantaged backgrounds. For these reasons, it could be a mistake if, in our defensiveness, we fail to acknowledge the economic and social benefits of (at least partially) sharing a "culture" with the (white) people we interact and work with. Finally, we might want to consider the possibility that Shelby Steele is right when he suggests that in our readiness to defend cultural particularity, we overlook the importance of seeing "human universals." Steele may be communicating something of value when he suggests that a world that paid more attention to our common humanity *would* be a better world: less conflictual, more harmonious, more egalitarian, more just.

Because neoconservative minorities such as Rodríguez and Steele base their conviction that minorities should be required to assimilate to a white, middle-class American norm upon their notion of what universal humanity is, it is worth looking at what neoconservatives mean when they refer to "human universals."

The neoconservative understanding of the relationship between collective (racial and, as such, particular) identity and individual (universal and, as such, raceless) identity is that the two are antithetical to each other. Specifically, they believe that racial group membership robs a person of an important aspect of her humanity—that is, her individuality. Steele, for example, sees racial identity as a "threat" to human individuality:

> When [middle-class blacks] first meet, we experience a trapped feeling, as if we had walked into a cage of racial expectations that would rob us of our individuality by reducing us to an exclusively racial dimension. We are a threat, at first, to one another's uniqueness.[6]

Furthermore, neoconservative minorities assume individuality to be a property of those persons who, because they are not identified with a racial collective, can be differentiated from the crowd and can exercise their civic rights. By contrast, those persons who are seen as unindividuated members of a collectivity are perceived to be somehow deficient: they lack a public identity and consequently lack human agency. Richard Rodríguez conveys this idea in his discussion of undocumented Mexican workers, where his formulations suggest that he believes that in order for a person to be considered truly human, she cannot be identified with a racial or ethnic collective:

> On two occasions, the contractor hired a group of Mexican aliens. . . . In all, there were six men of varying age. . . . They came and they left in a single old truck. Anonymous men.

> Their silence stays with me now. The wages those Mexicans received for their labor were only a measure of their disadvantaged condition. Their silence is more telling. They lack a public identity. They remain profoundly alien. Persons apart.[7]

In Rodríguez's view, these "anonymous" Mexicans cannot be differentiated from one another: they travel together and remain collectively silent. Moreover, the lump-sum wages they receive measure their inability to advocate, as individuals, on their own behalf. Because "those Mexicans" lack a "public identity," because they cannot speak for themselves, they remain "profoundly alien." Thus, from Rodríguez's neoconservative minority perspective, the Mexicans are deficient in an important element of their humanity—that is, their individuality. Shelby Steele expresses a similar idea somewhat differently in the following passage:

> In the deepest sense, the long struggle of blacks in America has always been a struggle to retrieve our full humanity. But now the reactive stance [that is, black identity] we adopted to defend ourselves against oppression binds us to the same racial views that oppressed us in the first place. Snakelike, our defense has turned on us. I think it is now the last barrier to the kind of self-possession that will give us our full humanity, and we must overcome it ourselves.[8]

What the above passages illustrate is that underlying the neoconservative minority bias against racial group membership is a specific conception of what it means to be human. By setting collective (racial and, as such, particular) identity in opposition to individual (universal and, as such, raceless) identity, Rodríguez and Steele configure cultural, racial, or ethnic particularity as supplemental—even inimical—to universal humanity. In the following passage, for instance, Steele portrays racial specificity as additional—not intrinsic—to the "human universals":

> In the writing [of *The Content of Our Character*], I have had both to remember and forget that I am black. The forgetting was to see the human universals within the memory of the racial specifics. One of the least noted facts in this era when *racial, ethnic, and gender difference* are often embraced as sacred is that being black *in no way spares one from being human*. . . . [I]n this book I have tried to search out the human universals that explain the racial specifics.[9]

According to Steele's view in the above passage, what is "human" transcends what are merely racial, ethnic, or gender trappings. In other passages, Steele takes a harsher view, portraying racial identity as harmful to human possibility:

> To retrieve our individuality and find opportunity, blacks today must—consciously or unconsciously—disregard the prevailing victim-focused black identity. Though it espouses black pride, it is actually a repressive identity that generates a victimized self-image, curbs individualism and initiative, diminishes our sense of possibility, and contributes to our demoralization and inertia. It is a skin that needs shedding.[10]

Steele's interesting choice of metaphors ("a skin that needs shedding") in an argument that advocates the end of *black* racial identity makes more explicit his underlying conception of what it means to be human. Throughout his book, Steele's ideal human appears as a deracinated (by default white), ungendered (by default male), unsexed (by default heterosexual), postcultural (by default American) individual; he appears to be devoid of particularity, and he possesses rational agency.[11] In all this, Steele's ideal human bears a telling resemblance to the European Enlightenment's all-knowing and unsituated subject of reason.

What I am suggesting is that neoconservative minorities such as Rodríguez and Steele accept the bourgeois heterosexual Euro-American male subject as the standard of universal humanity. They err, as Enlightenment thinkers typically have, by taking one particular manifestation of humanity and positing it as universal. They do this by setting the bourgeois heterosexual Euro-American male subject as the norm to which all other subjects must conform, even as they simultaneously disavow that subject's racial, gender, sexual, and cultural particularity. Rodríguez, Steele, Carter, and Chávez all understand "racial" identity as always referring to "black" or "Hispanic" (that is, non-"white") identity. In their writings, "white" identity does not appear as a "racial" identity. Although they acknowledge the existence of "white" people, they do not demonstrate an awareness that persons in the United States with pale skin undergo a racialization process that produces them as "white." Similarly, "male" does not appear as a gendered identity, while heterosexuality is simply assumed.

Neoconservative minorities consistently characterize particularity as that which deviates from the middle-class heterosexual white male norm. Rodríguez, for example, derides "gay studies, women's studies, ethnic studies" as areas of inquiry that do not contribute to a fundamental understanding of who "Americans" are. According to Rodríguez, the study of gays, women, or ethnics serves merely to "flatter" the groups in question.[12] By contrast, Rodríguez believes that the study of the European (or Euro-American) heterosexual male teaches us something fundamental about what it means to be

American. Rodríguez writes: "I need to know about seventeenth-century Puritans in order to make sense of the rebellion I notice everywhere in the American city. Teach me about mad British kings so I will understand the American penchant for iconoclasm."[13] The difference in Rodríguez's schema between (presumably heterosexual) "mad British kings" and "gays" is, apparently, the difference between sufficiency and excess: we need to know about one, but we do not need to know about the other. Thus, Rodríguez reinscribes the bourgeois heterosexual European or Euro-American male subject (here represented by seventeenth-century Puritans and mad British kings) as the unmarked standard from which gays, women, and ethnics deviate as a result of their sexual, gender, and racial particularities.[14]

Rodríguez and Steele further err in setting collective identity in opposition to individual identity. Collective identity is not antithetical to individual identity; rather, they are dependent on each other. It is as impossible to have a collectivity that is not made up of individuals as it is to have an individual who is not a member of some collective. This is because identity is inescapably relational: to know ourselves as *selves* requires us to know ourselves in relation to *others*. In the process of defining who we are, we describe ourselves as beings with certain recognizably human characteristics—characteristics shared by some and lacking in others. To the extent that we define ourselves as being like some people and not like others, we will identify ourselves in relation to a group—even if it means defining ourselves as being outside that group.

The neoconservative tendency to see individual identity as antithetical to collective identity betrays one of the characteristic weaknesses of liberal philosophical assumptions regarding the possibility of individual autonomy. As feminist philosopher Alison Jaggar has convincingly argued, such assumptions ignore the fact of human biology. Humans simply do not exist as autonomous and self-sufficient individuals acting from fully rational, conscious choice. From the moment of conception through the first few years of infant dependency and into adulthood, humans exist as emotionally and physically needy participant members of a larger social collective; their very survival is predicated on their membership in an interactive human society.[15]

Moreover, just as there are no individuals who are not members of some collective, so there are no members of a collective who are not at the same time individuals. Because every human being occupies an objective social location constituted by a multitude of categories of identity, every member of a given collective is likely to differ from every other member in one or more significant ways. This is why the social identities of individual members of a particular racial group cannot be assumed to be the same—race is but one aspect of social location.[16] Therefore, to assume (as neoconservative minorities do) that the act of identifying as African or Mexican American deprives a person of her individuality is to fall into the essentialist (and racist) logic of assuming that race makes up the totality of her being.

Neoconservative Minorities' Ideal of Assimilation

Rodríguez's and Steele's acceptance of the bourgeois heterosexual Euro-American male as the exemplar of universal humanity profoundly influences their conception of the best way to work toward a nonracialized society. This is because they uncritically embrace what they take to be the middle-class American cultural values synonymous with that norm. They see American society as an ideal society, and assume that if there are individuals who do not fit into American society, those individuals, and not society, need to change. As a consequence, neoconservative minorities equate assimilation to American mainstream culture with overall societal advancement. Steele, for instance, sees assimilation as highly desirable for promoting a better world:

> [T]he work ethic, the importance of education, the value of property ownership, of respectability, of "getting ahead," of stable family life, of initiative, of self-reliance, et cetera—are in themselves, raceless and even assimilationist. . . . These values are almost rules for how to prosper in a democratic, free enterprise society that admires and rewards individual effort.[17]

In the above passage, Steele implicitly suggests that the culturally and historically situated values held by middle-class Americans represent the pinnacle in human achievement.

Rodríguez, for his part, starts out by arguing that assimilation is a necessary good and ends up by viewing it as inevitable. In *Hunger of Memory*, Rodríguez argues vigorously for the value of assimilation to a white, middle-class American norm on the basis of the claim that those who are not fully assimilated are alienated from public life. In *Days of Obligation*, he suggests that assimilation is not necessary so much as it is certain:

> The best metaphor of America remains the dreadful metaphor—the Melting Pot. Fall into the Melting Pot, ease into the Melting Pot, or jump into the Melting Pot—it makes no difference—you will find yourself a stranger to your parents, a stranger to your own memory of yourself.[18]

Assimilation, Rodríguez implies, is a *natural* phenomenon: "I don't believe in assimilation any more than I believe in the sunrise. It happens. Assimilation happens, to coin a phrase."[19]

Unlike Steele and Rodríguez, Stephen Carter appears to recognize that other cultures may have other, equally valuable ways of approaching the world. He writes:

> The ideal of merit as the route to reward should not be confused with the very different proposition that the society in which we live today is one that gives out rewards that way. Similarly, not every standard accepted in *our* society is necessary for civilization in *every* society. Even the most confirmed cultural absolutist can hardly come away from such a book as Jomo Kenyatta's *Facing Mount Kenya* without conceding that others may have customs that work for them and not for us, and that forcing them to be like us would likely destroy perfectly moral, if somewhat different, cultures.[20]

However, having acknowledged that other—different—cultures may be "perfectly moral," Carter sets it aside as something that need not be considered further in his present discussion. The result is a gentle cultural relativism by virtue of which he refuses to consider the possible relevance of other societies' cultural practices for his own life. This basically anti-intellectual move is somewhat surprising coming from someone so concerned about getting out of the preformed intellectual "box" to which his racial identity supposedly consigns him. It is a move, moreover, that replicates his refusal in another section of his book to consider the "fairness" of the screening "standards" by which educational goods and economic resources get distributed. At one point he writes: "I put aside for the moment the question of the fairness of standards"; and later he says that "most professionals of whatever color are far too busy proving themselves to spend time quibbling over the fairness of standards for medical board certification or law firm partnership."[21]

Because he sets aside these important political and evaluative questions, Carter avoids the necessity of questioning his own values, and those of the dominant members of the society in which he lives. He assumes, for instance, both that "standards of excellence are a requisite of civilization," and that "we live in a world of brilliant scientific discoveries, remarkable acts of moral and spiritual courage, profound literary achievements, and outstanding professional performances." Carter's somewhat rosy view of the world (which is not false so much as only half true), allows him to proclaim that "we live in a world that cares about excellence, needs it, and should not be afraid to judge it."[22] The problem with Carter's argument is that he never addresses the difficult issue of how exactly we should go about judging "excellence." Instead, he presumes that whatever standards are already in use are culturally unbiased and provide an adequate method of judging merit and excellence. Rather than questioning the fairness of standards or examining the dominant values of the society he lives in, Carter suggests that we should turn our attention to cultivating what he calls "The Edge, what every professional driving toward the top of his or her chosen field wants to hold over all the others, the competition, who are grabbing for the same brass ring."[23] Carter thus fails to ask himself the really challenging questions, among which might be: Is competition a good in itself? Is it productive to want to "hold" things over other persons? Is "grabbing for the same brass ring" the model of human interaction we should all be striving for? In the end, by not considering seriously the viability of alternative values, Carter ends up affirming the primacy of bourgeois heterosexual Euro-American male cultural values as much as Rodríguez and Steele do.

Neoconservative minorities' a priori assumption that American society is not in need of reform and that all people are equally autonomous agents acting from fully rational, conscious choice leads them to take reductive approaches to solving complex social problems. Because they misjudge the absolute merit of American society, they make policy recommendations that hinder, rather than facilitate, the development of productive cross-cultural interaction. The most frequent solution they proffer to problems involving racial and economic inequality is that individual members of minority groups must simply work harder. Steele insists that "individual initiative" is "the only thing that finally delivers *anyone* from poverty."[24] Carter proposes, as an alternative (or remedy) to affirmative action, that blacks just "do better." He says that "the way to turn this potential liability [the stigma of affirmative action] into a powerful asset is to make our cadre of professionals simply too good to ignore."[25] Not surprisingly, the neoconservative minority perspective incorporates a blame-the-victim mentality. Chávez asserts that "only the Puerto Rican community can save itself, but the healing cannot begin until the community recognizes that many of its deadliest wounds are self-inflicted,"[26] while Steele piously declares that "if conditions have worsened for most of us as racism has receded, then much of the problem must be of our own making."[27] Such sanctimoniousness on the part of neoconservative minorities ignores the role of economic forces and government policies on the lives of ordinary working people: Chávez's "analysis" of the Puerto Rican situation fails to take into account the role of the U.S. government-sponsored Operation Bootstrap in the creation of a massive Puerto Rican underclass,[28] while Steele's attempt to conjure away racism through the incantatory repetition of the phrase "as racism has receded" has had little effect on the socioeconomic situation of blacks and Latina/os living in the United States today.[29] As a whole, neoconservative minorities seriously underread the degree to which economic forces in a capitalist society exert control over the material conditions of the lives of ordinary people.

A Realist Approach to Universal Humanity

My examination of the neoconservative minority approach to universal humanity reveals that the problem many Enlightenment critics have with the concept of the "universal" may actually be a problem with the way that concept has historically been described—specifically, with the particular *content* that has been ascribed to the "universal" human. A realist approach to identity suggests that cultural particularity is antithetical to universal humanity only when we have a culturally elaborated understanding of what universal humanity is. When, for example, the universal subject is figured implicitly as the bourgeois heterosexual European male, then any feature that diverges from that norm (such as homosexuality or female gender) will be seen as culturally particular and epistemically irrelevant. When, however, we acknowledge that the so-called universal subject that Enlightenment critics have been rejecting is actually the bourgeois heterosexual European (or, in the United States, Euro-American) male, then we are in a better position to see him as a cultural being—an embodied being grounded in a particular time and space.[30] Situating this grand subject of reason allows us to divest him of his universalist pretensions without doing away with the subject (and subject-based agency) altogether. The realist contention is that cultural particularity need not be antithetical to universal humanity as long as we have a conception of universal humanity that is *not* culturally elaborated. The task now is to formulate such a conception.

The realist suggestion proposed by Satya Mohanty in his book *Literary Theory and the Claims of History* is that we should follow Kant in understanding "reason" as a practical and universal human capacity. Rather than understanding reason as a fixed Enlightenment formula for achieving predetermined moral and political ends, Mohanty suggests that we see it as a universal human capacity that allows persons to continually evaluate their actions within the context of their ideas and experiences, and enables them to act purposefully in response to those on-going evaluations.[31] The advantage to recognizing that all humans are "rational" in this minimal way is that it allows us to conceptualize human universality in terms of a basic capacity shared by all humans, rather than as a comprehensive account of human nature. Under this view, one need not belong to a particular racial or cultural group in order to be considered worthy of human dignity and consideration; one need only be a part of an evolving cultural community composed of human beings who reflect upon and occasionally change their cultural practices. Moreover, this is a conception of universal humanity that invites specification and particularization but does not require either for support of the basic universalist claim.[32]

The minimal notion of universal humanity Mohanty argues for suggests both the possibility and necessity of cross-cultural communication. While realists such as Mohanty acknowledge the importance—and occasional necessity—of having a common language, common values, and common priorities, they also understand that it would be a mistake to assume that they know ahead of time what that language, those values, and those priorities should be. Too often the issue of diversity is discussed in either/or terms: either diversity is good, or it is not; either humans foster difference or they attempt to eradicate it. From a realist perspective, it is a mistake to think of our options for dealing with difference in these oppositional terms. Given the fact of human diversity, we need to take the project of cross-cultural communication seriously.

Of course, any project of cross-cultural communication requires that we attend to the nature of human difference. In order to do this, we need to be able to specify what the differences are, what those differences mean to the way we choose (or are forced) to live our lives, and whether or not the differences between individuals or groups can or even *should* be resolved. We need to be able to ask what difference a given difference makes. It is important for us to realize that while there are some differences we can live with, there are others we cannot. Moreover, for the sake of the healthy flourishing of humankind, we need to know which are which. Consider, for example, language difference. The consequences of language difference range from the realm of minor annoyance to a matter of life and death. For example, if you are in an elevator with two other people who are speaking a language you do not understand, your inability to understand them may make you feel vulnerable. You may wonder if they are talking about you (they may be) and you may be irritated. Strictly speaking, this is not a societal issue; it is your problem. You can choose whether or not to be annoyed. Not being able to understand everything everybody else says at all times is a consequence of language difference that society at large can live with.

There are other circumstances, however, in which it is imperative that two people share a language. It is fairly obvious, for instance, that a flight controller and the pilot of an aircraft attempting to land within that flight controller's jurisdiction must share some kind of language. It is similarly important that a doctor and a nurse be able to communicate with each other in an emergency-room situation. A plane crashing because the pilot cannot understand the flight controller's language, or a patient dying because the doctor and nurse cannot communicate with each other, is the consequence of language difference that society at large literally cannot live with. These are instances in which language difference becomes a societal issue, and in which the need for a common language is quite obvious. But what is not obvious is what that common language should be. There is no reason that the speakers of one language should be forced to switch to the other—it is quite possible that the two parties could both learn a third, neutral language, or that the two languages could be combined into a pidgin or creolized language. In actual fact, the issue of which language will prevail will most likely be decided by considerations of convenience or power—but it is not necessary that it be so.

Thus, the value of assimilation (insofar as it involves sharing a language, accepting received values, assuming customary habits of interaction) does not involve specifically the well-being of minorities so much as it resides in a legitimate need for productive human interaction. When minorities assimilate to white middle-class American culture, the effect is often that they learn to communicate more effectively with those who hold the keys to their economic well-being; the result is potentially rewarding for everyone involved. However, having acknowledged the value of sharing a common culture, the realist would nevertheless argue that it is a mistake to assume that productive human interaction is predicated on assimilation to a predetermined norm. There are two reasons for this. First is the damage that assimilation (when conceived of as forced unidirectional cultural change) wreaks on the psyches of those individuals who are forced to abandon their own culture.[33] Second is the loss of moral and epistemic possibility that follows in the wake of predetermined cultural homogeneity. From a realist perspective, people such as Richard Rodríguez, Shelby Steele, and Stephen Carter suffer from a failure of imagination—a failure that derives at least in part from the white American ethnocentrism and racism these men have internalized.[34] Consequently, they are unable to consider the possibility that other cultures may have different ways of approaching problems or social arrangements that are more beneficial to human flourishing. Neoconservative minorities assume ahead of time that the middle-class American values they hold are the best values there are. *However, there is no reason to assume that white middle-class American values represent the pinnacle of human achievement.* In fact, there is much evidence to suggest that they do not. To the extent that we are interested in working for a better world, then, our goal should be not assimilation, but rather multidirectional cross-cultural acculturation.

When neoconservative minorities point to the successes of "assimilated" minorities, they exhibit selective vision. While they see the value of cultural sharing, they fail to consider the emotional, psychological, and *epistemic* consequences of forced unidirectional cultural change. Objectively speaking, we live in a troubled society: one need only turn on the television, pick up the newspaper, or talk to one's neighbor to realize this. For this reason, if people do not fit into our society, we should consider the possibility that we need to change society instead of people. Moreover, contrary to Rodríguez's claim that assimilation is inevitable, cultural change is not always in the direction of assimilation. Cultural change always occurs, but more often in several directions.

The Value of Being *Asimilao*

In his essay "'Qué assimilated, brother, yo soy asimilao': The Structuring of Puerto Rican Identity in the U.S.," Juan Flores argues that Puerto Ricans living on the mainland do not assimilate as much as they grow together in a strong process of cultural convergence with blacks and other migrants from the Caribbean and Latin America.[35] Flores notes that while this growing together is often mistaken for assimilation, it is not directed toward incorporation into the dominant culture. What results, instead, is a pluralism that does not "involve the dissolution of national backgrounds and cultural histories but their continued affirmation and enforcement even as they are transformed."[36] It is only from this vantage point of cultural coalescence with other nondominant groups that Puerto Ricans move toward interaction with Anglo-American society at large. Flores argues that while Puerto Ricans who have undergone this cultural convergence can be readily distinguished from those who have more recently arrived from the island, it is nevertheless "not accurate to speak of assimilation" in connection with their cultural formation. He concludes:

> Rather than being subsumed and repressed, Puerto Rican culture contributes, on its own terms and as an extension of its own traditions, to a new amalgam of human expression. It is the existing racial, national and class divisions in U.S. society which allow for, indeed necessitate, this alternative course of cultural change.[37]

Invoking the main theme from Nuyorican poet Tato Laviera's poem "asimilao," Flores contends that while Puerto Ricans in North America undergo cultural change, they do not become assimilated in the sense of becoming culturally indistinguishable from middle-class white Americans. Rather, they adapt to their new surroundings by retaining some values and cultural practices and by changing others—absorbing other ways of being in the world from among the various cultural groups they come into contact with. They become, in other words, "*asimilao*."

Once we acknowledge that assimilation (when conceived of as forced, unidirectional cultural change) is not inevitable, then we are free to consider the possibility that neither is it necessarily desirable. I will go further and argue that assimilation to a predetermined norm can actually impoverish society by depriving people of the behavioral and moral insights they might gain as a result of their respectful interaction with people from different cultural backgrounds. To make this claim, I will draw upon Mohanty's realist idea that cultures are both repositories of and laboratories for behavioral and moral knowledge.[38]

To understand why assimilation to a predetermined norm can be epistemically and morally detrimental, we must first remember that cultural change is not arbitrary, but is a response to changing social and economic conditions. Although such cultural change may occasionally be forced (as in the case of government-sponsored assimilation programs), it can also occur as a result of (more or less) conscious choices on the part of cultural practitioners. To the extent that humans have some choice about how they will interact with their changing environment, "cultural practices—ways of living, of creating, of choosing to value one thing over another in our daily lives—are an essential form of moral inquiry." Cultures, Mohanty explains, "not only embody values and beliefs, they test and modify these values and beliefs in practical ways." [39] It is when we think of cultures as behavioral and moral laboratories that we can begin to understand how essential multiculturalism is to our society's ability to imagine and enact new behavioral and moral possibilities in the face of changing circumstances. Other people's preferred ways of living can provide us with models for other kinds of cultural practices—practices that we may not have thought of, or that we may not have had the opportunity to try—that may be more conducive to human flourishing, or more appropriate to changing circumstances, than some of our own.[40]

Mohanty's realist conception of multiculturalism as epistemic cooperation thus provides a strong justification for the preservation of cultural diversity. It allows us to see that cultural diversity is a valuable characteristic of an ideal society—for epistemic reasons, not merely sentimental ones. If we follow Mohanty in understanding cultural diversity as "the *best social condition* in which objective knowledge about human flourishing might be sought," then we will see that in protecting cultural diversity we are not merely avoiding a negative social consequence (inflicting violence on underrepresented groups), but promoting a positive one (nurturing the conditions that might lead to a better world).[41] Moreover, it is not necessary to argue that *every* multicultural situation *always* leads to human flourishing in order to defend the general principle that cultural diversity is conducive to humans' moral and intellectual growth.

The Epistemic Significance of Identity Politics

In conclusion, I want to turn to the implications of my argument for the practice of identity politics. Within politically progressive circles today, it is often taken for granted that identity politics as such are essentialist, theoretically retrograde, or even politically dangerous. I want to suggest that absolute dismissals of all kinds of identity politics are premature—even though such dismissals are frequently motivated by political convictions similar to those that motivate my own arguments. (For the purposes of this essay, I define identity politics as a social practice in which a person who identifies or is identified with a recognizable group makes arguments or takes action with the purpose of affecting social, economic, or educational policy relative to that group. Within this social practice, the identity of the political practitioner both motivates and is a central facet of the claim, argument, or action.) Without defending those forms of identity politics that are predicated on the disenfranchisement of others, and with full awareness that all identities are somewhat reductive and potentially co-optable, I nevertheless contend that *some* forms of identity politics that are undertaken by members of marginalized groups in the service of creating economic, social, and political equity between different groups are epistemically and morally justifiable.[42] Embedded in my argument is the idea that identity politics cannot be an end in themselves, but should be seen as a necessary step on the way toward creating economic, social, and political equity between different groups.

My reasons for defending identity politics by members of marginalized groups are primarily epistemological. To the extent that we, as cultural critics, are interested in gaining a more objective perspective upon our social world, we must give greater weight to socially marginalized identities and nondominant perspectives. Because the "institutions of social reproduction and cultural transmission—schools, libraries, newspapers, and museums, for instance—are oriented to the dominant cultural and social perspectives," and because those institutions transmit cultural information in ways that seem both natural and benign, their bias in favor of the dominant culture is often invisible.[43] For this reason, unless humans have access to alternative perspectives—perspectives that explicitly contradict the dominant one—they risk being arrested in the process of their intellectual and moral growth. This is also why we must pay attention both to marginalized identities and to the social processes that serve to make them marginal. Since identities are indexical—they refer outward to social structures and embody social relations—they are a potentially rich source of information about the world we share.

In another article I have argued at length that the recovery of the experiences of oppressed people and the examination of previously devalued cultures uncover knowledge and ways of living that, when shared with people who have not been oppressed or have not lived in the same way, allow oppressor and oppressed alike to have a more complex and adequate understanding of their shared world than either of them could have by themselves. I have further argued that as long as certain identities are devalued, those identities will be epistemically valuable and politically salient. I have shown that the recovery of the experiences of oppressed peoples and the examination of previously devalued identities are necessary steps on the road toward an adequate knowledge of social relations.[44] What I wish to add here is that the first step in the recovery of the experiences of oppressed people will involve a reexamination by oppressed peoples of their own lives. This is not standpoint epistemology in the sense of having nonoppressed people starting from the lives of oppressed people.[45] This project of self-examination must be carried out by oppressed peoples and then *shared* with people who have not been oppressed in the same way. Inasmuch as this examination is carried out by and from within a community of similarly oppressed people, they will necessarily practice identity-based politics.

It is my contention that neoconservative minorities—despite their unwillingness to acknowledge as much—are themselves participating in the process of self-examination entailed by identity politics. They are persons identified with recognizable groups (Mexican American and African American) who engage in social practices (such as writing books and granting interviews) in which they make arguments (against bilingual education or affirmative action) or take action (such as sponsoring legislation) with the purpose of affecting social, economic, or educational policy relative to their own groups. Moreover, their identities (political and racial) both motivate and are central to their claims, arguments, and actions. Both here and in my forthcoming book, *Learning from Experience: Realist Theory and Chicana/o Identity*, I have shown that neoconservative minorities are collectively participating in the creation of a discourse and an identity identifiable as "neoconservative minority." They are not iconoclastic individualists, but rather share a tendency to take similar positions in public debates concerning multicultural education, assimilation, and racial or ethnic identity. Furthermore, although they differ in the particulars, neoconservative minorities share several basic assumptions about the egalitarian nature of U.S. society and the necessity for minorities to assimilate to a white middle-class U.S. norm. For the purposes of illustration, I will briefly summarize some of the characteristic features of neoconservative minority identity politics. Neoconservative minorities have an ambivalent relationship to the minority communities with which they are identified by others. They simultaneously exploit their minority status for political and economic purposes (they allow themselves to be published and marketed as native informants) even as they attempt to disavow their "exemplary" minority status. As a general rule, neoconservative minorities overlook the structural and inegalitarian nature of society. They ignore the correlation between the likelihood of incarceration and nonwhite racial status, and that between poverty and female gender. Where neoconservative minorities do address such glaring social inequalities, they tend to locate the cause of such inequalities within the cultural character of the subordinated individual or group. Consistent with their focus on culture, neoconservative minorities have a liberal understanding of individual agency. Instead of seeing people as temporally and biologically limited beings with a variable measure of control over their lives, neconservative minorities tend to see *all* people as *equally* autonomous agents acting from fully rational, conscious choice. Although they invariably mention socioeconomic status as a factor influencing people's lives, they do not incorporate a class analysis into their interpretative frameworks, or deal adequately with the effect economic forces have on individual life chances. In several neoconservative minority narratives, class emerges as an issue only for the purpose of undermining the salience of race as a determining feature of social identity. Additionally, they fail to acknowledge that in a capitalist economy, some people—no matter how hard they work—will never attain middle- or upper-class status for the simple reason that capitalism requires an exploitable labor force. As a result of their tendency to overlook the structural nature of society, neoconservative minorities have idealist conceptions of identity. By undermining or ignoring the political, economic, and social salience of race and gender, they focus on culture (language, habits of interaction, family structure, living arrangements) as the only determinant of social identity. They assume that if a person changes her culture, she can change her social identity (and, by extension, her life chances). Finally, neoconservative minorities' focus on culture leads them to champion assimilation (forced unidirectional cultural change) to a white middle-class American norm. They argue against multicultural education, affirmative action, and bilingual education in the belief that such programs hinder rather then promote the assimilation of minorities into American mainstream society—a society about which they are wholly uncritical.

Understanding neoconservative minorities as practitioners of identity politics has helped me to appreciate their arguments for assimilation—which I recognize as having been developed through self-reflection about the meanings of their own racialized identities—as suggestions for the best way to end or minimize race-based discrimination and inequality in our society. I do not, for the reasons enumerated in this essay, agree with the majority of their suggestions, nor do I admire most of the political and rhetorical strategies they employ in their efforts to negotiate their own racialized identities. I do, however, defend their practice of identity politics in the service of creating economic, social, and political equity between different racial groups. Moreover, because I see neoconservative minorities as fellow travelers in this worthy social, political, and epistemological project, I have been spared the necessity of either accepting or rejecting their suggestions outright. Instead, I have been able to consider the merits of their perspective, evaluate their arguments, and, by identifying the sources of their errors, work toward figuring out less reductive and more effective ways of approaching the problems of race-based (and other forms of) discrimination and inequality. The project of evaluation and engagement with the arguments of neoconservative minorities is what has led me to suggest, as an alternative to assimilation, the value of being *asimilao.*

Notes

1. By considering the merits of neoconservative minority discourse, I do not intend to overlook, downplay, or endorse the many problematic aspects of their perspective. I do, however, want to allow for the possibility that neoconservative minority accounts such as Richard Rodríguez's *Hunger of Memory: The Education of Richard Rodríguez* (New York: Bantam Books, 1983), Shelby Steele's *The Content of Our Character: A New Vision of Race in America* (New York: St. Martin's Press, 1990), Stephen Carter's *Reflections of an Affirmative Action Baby* (New York: Basic Books, 1991), and Linda Chávez's *Out of the Barrio: Toward a New Politics of Hispanic Assimilation* (New York: Basic Books, 1991) are attractive to most white (and some nonwhite) Americans for reasons *other* than simple racism.
2. In this essay, I use the term *assimilation* to refer to forced unidirectional cultural change to a white middle-class American norm.
3. For more on the postpositivist realist theory of identity, from which I derive my theoretical framework, see Satya Mohanty, *Literary Theory and the Claims of History: Postmodernism, Objectivity, Multicultural Politics* (Ithaca: Cornell University Press, 1997), especially ch. 7; and Paula Moya and Michael Hames-García, eds., *Reclaiming Identity: Realist Theory and the Predicament of Postmodernism* (Berkeley: University of California Press, 2000).
4. See Rodríguez's discussion about the purpose of education in his book *Days of Obligation: An Argument with My Mexican Father* (New York: Penguin, 1992). He writes: "The classroom will teach us a language in common. The classroom will teach us a history that implicates us with others. The classroom will tell us that we belong to a culture" (167). Also, in an August 1994 interview Rodríguez talked about what he sees as the function of the American educational system: "What the classroom should insist on is that [little Johnny] belongs to a culture, a community, a tradition, a memory, and that in fact he's related to all kinds of people that he'll never know. That's the point of education. . . . Education is not about self-esteem. Education is demeaning. It should be about teaching you what you don't know, what you yet need to know, how much there is yet to do." Virginia Postrel and Nick Gillespie, "On Borders and Belonging: A Conversation with Richard Rodriguez," *Utne Reader,* March-April 1995, 76–79.
5. Rodríguez, *Hunger of Memory*, 26, 35.
6. Steele, *Content of Our Character*, 22–23.
7. Rodríguez, *Hunger of Memory*, 134, 138.
8. Steele, *Content of Our Character*, 35.
9. Ibid., xi, emphases added.
10. Ibid., 172.

11. Renato Rosaldo uses the term *postcultural* to refer to dominant members of the North American middle class. His point is that people who belong to a dominant First World culture are often unable to see themselves as cultural beings. Because how and what they do seem to them to be the "obvious" and "right" way to do things, and because they are unable to imagine themselves as possible objects of an anthropological gaze, they appear to themselves as "people without a culture." Under this view, immigrants have culture while those who have assimilated have moved beyond culture (209–10). Renato Rosaldo, *Culture and Truth: The Remaking of Social Analysis* (Boston: Beacon Press, 1989).
12. Rodríguez, *Days of Obligation*, 169.
13. Ibid.
14. Curiously, although Rodríguez argues against gay studies, women's studies, and ethnic studies, he inadvertently suggests their value. He writes, "Did anyone attempt to protect the white middle-class student of yore from the ironies of history? Thomas Jefferson—that great democrat—was also a slaveowner. Need we protect black students from complexity? Thomas Jefferson, that slaveowner, was also a democrat. . . . Once you toss out Benjamin Franklin and Andrew Jackson, you toss out Navajos. You toss out immigrant women who worked the sweatshops of the Lower East Side. Once you toss out Thomas Jefferson, you toss out black history" (*Days of Obligation*, 169–70). The irony behind what Rodríguez says is that American history, as it has traditionally been taught to those "middle-class students of yore" (and to everybody else), did precisely what he suggests it did not—that is, it protected them from the ironies of history. For a powerful critique of the inadequacies of historical education in the United States, see sociologist James W. Loewen's best-selling book *Lies My Teacher Told Me: Everything Your American History Textbook Got Wrong* (New York: Simon and Schuster, 1996). What Rodríguez's discussion of education suggests is that he misunderstands the aims and contributions of gay, women's, and ethnic studies programs. It is partly as a result of the growth of black and other ethnic studies programs that we now question the myth of the founding fathers as the great and beneficent protectors of democracy and freedom. Moreover, without the establishment of women's studies programs, it is highly unlikely that sufficient resources would have ever been dedicated to a study of immigrant women in the sweatshops of the Lower East Side such that we might have a more adequate understanding of the role of women's labor in the shaping of the U.S. economy. Contrary to what Rodríguez suggests, gay studies, women's studies, and ethnic studies programs have never been interested in "tossing out" Benjamin Franklin and Andrew Jackson. They have never exclusively devoted themselves to "instill[ing] in children a pride in their ancestral pasts," or producing a "pageant of exemplary slaves and black educators," even though it is well accepted in educational circles that self-esteem is an important element in successful educational efforts (*Days of Obligation*, 169). Their epistemological and educational mission has always been corrective. By their very nature, they—as much as or more than any other area of study—have been actively engaged in exploring the ironies of history.
15. See Alison Jaggar's *Feminist Politics and Human Nature* (Totowa, N.J.: Rowman and Littlefield, 1983), esp. 41.
16. By "social location" I mean to refer to the particular nexus of gender, race, class, and sexuality (and other, less salient social constructs) in which a given individual exists in the world.
17. Steele, *Content of Our Character*, 95.

18. Rodríguez, *Days of Obligation*, 161.
19. Rodríguez, quoted in Rena Pederson, "Diversity and Assimilation," *Dallas Morning News*, April 4, 1995, 2J.
20. Carter, *Reflections* 231–32.
21. Ibid., 51, 90.
22. Ibid., 231.
23. Ibid., 90.
24. Steele, *Content of Our Character*, 16.
25. Carter, *Reflections*, 86.
26. Chávez, *Out of the Barrio*, 159.
27. Steele, *Content of Our Character*, 15.
28. For more on how U.S. economic policy has influenced the lives and economic opportunites of Puerto Ricans, see Virginia Sánchez Korrol, *From Colonia to Community: The History of Puerto Ricans in New York City* (Berkeley: University of California Press, 1983), James L. Dietz, *Economic History of Puerto Rico: Institutional Change and Capitalist Development* (Princeton: Princeton University Press, 1986), and Raymond Carr, *Puerto Rico: A Colonial Experiment* (New York: New York University Press, 1984).
29. See Steele's chapter "Race-Holding" in *Content of Our Character*, in which he repeats this phrase or a variation of it no fewer than six times. My point is that Steele relies on mere repetition to convince his reader of the truth of this claim without providing any substantive evidence that it is so.
30. My point holds for any culturally elaborated understanding of universal humanity, whether that subject be the bourgeois heterosexual European male or, let us say, a proletarian lesbian Asian female. Historically, of course, the so-called universal subject has been equated with the bourgeois heterosexual European male, which is why it is so difficult for us to see him as a particular being.
31. Mohanty, *Literary Theory and the Claims of History*, 139, 199, 248.
32. Ibid., 199–200.
33. Ofelia Schutte, in her contribution to this volume, argues that when assimilation leads to an indifference toward the preservation of diversity as constituted by ethnic group membership, it functions to "deprive human beings of prosperous conditions by which they can be recognized for their specific linguistic and historical-cultural achievements and contributions." Moreover, to refuse such recognition is to "inflict a degree of violence on them." Charles Taylor makes a similar argument: "Nonrecognition or misrecognition can inflict harm, can be a form of oppression, imprisoning someone in a false, distorted, and reduced mode of being" (Taylor, "The Politics of Recognition," in Amy Gutmann, ed., *Multiculturalism* [Princeton: Princeton University Press, 1994], 25). The idea behind such calls for recognition is that to erase a culture (by destroying or refusing to recognize it) is effectively to deny the full humanity of those people who have been socialized within it.
34. Because he never questions the value of assimilation, Rodríguez cannot account for why so many Latina/o educators with advanced degrees in their field have what he represents as such nefarious designs on their communities of origin. Consequently, he lets slander do the work of argumentation in dismissing their substantive claims. Rodríguez calls bilingual education a "scheme" perpetrated by "middle-class ethnics" who are "filled with decadent self-pity, [and] obsessed with

the burden of public life" (*Hunger of Memory*, 11, 27). Rodríguez suggests that "foreign-language bilingualists" are naive and dangerous—naive because they do not realize that one cannot be "a public person while remaining a private person," and dangerous because "they romanticize public separateness and they trivialize the dilemma of the socially disadvantaged" (*Hunger of Memory*, 33, 26, 34, 27).

35. Juan Flores, "'Qué assimilated, brother, yo soy asimilao': The Structuring of Puerto Rican Identity in the U.S.," in *Divided Borders: Essays on Puerto Rican Identity* (Houston: Arte Publico Press, 1993), 191–92.
36. Ibid., 192.
37. Ibid.
38. See Mohanty, *Literary Theory and the Claims of History*, esp. 240–42.
39. Ibid., 240.
40. I recognize that humans' ability to modify their cultural practices in accordance with their evolving values and beliefs will vary across time, space, and circumstance. I understand that some people, because of the objective social locations they occupy, will be less autonomous and more affected by economic, social, or cultural constraints than some others. Furthermore, I acknowledge that what we might subjectively experience as an act of individual choice might be influenced by larger historical and economic forces. Nevertheless, I reject as unfounded the claim that any or all of us are so completely overdetermined that some degree of voluntary and liberatory cultural change is impossible. It is in this spirit that I embrace Mohanty's conception of multiculturalism as epistemic cooperation.
41. Mohanty, *Literary Theory and the Claims of History*, 243.
42. I see my position as being consistent with the one taken by Ofelia Schutte in her contribution to this volume. Schutte explains that the fact that "the words *woman* and *Hispanic* may be politicized or commercialized well beyond [her] taste, and even contrary to it, does not lead [her] to stop describing herself by use of these terms." What we understand is that these (and other) terms do important work for her insofar as they allow her to situate herself in relation to others. Schutte reconciles herself to the limitations of each identity category by adopting the principle of recognizing the internal heterogeneity of the groups with which she identifies. This principle allows her to identify as a member of a group without being coerced into compliance with its normative type. A similar logic attends Schutte's defense of retaining ethnic/cultural identifications. While she recognizes the potential dangers posed by group identifications, she also recognizes the value—which is supported by a broader principle of social justice—of "having a substrate of differentiating elements in cultures . . . that challenge the narrow-mindedness of patterns of behavior inherited from the past."
43. Mohanty, *Literary Theory and the Claims of History*, 237.
44. See my essay "Postmodernism, 'Realism,' and the Politics of Identity: Cherríe Moraga and Chicana Feminism," in M. Jacqui Alexander and Chandra Talpade Mohanty, eds., *Feminist Genealogies, Colonial Legacies, Democratic Futures* (New York: Routledge, 1997).
45. I am indebted for this insight to Brent Henze's essay "Who Says Who Says? The Epistemological Grounds for Agency in Liberatory Political Projects," in Paula M. L. Moya and Michael R. Hames-García, eds., *Reclaiming Identity: Realist Theory and the Predicament of Postmodernism* (Berkeley: University of California Press, 2000).

The Larger Picture 5

Hispanics/Latinos (and Latino Studies) in the Colonial Horizon of Modernity

Walter D. Mignolo

Think of two parallel lines. They do not touch each other. My paper is an argument to connect two such lines. One line is ethnicity and race; the other, cultures of scholarship. The question is simply one of knowledge and human interest. Since this is not geometry, I need to place these parallel lines in the context of history. Thus, I am approaching the topic of this volume from a historical perspective. I do not claim that history can teach us the future. I claim that there is a historical explanation that has been overlooked for the prominence of ethnoracial identity and identification during the last thirty years. It is not history that will teach us the future, but the requitals of what official histories have silenced in the past.[1] My argument is not cast in a national perspective, neither Spanish peninsular nor that of any particular Latin American country. Rather, I adopt the perspective of modern world system analysis,[2] which I will render as modern/colonial world system perspective, to examine the very constitution of the categories we are dealing with today in the United States.[3] Thus, I discuss the making of a Hispanic/Latino category in relation to the larger picture in the Americas, where it interacts with the categories of "Afro-American," "Amerindian," and "Native American." There are reasons, in the very process of the modern/colonial world system, for focusing on these categories and leaving aside, for the moment, other ethnic labels.[4] These reasons will become clear later. Although some of the papers included in this volume question historical configuration (Pogge), and others do not directly take it into account

(Young), I believe that, on the contrary, structural differences cannot be dealt with adequately without paying due attention to their historicity. Public policy is necessary to redress the inequality and inequities of the present, but it is not good enough to change and satisfy subjectivity. The historicity of public policy is embedded in the coloniality of power and the colonial difference of the modern/colonial world system in which we live. For the sake of clarification, I add that here I talk about coloniality as the invisible but unavoidable other side of modernity. Moreover, the coloniality of power and colonial difference are not strictly of the past, but are still at work in the present.[5] Global colonialism, driven by financial markets, is no less a type of colonialism than Christian or British colonialism, driven by the goal of Christianizing or civilizing the world.[6]

Let me start with three issues. The first is a thesis: that the conception and perception of Hispanics/Latinos has its principal articulation in 1898, during the war between an emergent imperialist power (the United States) and an empire in decline (Spain), intermingled with national struggles for independence (in Cuba and Puerto Rico). In 1848, during the war between the United States and Mexico and the displacement of the frontier toward the South, a significant number of Mexicans were unwillingly left within the United States. The idea of the "Spanish Borderlands" was introduced by historian Herbert Eugene Bolton in 1921.[7] Bolton's view, and this is part of my thesis, was articulated around the ideology and the civilizing mission of the Aryan race that was rearticulated in 1898 during the Spanish-American War and in connection with a revamping of manifest destiny.[8] I will further argue that if the current perception and conception of Hispanics/Latinos has its historical roots in 1898, it also has its historical framework in what I call, based on Wallerstein, the modern/colonial world system. I accept the framework, but at the same time, I depart from it on the grounds that modern world system conception, as it is termed today, was and still is blind to the coloniality of power and colonial difference.

The second issue is an epistemic one that I would like to relate to the ethnoracial one implied in the first thesis. It is that 1898 was also an important date in the formative process of Latin American studies in and from the American perspective, in relation to the Caribbean and Central America.[9] After World War II, Latin American studies was articulated with area studies, and since the 1970s, it has entered into a conflictive dialogue with Latino studies; today it is being restructured around the Ford Foundation's interest in, and generosity toward, rethinking area studies.[10] Thus, my contribution to the discussion here is not only to keep it cross-disciplinary, but to question the very foundation of disciplinarity from the perspective of the coloniality of power and colonial difference. Colonial difference is at work here as "epistemic difference" and has much to do with the perception and conception of Hispanics/Latinos in academic life and in cultures of scholarship. I would like to add that my own essay is located in between Latin American and Latino studies and is, at the same time, a critique of the current epistemic limits of Latin American studies from the perspective of Latino studies. I am not treating Hispanics/Latinos as a subject of studies or reflection, but as a perspective from which to think. I will not be talking about "those groups," whose rights and justice we are reflecting upon here as if we were not part of any of them; rather I would like to bring to the foreground the "group" from which each of us talks about "group rights." I will be talking therefore as a Latin Americanist and, if I daresay, as a Latinist or "Hispanicist." As you may know, this is not a question of essences, but a question of choice. I could have chosen not to raise this issue and to talk instead about ethnic identities and group rights as if disciplinary locations were uncontaminated with any ethnic or group rights. I will explore later the differences between Latin American and Latino studies. For the time being, I would just like to add that my argument will be developed from a Hispanic/Latino and subaltern perspective on disciplinary knowledge in relation to area-studies paradigm.

The third issue is a set of questions that try to bring together the first two. What can we learn from the first two issues about the location of "Hispanics/Latinos" in the multicultural debate that is still alive and well in the United States, although not limited only to that country? To avoid the easy misconception that multiculturalism is strictly an American problem, or that if it is found elsewhere, it is either a result of or has at least been influenced by U.S. multiculturalism, I would like to quickly recall the debate that has been going on in Bolivia. For a number of years now, Bolivian intellectuals have been discussing multiculturalism and plurilingualism (where Aymara, Quechua, and Spanish have been coexisting for five hundred years)[11] independently of discussions in the United States and in opposite historical and social conditions than those of the United States.[12] Multiculturalism and plurilingualism in Bolivia were prompted not so much by immigration as by colonial legacies and the colonial difference implanted in the Andes since the sixteenth century. This piece of information is not trivial, since among the thirty million or so "Hispanics/Latinos" in this country, there are already a significant number of Amerindians (Mixtec, Zapotec, Quechua, Mam, Ixil, Kanjobale, and so on) who are neither "Hispanic" nor "Latino."[13] Furthermore, the designation "Hispanic/Latino" also hides from view the large number of Afro-Latin Americans in Brazil, Colombia, Cuba, Haiti, Guadeloupe, and Martinique. Clearly, then, the "Hispanic/Latino" label responds to and is a legacy of imperial conflicts and other legacies resulting from the making and classification of the nonimperial world. There are also Afro-Latinos in conditions similar to the Amerindians, for example, Afro-Americans not from the United States. This situation is even more complicated.

This scenario allows me to come to two propositions. The first is the need to consider the Americas, for the future, beyond the nineteenth-century distinctions between Anglo and Hispanic/Latino. "Hispanic" and "Latino" place the accent first on the language and the white/creole population, thereby excluding the black/creole population in Latin America, particularly in Colombia, Brazil, and the Caribbean. The second is that the Hispanic/ Latino question begs a larger one: the division between the two Americas, one Latin, the other Anglo, with a Latin/Anglo Caribbean in the middle. Thus, is it possible to construct a future dealing with the question of the coloniality of power and the world hegemony of the United States? How can we construct a more practical future that focuses on Hispanics/ Latinos (including Latin American Amerindians, Afro-Latin Americans) in the United States and that will detach geohistorical and racial identifications from citizenship?[14] My proposal is to think in terms of "critical assimilation" (see Moya's essay in this volume), by which I mean assimilation in dissent toward social transformation, not only in academia but in the realm of public policy. If we disengage the state from the nation (a topic I will return to later), and also the state from the hegemonic idea of the nation (as in the nation-state), it becomes necessary to imagine a state that performs its managerial functions on the bases of border thinking and border politics from the perspective of subalternity, a necessary condition for assimilative criticism. The modern state, on the contrary, operates on the basis of a territorial imaginary and the belief that there is a one-to-one relation between the state and the nation. Critical assimilation, from a subaltern perspective, should be a relentless claim for group rights, for justice, and for the erasure of the colonial difference embedded in the idea of the one-to-one relation between state and nation. The presupposition that the nation belongs to and is defined by those who hold the power, and consequently the values that shall be embraced in assimilation, is a presupposition sustained precisely by the colonial difference. To erase the colonial difference is to erase the infrastructure that calls for assimilation to the hegemonic values and to reimagine the state as an administrative and legal structure dissociated from any particular nation and operating, so to speak, on the borders of the nations.

Now back to area studies. Area studies reproduced the colonial difference set up by occidentalism and orientalism in cultures of scholarship.[15] Latino studies scholars and intellectuals are in a parallel epistemological position to that of intellectuals and social scientists in Latin America, linking cultures of scholarship with the sociohistorical situations they engage. Latin Ameri canists in the United States are in a strange position because the object of study is somewhat removed from their daily lives. One way to get closer to it is to take into account our situation as Hispanics/Latinos/Latin Americans, or whether you are Hispanic/Latino or not, to start from the fact that Latin America is not only "down there" but "up here." This is also what I mean when I suggest that Latin American studies should be rethought from the epistemic perspective introduced by the "study" of Latin America, bypassing the political implications that such studies may have within the United States, within and without academia. Being a practitioner of Latin American or Latino studies in the United States implies that one is at the same time a practitioner of American studies.[16] This is the only way I see for Latin Americanists in the United States to match and occupy a parallel position to their counterparts in Latin America and to avoid reproducing area studies ideology. If this imbalance is not redressed, even Latin Americanists in the United States, including those from the left, will continue reproducing the colonial difference. Whereas Latin Americanists with a Hispanic or Latin American education and training "lack" the American experience, Latin Americanists with an American or northern European education and training "lack" the education, training, and living experience of Latin America. Latin American studies could capitalize on this dichotomy. This is precisely what Latino studies offers at this point: not only thinking the borders but thinking from the borders, and consequently underlining the colonial difference implied in the dichotomy of Latin American and American studies. Latino studies has created its own distinctive place between both of them. Yet this is not an altogether separate space. It is border thinking from a subaltern perspective. It is thinking from, and outside, the disciplines in confrontation with the canonicity of disciplinary norms.[17]

Hispanics/Latinos and the Colonial Difference

Aníbal Quijano, a Peruvian sociologist and historian, introduced the notion of the coloniality of power and defined it in terms of two fundamental axes.[18] Both axes presuppose the idea and the framework of Wallerstein's modern world system and allow us to go beyond it. This implies a modification of Wallerstein's modern world system metaphor as far as it is conceived and perceived from inside its very imaginary.[19] Quijano's concept of the coloniality of power opens up the possibility of looking at modernity from the perspective of coloniality, and thinking *from* the colonial difference, not just *about* it. This move is crucial not only for understanding Hispanics/Latinos today, but also for understanding the issues of multiculturalism that have been shaped by the colonial difference.

Quijano and Wallerstein coauthored an article in which the complementarity and differences between them come across clearly.[20] Their argument focuses on the central dimension of the Americas in the configuration of the modern/colonial world and the constitution of the Atlantic commercial system. In his own articles Quijano makes the same point, but changes "America" to "Latin America" and states that capitalist modernity and Latin America were born the same day.[21] The colonial difference here is at work in the double historical perspective: Wallerstein's from inside the system, Quijano's from its exterior borders. They are located on opposite sides of the colonial difference, although neither of them is outside the system. In any event, the Atlantic emerged as a commercial circuit in the sixteenth century (and when it did, it was marginal in relation to the center of power from China to the Middle East and North Africa) and connected the margins of Europe with other commercial circuits (Anáhuac, Tawantinsuyu) that were unknown from the perspective of Europe, China, or the Middle East. Anáhuac and Tawantinsuyu became the "Indias Occidentales" under Spanish rule, and "Americas" for the white creole population in the Americas as well as for European intellectuals outside of Spain toward the end of the eighteenth century. This is the moment of articulation of an imaginary, in this case the imaginary of the modern/colonial world, whose history helps in understanding the location of Hispanics/Latinos in the United States. This history is not the history of Hispanicity and Latinity, but the history of its own constitution and from its own perspective. I will further argue in my second point about the disciplines (Latin American studies and Latino studies) that it is precisely this history that gives Latino studies an epistemological potential that is crucial for the future of cultures of scholarship and for overcoming the colonial and epistemological difference embedded in area studies. I am making this argument as both a Latin Americanist and a Hispanic in the United States.

The two axes along which Quijano defines the coloniality of power are the ethnoracial (and its consequences, class and gender/sexuality) foundation of the modern/colonial world system and the subalternization of knowledge. The coloniality of power establishes the colonial difference, and through it the particular articulations of subalternity within communities of knowledge. The ethnoracial foundation of modernity can be located in the classification of the colonial world whose basic principles were established in the sixteenth century and altered thereafter by successive colonialisms. Immanuel Kant's planetary distribution of people by color and continents is a powerful moment in the imaginary of the modern/colonial world system. Kant decided that red people were located in the Americas, yellow in Asia, black in Africa, and white in Europe.[22] Apparently Kant took this classification from the second edition of Linnaeus's *General System of Nature* (1740). As a consequence of this legacy and of the modern/colonial world, I have to check "Hispanic" and "white" on any government form: by Linnaeus's and Kant's logic, "whites" cannot be "Hispanics." This seems to be an obvious foundation for what Hollinger labels the "ethnoracial pentagon," to which "Hispanics" have been added (see page 117). Whereas the basic ethnoracial principles in the sixteenth century were established from a religious and legal/theological perspective and involved mainly Christians, Moors, and Jews, on the one hand, and Spaniards and Amerindians, on the other, the nineteenth century reconverted and adapted these principles to the new circumstances. The earlier Christian ethnoracial foundation was changed into a secular form during the nineteenth century in which, with the colonial hegemony of England, the idea of "whiteness" attached to the Anglo-Saxon and Teutonic race began to emerge. Hannah Arendt makes an important point about Count Arthur de Gobineau's *Essais sur l'inégalité des races humaines* (1853). Responding to a discussion taking place mainly in Germany and France, which began at least half a century before his book was published, Gobineau was searching for a definition and creation of a new elite to replace the aristocracy. Instead of princes, he proposed a "race of princes," the Aryans, whom he said were in danger of being submerged through democracy by the lower non-Aryan classes.[23] Curiously enough, Gobineau's fear was later converted into the idea of a planetary democracy that could be managed by Aryans. This idea of "whiteness" was consolidated and played a fundamental role in one of the major transformations of the modern/colonial world system: the emergence of the United States, a former colony, as a new world power. The pivotal date of this transformation is 1898. This date displaced the balance of power within the modern/colonial world system in the sense that a postcolonial nation such as the United States inverted the order of domination. Spain, Latin America, and the Caribbean were reconfigured along a North-South axis rather than an East-West one. The framework for modern Hispanics/Latinos was thus established.

The second axis around which Quijano defines the notion of the coloniality of power is in the domain of knowledge. Parallel to the ethnoracial classification of the world was the classification of languages and knowledges. Early missionaries did a wonderful job describing and admiring the achievements of Incas, Aztecs, and Mayas, at the same time reducing their knowledge to objects of description that were epistemologically unsustainable. The idea of enriching the Renaissance order of knowledge, the trivium and the quadrivium, with the knowledge of Amerindian civilizations never crossed the mind of the most enlightened missionaries and men of letters. Amerindian knowledge became an object of admiration and description (as is evidenced by the monumental work of Bernardino de Sahagún) while the epistemology of the European Renaissance was assumed to be the natural perspective from which this knowledge could be described and suppressed. This same process was reiterated after the Enlightenment, when the concept of reason opened up a new description, conception, and justification of knowledge in a secular world; reason gradually became associated with northern Europe, and indirectly with "whiteness."[24]

However, I am jumping too far ahead here. Before getting to the end of the road, I would like to recall that the debate over the New World originated at the moment when French philosophers and scientists, rather than Spanish missionaries, described the nature of the New World as either extremely exuberant or lacking, but in either case not mature and balanced. Leclerc de Buffon formulated a reclassification of peoples and their differences in relation to nature based on European peoples as a point of reference. The tensions between all men being equal and different began to be resolved by a chronological order that culminated in Hegel's philosophy of history. The present Europe was both the reference point and the point of arrival for all the different "races" of men who were equal but not yet at the point of arrival in civilization.[25] Yet what should interest us the most is the meaning that "whiteness" acquired in America as a result of the abolition of slavery in the British possessions in the Caribbean (1834) and in the United States during the Civil War.[26] These two events brought together in an unprecedented way the legacies of the sixteenth-century slave trade and the rearticulation of races around color. Yet between the Enlightenment's secularization of racial distinction and its translation to color, the historical moment in which England confronted the "right of men" with the "right of the Englishmen" has to be taken into account.[27]

The visible aspect of the coloniality of power is the colonial difference secured around the ethnoracial and epistemological foundation of the modern/colonial world system. Coloniality of power and colonial difference are helpful in explaining why 1898 is a crucial date for understanding current conceptions and perceptions of Hispanics/Latinos in the United States. Before getting to this point, however, I need to discuss further the ethnoracial foundation of modernity in the sixteenth century—that is, to expand on one of the axes of coloniality of power and make further connections with the transformation of the ethnoracial classificatory system from the sixteenth to the eighteenth centuries.

Two ethnoracial classificatory principles were at work in the sixteenth century. One was "purity of blood,"[28] the other the "rights of the people."[29] "Purity of blood" was a principle of control and marginalization that established Christian and Castilian territoriality. The idea of "rights of the people" was a forerunner of the "rights of men and of citizenship." The first established the colonial difference in ethnoracial terms in the Mediterranean; the second, in the Atlantic. The "rights of the people" responded to politics of integration and assimilation; "purity of blood" responded instead to the politics of exclusion. This logic is still at work today, although with different "contents," and sometimes it remains unspoken. People seldom talk about "purity of blood" today, although it is still at work indirectly in social and institutional conversations. On the other hand, the "rights of the people" has been rearticulated as the "rights of men and of citizens" and later as "human rights." Lately, "human rights" has acquired more specific denominations, such as "linguistic rights," "indigenous rights," and so on.

In the sixteenth century Amerindians were declared servants of God and vassals of the Spanish king. As such, at least legally and in principle, they could not be enslaved. These principles indirectly increased the need for slaves to work in the plantations and in the mines. Slaves did not have the advantage that Amerindians possessed—they were neither servants of God nor vassals of the king of Spain. In the seventeenth century slavery became important in British and French possessions in the Americas and the Caribbean. African slavery is a phenomenon of the modern/colonial world system. Slaves completed the ethnoracial foundation of modernity in the Mediterranean and in the Atlantic. As Manning points out, "it is only with the New World that one can explain the European demand for a large number of slaves."[30] If *mestizaje* became an important issue in Latin America, its conceptual framework was established in the early years of the sixteenth century. Christians, Jews, Moors, and *conversos* provided the initial historical context. Spaniards, British, creoles (or "first Americans" in the United States), Amerindians, and African slaves provided the subsequent one. The foundation of the modern/colonial world system changed content and appearance, but the logic remained the same until the sixteenth century, when the Atlantic became, and was constituted as, a new commercial circuit. This logic is valid for the Americas in general, including the Caribbean. The division, distinctions, and differentiation were and still are consequences of the colonial difference and coloniality of power. Thus, the historical argument is not one that presupposes an Anglo North America and a Latin South America, with a Caribbean in between, but an argument that looks at the racial and epistemological configurations of continental divides. Through this logic we can understand Hispanic/Latinos' locations in the United States today. History by itself is not helpful in anticipating and orienting the future, but the way we tell it is. Official and hegemonic histories have already anticipated it in a way that is not advantageous for all involved. This is why we have the emergence of subaltern studies in South Asia and historians such as David Hollinger reflecting on the conditions for a post-ethnic America.[31]

We have the elements necessary to understand the importance of 1898 in the colonial horizon of modernity, and its significance for the locations of Hispanics/Latinos today. U.S. Representative Charles Cochran, speaking in 1898 about the annexation of Hawaii, stated that the annexation was "only another step in the onward march of liberty and civilization" and "toward the conquest of the world by the Aryan races." He added that the "reign of the Aryan, with justice, enlightenment and the establishment of liberty, shall penetrate to every nook of the habitable globe."[32] Discourses of legitimization of the war against Spain in Cuba and Puerto Rico were cast in similar terms. The Anglo-Saxon white became the point of reference for the classification of the population in terms of race. Races other than white were found dangerous or lacking; for example, the vigorous Slavs were considered dangerous.[33] Not only non-European peoples but also Latins (Spanish, Italian, Portuguese) were deemed lacking in relation to the standards set by the civilized white Europeans.[34] Gobineau's belief that Teutonics, and above all Anglo-Saxons, were the "purest" Aryan denominations on the entire planet was important to justify the distinction between Spanish-Aryan and Anglo-Aryan. In effect, this helped to distinguish between Anglo-Saxon white and Spanish-Christian white.[35] The colonial difference was rearticulated again at two levels, the interior and exterior borders of the modern/colonial world system. Europeans of Latin origin were cast in a subaltern category, a location that Spain began to occupy toward the end of the eighteenth century and more so after the Napoleonic invasion. In 1898 Spain not only lost the war but also moved a step further down in the classification of races. Spain was condemned in the name of white supremacy. The Inquisition (strictly related to the "purity of blood" principle, which served as its institutional control) was perceived as a cause of Spanish decay. In the study of the history of conflicts between England and Spain, the Inquisition has been articulated as a reason for the superiority of the British over the Spanish.[36] Cubans and Puerto Ricans were twice demoted—first because of their Latin descent, and then because of their *mestizaje* with Amerindians or Afro-Americans.

The supremacy of the white race at the time was proclaimed, curiously enough, by creoles, Cubans, and Puerto Ricans who were arguing for national independence. The same idea was also stated by the Argentinian Domingo Faustino Sarmiento a half century earlier in his classic book *Facundo, or Civilization and Barbarism* (1845). Although Sarmiento's work predates Gobineau's, the application of racial logic to a secular world was under discussion and well advanced even in the eighteenth century.[37] What becomes clear at this juncture is that while Gobineau was influential both in the United States and in Latin America, in the second half of the nineteenth century a distinction between Latin Christian white and Anglo-Saxon white was manifested. There was a collaboration between Cuban, Puerto Rican, and U.S. intellectuals as they all celebrated the fact that the Americas were finally independent from Europe. The Western Hemisphere was finally on its own, but the articulation of the civilizing mission with the revamping of manifest destiny reordered the modern/colonial world system and put Latin America at odds with it. Spanish America, once on the western margin of Europe, now became the southern margin of the United States. The colonial difference was reconverted on one of the axes of the coloniality of power (ethnoracial classification) and the location of Hispanics/Latinos was decided.

The Colonial/Epistemological Difference: Area Studies, Latin American Studies, and Latino Studies

The study of Latin America within the United States also has its point of reference in 1898, with the expansion of the United States to the Caribbean and Central America. Although racial prejudice against Spaniards and Mexicans can be traced back to the beginning of the nineteenth century, these prejudices were based on the Black Legend rather than on the rearticulation of white supremacy that occurred after the publication of Darwin's *On the Origin of Species* in 1849, one year after the Guadalupe Hidalgo Treaty.[38] Toward the end of the nineteenth century, the discourse on white supremacy brought manifest destiny together with the "survival of the fittest," which changed the national rhetoric of 1848 into an imperialist discourse.[39] In the first decades of the twentieth century, the Bolton School at Berkeley redressed the difference between people of Hispanic and Mexican descent.[40] The former were defined in terms of past glory, the latter in terms of present decay. If the Bolton School put the Southwest borderlands on the map of the United States—and from that perspective its contribution is valuable—the historians who emerged after 1898 and the expansion toward Central America left it as a past curiosity. The *Hispanic American Historical Review* (founded in 1918) became the instrument of this new interest and was influential until World War II. The panorama of cultures of scholarship on Latin America and in the United States drastically changed after the Cuban revolution, with the foundation of the Latin American Studies Association (LASA) and the establishment of area studies as the expression of an American perspective on the rest of the world. However, from Davis to LASA, going through Bolton and its legacy, the study of Latin America was primarily a matter of politics and cultures of scholarship in the United States, with little influence on scholars living and thinking in Latin America.

I presented this schematic story in order to explain the second axis (the epistemic one) of the coloniality of power and the change in the colonial/epistemological difference, and find the connection with the first, the ethnoracial axis. First of all, area studies during the cold war was a reconversion of occidentalism in the sixteenth and seventeenth centuries, and of orientalism in the late eighteenth and nineteenth centuries. While occidentalism was the consequence of Spanish and Portuguese missionaries and men of letters who placed the Indias Occidentales as the extreme of an arising Western consciousness, orientalism (which presupposed occidentalism) was the consequence of civilization studies and the new relationships that Europe (this time England and France) established with the East. In the 1970s area studies redistributed the former distinctions between East and West, took the planet as the field of study, and introduced a new axis between North and South. This was a substantial relocation of the colonial/epistemological difference, with serious consequences for Hispanics/Latinos in academia and for Latino studies as an emerging field.

This scenario complements the one described by political scientist Carl Pletsch in his classic article concerning the distribution of scientific labor during the cold war.[41] According to Pletsch, area studies distributed scientific labor in relation to the classification of the world into the First, Second, and Third Worlds. The coloniality of power and colonial difference, in both their ethnoracial and epistemological foundations, were clearly at work in the geopolitical distribution of the world and in the consequent distribution of scientific labor. According to Pletsch, sociology and economics were the disciplines whose domain of study was the First World. The Second World was the domain mainly attributed to political science. The Third World became the domain primarily of anthropology. Latin America, for the reasons explained above, became not only part of the Third World but also part of the world in which Spanish and Portuguese were the main languages, at a time when Spanish and Portuguese were no longer the languages of hegemonic scholarship. Latin Americanists in the United States, from both the right and the left, remained blind to the colonial difference. However, this does not mean that they were unaware of colonialism or of the colonial period in Latin America. Some of them, primarily those of a liberal persuasion, worked either directly or indirectly along the lines of the United States's ideology of development and modernization toward Latin America. Those of the leftist persuasion devoted their time to criticizing American policies for development and modernization.[42] Yet this was primarily a debate *about* Latin America *among* American scholars in the social sciences, in which no

Latin American intellectuals participated, nor was production of knowledge in Latin America taken into account. According to the tripartition of the world by area studies, Latin America was considered a place where culture, but not science or culture of scholarship, was produced.

Latin American studies, in its liberal and leftist version, was (and in part still is) blind to (and consequently reproduced) the colonial and epistemological difference, even when the colonial period became an object of study. Knowledge produced in Latin America was subalternized, and the subalternization of knowledge was due to the location of Latin Americans, after 1898, in the ethnoracial and epistemological organization of the world. I perceive here complicity between whiteness and epistemology, and between color and culture. It is precisely this equation that Latin American studies, in general, continues to reproduce. Thus, there is the perception in the field that Latin American studies has a scholarly edge in relation to Latino studies, which is perceived as more political, essayistic, and literary than "scientific," even though books such as the one recently edited by Frank Bonilla,[43] among many others,[44] prove that this is not the case. Reports on Latino studies scholarship since the 1970s provided by sociologist Joan Moore, political scientist John A. García, and historian Richard Griswold del Castillo show not only the rigor of Latino studies scholarship, but also the serious challenges Latino studies presents to the canonical research projects and agendas of the social sciences.[45] Yet it is certainly the imaginary of the colonial difference that permeates the view of the two fields. The emergence of Latino studies in the 1970s began to alter this panorama. Today, approximately thirty years later, it is possible to think that Latino studies, contrary to the current view from outside, is the necessary place for the transformation of area studies, including Latin American studies, and for the erasure of the colonial/epistemological difference.

There are at least two roads that frame the emergence of Latino studies in the 1970s and its situation at the end of the 1990s, and explain why Latino studies' awareness of the colonial difference establishes a new perspective in relation to Latin American studies. One of the reasons for the creation of Latino studies was the pressure exerted by social movements linked to claims of civil rights and the emergence of a new Chicano consciousness, although Latino studies is of a later conceptualization.[46] When John García, as a political scientist and Latino, observes that "the origins of Latino studies lies with, and remains connected to, the realities and relationships of persons of Latino origin living in the United States" and further adds that "the intellectual interests in the Latino communities have much of their bases in the identification, analysis and understanding of the Latino experience in the United States," he is pointing to a crucial epistemological issue that distinguishes Latino studies from Latin American studies.[47] The identification between the subject and object of study brings to the foreground the colonial difference. Here, the term *identification* does not mean that the colonial difference is something to be studied (like the colonial period), but is rather the very foundation of Latino studies itself. This is not the case with Latin American studies as we'll see. Furthermore, "identification" does not mean abandoning the possibility of "objective" knowledge. Rather, it means to critically question an epistemological belief (for example, the objectivity of knowledge) that is a consequence of coloniality of power and colonial difference.

The second road that frames the emergence of Latino studies involves its interdependence with Latin American studies. Let us take for example the discussion at Stanford of the pros and cons of dependency theory as reported by Bonilla.[48] What happened at Stanford during the '70s is relevant in three different ways. First, it is significant that Cardoso himself (and not Gunther Frank) was advocating dependency theory—that is, that a Latin American intellectual was *expressing* it, rather than a Latin Americanist *describing* it. Cardoso himself wrote a wonderful article in the 1970s on the consumption of dependency theory in the United States, in which he observed that dependency theory was deprived of its dialectical and political dimension and translated into the scientific language of the social sciences.[49] Such a translation was a clear reproduction of the colonial/epistemological difference manifested in the superiority and objectivity of the social sciences as practiced in the United States that erased the political motivations of dependency theory in the first place. "Objective" scientific criteria overruled the social and historical necessities that conditioned the emergence of dependency theory in Latin America. Thus, the consumption of dependency theory in the United States twice revealed the colonial difference. On the one hand, at the disciplinary level, it confronted the practice of the social sciences in the First and Third Worlds; on the other hand, it revealed the colonial difference in the domain of area studies, since in order for dependency theory to exist in the United States it had to be translated by sociologists and Latin Americanists.[50]

The emergence of Latino studies began to cut across the colonial difference and to offer a space in which an epistemological potential was emerging, no longer caught in the colonial difference and driven by the coloniality of power. I would say that Latino studies served to legitimize the colonial difference. By progressing the "identification" between the ethnoracial and the epistemological, Latino studies became a critical position of the complicities between ethnicity and cultures of scholarship in the modern/colonial world. The Gulbenkian report touched upon this when describing the origin of the social sciences in the middle of the nineteenth century.[51] Yet the report itself fell short of the projected vision and solution, as once the problem was recognized, the report's suggested solutions reproduced the epistemological foundation of the problem. How to universalize sociology, once the complicity between sociology and colonialism has been recognized, is certainly not the question that should be asked. Sociology (as well as other disciplines) has significantly contributed to human knowledge, but it has also subalternized others. The question, then, is not how to universalize sociology, but how to erase the colonial difference embedded in cultures of scholarship and how to think in terms of knowledge rather than in terms of disciplines—to accept, finally, that sustainable knowledge does not have to be produced, out of necessity, in the disciplinary framework of Western scholarship. The institutional situation of Latino studies has not changed very much. According to Cabán, twenty-five years ago Puerto Rican and other ethnic/national minority studies were unwelcome "and relegated to practical exile at the margins of the university." Now, these departments remain understaffed and underfunded, and they are accepted as the price the new corporate university has to pay to sustain a façade of tolerance.[52] While this is true, the institutional situation should not obscure the epistemological difference that Latino studies has introduced. Historical conditions have changed for both Latin American studies and Latino studies. Today, the potential articulation between Latin American studies and Latino studies can be pursued on two fronts: one, by pushing to the limits the question of "identification" in cultures of scholarship; two, by pushing to the limits the geopolitical changes introduced by globalization, and consequently the porosity established between areas of studies and studying areas, between knowledge and the known. In the conversations about rethinking area studies after the end of the cold war, a distinction was introduced between "area-based knowledge" and "discipline-based knowledge." While this distinction is helpful in moving us beyond the area/object-of-study Third World and discipline/knowing-subject First World, it still presupposes that "disciplines" are neutral in relation to "areas." This reconfiguration has important consequences for the debates on multiculturalism and for the locations of Hispanics/Latinos in it. The debates on multiculturalism, as far as Hispanics/Latinos are concerned, presuppose two distinct entities: Hispanic/Latin America, on the one hand, and Anglo America, on the other. Latin American studies was constituted under, and still remains under, this presupposition. Once the geopolitical distribution of the Americas is challenged, not only Latin American studies but also American studies will be called to trial, as José Saldívar has been insisting since the early 1990s.[53] Globalization and the end of the cold war created new conditions for rethinking cultures of scholarship and area studies.

Thinking from "Latinidad" implies the critical assumption of colonial difference, rather than making colonial difference a topic or issue to be described, narrated, and finally removed from and by a transcendental or nonhistorically located epistemological position. "Identification" means a particular engagement, in Latino studies, between the scholar or social scientist and the community or communities with which he or she identifies, which parallels the situation of the scholar or social scientist in Latin America. There are no "Latin Americanists" in Latin America in the sense that area studies defined and identified the expert and specialist in a given area. However, there are intellectuals engaged in producing knowledge for the need of social transformation or for preventing such transformations. The recognition of the ratio between disciplines, social identification, and local histories in the case of Latino scholars in the United States and Latin American scholars in Latin America invites us to undo and redo the epistemological dislocation of Latin American studies vis-à-vis Latino studies and Latin American scholars engaged in the sociohistorical situation from and about which they produce and transform knowledge. The equation between place and knowledge can no longer be avoided and disguised under the assumptions of epistemic universality. Once this step is taken and the colonial difference is recognized, very productive alliances could be established between Latino/Latin Americanists in the United States and Latin American intellectuals explicitly addressing the colonial difference and the coloniality of power (for example, Quijano, Dussel, Rivera Cusicanqui, Stavenhagen, González Casanova, Barragán, and so on). In such alliances, the "area" or the "national" will no longer serve as the reason for dividing knowledge from the known. As far as the colonial difference is recognized as a locus where coloniality of power is exercised, the colonial difference is at work at every level and involves Latin Americanists, Latinos, and Latin Americans.

It is a common saying among scholars in Latin American and Latino studies, and Latin American intellectuals interested in these issues, that the "Latino" label obscures the national particularities of various groups and therefore hides the differences among "Latinos" themselves. This is an accurate statement. The same argument can be made about the "Latin American" label since it hides the particularity of each country. Yet I hear this latter argument much less often than the former. Why is it that there is more concern about dividing "Latinos" than about doing the same with "Latin Americans"? I do not think that this basic truth should occupy much time and discussion. It is a starting point. The main issue is somewhere else. I would suggest that the main question is what happens when people from local histories (national or not) in Latin America come to the United States. Do they maintain their alliances according to their national community of origin, or do they establish other alliances as well? In a manner of speaking, they manage to do both. Agustín Lao-Montes distinguishes four different and overlapping political ideologies of Latinidad (ethnic Keynesianism, Latino grassroots populism, Hispanic neoconservatism, Latino/America vanguardism) emerging from the massive migrations from Latin America and the Caribbean to New York in the past twenty years.[54] Laguerre, having studied Haitian migration to the United States during and after the revolution (1804), during the U.S. occupation (1915–1934), and during and after Duvalier's regime (1957–1986) shows the transnational character of these migrations as they relate to the homeland.[55] Grosfoguel mapped Puerto Rican migrations to the United States in different stages during the twentieth century.[56] Massive migrations related to globalization explain the fact that in the 1970s, for very clear historical reasons, Puerto Ricans and Chicanos were the strongest communities of "Hispanics," one of the categories of the ethnoracial pentagon introduced in 1977 by the state government.[57] That is why, in the early 1970s, there was no such thing as "Latino studies." Instead, there were "Chicano studies" and "Puerto Rican studies."[58]

So my question is: What happens to people coming to the United States from different places in Latin America? Whatever happens in their personal lives and according to their (our) particular stories and "original" nationalities, the main issue is whether to assimilate and become Anglo-American white, to resist and remain marginal, or to work toward overcoming the colonial difference from the colonial difference itself. The last option involves at least two general activities, if not activism: social movements and cultures of scholarship. Chicano studies and Puerto Rican studies in the 1970s responded to the need of social movements and, as a result, appeared suspicious to university administrations and not scholarly to practitioners in the social sciences and the humanities (as well as to Latin Americanists). The situation has changed in the 1990s, and Latino studies is responding more to global changes and the norms of cultures of scholarship.[59] However, Latino studies has contributed (among other newly emerging academic programs such as Afro-American, women's, gay, and ethnic studies) to transform cultures of scholarship by linking the ethnic identification of the scholar with the domain of study. This move allows for a political and transformative power in cultures of scholarship that was not possible within area (and Latin American) studies. As Cabán has observed, Latin American studies is organized from the top down, while Latino studies is organized from the bottom up (or from below). A place of encounter between the two is the colonial difference, the moment in which Latin American studies follows the example of Latino studies and takes the colonial difference seriously and critically, for which Quijano's coloniality of power offers a point of reference and departure. This will be the moment when Latin America ceases to be an object of study and would be replaced by the colonial difference as the point of articulation of the very historical *being* of "Latin America" in the modern/colonial world.

Uncoupling the Nation from the State: Multiculturalism, Colonial Difference, and the Politics of Knowledge

The final issues I would like to explore are the connections and consequences of bringing together the two axes of the colonial difference, the ethnoracial and the epistemic. I begin by asking the following question: When the multiculturalism issue is addressed in a scholarly debate, with which ethnoracial group is the author of a given article, or speaker in a given context, aligned? I have the impression that in cases such as Latino studies, there is always an explicit connection between the "Latinidad" with which the scholar identifies and the domain of studies and reflection, while in other contexts (particular disciplines or area studies) such identification remains suspended. Latin Americanists do not necessarily identify themselves as Latin Americans.

Hollinger locates multiculturalism in the 1990s as the natural outcome of a state governmental policy of classifying the U.S. population and immigration in the 1970s into what he calls the "ethnoracial pentagon": "white (Caucasian or, later, European-American), Hispanic (Latino), black (Afro-American or, later, African-American), Indian (Native American or, later, Indigenous Peoples), and Asian-American (including Pacific Islander)."[60] Kant's planetary classification is now concentrated within the United States. In the process, four races have been changed into five ethnicities. The difference is the emergence of "Hispanics." Yet why are "Hispanics" not considered "white"? It goes without saying that the erasure of national difference under "Hispanic/Latino" is not something with which only this group shall be concerned. It happens to each of the categories of the ethnoracial pentagon. The historicity of the ethnoracial pentagon is relevant. By historicity, I mean not only the conditions of its constitution in 1977, but the long-term institutional memory that made it a natural distinction from the perspective of the state and for whites/Caucasians, one of the pillars of the pentagon. However, a subtle distinction is not made, one that is crucial to place Hollinger's discourse: the distinction between Anglo-Americans and Euro-Americans. I suspect that Anglo-Americans are not subject to immigration policy since they are the citizens of the state that distinguished between "Anglo-Americans" (citizens) and "Euro-Americans" (immigrants). The presence of Euro-Americans in the ethnoracial pentagon points toward the

European immigration at the end of the nineteenth century and beginning of the twentieth century. "Anglo-American" appears, then, as an empty signifier outside the ethnoracial pentagon, the place from where the pentagon is "named." In that sense, the pentagon is not equally distributed for the first category ("white/Euro-American"); this is the category included in the locus of enunciation (Anglo America) whence the other four ethnoracial categories are established. This is Hollinger's implicit identification, which is indeed not an identification. Hollinger can describe the category "white/Euro-American" as one of the five categories and, at the same time, inhabit it. His claim for a postethnic America is not a discourse located in and from the borders, but in and from a "will to descend" that Hollinger can identify only in each of the particular four ethnicities (Native Americans, Hispanics/Latinos, Afro-Americans, Asian Americans). Hollinger is not only blind to the colonial difference but also to the very fact that his own "will to descend" is located in the European Enlightenment. I am making a strong claim here and asserting that hegemonic disciplines and disciplinary positions are implicitly associated with "whiteness." Hollinger's claim for a postethnic America is a noble one, and I can endorse it in its nobility. However, I have serious reservations concerning the way Hollinger formulates it. One of these reservations is that Hollinger's postethnic America will be an America in which benevolent assimilation (and not critical and dissenting assimilation) is called for.

The curious corollary of Hollinger's noble claims for a postethnic America is the fact that such a claim can be made from only one of the ethnoracial points of the pentagon. Yet in Hollinger's prose the claim is made in such a manner that it appears to be enunciated from a neutral perspective or from a neutral place located outside the ethnoracial pentagon itself. From such an apparently neutral position, Hollinger is able to criticize the "will to descend" as if his arguments were not grounded in his own unmentioned "will to descend," which in turn is grounded in Enlightenment values and Anglo-Saxon group rights, from early in the modern/colonial world system. I am not arguing that it is wrong for Hollinger to defend those values. I respect his position when he says that "defenders of the culture of the West need to state clearly that this culture is to be affirmed because it is valuable, not because it is Western."[61] I do argue that this is a statement in which his own "will to descend" is stated but not self-recognized, and that it may be difficult to reach a postethnic America guided by the principles of one ethnic group, in this case, the leading group of the ethnoracial pentagon in which the project is inscribed. Hollinger's claim for a postethnic America is noble yet suspicious, since it is made from the hegemonic perspective of the white/Anglo-American component of the pentagon. Could a similar claim from a

Hispanic/Latino perspective be entertained? Are Hispanics/Latinos (or Afro-, Native, and Asian Americans) in a position to make such claims? They are not, because theirs is a position of subalternity.

In this regard, I would like to add that a postethnic America cannot be achieved without dispelling and superseding the colonial difference from the perspective of the colonial difference itself. Otherwise it will result in blind assimilation or open repression. To that effect, a position of "critical assimilation" must be taken from the perspective of subaltern ethnoracial groups. By critically engaging the hegemonic ethnoracial perspective, in the public sphere and academia, and working toward social transformations, a postethnic America could be an obtainable horizon. Of course, we cannot lose sight of the larger picture and must understand that a postethnic world is the final destination; this cannot be modeled on a postethnic America as mapped by Hollinger. A condition necessary to reach this goal would be to twice disengage the nation-state: first, to uncouple the state from the nation (for example, the ethnoracial pentagon); second, to disengage the state from the natural and hegemonic nation, the Anglo-Saxon nation on which it rests. These conditions should be applied not just to the United States, but to the entire modern/colonial world. If the ethnoracial foundation of the modern/colonial world was one of the axes on which coloniality of power established the colonial difference, then dispelling and superseding it are not just a question of one country, even if that country is currently considered the leading country. The entire world that was shaped by the ethnoracial axis of the coloniality of power shall become the location of decolonizing projects that attempt to erase colonial differences, ethnoracially and epistemologically.

Since the cards have already been marked by coloniality of power, the colonial difference, and the complicity between ethnoracial foundations and the subalternization of knowledge, what are the political options for Hispanics/Latinos in the United States? One, of course, is to play the game of assimilation, as Richard Rodríguez proposes. This option repeats, on the one hand, the decision made by nation builders and ideologues in Latin America in the nineteenth century, and today it supports the neoliberal global designs for homogenization of the planet. Another option is to resist and remain in the margins or isolated, as was the case until recently for many Amerindian communities in Latin America. A third option, the one I favor, is a resistant or critical assimilation, which is also the path chosen by indigenous movements in Latin America, such as the Paeses in Colombia or the Zapatistas in Mexico. I assume that in all these cases, the first condition that must be met is to become citizens. To have representation in the government and in state institutions is the second. Yet both are linked to the colonial difference and the construction of subjectivity among the groups in question for which citizenship and state representation is a necessary, but not sufficient, condition. The issue is then, under present circumstances, to become X (belonging to the state through citizenship) but at the same time to remain Z (ethnic national belonging through knowledge, education, subjectivity, memories, and, above all, intervention in the organization of the state)—that is to say, to become a regular member of the state (which is minimally achieved through citizenship) and to remain Hispanic/Latino. This could be translated as maintaining the right of difference, because as human beings and as members of the state we are all equal, according to my understanding of the Zapatistas' dictum: because we are equal we have the rights to the difference. At this point, the difference is no longer a colonial difference that reproduces inequalities and inequities, but a creative difference that contributes to the enrichment and the expansion of the domain of human interactions.

This is where Appiah's distinction between cultural diversity and diversity of identity is useful.[62] Appiah strongly reacts against diversity of identity understood as a forced allocation of identity. In education, diversity of identity will imply that the descendants of a given cultural group are educated according to what is presupposed as the particular features and history of that group. Cultural diversity, instead, will transmit to everybody what "belongs" to everybody else without identifying a given group of people with a given culture. There is no question in my mind that the coloniality of power and colonial difference as they shaped the history of Hispanics/Latinos and what they are today in the United States shall be discussed, transmitted, and taught parallel to the history of the Anglo-American, Afro-American, Native American, and other ethnonational histories that have become relevant for the United States. This is, in other words, the history of the modern/colonial world system and the enactment of colonial difference that involves not only teaching and research, but also public policy and justification of the claims of group rights, when the groups in question claim, on the one hand, ethnoracial rights and struggle, on the other hand, to overcome the social hierarchies produced by colonial difference.

Closing Remarks

Overcoming the colonial difference in any country, be it the United States, Bolivia, France, or the former Yugoslavia, is a crucial task for the future that cannot be dictated from the perspective of hegemonic groups and from the knowledge provided by mainstream social sciences and top-bottom area studies. *The underlying principles here are that the politics of recognition includes not just the right to be recognized as different, but mainly the right to be recognized as equal.* Consequently, the politics of recognition is only the first step toward the most important one, that is, the recognition not only of equality but also of equity, as Iris Marion Young argues in this volume. From here, it is possible to derive a position of "critical assimilation" as the right to be different because we are all equal, as the Zapatistas taught us. However, if this is one possible way of thinking beyond the colonial difference as established by the first axis of the coloniality of power, how do we move from here to the second axis, to cultures of scholarship and to the colonial/ epistemological difference? I do not have space here to go into an argument that I developed elsewhere, but I would like to end with the following.[63] Overcoming the colonial differences and coloniality of power require, among other things, a new epistemology that I conceive as "border thinking." Subaltern knowledges have always been recognized as different, never as equal, since these knowledges were linked with ethnicity. Thus, we had the "epistemic" colonial difference. That is why we had occidentalism, orientalism, and area studies. To remain within the epistemology of the modern/colonial world system implies epistemic assimilation. On the other hand, to claim the purity of subaltern knowledges implies an epistemological self-marginalization. Here too, the principle of "critical assimilation" that we can think of in terms of ethnoracial configuration, the first axis of the coloniality of power, could be extended to the domain of epistemology, the second axis of the coloniality of power. Critical epistemological assimilation can then be conceived as border thinking from the perspective of subaltern knowledges.[64] Latin American studies can hardly do the job at this point because of the top-bottom self-constitution in the context of area studies and the social sciences. The epistemological potential of Latino studies (or ethnic studies) is indeed located at the crossing of the two axes of the coloniality of power. It is an epistemological potential that can assist in overcoming the coloniality of power, ethnoracially and epistemologically, and the colonial difference.

Notes

1. See Michel-Rolph Trouillot, *Silencing the Past: Power and the Production of History* (Boston: Beacon Press, 1995).
2. Immanuel Wallerstein, *Geopolitics and Geoculture: Essays on the Changing World-System* (Cambridge: Cambridge University Press, 1991).
3. Walter D. Mignolo, *Local Histories/Global Designs: Coloniality, Subaltern Knowledges and Border Thinking* (Princeton: Princeton University Press, 2000).
4. Suzane Oboler, *Ethnic Labels/Latino Lives: Identity and the Politics of (Re)presentation in the United States* (Minnneapolis: University of Minnesota Press, 1994).
5. Aníbal Quijano, "Colonialidad del poder, cultura y conocimiento en América

Latina," *Anuario Mariateguiano* 9 (1997): 113 21, and "The Colonial Nature of Power and Latin America's Cultural Experience," in R. Briceño-León and H. R. Sonntag, eds., *Sociology in Latin America, Proceedings of the ISA Regional Conference for Latin America*, Venezuela, July 7–9, 1997 (International Sociological Association, 27–38).

6. Walter D. Mignolo, "Globalization, Civilization Processes and the Relocation of Languages and Cultures," in F. Jameson and M. Miyoshi, eds., *The Cultures of Globalization* (Durham: Duke Unversity Press, 1998), 33–53.
7. David Weber, "The Idea of the Spanish Borderland," in David Thomas, ed., *Columbian Consequences: The Spanish Borderlands in Pan-American Perspectives* (Washington, D.C.: Smithsonian Insitution Press, 1991), 3: 3–20, and "Turner, the Boltonians and the Borderland," in *Myth and the History of the Hispanic Southwest* (Albuquerque: University of New Mexico Press, 1988), 33–54.
8. Reginald Horsman, *Race and Manifest Destiny: The Origins of American Racial Anglo-Saxonism* (Cambridge, Mass.: Harvard University Press, 1981).
9. Mark T. Berger, *Under Northern Eyes: Latin American Studies and U.S. Hegemony in the Americas, 1898–1990* (Bloomington: Indiana University Press, 1995), 25–65.
10. Howard F. Cline, "The Latin American Studies Association: A Summary Survey with Appendix," *Latin American Research Review* 2, 1 (1966): 57–79; J. Stanley Heginbotham, "Rethinking International Scholarship," *Items* (Social Science Research Council) 48, 2–3 (1994): 33–40; Edmundo F. Fuenzalida, "The Reception of 'Scientific Sociology' in Chile," *Latin American Research Review* 18, 2 (1983): 95–113; Gilbert W. Merkx, "Foreign Area Studies Back to the Future?" *LASA Forum* 26, 2 (1995): 5–8.
11. See the two collections edited by Carlos F. Toranzo Roca, *Diversidad Etnica y Cultural* (La Paz: Instituto Latinoamericano de Investigaciones Sociales, 1992), and *Lo pluri-multi o el reino de la diversidad* (La Paz: Instituto Latinoamericano de Investigaciones Sociales, 1992); Silvia Rivera-Cusicanqui, "Mestizaje colonial andino: Una hipótesis de trabajo," in X. Albo, ed. *Violencias encubiertas en Bolivia*, vol. 1: *Cultura y Política* (La Paz: CIPCA, 1993), 55–96.
12. Charles Taylor, "The Politics of Recognition," in Amy Gutmann, ed., *Multiculturalism: Examining the Politics of Recognition*, 2nd ed. (Princeton: Princeton University Press, 1994), 25–73; Michael Walzer, *On Toleration* (New Haven: Yale University Press, 1997); Nathan Glazer, *We Are All Multiculturalists Now* (Cambridge: Harvard University Press, 1997).
13. Stefano Varese, "Parroquialismo y globalización. Las etnicidades indígenas ante el tercer milenio," in S. Varese, ed., *Pueblos indios, soberanía y globalismo* (Quito: Abya-Yala, 1996), 15–30.
14. For an analysis on "Latinos" in the U.S. and racial issues related to coloniality of power see Roman Grosfogel and Chloe S. Georas, "'Coloniality of Power' and Racial Dynamics: Notes towards a Reinterpretation of Latino Caribbeans in New York City," in *Identities* (forthcoming, 2000).
15. Fernando Coronil, "Beyond Occidentalism: Toward Nonimperial Geohistorical Categories," *Cultural Anthropology* 11, 1 (1996): 52–87; Walter D. Mignolo, "Postoccidentalismo: Las epistemologías fronterizas y el dilema de los estudios (latinoamericanos) de áreas," *Revista Iberoamericana* 62, 176–77 (1996): 679–96; Edward Said, *Orientalism* (New York: Vintage Books, 1978).
16. José Saldívar, *The Dialectics of Our America: Genealogy, Cultural Critique and Literary History* (Durham: Duke University Press, 1992).

17. Richard Griswold del Castillo, "History from the Margins: Chicana/o History in the 1990s," occasional paper no. 28, Julián Samora Research Institute, Michigan State University, 1997, 2.
18. See Quijano, "Colonialidad del poder, cultura y conocimiento en América Latina," and "The Colonial Nature of Power and Latin America's Cultural Experience."
19. See Wallerstein, *The Modern World-System* (New York: Academic Press, 1974), as well as his "World-System Analysis," in A. Giddens and J. H. Turner, eds. *Social Theory Today* (Cambridge: Polity Press, 1987). See also his *Geopolitics and Geoculture.*
20. Aníbal Quijano and Immanuel Wallerstein, "Americanity as a Concept, or the Americas in the Modern World-System," *ISSA* 1 134 (1992): 549–54.
21. Quijano, "The Colonial Nature of Power and Latin America's Cultural Experience."
22. Immanuel Kant, *Anthropology from a Pragmatic Point of View*, trans. V. L. Dowdell, rev. and ed. H. H. Rudnick (Carbondale: Southern Illinois University Press, 1978 [1792]).
23. Hannah Arendt, *The Origins of Totalitarianism* (New York: Harcourt Brace, 1976 [1948]).
24. Kant, *Anthropology from a Pragmatic Point of View.*
25. Antonello Gerbi, *La disputa del Nuevo Mundo. Historia de una polémica*, 1750–1900, trans. Antonio Alatorre (México: Fondo de Cultura Económica, 1982 [1955]), 7–46.
26. Theodore W. Allen, *The Invention of the White Race*, vol. 2: *The Origin of Racial Oppression in Anglo-America* (London: Verso, 1997).
27. Arendt, *The Origins of Totalitarianism*, 175–80; Allen, *The Invention of the White Race*, vol. 2.
28. Albert A. Sicroff, *Les controverses des statuts de "pureté de sang" en Espagne du XVème au XVIIème siècle* (Paris: Didier, 1960); Haim Beinart, *Los conversos ante el tribunal de la Inquisición* (San Juan: Río Piedras Ediciones, 1983).
29. Demetrio Ramos et. al. Francisco de Vitoria y la Escuela de Salamanca. La Etica en la Conquista de America (Madrid: Consejo superior e Invertsglacione Científica, 1984).
30. Patrick Manning, *Slavery and African Life: Occidental, Oriental and African Slave Trades* (Cambridge: Cambridge University Press, 1990), 30.
31. D. A. Hollinger, *Postethnic America: Beyond Multiculturalism* (New York: Basic Books, 1995).
32. Quoted by Anders Stephanson, *Manifest Destiny: American Expansion and the Empire of Right* (New York: Hill and Wang, 1995), 89.
33. Henry Cabot Lodge, "For Intervention in Cuba," in *Annals of America,* vol. 12: *1895–1904. Populism, Imperialism and Reform* (Chicago: Encyclopaedia Brittanica, (1976 [1895]), 85–87.
34. John William Burgess, *Political Science and Comparative Constitutional Law* (Boston: Ginn and Company, 1893).
35. Frank Hamilton Hankins, *The Racial Basis of Civilization: A Critique of the Nordic Doctrine* (New York: A. A. Knopf, 1928), 47–48.
36. M. S. Furnefold, "For the Restoration of White Supremacy in North Carolina," in *Annals of America,* vol. 12: *1895–1904: Populism, Imperialism, and Reform* (Chicago: Encyclopaedia Brittanica, 1976 [1898]), 229–31.

37. Arendt, *The Origins of Totalitarianism.*
38. Ramón Eduardo Ruiz, ed., *The Mexican War: Was It Manifest Destiny?* (Hinsdale, Ill. : Dryden Press, 1963); Robert W. Johannsen, *The Halls of the Montezumas: The American War in the American Imagination* (New York: Oxford University Press, 1985).
39. A. Beveridge, "The Taste of Empire," in *Annals of America, vol. 12: 1895–1904: Populism, Imperialism and Reform* (Chicago: Encyclopaedia Britannica, 1976 [1898], 198–202.
40. Herbert E. Bolton, *The Spanish Borderlands: A Chronicle of Old Florida and the Southwest* (Albuquerque: University of New Mexico Press, 1921); Weber, "The Idea of the Spanish Borderland."
41. Carl Pletsch, "The Three Worlds, or the Division of Social Scientific Labor, circa 1950–75," *Comparative Studies in Society and History* 23, 4 (1981): 565–90. See also Mignolo, "Postoccidentalismo," and "Colonial and Postcolonial Discourse: Cultural Critique or Academic Colonialism?" *Latin American Research Review* 28, 3 (1993): 120–31.
42. Berger, *Under Northern Eyes.*
43. Frank Bonilla, Edwin Meléndez, Rebecca Morales, and María de los Angeles Torres, *U.S. Latinos, Latin Americans and the Paradox of Interdependence* (Philadelphia: Temple University Press, 1998).
44. Juan Flores, "Latino Studies: New Contexts, New Concepts." *Harvard Educational Review* 67, 2 (1997): 208–21. Tomás Almaguer, *Racial Fault Lines: The Historical Origin of White Supremacy in California* (Berkeley: The University of California Press, 1984). David Montejano, *Anglos and Mexicanos in the Making of Texas: 1836–1986* (Austin: The University of Texas Press, 1987). José E. Limón, *Dancing with the Devil: Society and Cultural Poetics in Mexican American South Texas* (Austin: The University of Texas Press, 1994). Silvia Pedraza, *Political and Economic Migrants in America: Cubans and Mexicans* (Austin: The University of Texas Press, 1985).
45. Joan Moore, "Latino/a Studies: The Continuing Need for New Paradigms," occasional paper no. 29, Julián Samora Research Institute, Michigan State University, 1997; John García, "Latino Studies and Political Science: Politics and Power Perspectives for Latino Communities and Its Impact on the Discipline," occasional paper no. 34, Julián Samora Research Institute, Michigan State University, 1997; Griswold del Castillo, "History from the Margins."
46. Flores, "Latino Studies: New Contexts, New Concepts"; Moore, "Latino/a Studies: The Continuing Need for New Paradigms."
47. García, "Latino Studies and Political Science."
48. Frank Bonilla, "Rethinking Latino/Latin American Interdependence: New Knowing, New Practice," in Bonilla et al., eds., *U.S. Latinos, Latin Americans and the Paradox of Interdependence*, 217–30.
49. Fernando Enrique Cardoso, "The Consumption of Dependency Theory in the United States," *Latin American Research Review* 12, 3 (1977).
50. Berger, *Under Northern Eyes.*
51. I. Wallerstein, C. Juma, E. Fox Keller, J. Kocka, D. Lecourt, V. Y. Mudimbe, K. Mushakoji, I. Prigogine, P. J. Taylor, and M.-R. Trouillot, *Open the Social Sciences*, report of the Gulbenkian Commission on the Restructuring of the Social Sciences (Stanford: Stanford University Press, 1996).
52. Pedro Cabán, "The New Synthesis of Latin American and Latino Studies," in

Bonilla et al., eds., *U.S. Latinos, Latin Americans and the Paradox of Interdependence*, 204; Bonilla, "Rethinking Latino/Latin American Interdependence: New Knowing, New Practice"; Suzanne Oboler, "Anecdotes of Citizen's Dishonor in the Age of Cultural Racism: Toward a (Trans)national Approach to Latino Studies," forthcoming.

53. Saldívar, *The Dialectics of Our America*, and his "Nuestra America's Borders: Remapping American Cultural Studies," in J. Belnap and Raúl Fernández, eds., *José Marti's "Our America": From National to Hemispheric Cultural Studies* (Durham: Duke University Press, 1998), 145–78.
54. Agustín Lao-Montes, "Introduction," in Arlene Dávila and Agustín Lao-Montes, eds., *Mambo Montage: The Latinization of New York City* (New York: Columbia University Press, forthcoming).
55. Michel S. Laguerre, *Diasporic Citizenship: Haitian Americans in Transnational America* (New York: St. Martin's Press, 1998).
56. Ramón Grosfoguel, "The Divorce of Nationalist Discourses from the Puerto Rican People: A Sociohistorical Perspective," in F. Negro-Muntaner and R. Grosfoguel, eds., *Puerto Rican Jam: Essays on Culture and Politics* (Minneapolis: University of Minnesota Press, 1997), 57–76.
57. Oboler, "Anecdotes of Citizen's Dishonor in the Age of Cultural Racism."
58. Flores, "Latino Studies: New Contexts, New Concepts."
59. Ibid.
60. Hollinger, *Postethnic America: Beyond Multiculturalism*, 5; see also his "The Will to Descent: Culture, Color, and Genealogy," lecture delivered at the National Humanities Center, Durham, N.C, 1997 (mimeo), 6.
61. Hollinger, *Postethnic America: Beyond Multiculturalism*, p. 128.
62. Anthony Appiah, "The Multicultural Misunderstanding," *New York Review of Books* 44, 15 (1997): 30–36.
63. Mignolo, *Local Histories/Global Designs.*
64. Ibid.

"It Must Be a Fake!" 6

Racial Ideologies, Identities, and the Question of Rights

Suzanne Oboler

As this century with its bloodstained record draws to a close, the nineteenth century dream of one world has reemerged, this time as a nightmare. It haunts us with the prospect of a fully homogenized, technologically controlled, absolutely hierarchized world, defined by polarities like the modern and the primitive, the secular and the non-secular, the scientific and the unscientific, the expert and the layman, the normal and the abnormal, the developed and the underdeveloped, the vanguard and the led, the liberated and the salvable.

—Ashis Nandy

About two and a half years ago Luis Gutiérrez, a Puerto Rican congressman from Chicago, was standing in line with his sixteen-year-old daughter and his niece, waiting to get into the Capitol to show them his office there. They had just been to "a tribute to all the veterans of the all–Puerto Rican 65th Army Infantry Regiment of the Korean War, including the 743 soldiers who were killed and the 2,797 who were wounded in that conflict." As a result, his daughter and niece were carrying small Puerto Rican flags. Gutiérrez told them to roll the flags up, thinking (mistakenly, as it turned out) that they were not allowed to bring flags into the Capitol. The girls did roll up the flags, but "they got caught in the rollers of the conveyer belt and unfurled." A Capitol police security aide, Stacia Hollingsworth, saw the unfurled flags and, according to the congressman, "yelled in [my] ear: 'Those flags cannot be displayed!'"

The *Chicago Tribune* journalists reporting the incident, David Jackson and Paul de la Garza, tell us that "Gutiérrez was embarrassed, but told his daughter to get rid of the flags, saying, "You know what the rules are."[1]

Overhearing him, Hollingsworth asked: "Who are you that you know what the rules are?" When he told her he was Luis Gutiérrez, a member of Congress, she replied, "I don't think so."

So Gutiérrez showed her his congressional ID card. Her immediate response was to say, "It must be fake." And then she added, "Why don't you and your people just go back to the country you came from?"

According to Jackson and de la Garza, "Gutiérrez was stunned. 'It wasn't like on a side street in Chicago,' he said. 'This was in the middle of the gallery. In the Capitol. Where I work. Can you imagine how humiliating this was in front of my 16-year-old daughter?' At that point, a Capitol Police dignitary protection officer rushed over, recognized Gutiérrez and pulled the aide aside. He told Gutiérrez he saw what happened and suggested that Gutiérrez file a complaint."[2]

The exchange between Congressman Gutiérrez and the Capitol security aide raises at least four related issues that characterize the situation of Puerto Ricans and, more generally, of Latinos in the United States today. First—and although it is important to note that his racial characteristics are never explicitly stated in the article—Gutiérrez clearly did not look like a member of the U.S. Congress, which is largely made up of white males. Second, since he did not look like a congressman, he could not be trusted. Hence the aide assumed he had "faked" his congressional ID card. Third, Gutiérrez's visual features marked him as foreign to the image of people who belong in the United States. As such, he was told that he was neither recognized as a U.S. citizen nor welcome in this country. And finally, this relatively insignificant tale exemplifies the lack of awareness of the long historical presence and citizenship status both of Puerto Ricans (officially U.S. citizens since 1917) and, more generally, of the majority of the population today officially known as "Hispanics" in the United States.

Minimally, Congressman Gutiérrez's experience suggests the extent to which racism in the United States ensures that, unlike white Americans, Latinos constantly have to prove their citizenship and to insist on their rights—including their "right to have rights" as citizens of this society.[3] In fact, the very symbolism of this exchange having taken place at the entrance to the building housing the U.S. Congress is illuminating, for it points to the ongoing emphasis on racial features and phenotype in defining membership in the nation's legislature, where the very meaning of national belonging is negotiated and the experience of representative democracy is recorded into the laws that reinforce the belief in a community of equals in the United States.

One conclusion we can draw from the Gutiérrez family's experience is that in spite of both the end of legal segregation brought about by the 1954 *Brown* v. *Board of Education* decision and of the civil rights movements of the 1960s and 1970s, racism continues to interfere with the possibility of creating a community of equals—and its modern synonym, citizenship—in the United States. Indeed, this encounter reminds us yet again that while citizenship may be commonly understood as a legal status, it is above all a political reality. As such, it cannot be fully understood without taking into account the specificity of the context within which it is understood and differentially experienced in people's daily lives.

The aim of this volume is to better understand the interrelated questions of ethnic identity, culture, and group rights, specifically as these refer to the situation of Hispanics/Latinos in the United States. In addressing these questions, the focus of this essay is not so much Latino ethnic identity itself as it is the context of ongoing racism within which it is defined. Similarly, this paper does not directly address the debate on the validity of group or individual rights as much as it does the persistence of racism in both the United States and the broader international community as a whole.

In other words, the aim of this essay is to describe and clarify the national and global context within which we can discuss the ethnic identity, culture, and group rights of Hispanics/Latinos. I argue that it is a context in which, increasingly, racism and xenophobia shape both the meaning and social value attributed to individuals' ethnic identities and to their lived experience of national belonging in contemporary U.S. society. Insofar as citizenship is the political expression of national belonging, my aim is to clarify the contemporary role of racism in the decline of citizenship and in ensuring the impossibility of belonging to a national community of equals, both in U.S. society and in the broader international context.[4]

I begin with a brief outline of the historical development of citizenship in the United States. It is a history that, from the beginning, has been permeated by a virulent racial ideology long characterized by pseudoscientific, biologically deterministic interpretations of human difference. I argue that following the end of legal discrimination in the post–World War II period, a new racial ideology, similar to that found in Latin American societies, has emerged in the United States. It is an ideology that is generating new kinds of social relations, which are in turn increasingly differentiating people's experience and sense of belonging, with serious consequences for both the political reality and the social value of citizenship.

In the second part of this essay, I examine the implications of this new ideology of social racism in U.S. society in relation to the official ethnic labels—"Asian American," "Hispanic," "African American" and "black," "Native American," and "white European"—initially created for the U.S. Census by the Office of Management and Budget in 1977. Here I suggest that any discussion of rights—and hence of the interaction of racism and citizenship in the current U.S. context—has to take into account that these government-created ethnic and racial categories are first and foremost bureaucratic neologisms of the state. Given the current backlash against affirmative action, bilingual education, and the rights of both documented and undocumented immigrants, I argue that what we are seeing today is the emergence of laws and practices that although ostensibly aimed against foreigners, increasingly have detrimental repercussions for all citizens and residents of the United States.

This is the context within which I believe we should be discussing the question of the ethnic identity, culture, and rights of Latinos. Let me turn first, then, to the development of the political meaning of citizenship as it has been shaped by its interaction with race in the course of United States history.

Citizenship as a Political and Historical Construction

In considering the experience of Congressman Gutiérrez or, more generally, of Latinos in the United States, it is important to keep in mind that the concept of citizenship was never defined by the founding fathers in the Constitution. Instead, they spoke of "the people of the United States" and rarely mentioned the word *citizen*.[5] Therefore, the political reality and social value of citizenship became contingent on a series of laws and/or court cases that at various times in the nation's history either reinforced or challenged each other. At the same time, both the laws and the courts ultimately aimed at specifying the role and implications of "race" in determining who could be a citizen, as well as in clarifying the responsibility of the state to the citizenry.[6]

The Dred Scott case of 1857, for example, argued that the founding fathers did not mean to include blacks when they spoke of "the people of the United States." The subsequent Civil Rights Act of 1866 was specifically designed to reverse the Dred Scott decision, and was followed by the Fourteenth Amendment, ratified in 1868, which, for the first time in U.S. history, created a *national* citizenry and established the principle of equality under the law for all people born in the United States.[7] It is important to note that in adding the Fourteenth Amendment to the Constitution, the 1868 Congress was not only acknowledging the inclusion of African Americans into the polity. It was also—and perhaps more significantly—*explicitly* expanding the previous, more restricted understanding of the national community to include the idea that *all* categories of citizenship and of rights have to be publicly discussed in relation to all persons involved, rather than in relation to only one or another population group.

Less than two decades later, however, the *Plessy* v. *Ferguson* decision in 1896 effectively challenged that amendment. Ruling that "legislation is incapable of eradicating racial instincts," the Supreme Court established racial segregation as the law of the land for the next sixty years.[8] The *Brown* v. *Board of Education* decision ended legal segregation in 1954, thus countering the *Plessy* ruling by pointing to the ways that the psychological damage created by segregation prevented black children's access to equal opportunity. But it took the subsequent civil rights movements of the 1960s to create the various civil rights acts specifically aimed at enforcing the *Brown* decision.[9]

From this perspective, the policies enacted in the last thirty years of the twentieth century represent a new attempt to create a national community of equals—an attempt grounded in the explicit acknowledgment of the historical role of race in shaping the political reality and social value of citizenship.[10]

Nowhere is this more clearly stated than in President Johnson's speech at Howard University in 1965, in which he emphasized the need to create policies aimed at ensuring "not just freedom but opportunity, not just legal equity but human ability, not just equality as a right and a theory, but equality as a fact and as a result." Indeed, in pitting his call for concrete and measurable progress on race against the abstract ideals of "equality as a right and a theory," Johnson pointed to the extent to which citizenship has to be understood not so much as a legal construct, but above all as a political reality that shapes the lived experience of all citizens in the United States. Referring to the passage of the Voting Rights Act as "the end of the beginning," Johnson goes on to define its implications for citizenship, in both political and socioeconomic terms:

> That beginning is freedom. And the barriers to that freedom are tumbling down. Freedom is the right to share fully and equally in American society to vote, to hold a job, to enter a public place, to go to school. It is the right to be treated in every part of our national life as a person equal in dignity and promise to all others.
>
> But freedom is not enough. You do not wipe away the scars of centuries by saying "Now you are free to go where you want, do as you desire, and choose leaders you please." You do not take a person who, for years, has been hobbled by chains and liberate him, bring him up to the starting line of a race and then say, "you are free to compete with all the others" and still justly believe that you have been completely fair.
>
> Thus, it is not enough to just open the gates of opportunity. All our citizens must have the ability to get through those gates.[11]

Johnson's words clearly suggest that the initial impetus for creating policies such as affirmative action wasn't limited solely to ensuring racial minorities' access to full citizenship. Rather it was aimed at finally keeping the promise of citizenship—that is, the promise to create a national community of equals, initially made through the 1866 Civil Rights Act and enshrined in the Constitution through the Fourteenth Amendment.

Yet, more than thirty years later, the nation is witnessing a growing racist backlash against the gains made by the civil rights movement. This is evident in the state-supported antiwelfare policies designed to undermine those gains, in popular support for anti-affirmative-action propositions passed in the states of California (1996) and Washington (1998), and in legislative proposals stemming from the rising anti-immigrant sentiment—particularly against Latinos—around the country.[12] It is particularly apparent in the increasing number of violent attacks by both police and citizens against individuals from racial minority groups.[13] In short, we do not have a community of equals today.

Clearly, affirmative action, like any political solution created by human beings, is not perfect, and like any public policy, its implementation can be improved. Yet given the present context of violence targeted primarily if not specifically against racial minorities, and in view of the wholesale destruction of the institutions that others have built in the past (the Republican Party's dismantling of the judicial system throughout 1998 and its increasingly open disdain for representative democracy being cases in point)[14]—it is equally clear that we cannot allow the elimination of the only policy aimed at addressing the persistence of racially based inequality and intolerance. In fact, it is imperative that everything be done to protect policies such as affirmative action, which currently ensures at least minimal compliance with the civil rights legislation of the 1960s. This is particularly necessary in view of the fact that there are currently no other available proposals that meet this policy's original objective: the establishment of "equality as a fact and as a result" in U.S. society.[15] Indeed, given the lack of viable political alternatives, I would argue that protecting any measure designed to counteract the persistence of racism has become, today, a responsibility of citizenship.

From this perspective, the question, then, is not whether we continue affirmative action.[16] The problems confronting this country today are much more complex. As the following pages suggest, instead of a community of equals, we increasingly have a rigid socioracial hierarchy of "ethnic groups," similar to what we find in Latin American societies, yet with one important difference: in the United States, this hierarchy is reinforced by the state's official categorization of the population into racialized "ethnic" groups and its strategic and discretionary distribution of resources in those terms. So, again, the salient issue is not affirmative action: rather, it is the persistent role of racism in shaping the political reality of citizenship in the United States.

Racism, after all, is an ideology that has plagued the modern world, particularly in the twentieth century. It is an ideology that looks for and reinforces biological and visual manifestations of difference in order to justify socioeconomic inequality. As Peter Wade reminds us:

> Races, racial categories, and racial ideologies are not simply those that elaborate social constructions on the basis of phenotypical variation—or ideas about innate difference—but those that do so using the particular aspects of phenotypical variations that were worked into vital signifiers of difference during European colonial encounters with others.[17]

Like the practice of racial discrimination, then, "race" is not a fact of nature but rather solely a social construct. Racism is, above all, proof of the success of a socially constructed artifice, rooted in nineteenth- and twentieth-century ideological practices that justified the enslavement of and discrimination against one group by another. To this day, racism—the legacy of slavery— continues to structure the social hierarchies of all the nations of the Americas and to be "a fundamental organizing principle, a way of knowing and interpreting the social world."[18]

Like citizenship, race is also not a static concept.[19] As a result of the discrediting of scientific racism underlying Nazism during World War II, its contemporary meanings and social value have gradually changed both in the United States and abroad.[20] Certainly at the end of the twentieth century, the world as a whole has witnessed the disappearance of legal discrimination and, consequently, the seeming attenuation of racism in the political sphere of every society. Yet, paradoxically, the end of legal discrimination has signaled the unchallenged entrenchment of racism in social relations, particularly in the private sphere.

In the United States, the dualistic black/white biological racism that justified legal segregation until 1954 has been undermined over the past four decades by the emergence of a new ideology of "social racism," embedded in a new kind of social relations that are reminiscent of those found in Latin America. The emergence of this ideology of social racism in the United States is particularly apparent in the growing adherence to the idea of racial mixture[21] (or biracialism—in Latin America, it is called *mestizaje*), leading some to stress that social class rather than race is the key to understanding and solving the ongoing problem of poverty and deprivation of large sectors of the population, including racial minorities, in the United States. Reinforced by those who point to what one prominent mainstream magazine defined in 1990 as "the browning of America,"[22] this perceived belief in the "declining significance of race"[23] has since been reinforced by the growing emphasis on the need to explicitly (re)define and stress American nationality as the basis for national unity.

The emphasis on national unity and the simultaneous insistence on the insignificance of biologically determined racial characteristics have long defined the meaning and social value of "race" and, hence, race relations in Latin America. As Magnus Mörner explains, "During the national period, racial distinctions no longer necessarily reflected the genetic composition of individuals; rather they were based on a combination of cultural social and somatic considerations."[24] The term *mestizo* (mixed blood) came to refer to cultural and social fusion, thus replacing the connotation of "biological fusion" inherent in the term *miscegenation.*[25]

In the course of the twentieth century, Latin American racial ideologues increasingly modified and eventually rejected the notion of scientific racism that their U.S. colleagues consistently articulated at various inter-American conferences on eugenics.[26] Contrary to the biological determinism that historically has pervaded U.S. race relations, Latin American intellectuals and scientists alike understood "race" in social terms—specifically in terms of the belief in the existence of higher and lower cultures, which could clearly be assimilated into a national socioracial hierarchy organized and (in)visibly marked by skin color and phenotype. While the choice of terms, like their connotations and uses, continues to be debated throughout the continent, recent Latin American scholarship leaves no doubt that this hierarchy of cultural differences, which ensures both that "everyone knows their place" and the impossibility of forging national communities of equal citizens, has historically been grounded in what the Peruvian anthropologist Marisol de la Cadena has defined as "silent racism."[27]

As I suggest in the following pages, this Latin American ideology of social racism, with its emphasis on the unifying force of nationality to the detriment of racial considerations, appears to be increasingly accepted in U.S. society, superimposed on—although not replacing—the biologically based black/white dualism that has been dominant for much of the nation's history. Nathan Glazer puts it well: "Insistence in our schools that we are all Americans and nothing less, that the changes that fully incorporate blacks have already occurred, that blacks are only Americans of darker skin, while true enough in law, is contradicted by reality."[28] In so doing, it is reinforcing the impact of the *Loving* v. *Virginia* Supreme Court decision, which lifted the two-hundred-year-old prohibition on biracial marriages in 1967, and thus clarifying the extent to which the persistence of racism ensures the impossibility of citizenship not only in the United States but also throughout the hemisphere. Let me explain this point through the case of "Hispanics" in the United States.

The Label "Hispanic" and the Question of Rights

In 1977 the U.S. Office of Management and Budget's Directive 15 created five racial/ethnic categories: white, Asian or Pacific Islander, black, American Indian or Alaskan native, and Hispanic.[29] These ethnic labels are best described as "masterpieces of ambiguity," to borrow a phrase coined in a different context by Maria Eugenia Matute Bianchi. For the 1990 census, for example, "Hispanics" were defined in the following terms:

> A person is of Spanish/Hispanic origin if the person's origin (ancestry) is Mexican, Mexican-Am., Chicano, Puerto Rican, Dominican, Ecuadoran,

> Guatemalan, Honduran, Nicaraguan, Peruvian, Salvadoran; from other Spanish-speaking countries of the Caribbean or Central or South America; or from Spain.[30]

The effects of differentiating and, in effect, racializing the entire U.S. population through these ethnic categories have been contradictory. Undoubtedly it has allowed us to track the progress toward political inclusion of racial minorities, as well as of women, since the end of legal segregation. But it has simultaneously reinforced the belief in the superiority of whiteness and "white privilege," making explicit the continuing existence of a socioracial hierarchy in a society that historically, and to this day, proclaims its adherence to the belief in equality for all. In fact, unlike past perceptions and beliefs that U.S. society was a "melting pot," there is today an implicit acknowledgment of an organized socioracial hierarchy, with whites at the top and blacks and Latinos alternating at the bottom. It is a hierarchy whose dominant theme, as Etienne Balibar puts it, "is not biological heredity but the insurmountability of cultural differences, a racism which at first sight does not postulate the superiority of certain groups or peoples in relation to others but only the 'harmfulness of abolishing frontiers, the incompatibility of life-styles and traditions.'"[31]

In short, the official creation of these ethnic categories has ensured that, as in Latin America, everyone "knows his (or her) place" in U.S. society. And as in Latin America, the outcome is the impossibility of establishing an expanded community of equals in the United States. This assertion is reinforced by the following five interrelated points.

1. The vagueness of the census definition has led to many debates in this country concerning who is a Hispanic and on what grounds. This debate includes questions such as whether citizens from Latin America's sovereign nations currently living in the United States are "as Latino" as those born in the United States.[32] Should this distinction be made? Given the vagueness of the wording and its consequences for public policy, social and race relations, and individuals' daily lives, it is essential that we acknowledge that in the United States, the term *Hispanic*—as originally conceived by the state in the 1970s and currently understood—is first and foremost a bureaucratic invention, used for census data collection. Like its grassroots alternative designation *Latino*, the term *Hispanic* does not refer to, and is in no way tied to, an actual historical, territorial, or cultural background or identity of any of the national-origin groups or ethnic populations it encompasses in the United States. Instead, it comprises the populations of all the Spanish-American nations and of Spain. I should add that we can see the same kind of homogenization with similar implications in relation to all the other ethnic categories.

2. The term *Hispanic*, like other ethnic labels, is here to stay. And from this point of view, the Hispanic (or Latino) experience and identity in the United States cannot be understood outside of the context of the relations that colonized citizens (such as the Puerto Ricans) and conquered peoples (such as sectors of the Chicano population) have historically had with the U.S. government. This context conflated race and nationality and, in 1977, allowed for the official designation of the ethnic label Hispanic which homogenized all people of Latin American descent.[33] Nor can it be understood outside of the context of the historical and very specific differences that mark U.S. relations with each of the various Latin American nations. These relations invariably differentiate the sociopolitical experiences of each national population in this country.[34] But it is also important to note that this is an unprecedented historical moment in the history of the hemisphere and of its populations, for it is the first time that there has been a significant meeting of the various national populations of Latin America in one country, which, perhaps ironically, happens to be the United States.

3. The emphasis on ethnicity, and more particularly on ethnic labeling, is directly related to the distribution and withdrawal of resources and opportunities. Yet the establishment of these official categories has not significantly improved either the social and economic conditions or society's attitudes and perceptions toward people of Latin American descent. [35] Indeed, according to a recent news release by the National Council of La Raza, "Hispanics now have the highest poverty rate of any major ethnic or racial group in the U.S."—albeit still closely followed by African Americans.[36]

This points to the contradictory role that labels are playing today. On one hand, these labels do allow us to track and compare poverty and illiteracy rates among racial groups, to measure the nation's progress toward what Johnson called "equality as a fact and as a result." On the other, the labels are not improving the social or economic conditions in which people live. Instead, the label "Hispanic" marks all Latinos as culturally and socially inferior, as having "bad values" that are perceived to be related to their "foreign"—un-American—origins (a point to which I will return at the end of this paper). Hence, as the case of Congressman Gutiérrez suggests, on the basis of their "un-American" cultural and linguistic difference, as well as of their racial markings, the label is in fact serving to locate all "Hispanics" as a group in a hierarchy in which—to paraphrase Verena Stolke—social inequalities are naturalized on the basis of racial, gendered, and cultural characteristics.[37]

4. The label "Hispanic," like the categories "Asian American" and "African American," exemplifies the impact of globalization in "minoritizing" all populations from Asia, Africa, and Latin America in the United States.[38] The

minoritization of the Third World and the simultaneous emphasis on ethnic-group belonging rather than on citizenship (that is, Hispanic first, American second) has resulted in a variety of complex responses by both Latinos and non-Latinos to the growth of the Latino population in the United States. These are visible in the heated and often acrimonious debates on, and subsequent passage of, anti-immigrant, anti-affirmative-action, and anti-bilingual-education propositions in California and elsewhere, as well as in the proposals for similar bills in Congress. One of the consequences of this is that it now seems natural that the burden and responsibility of protecting both the human and the citizenship rights of individuals lie solely with the particular "ethnic group" to which they ostensibly belong, rather than with the national society as a whole, or with the state, for that matter.

For example, it is now up to the particular ethnic group—in this case "Hispanics"—rather than the larger society to make public responses to the injustices perpetrated upon all people of Latin American descent, regardless of their citizenship status. Certainly it no longer matters whether these injustices refer to the discrimination and deepening poverty of Latinos as a group or to the murder of individuals—for example, the killing of the Puerto Rican Anthony Baez by the New York City police or the killing of the Mexican-American adolescent Ezequiel Hernandez by the National Guard. Certainly it has always been up to the African-American community to demand justice for many blacks harassed, maimed, or murdered by the police and citizens of this country. Since the response to each racist attack is now assumed to be the responsibility of the particular racial group involved, the rest of the nation is increasingly becoming silent and turning its back on the ongoing racial violence against minorities.

Not surprisingly, the consequent decline of citizenship is leading sectors of the minority populations to build on and/or reinforce their own "imagined communities" within their respective groups.[39] Indeed, while the labels have served to homogenize the individual experiences of minorities, the consequence of society's continuing indifference to difference is that minorities today are also redefining the political reality of the labels. For example, insofar as "immigrants, even those who are legal residents and citizens, are being re-imagined as less deserving members of the community,"[40] sectors of the Latino populations are reinterpreting the label in hemispheric and transnational terms.[41] Thus, as a result of the current backlash against the gains of the civil rights period and the consequent undermining of the Fourteenth Amendment's promise of citizenship, the labels today are beginning to contribute to a sense of "cultural citizenship" among growing numbers of disenfranchised minority populations.[42] In so doing, the labels are both redefining the meaning of belonging and enabling minorities to engender a collective response to the particular incidents and issues affecting each group—including, but not limited to, attacks against racially marked individuals. In short, given the gradual demise of citizenship, mainstream society's hierarchized emphasis on the "browning of America" is redefining the meaning of belonging along essentializing racial lines. In the process, it is pointing to the extent to which the state-imposed categories increasingly undermine the possibility of constructing a community of equals in the United States.

5. Finally, it is important to note that the growth of the populations of Latin American descent in the United States and its racialization as a homogeneous "Hispanic ethnic group" are taking place in a larger global context, which I believe frames the entire debate on the ethnic identity, culture, and rights of Latinos. Clearly, the international context of this post–Berlin Wall decade has immersed all democracies in a process of expanding the scope of citizenship. Yet there has been relatively little, if any, sign of a significant and structured general debate within or among the older democracies about how to define the very notion of a collectivity—of a national citizenry—in the new global context.[43] Instead, the historically inherited structures of citizenship rights—like the very political reality of citizenship itself—are being brought into question,[44] with little effort made toward creating new international agreements and institutions (or at least reinforcing those that exist) in order to fully guarantee the human and political rights of the world's population.

In this context a new legal category has emerged—a category that, at least in name, draws attention to the paucity of existing political solutions through which to address the lack of rights of a growing sector of the world's migrant populations (including many of those known as U.S. Latinos). I am referring to the term *denizen*, which, as Walter Truett Anderson notes, refers to "people who aren't exactly citizens, but who aren't exactly foreigners either." In Western Europe "many of these people are long term residents who were recruited as guest workers and, like the man who came to dinner, they have stayed." They remain because, for better or for worse, they "have no other choice"; because they have a better opportunity to provide for their families, whether in their new countries or through remittances to their homeland; or simply because they "like it where they are." But, above all, they stay because "the 'host' countries are not quite up to massive deportations."[45]

From this perspective, denizens are both a symptom of the decline of citizenship and a contributing factor to it—and as such, they put into question the entire issue of "rights" as paradigmatic of citizenship. Certainly the debates in California on Proposition 187 in 1994 and, more recently, Proposition 227 leave no doubt that the presence of denizens in the United States has forced the state to specify its obligation to provide for such basic human needs as medical care, housing, and education. As Anderson correctly points out, protecting the rights of denizens does involve both national policy and "the obligations that countries have as signatories to the various treaties based on the post–World War II Universal Declaration of Human Rights."

But at the heart of the issue of denizenship is the contradiction that Hannah Arendt first discussed specifically in relation to the plight of World War II's refugees: that is, the contradiction between citizenship rights, grounded in the sovereignty of each nation, and human rights, which from their origin were defined in supranational terms, and thus have always put the very notion of national sovereignty into question.[46]

Indeed, it is important to note that the reluctance to address the needs of denizens is not a problem limited to the United States.[47] This reluctance, like the racist underpinnings of contemporary state actions against noncitizens, is apparent throughout the developed world—for example, in France's decision to refuse automatic birthright citizenship to its predominantly second-generation immigrants from North Africa, in Spain's agreement to contain the entry of Africans into Europe as a condition for its inclusion in the European Union, and in the Czech Republic's decision in the summer of 1998 to build a wall separating the Roma from the nongypsy population.[48]

Seen in this broader, international context, current efforts to curtail the entry and/or permanence of Latin Americans in the United States, while clearly racist in intent, are not anomalies either in tone or in substance.[49] And in fact, some attempt is being made to gradually codify their rights in different ways in international treaties and law. Yet both within and beyond the United States, recent state actions suggest a reluctance to allow the fifty-year-old Declaration of Human Rights to prevail over the rights of the state to insist on its sovereignty and to decide who can actually enter its territory, the grounds under which individuals can remain within its borders, and the obligations of the host society to ensure the well-being of noncitizens within its territory. In short, as James Hathaway has argued in the context of refugee rights, "strict respect for sovereignty, coupled with a willingness to disregard that norm only when some form of self-interest stirs powerful states into motion, has meant that there is a huge dichotomy between the rhetoric and the reality of human rights law."[50] At the same time, contemporary state actions also reflect a general trend by the states of the developed world to challenge grassroots demands for the creation of mechanisms through which the rights of noncitizens, or denizens, are protected and guaranteed.[51]

The difficulties that grassroots organizations are having in successfully challenging these trends is at least partially due to the lack of human rights organizations that have significant political legitimacy in the international arena.[52] But the case of the United States makes it clear that it is also (and perhaps primarily) due to the demise of the political sphere, a result of both the political exclusion of denizens and the disenfranchisement of a growing number of racial minorities through poverty and criminalization.[53] Consider, for example, the following discussion of Mexican immigrants in California, by Jorge Castañeda:

> Through no fault of its own, undocumented Mexican immigration is contributing to the "de-democratization" of California society. . . . By the end of the twentieth century, the richest state in the world will have a terribly skewed political system, with a foreign plurality that works, consumes, and pays taxes but does not vote, run for office, organize or carry much political clout.[54]

Key to the demise of the political sphere, then, is the ongoing partial and targeted globalization of key economic institutions, which, as Castañeda goes on to suggest, is increasingly ensuring dedemocratization, economic inequality, and social polarization in the United States. Indeed, it is important not to underestimate the fact that only institutions related specifically to the financial sector are actually being globalized.[55] After all, the financial sector is the least capable of either ensuring or protecting rights, since its operation is neither contingent upon nor concerned with the kinds of democratizing policies entailed in ensuring the maintenance, much less the extension, of either political or social rights to individuals and groups. In short, the current partial and targeted globalization of key economic institutions is increasingly obstructing the state's ability to guarantee the rights of its own population.

This limited globalization has dangerous political consequences for the very principle of democracy around the world. In the name of its borders, for example, the United States now has counterterrorism provisions, aimed at immigrants, that override the rights of all populations. In a context in which all Third World populations are being minoritized, and in which there is strong popular support for legislative and popular attacks against all nonwhite immigrants, these provisions both reflect and reinforce the perception and redefinition of all racial minorities as a threat to "national security."[56]

Conclusion

Ethnic labels such as "Hispanic" allow us to identify a racial hierarchy that, now rationalized in essentializing "cultural" terms, accounts for the ongoing (in)visibility of people of Latin American descent. In so doing, it is reinforcing inequalities not only within the United States, but also—as a result of the consequent minoritization of the entire Third World—between the Western developed nations and the developing world. From this perspective, while the state-imposed categories increasingly undermine the possibility of constructing a community of equals, they simultaneously highlight the process by which the United States is moving in the direction of a rigid, class-based society—a society in which, as in Latin America, the lack of social mobility, like the concomitant widening gap between the rich and the poor, can be explicitly rationalized along ethnic and racial lines.[57]

Ultimately, the persistence of racism and of the ongoing racialization practices in the United States and abroad has put us in a quandary. On the one hand, we are confronted with the question of the very viability of focusing the analysis of the concept of rights—whether we are referring to group or individual rights—exclusively within the old parameters of national boundaries. On the other, given the absence of legitimized international institutions that protect the human rights of all individuals, regardless of citizenship, we need to find new ways of reinforcing the institutions of citizenship, even while we simultaneously create new ways of safeguarding human rights in an increasingly transnational world.

Overcoming the polarities described by Ashis Nandy at the beginning of this essay may be one way to begin to address this impasse.

Notes

1. David Jackson and Paul de la Garza, "Rep. Gutiérrez Uncommon Target of a Too Common Slur," *Chicago Tribune*, April 18, 1996, 1.
2. I first read a summary of this story in Kevin R. Johnson's thought-provoking essay "Citizens as Foreigners," in Richard Delgado and Jean Stefancic, eds., *The Latino/a Condition: A Critical Reader* (New York: New York University Press, 1998), 198–201.
3. The phrase "the right to have rights" was originally coined by Hannah Arendt to emphasize the condition of rightlessness and consequent plight of refugees in the postwar period. See *The Origins of Totalitarianism* (New York: Harcourt Brace and Company, 1979), 296.
4. Stuart Hall and David Hall, "Citizens and Citizenship," in Stuart Hall and Martin Jacques, eds., *New Times: The Changing Face of Politics in the 1990s* (New York: Verso, 1990), 173–90.
5. Alexander Bickel, *The Morality of Consent* (New Haven: Yale University Press, 1975).
6. For a thought-provoking interpretation of the social implications of the Court's decisions, cf. Kimberlé W. Crenshaw, "Color Blindness, History and the Law," in Wahneema Lubiano, ed., *The House That Race Built: Black Americans, U.S. Terrain* (New York: Pantheon Books, 1997), 280–88.
7. Eric Foner and Olivia Mahoney, *America's Reconstruction: People and Politics after the Civil War* (New York: HarperCollins, 1995), 80.
8. Bickel, *The Morality of Consent.*

9. Harvard Sitkoff, *The Struggle for Black Equality, 1954–1992* (New York: Hill and Wang, 1993).
10. Meta Mendel-Reyes, *Reclaiming Democracy: The Sixties in Politics and Memory* (New York: Routledge, 1995); William H. Chafe, "The End of One Struggle, the Beginning of Another," in Charles W. Eagles, ed., *The Civil Rights Movement in America* (Jackson: University Press of Mississippi, 1986), pp.127–48.
11. Lyndon B. Johnson, "To Fulfill These Rights," in George Curry, ed., *The Affirmative Action Debates* (Reading, Mass.: Addison-Wesley, 1997), 16, 24.
12. Elizabeth Martínez, *De Colores Means All of Us: Latina Views for a Multi-Colored Century* (Boston: South End Press, 1998), 68–80; Leo Chavez, "Immigration Reform and Nativism: The Nationalist Response to the Transnationalist Challenge," in Juan F. Perea, ed., *Immigrants Out! The New Nativism and the Anti-Immigrant Impulse in the United States* (New York: New York University Press, 1997), 61–77.
13. Ineke Haen Marshall, "Minorities, Crime and Criminal Justice in the United States," in I. H. Marshall, ed., *Minorities, Migrants and Crime: Diversity and Similarity across Europe and the United States* (Thousand Oaks, Calif.: Sage Publications, 1977), 1–35.
14. Referring to the debates in both the Judiciary Committee and the House of Representatives on impeachment (December 18 and 19, 1998), the editorial page of the *Washington Post* begins by noting that "the comity on which national political life depends has pretty plainly been lost." It ends its somber editorial by quoting the words of a congressman, following the impeachment debates: "Rep. Peter King of New York, one of the few Republicans to buck his own party, yesterday lamented that the House is, with its impeachment vote, 'continuing our spiral toward a government subject to the whims of independent counsels, and based in the frenzied politics of the moment, rather than a government of immutable principles and transcendent institutions.'" Similarly, a news analyst for the *New York Times* asserted, "The deadly sweep of the scythe of neo-Puritanism appears unstoppable," thus suggesting the impossibility, and hence inevitable decline, of the political process. Indeed, at various points in both the Judiciary Committee hearings and the House debates, Representatives Conyers, Waters, and Frank referred to the Republicans' handling of the impeachment process as "a coup d'état."
15. The lack of concrete alternative policies was recently underscored by the report of the President's Race Relations Advisory Board; John Hope Franklin et al., *One America in the Twenty-first Century: Forging a New Future: The Advisory Board's Report to the President* (Washington, D.C.,1998). In analyzing the report's conclusions, Steven A. Holmes noted, "A number of scholars and civil rights advocates said the board had squandered an opportunity to make a bold contribution to stimulating an informed discussion of race that moved beyond the familiar positions of liberals and conservatives." Steven A. Holmes, "Clinton Panel on Race Urges Variety of Modest Measures," *New York Times*, September 17, 1998, A1.
16. George Curry, ed., *The Affirmative Action Debates* (Reading, Mass.: Addison-Wesley, 1997). For a discussion of some of the issues involved in the debate on affirmative action as it refers specifically to the case of Hispanics, cf. Jorge J. E. Gracia, "Affirmative Action for Hispanics? Yes and No," in this volume.
17. Peter Wade, *Race and Ethnicity in Latin America* (London: Pluto Press, 1997), 15.
18. Howard Winant, *Racial Conditions: Politics, Theory, Comparisons* (Minneapolis: University of Minnesota Press, 1994), 2; Michael Banton, *Racial Theories* (Cam-

bridge: Cambridge University Press, 1987); Wade, *Race and Ethnicity in Latin America*, 6–15.

19. Michael Omi and Howard Winant, *Racial Formation in the United States: From the 1960s to the 1980s* (New York: Routledge, 1986).
20. In this respect, Antonio Tabucci reminds us of the extent to which the Nazi regime concocted pseudoscientific theories of racial purity and resorted to scientific practices in its eradication of those it deemed "impure": "More than six million Jews, approximately one million gypsies and a number, which historians have yet to tabulate, of artists, intellectuals, homosexuals and undesirables considered to be racially impure, were scientifically gassed with Zyklon B (a scientifically-achieved chemical substance) and incinerated in furnaces with the highest of temperatures (another technical-scientific invention)—although not before their living bodies were used for an entire series of infamous experiments, which were also deemed scientific." Antonio Tabucci, "En busca de un tribunal," *El Pais Semanal* special edition: "50 Aniversario de la Declaración de Derechos Humanos," *Diario El País* (Madrid, Spain), December 6, 1998 (http//www.elpais.es/p/d/especial/derechos/princi.htm); translation is mine.
21. Maria P. P. Root, ed., *The Multiracial Experience: Racial Borders as the New Frontier* (Thousand Oaks, Calif.: Sage Publications, 1996); Tania Hernandez, "'Multiracial' Discourse: Racial Classifications in an Era of Color-Blind Jurisprudence," *Maryland Law Review* 57, 1 (1998): 97–173.
22. William A. Henry III, "Beyond the Melting Pot," *Time*, April 9, 1990, 28 ff.; Peter Brimlow, *Alien Nation: Common Sense about America's Immigration Disaster* (New York: Harper Perennial, 1996).
23. William J. Wilson, *The Declining Significance of Race: Blacks and Changing American Institutions* (Chicago: University of Chicago Press, 1980).
24. Magnus Mörner, ed., *Race and Class in Latin America* (New York: Columbia University Press, 1965), 3, 5.
25. Leslie Rout, *The African Experience in Spanish America* (New York: Cambridge University Press, 1976); Charles R. Hale, ed., "Mestizaje," special issue of *Journal of Latin American Anthropology* 2 (1996); Richard Graham, ed., *The Idea of Race in Latin America, 1870–1940* (Austin: University of Texas Press, 1990); Minority Rights Group, *No Longer Invisible: Afro-Latin Americans Today* (London: Minority Rights Group, 1995).
26. Nancy Leys Stepan, *"The Hour of Eugenics": Race, Gender and Nation in Latin America* (New York: Cornell University Press, 1996), 171–96.
27. Marisol de la Cadena, "Silent Racism and Intellectual Superiority in Peru," *Bulletin of Latin American Research* 17, 2 (1998): 143–64. See also José Rufino dos Santos, "O Negro Como Lugar," in Marcos Chor Maio and Ricardo Ventura Santos, eds., *Raça, ciência e sociedad* (Rio de Janeiro: Editora Fiocruz, 1996), 219–24.
28. Nathan Glazer, *We Are All Multiculturalists Now* (Cambridge: Harvard University Press, 1997), 158.
29. Jack Forbes, "The Hispanic Spin: Party Politics and Governmental Manipulation of Ethnic Identity," *Latin American Perspectives* 19, 4 (1992): 59–78.
30. U. S. Bureau of the Census, *Development of the Race and Ethnic Items for the 1990 Census* (New Orleans: Population Association of America, 1988), 51.
31. Etienne Balibar, "Is There a Neo-Racism?" in Etienne Balibar and Immanuel Wallerstein, *Race, Nation, Class: Ambiguous Identities* (New York and London: Verso, 1992), 21.
32. This question is not fortuitous, as evidenced on the one hand by the ongoing dis-

tinction made by students on campuses across the country between U.S. Latino organizations and those of the Latin American student organizations housing Latin American—that is, "foreign"—students, and on the other by the insistence on "internationalizing minorities" in mainstream U.S. society, conflating all aspects of Latin American national cultures and identifying them as "Latino." See Martha Giménez, "Minorities and the World-System: Theoretical and Political Implications of the Internationalization of Minorities," in Jane Smith et al., eds., *Racism, Sexism and the World-System* (Westport, Conn.: Greenwood Press, 1988), 39–56. A recent example of this is the way that the dancers in *Forever Tango*, an Argentinian dance production that opened recently in a Broadway theater, are referred to as "Latino artists" by the mainstream press. Cf. Luisita López Torregrosa, "Latino Culture Whirls onto Center Stage," *New York Times*, March 26, 1998, E1, E6.

33. Suzanne Oboler, *Ethnic Labels/Latino Lives: Identity and the Politics of (Re)presentation in the United States* (Minneapolis: University of Minnesota Press, 1995).
34. Although acknowledging that foreign policy does not account for all policy decisions, Christopher Mitchell convincingly argues that "concerns and actions of the U.S government rooted in international relations have tended to shape significant decisions about designating migrants from the Western Hemisphere to enter and/or remain in the United States." Christopher Mitchell, "Introduction," in Christopher Mitchell, ed., *Western Hemisphere Immigration and United States Foreign Policy* (University Park: Pennsylvania State University Press, 1992), 6. Indeed, the consequences of Mitchell's argument for U.S. Latinos are particularly apparent when considering U.S. foreign policy and relations toward Latin American nations specifically as these affect the diverse ways in which each Latin American population is received in this nation. The latter include Cubans forced into exile since the early 1960s; more recent refugee populations, including Nicaraguans, Guatemalans, and Salvadoreans; and those often characterized as "economic immigrants," such as Dominicans, Mexicans, or diverse South American nationals. On the complexity of the relationship between Latinos and Latin Americans in the current era of globalization, see the essays in Frank Bonilla, Edwin Meléndez, Rebecca Morales, and María de los Angeles Torres, eds., *U.S. Latinos, Latin Americans and the Paradox of Interdependence* (Philadelphia: Temple University Press, 1998).
35. The statistics are alarming: "Census data show that for the first time the poverty rate among Hispanic residents of the United States has surpassed that of blacks. Hispanic residents now constitute 23 percent of the country's poor, up eight percentage points since 1985. Of all Hispanic residents, 30 percent were considered poor in 1995, meaning they earned less than $15,569 for a family of four. That is almost three times the percentage of non-Hispanic whites in poverty. Of the poorest of the poor, those with incomes of $7,500 or less for a family of four, 24 percent were Hispanic. . . . Overall, income for Hispanic households has dropped 14 percent since 1989 to under $22,900, from about $26,000, while rising slightly for black ones." Significantly, the article goes on to emphasize, "Nor do the data simply reflect the recent influx of illegal Hispanic immigrants." Carey Goldberg, "Hispanic Households Struggle amid Broad Decline in Income," *New York Times*, January 30, 1997, 1.
36. National Council of La Raza, *NCLR Joins Poverty Dialogue Project*, May 1, 1998. http://nclr.policy.net/proactive/newsroom/release.vtml?id=17024.
37. Verena Stolke, "Is Sex to Gender as Race Is to Ethnicity?" in Teresa del Valle, ed., *Gendered Anthropology* (New York: Routledge, 1994), p. 30.

38. Giménez, "Minorities and the World-System."
39. Benedict Anderson, *Imagined Communities: Reflections on the Origin and Spread of Nationalism* (New York: Verso, 1983).
40. Leo Chavez, "Immigration Reform and Nativism: The Nationalist Response to the Transnationalist Challenge," in Juan F. Perea, ed., *Immigrants Out! The New Nativism and the Anti-Immigrant Impulse in the United States* (New York: New York University Press, 1997), 77.
41. Jorge Duany, "Reconstructing Racial Identity: Ethnicity, Color, and Class among Dominicans in the United States and Puerto Rico," and Helen I. Safa, "Introduction," both in Helen Safa, ed., "Race and National Identity in the Americas," special issue of *Latin American Perspectives* 25, 3 (1998).
42. William Flores and Rina Benmayor, eds., *Latino Cultural Citizenship: Claiming Identity, Space, and Rights* (Boston: Beacon Press, 1997).
43. Saskia Sassen, *Losing Control? Sovereignty in an Age of Globalization* (New York: Columbia University Press, 1996).
44. Ronald Beiner, *Theorizing Citizenship* (New York: State University of New York Press, 1995); Gershon Shafer, *The Citizenship Debates: A Reader* (Minneapolis: University of Minnesota Press, 1998).
45. Walter Truett Anderson, "'Denizens' to Become the New Citizens of the World," *Philadelphia Tribune*, April 29, 1997, 6A.
46. "The secret conflict between state and nation came to light at the very birth of the modern nation-state, when the French Revolution combined the declaration of the Rights of Man with the demand for national sovereignty. The same essential rights were at once claimed as the inalienable heritage of all human beings and as the specific heritage of specific nations, the same nation was at once declared to be subject to laws, which supposedly would flow from the Rights of Man, and sovereign, that is, bound by no universal law and acknowledging nothing superior to itself. The practical outcome of this contradiction was that from then on human rights were protected and enforced only as national rights." Arendt, *The Origins of Totalitarianism*, 230; see also Shafer, *The Citizenship Debates: A Reader.*
47. Nestor Rodríguez, "The Battle for the Borders: Autonomous Migration, Transnational Communities and the State," in Susanne Jonas and Suzie Dod Thomas, eds., *Immigration: A Civil Rights Issue for the Americas* (Wilmington: Scholarly Resources, 1999), 131–44; Chavez, "Immigration Reform and Nativism"; Rainer Baubock, Agnes Heller, and Aristide R. Zolberg, eds., *The Challenge of Diversity: Integration and Pluralism in Societies of Immigration* (Avebury: Ashgate, 1996).
48. Cf. *Migration News* 3, 9 (September 1996), http://www.undp.org/popin/popis/journals/migratn/mig9609.html; Jane Perlez, "A Wall Not Yet Built Casts the Shadow of Racism," *New York Times*, July 2, 1998, A4; Alan Travis, "Fortress Europe's Four Circles of Purgatory," *The Guardian* (London), October 20, 1998, 19; Linda Grant, "In the Ghetto," *The Guardian*, July 25, 1998, 16. Indeed, one recent news report suggests that the European nations are using the example of the United States in defining their rules, and discusses points of convergence and divergence in the implementation of immigration controls on the two continents. Cf. Carl Honore, "Fortress Europe: E.U. Looks to the U.S.-Mexico Experience for Guidance," *Houston Chronicle*, December 7, 1998, A13.
49. Consider, for example, the following report by the Associated Press, subtitled "Proposed Border Rule Dies," documenting the Senate's rejection of a proposal to

tighten the U.S.-Canadian border: "A proposed immigration rule change that would have made crossing the U.S.-Canadian border much tougher has been scrapped by the Senate Appropriations Committee, Sen. Patrick Leahy, D-Vt., said in Montpelier, that state's capital. At issue were provisions in the 1996 immigration overhaul law that were going to force the Immigration and Naturalization Service to check everyone entering and leaving the United States starting in October. Leahy said the rules were meant mainly for the Mexican border." Associated Press. "Proposed Border Rule Dies," *Star Tribune* (Minneapolis), June 26, 1998, 9A.

For other recent reports on the U.S. Canadian immigration, see Sharon Schmickle, "Dispute over Canada Border Restrictions Heats Up in Congress," *Star Tribune* (Minneapolis), July 31, 1998, 16A; Dena Bunis and Heather Macdonald, "Equity Goes South in Border-Check Plan: Immigration Proposals Call for Stricter Enforcement at the Mexican Border than at the Canadian Line, and Would Split the INS," *Orange County Register*, October 10, 1998, A17. Indeed, those who still believe that the official U.S. debates on immigration are not racially motivated might benefit from reading a recent collection of essays by Elizabeth Martínez, in which she argues, "Race and class link the documented and undocumented tightly, negating legalistic differences. When a cop or migra agent arbitrarily arrests a dark-skinned Latino who looks poor, he or she doesn't really care whether the person has the right piece of paper or not." Elizabeth Martínez, *De Colores Means All of Us.*

50. James Hathaway, "New Directions to Avoid Hard Problems: The Distortion of the Palliative Role of Refugee Protection." *Journal of Refugee Studies* 8, 3 (1995): 288–94.
51. In the United States, these efforts include tightening controls at the U.S.-Mexican border; the denial of social, educational, and medical services to noncitizens, whether through welfare legislation, Proposition 187 (1994), or, more recently, Proposition 227 (1998); and the proposal to change the Fourteenth Amendment of the Constitution, which guarantees citizenship to all those born in the United States.
52. Pablo De Greiff, "International Courts and Transitions to Democracy," *Public Affairs Quarterly* 12, 1 (1998): 79–99.
53. Angela Y. Davis, "Race and Criminalization: Black Americans and the Punishment Industry," in Wahneema Lubiano, ed., *The House That Race Built: Black Americans, U.S. Terrain* (New York: Pantheon Books, 1997), 264–79; Marshall, "Minorities, Crime and Criminal Justice in the United States."
54. Jorge Castañeda, *The Mexican Shock* (New York: New Press, 1995), 21.
55. Sassen, *Losing Control? Sovereignty in an Age of Globalization*; see also Pedro Cabán, "The New Synthesis. Latin American and Latino Studies. Refurbishing or Challenging Hegemony in the Academy," paper presented at the Inter-University Program for Latino Research conference "The Global Society and the Latino Community," Bellagio, Italy, December 12–16, 1994.
56. The consequences of this are not solely political, of course. As Cabán has noted, "Politicians play on fears of a vulnerable working class and deliberately misinform workers that their economic well-being is threatened by the virtual slave labor of Mexicans and Central Americans." Cabán, "The New Synthesis."
57. According to Wendy Berry, program officer at the Twentieth Century Fund Foundation, "In 1995, 47.2 percent of the nation's financial wealth was held by the top one percent of Americans, up almost 2 percent from 1992." Wendy Berry, "America's Wealth Pyramid," *Washington Post*, letter to the editor, January 6, 1999, A24.

PART 2

HISPANIC / LATINO IDENTITY, POLITICS, AND RIGHTS

Structure, Difference, and Hispanic/Latino Claims of Justice

7

Iris Marion Young

What do Hispanics/Latinos want? I retain the undecidability of the group label that Jorge Gracia has modeled in the title of his latest book.[1] Many today would likely answer that the claims of Hispanics/Latinos in the political struggles and debates of the United States are a form of identity politics. On this interpretation, what Hispanics/Latinos want from other Americans are public policies of recognition of their specific group identity as Hispanic/ Latino. Political mobilization of Hispanics/Latinos seeks public sites for the assertion and expression of Hispanic/Latino identity, respect by others for this identity, the freedom to live out that identity, and public support for the maintenance and flourishing of the cultural bases of this identity. Some would go even further and claim that political mobilization of Hispanics/ Latinos involves promoting the self-regarding interests of this identity group in competition with other groups for the scarce resources of political office, places in graduate school, professional jobs, and public subsidies. Such a viewpoint suggests that Hispanic/Latino political mobilization consists in putting loyalty to Hispanics/Latinos above all—for example, promoting Hispanic/ Latino political candidates just because they are Hispanic/Latino. On this interpretation, identity politics is simply another self-regarding interest group politics with a layer of cultural respect and appeal to liberal guilt.

In this paper I challenge this image of Hispanic/Latino political mobilization. On the whole, this image fails to depict the claims of justice that Hispanics/Latinos have made and continue to make on American society.

This paper neither articulates a general theory of justice nor justifies in detail the claims of justice that I perceive Latino/Hispanic movements make. My project here is much more modest, namely, to distinguish among certain claims of justice, and to distinguish claims that appeal to justice from other kinds of political claims.

Most particularly, claims of justice are normative in a way that assertions of self-interest are not. Individual and collective political actors do often use institutions to further what they define as their own best interests, without concern for the interests of others. In doing so they feel no obligation to try to persuade others that they *deserve* certain benefits or policy outcomes, nor do they care to appeal to principles or norms that the others might accept.

Sometimes political actors make appeals to justice, however. When they do so they claim that what they seek in the political arena is right from a moral point of view, in terms of equity, fairness, freedom, or other collective values of mutual respect and social cooperation. When they put their claims in terms of entitlement rather than in terms simply of what they want, they implicitly accede to a requirement that they be accountable to others for these claims. When political actors assert that a particular course of action would promote justice and should be followed for that reason, they must engage with others in justifying these claims in terms that they think the others should find acceptable from the point of view of society-wide issues of fairness.

Issues brought under the label of a politics of recognition are indeed about justice. It rarely happens, however, that such issues of freedom of cultural expression and respect for difference are detached from structural inequalities or disadvantages in the distribution of goods, the division of labor, or institutionalized positions of power and prestige. I will argue here that the best interpretation of Hispanic/Latino claims of justice concerns such issues of structural inequality. I will review three issues of injustice relevant to understanding the political claims of Hispanic/Latino movements: (1) citizenship and belonging, (2) language support, and (3) racism, stereotyping, and discrimination. I show how each of these sets of issues relates to people structurally positioned as Hispanic/Latino, and that the claims of justice they carry refer in large degree to issues of substantive equal opportunity.

This essay aims to distinguish a politics of difference, where structural difference built upon perceived cultural difference is the main issue, from the conceptualization many have of identity politics. The paper ends, however, by briefly exploring some understandings of identity politics that do properly describe Hispanic/Latino political mobilization for the sake of justice. In most respects, however, the phrase "identity politics" trivializes Hispanic/

Latino political mobilization and obfuscates its purposes. To the extent that some within Hispanic/Latino political movements accept this label and description, they may contribute to this confusion and trivialization.

Critiques of Identity Politics

A politics of difference, as I understand it, consists of claims by political movements that justice is best served by acknowledging the cultural and structural social groups differentiating a society, and by attending to how differences of culture or structural social position produce conflict and condition relations of privilege and relative disadvantage. Accommodating and sometimes compensating for the consequences of social differentiation are necessary for achieving equal respect and the genuinely equal opportunity for every person to develop and exercise her or his capacities and participate in public life.

The politics of difference expresses skepticism about appeals to a common good. Such appeals might be legitimate in societies without social inequality. Under circumstances of social differentiation and inequality, however, dominant interpretations of a common good too often reflect the perspective and interests of only some groups. The politics of difference resists approaches to law and justice that claim citizens should be considered formally equivalent and should come under identical policies and rules applied in the same way to all. Because of socially constituted differences in situation or opportunity, applying formally equal principles often produces or reinforces material inequality and disadvantage. The idea that citizens should put aside their experienced specificities and engage in political discussion only by appealing to what they have in common, on this view, misses how the public expression of socially differentiated experience and perspective deepens everyone's understanding of the society, its problems, and what may be needed to try to address them in the most just way.[2]

At least three streams of democratic theorists recently have criticized the politics of difference, claiming that it is merely divisive and selfish: a neorepublican stream, a nationalist stream, and a socialist stream. Each construes group-specific justice claims as assertions of group identity, and each criticizes this "identity politics" for displacing "real" political issues, producing intractable conflict, and destroying the public sphere by giving groups warrant to stay in their parochial enclave.

For Jean Elshtain, workable democracy involves active citizens in a vibrant civil society who cooperate in a public spirit that seeks their common good. Democratically committed citizens must adopt a public orientation of commitment and responsibility in which they leave behind what differentiates them. Workable democratic communication and decision making, according to Elshtain, require that citizens be able to transcend the parochialism of their private associations, affections, and affiliations.

Recent movements asserting the importance of attending to social group difference, such as feminism, gay rights activism, or post-civil-rights African-American activism, do not, in Elshtain's view, display such public-spiritedness. Blacks or Latinos or Native Americans claim that American history has left a legacy of discrimination and disadvantage reproduced in schools, workplaces, and public policy, but in their claims for redress, according to Elshtain, they ignore their responsibilities for promoting the common good of everyone. Abandoning a public commitment to a common good, these movements have turned politics into a cacophony of self-interested demands for recognition and redress, where groups within their private identities are unwilling or unable to communicate and cooperate.[3]

David Miller similarly reduces a politics of difference to the public assertion and recognition of group identity, whether sexual, cultural, or ethnic. He does not entirely reject the idea that minority cultures should receive public recognition and expression. To the extent that some groups tend to be excluded from full participation in public deliberation, he agrees that special representation for groups may sometimes be necessary. A politics of difference taken too far in this direction, however, endangers the national identity that ought to be the primary focus of political debate. Groups that wish to make claims on one another for justice can do so effectively, Miller argues, only on the basis of sharing a common national identity. That national identity is the basis of the trust among groups necessary to an orderly and human democratic government. Individuals can develop and express their ethnic and other group identities, such as their gender identity, Jewish identity, or Hispanic/Latino identity, but the national identity must be universal and neutral, as the commitment to a common political culture that transcends these specificities.[4]

Claims that political attention to social group difference damage a needed unity are not surprising coming from republican or nationalist principles. That some writers associated with an anticapitalist left make similar claims is more surprising. Feminist, indigenous, or antiracist movements and claims for justice, according to leftists such as Todd Gitlin or David Harvey, have splintered progressive politics into separatist enclaves. Attention to issues such as sexual harassment, police brutality, or language discrimination diverts egalitarian socialists from a focus on the power of capitalism that oppresses all of the groups. Concern with culture and identity freezes different groups in opposition to one another, rather than uniting everyone who has reason to oppose the power that corporate imperatives have over the lives of most people. As the gap between rich and poor grows and increasing numbers of people worldwide are hurled into poverty or economic insecurity, emancipatory politics requires that all who are interested in justice put aside their particular claims of race or ethnic oppression and unite behind the common dream of a society that meets everyone's basic needs. The politics of difference only deflects from such concerns. Those group-based claims are particularist and self-regarding, unlike the claims of working-class struggle, which transcend those group particularities toward a vision of universal human emancipation.[5]

Due to interpretations such as these, the label identity politics has acquired a negative connotation in much conservative, liberal, and radical discourse. Others in group-based social movements, such as those of Hispanics/Latinos, on the other hand, have affirmed this label as naming the basis of their mobilization and concerns. I want to argue, however, that a politics of difference should resist reduction of its political claims to questions of identity. Issues of cultural identity and group solidarity are certainly relevant to a politics of difference but are only one element in larger claims of justice. As many within these movements have argued, interpretation of a politics of difference as identity politics runs a risk of thinking of social groups as fixed and bounded entities separate from others in basic interests and goals. Let me then try to sort out what is and is not appropriate about the label "identity politics" to describe Hispanic/Latino political mobilization in the context of the United States, and indicate some of the negative consequences of too narrow a conceptual focus on identity.

Social Group Difference Is Not Identity

Those who reduce group difference to identity implicitly use a logic of substance to conceptualize groups. Under this logic a group is defined by a set of essential attributes that constitute its identity as a group. Individuals are said to belong to the group insofar as they have the requisite attributes. On this sort of account, the project of defining Hispanics/Latinos as a group consists of identifying one or more personal or social attributes that make the group what it is, and which those said to be members of the group share, such as biological connection, language, national origin, or celebration of specific holidays. Much recent theoretical reflection on a politics of difference, however, has subjected such group essentialism to significant criticism.

Whether imposed by outsiders or constructed by insiders to the group, attempts to define the essential attributes of persons belonging to social groups fall prey to the problem that there always seem to be persons without the required attributes whom experience tends to include in the group or who identify with the group. The essentialist approach to defining social groups freezes the experienced fluidity of social relations by setting up rigid inside-outside distinctions among groups. If a politics of difference requires such internal unity coupled with clear borders to the social group, then its critics are right to claim that such a politics divides and fragments people, encouraging conflict and parochialism.

A politics that seeks to bring oppositional groups together on the basis of a group identity all members share, moreover, must confront the fact that many people deny that group positioning is significant for their identity. Some women, for example, deny reflective awareness of womanly identity as constitutive of their identity, and they deny any particular identification with other women. Some Americans with Latino backgrounds deny the existence of a Latino or Hispanic identity and claim that having a Latino background is not important to their personal identities. Even when people affirm group affinity as important to their identities, they often chafe at the tendency to enforce norms of behavior or identity that essential definitions of the group entail.

Third, the tendency to conceive group difference as the basis of a common identity that can assert itself in politics implies for many that group members all have the same interests and agree on the values, strategies, and policies that will promote those interests. In fact, there is usually wide disagreement on political ideology among people in a given social group. Though members of a group oppressed by gender or racial stereotypes may share interests in the elimination of discrimination and dehumanizing imagery, such a concern is too abstract to constitute a strategic goal. At a more concrete level members of such groups usually express divergent and even contradictory interests.[6] Hispanics/Latinos in the United States, for example, are widely divergent in political ideology and principles.

The most important criticism of the idea of an essential group identity that members share, however, concerns its apparent denial of differentiation within and across groups. Everyone relates to a plurality of social groups; every social group has other social groups cutting across it. The group "men" is differentiated by class, race, religion, age, and so on; the group "Muslim" is differentiated by gender, nationality, and so on. The group "Hispanic/Latino" is differentiated by gender, race, sexuality, national origin, class, and many other identity markers. If group identity constitutes individual identity and if individuals can identify with one another by means of group identity, then how do we deal theoretically and practically with the fact of multiple group positioning? Is my individual identity somehow an aggregate of my gender identity, race identity, and class identity—like a string of beads, to use Elizabeth Spelman's image?[7] Spelman, Lugones, and others also argue that the attempt to define a common group identity tends to normalize the experience and perspective of some of the group members while marginalizing or silencing that of others.[8] Hispanics/Latinos who transgress heterosexual norms, for example, are easily marginalized by an effort to define authentic or essential Hispanic/Latino culture and values.

Some of these problems with attempting to define a group identity can be mitigated by conceptualizing groups with a relational rather than substantive logic. Any group consists of a collection of individuals who stand in determinate relations with one another because of the actions and interactions of both those associated with the group and those outside of or at the margins of the group.[9] Considered relationally, a social group is a collective of persons differentiated from others by cultural forms, practices, special needs or capacities, structure of power, or privilege. The attributes by which some individuals are classed together in the "same" group appear as similar enough to do so only by the emergent comparison with others who appear more different in that respect. Relational encounter produces the perception of both similarity and difference. Before Captain Cook landed on the islands now called New Zealand, for example, there was no group anyone thought of as Maori. The people who lived on those islands saw themselves as belonging to dozens or hundreds of groups with different lineages and different relations to specific natural resources. Encounter with the English, however, gradually changed the perception of their differences; the English saw them as similar to each other in comparison to the English, and they found the English more different from them than they felt from one another.

In a relational conceptualization, what makes a number of people a group is less some set of attributes its members share than the relations in which they stand to others. On this view, social difference may be stronger or weaker, more or less salient, depending on the point of view of comparison. A relational conception of group difference does not need to force all persons associated with the group under the same attributes. Group members may differ in many ways, including how strongly they bear affinity with others of the group. A relational approach, moreover, does not designate clear conceptual and practical borders that distinguish one group decisively from others. Conceiving group differentiation as a function of relation, comparison, and interaction, then, allows for overlap, interspersal, and interdependence among groups and their members.[10]

Jorge Gracia proposes a complex and subtle relational interpretation of the meaning of that group he gives an undecidable name, "Hispanic/Latino." As I understand his theoretical strategy, there are many people in the world rightly associated with the group "Hispanic/Latino," but not because they share a particular set of attributes—whether race, nationality, language, or religion. What defines the group instead is the relation its members have to the long and determinate history of Iberian colonization of the Americas and the subsequent development of Latin America in relation to English and

French Americas. People who identify as or are identified as Hispanic/Latino enact affinities with one another on the basis of their understanding of themselves as positioned by and in these historical relationships.[11]

I am arguing, then, that describing whatever political claims Hispanics/Latinos make in American public life as "identity politics" is misleading because there is no simple group identity that can be expressed in that public. Social group differentiation concerns the relations in which persons stand—finding more cultural affinities with some than with others, for example. The relational meaning of Hispanic/Latino group difference in the United States, for example, is a function not only of affinity relations between those called Hispanic/Latino; the social positions of these persons are also conditioned by relation to the constitutive outside of an Anglo-European group designation whose cultural and historical affinities have dominated American politics and economics since their founding. In the context of the United States, those identified as Hispanic/Latino have been defined not simply as different but lesser. They have often been positioned by Anglo society as exploitable for menial labor; their language, history, and forms of affinity groups have been denigrated and stereotyped. Shortly I will explain how this Anglo domination produces structural positioning and inequality that describes the basis of Hispanic/Latino political claims better than a simple experience of cultural identity does.

Structural Difference and Inequality

In the context of politics and society in the United States, I suggest that Hispanics/Latinos do not constitute a single cultural group, but rather are better thought of as a *structural* social group. Appeal to a structural level of social life, as distinct from a level of individual experience and action, is common among social critics.[12] Appeal to structure invokes the institutionalized background that conditions much individual action and expression, but over which individuals as such have little control. Yet the concept of structure is notoriously difficult to pin down. I will define social structure, and more specifically structural inequality, by accumulating elements from different accounts.

Marilyn Frye likens oppression to a bird cage. The cage makes the bird entirely unfree to fly. If one studies the causes of this imprisonment by looking at one wire at a time, however, it appears puzzling. How does a wire only a couple of millimeters wide prevent a bird's flight? One wire at a time, we can neither describe nor explain the inhibition of the bird's flight. Only a large number of wires arranged in a specific way and connected to one another to enclose the bird and reinforce one another's rigidity can explain why the bird is unable to fly freely.[13]

At a first level of intuition, this is what I mean by social structures that inhibit the capacities of some people or enable others. An account of someone's life circumstances contains many strands of difficulty or difference from others that, taken one by one, can appear to be the result of either decisions, preferences, or accidents. When considered together, however, and when compared with the life story of others, they constitute a net of reinforcing relationships. Let me illustrate.

Susan Okin gives an account of women's oppression as grounded in a gender division of labor in the family.[14] She argues that gender roles and expectations structure men's and women's lives in thoroughgoing ways that result in disadvantage and vulnerability for many women and their children. Institutionally, the entire society continues to be organized around the expectation that children and other dependent people ought to be cared for primarily by family members without formal compensation. Good jobs, on the other hand, assume that workers are available at least forty hours per week year round. Women are usually the primary caretakers of children and other dependent persons, due to a combination of factors—their socialization disposes them to choose to do it, and/or their job options pay worse than those available to their male partners, or their male partners' work allows them little time for caregiving. As a consequence, the attachment of many women to the world of employment outside the home is more episodic, providing lower status and pay than men's. This fact in turn often makes women dependent on male earnings for primary support of themselves and their children. Women's economic dependence gives many men unequal power in the family. If the couple separates, moreover, prior dependence on male earnings coupled with the judicial system's assumptions make women and their children vulnerable to poverty. Schools, media, and employers' assumptions all mirror the expectation that domestic work is done primarily by women; these assumptions in turn help reproduce those unequal structures.

This is an account of the structural inequality of gender. One can tell analogous stories of structural inequalities of class or racial position, and I will do so shortly with specific reference to Hispanics/Latinos. At this point, however, I wish to systematize the notion of structure by building up definitions from several social theorists. Peter Blau offers the following definition: "A social structure can be defined as a multidimensional space of differentiated social positions among which a population is distributed. The social associations of people provide both the criterion for distinguishing social positions and the connections among them that make them elements of a single social structure."[15] Blau exploits the spacial metaphor implied by the concept of structure. Individual people occupy varying positions in the social space, and their positions stand in determinate relation to other positions. The structure consists of the connections among the positions and their relationships, and the way the attributes of positions internally constitute one another through those relationships. The position of supervisor in a workplace hierarchy is constituted by relationship to determinate subordinates, and their positions are constituted by relations to the supervisor position.

For purposes of inquiring about claims of social justice, we are not interested in such specific positions as foreman on the automobile assembly line, but in more generalized positions that constitute the more basic structure of a whole society. Basic social structures consist of determinate social positions that condition people's opportunities and life chances. These life chances are constituted by the ways the positions are related to one another to create systematic constraints or opportunities that reinforce one another like wires in a cage. Structural social groups are constituted through the social organization of labor and production, the organization of desire and sexuality, the institutionalized rules of authority and subordination, and the constitution of prestige. Structural social groups are relationally constituted in the sense that one position does not exist apart from its differentiated relations to other positions. A position in the social division of labor, for example, is what it is only in the context of the total organization of productive activity to which it is related.

It is certainly misleading, however, to reify the metaphor of structure, that is, to think of social structures as entities independent of social actors, lying passively around them and easing or inhibiting their movement. On the contrary, social structures exist only in the action and interaction of persons; they exist not as states, but as processes. Thus Anthony Giddens defines social structures in terms of rules and resources recursively implicated in the reproduction of social systems.[16] In the idea of the duality of structure, Giddens theorizes how people act on the basis of their knowledge of preexisting structures, and in so acting people reproduce those structures. We do so because we act and interact according to rules and expectations and because our relationally constituted positions make or do not make certain resources available to us. Caste positions, for example, inhere in a rigid social structure that conditions much about the behavior, privileges, and opportunities of persons. The castes do not exist, however, except as enacted and reenacted in minute rituals of deference and superiority enforced through distributions, material dependencies, and threats of force.

Defining structures in terms of the rules and resources brought to actions and interactions, however, makes the reproduction of structures sound too much like the product of individual and intentional action. The concept of social structure should also include the conditions under which individuals act, which are often a *collective* outcome of action impressed onto the physical environment. Jean-Paul Sartre calls this aspect of social structuration the "practico-inert."[17] Most of the conditions under which people act are sociohistorical: they are the products of previous actions, usually products of many coordinated and uncoordinated but mutually influenced actions over them. Those collective actions have produced determinate effects on the environment that condition future action in specific ways. As I understand the term, social structures include this practico-inert not only in the physical organization of buildings, but also in modes of transport and communication; the practico-inert can encompass even trees, rivers, and rocks and their relation to human action.

Reference to such material aspects of social structures helps lead us to a final aspect of the concept. The actions and interactions that take place among persons differently situated in social structures take place not only on the basis of past actions whose collective effects mark the physical conditions of action. They also often have future effects beyond the immediate purposes and intentions of the actors. Structured social action and interaction often have collective results that no one intends and which may even be counter to the best intentions of the actors.[18] Even if no one intends them, they become given circumstances that help structure future actions.

In sum, structures refer to the relations of basic social positions that fundamentally condition the opportunities and life prospects of the persons located in those positions. This conditioning occurs because of the way that actions and interactions in one situation reinforce the rules and resources available for other actions and interactions involving other people. The unintended consequences of the confluence of many actions often produce and reinforce such opportunities and constraints, and these frequently make their mark on the physical conditions of future action as well as on the habits and expectations of actors. This mutually reinforcing process means that the positional relations and the way they condition individual lives are difficult to change.

Structural inequality, then, consists of the relative constraints on freedom and material well-being that some people encounter as the cumulative effect of the possibilities of their social positions, as compared with others who, because of their social position, have more options or easier access to benefits. These constraints or possibilities by no means determine outcomes for individuals in their ability to enact their plans or gain access to benefits. Some of those in more constrained situations are particularly lucky or unusually hardworking and clever, while some of those with an open road have bad luck or squander their opportunities by being lazy or stupid. Those who successfully overcome obstacles, however, nevertheless cannot be judged as equal to those before whom few obstacles have loomed, even if at a given time they have roughly equivalent incomes, authority, or prestige.

Hispanics/ Latinos and Structural Inequality

I am arguing that an understanding of Hispanics/Latinos as a single social group in the context of the United States is better conceptualized in terms of structural position than cultural identity. Members of this group are positioned in a system of structural relations with constraints and enablements that often have far-reaching consequences for their opportunities for well-being. A Hispanic/Latino politics of difference is primarily about making claims of justice that refer to the differentiated social conditions they experience within American structural relations. I find three general categories of structural relations most important: (1) citizenship and social belonging, (2) linguistic opportunity, and (3) racialized discrimination and stereotyping. These three aspects of American social relations are logically distinct, but are often empirically linked and reinforcing for this group. Persons associated with the group "Hispanic/Latino" are not positioned identically with respect to these three sets of relations, but nearly all find their lives conditioned by at least one of them.

Saying that Hispanic/Latino politics should be understood primarily as a response to structural inequality does not imply that cultural difference is distinct from or irrelevant to the structural positioning of Hispanics/Latinos. Most of those who identify as or are identified by others as Hispanic/Latino in the United States have cultural backgrounds and contemporary lived culture that they and others experience as different in some determinate ways from a dominant Anglo culture. Most also experience determinate historical and cultural differences, however, from many others who identify or are identified as Hispanic/Latino. People of Cuban descent are culturally different from Chicanos, for example, and both are culturally different from Salvadoran refugees. What makes it sensible to say that they are nevertheless a single group, then, is not a common culture or history, but rather the fact that social structures similarly position them largely on the basis of their otherwise divergent cultural backgrounds. Let us now explore these three conditions that contribute to the structural positioning of Hispanics/Latinos, and the sorts of justice claims they generate.

Citizenship and Belonging

Whatever their legal citizenship status, and however many generations of American citizens they can trace in their ancestry, Hispanics/Latinos in the United States are liable to be treated as foreigners.[19] Especially if they are brown-skinned, or "look" Indian, or speak English with what others perceive as a Hispanic accent, they are liable to be treated as not belonging to their communities and societies in a full sense, and they often do not feel that they belong. In addition to such feelings of exclusion and marginalization, their positioning can prompt some of these people to care less than others about social connections outside their immediate affinity groupings, and to lack confidence that they can participate effectively in the wider society. Besides relations of social belonging or not belonging, the positioning of Hispanics/Latinos concerns rights of social membership or the lack thereof. Noncitizen residents in the United States do not have the same rights as citizens. What rights society should recognize for noncitizens is an important and highly contested issue of justice for Hispanics/Latinos.[20] This is an issue that affects most Hispanics/Latinos, and not only noncitizens, because even citizens positioned as foreigners are liable to have their rights challenged or unprotected. All Hispanics/Latinos are liable to have more difficulty than others in registering to vote, accessing public services, asserting their rights in the criminal justice system, or challenging employer policy. Being positioned as foreigners or outsiders thus can have determinate material consequences for their economic, social, and political opportunities.

The claims of justice that arise from being positioned as foreigners thus concern the recognition of civil and political rights, inclusive respect as social members, and liberty and opportunity to pursue projects without harassment. Such claims of justice affect all U.S. residents who are not citizens or are liable to be treated as foreigners, of course, including many who are not Hispanic/Latino. It seems to me, however, that Hispanics/Latinos are uniquely positioned as permanently foreign immigrants in the imagination of Anglo Americans. This intuition is connected to the issues of racism that I will discuss shortly.

Language

The Spanish language helps position many as Hispanic/Latino. Many Hispanics/Latinos speak Spanish better than English, including many who are American citizens and legal residents. Language is a vital tool for achieving one's goals. In most workplaces, to be effective and efficient a person must have significant oral and written communication skills in a language shared with coworkers. Without the ability to understand and communicate in the language of newspapers and other publications, television, city council meetings, and so on, political participation is difficult. Language is also an intrinsic aspect of personal and cultural identity. Through the subtleties of language—tone, idiom, phrasing—a person forms and expresses her "personality": her sense of humor, her intelligence, her creative energy.

Through embodied elements of language such as accent, vocabulary, connotation, and slang, persons express enjoyable and sometimes exclusive particularist affinities with one another.

Language is a major vehicle of belonging, political cooperation, economic opportunity, and personal expression. Learning a second or third language to the extent of becoming competent in it in all these ways is difficult, and requires considerable time and resources. I find that there are two sorts of justice claims involving language that Hispanics/Latinos make or might make. The first I construe as a claim of linguistic recognition. The second concerns linguistic equality.

One form of a claim of multiculturalism as a claim of justice that has been made by some Hispanics/Latinos in the past, but seems to be more muted today, says that U.S. society should recognize Spanish as one of its constituent languages. This is a claim of recognition, as Charles Taylor uses that term, and the analogy with the Québécois case is strong. Many Hispanics/Latinos live in territories that were once independently Hispanic, and which the Anglo-American state incorporated by force. Other Hispanic/Latino populations today have territories independent of the United States but nevertheless have experienced paternalistic political and/or economic domination by the United States. This history of incorporation and subsequent English-language domination gives Hispanics/Latinos a unique claim to the recognition of Hispanic/Latino language and cultures as a historical part of the United States. Connected with the issue of belonging, such a claim denies that the Spanish language is a "foreign" language. If education, signs, public services, publications, radio and television broadcasts, and so on were bilingual at least in those regions of the United States with sizeable Hispanic/Latino populations, members of this group would belong to U.S. society in a more complete and positive way.

This claim of recognition can rightly be called a form of identity politics. It seems to me, however, that especially under contemporary conditions of conservative backlash and economic retrenchment, this is neither the most voiced nor the most important claim. The main issues of justice involving language concern fairness and equal opportunity.

Those who do not speak or understand well the language of instruction, public debate, workplace interaction, social services, and bureaucracy are at a serious disadvantage compared with those who function well in the dominant language. Not only do they learn less, participate less effectively in politics or the labor market, and are relatively poorly served in shops and offices, but their lives are simply harder. Language difficulties make almost all social activities more difficult and time-consuming than they are for others. When institutions do not accommodate to language, those with limited skills in the dominant language are liable to suffer many hardships and disadvantages.

Hispanic/Latino justice claims regarding linguistic disadvantage, then, should be construed as primarily about compensating for the unfair disadvantages minority status produces in most areas of social and economic life. Institutions that serve Hispanics/Latinos should be required to offer services in Spanish—schools, health and social services providers, government offices, and so on. Speaking Spanish in these institutions need not be conceived of as multicultural recognition, but rather as a simple requirement of equal service; any significant linguistic minority in a region can plausibly make similar claims.

Language debate in the United States, moreover, usually fails to highlight another important justice claim: that there should be public support for learning the majority language. U.S. policy and Anglo practice expect people who belong to American society to speak English. A society that expects linguistic minorities to learn the dominant language in order to participate in political and economic life is obliged to provide extensive support for such language learning. Free or very inexpensive instruction for English proficiency is rare in the United States. For Hispanic/Latino welfare mothers being forced to look for jobs in many U.S. cities, for example, the issue is not recognition of and accommodation to their linguistic identity; they need extensive free instruction that enables them to function in a predominantly English-speaking workplace.

Racism, Stereotyping, Discrimination

Unless their surname suggests a non-Hispanic/Latino background and their looks and speech allow them to "pass" for Anglo if they choose, Hispanics/Latinos are liable to experience discriminatory treatment and stereotyping. To one degree or another, Hispanics/Latinos are liable to be inconvenienced, disadvantaged, or oppressed by racist structures. Anti-Hispanic/Latino racism takes many forms: assumptions that Hispanics/Latinos are inferior to Anglos in intelligence or character, that one can generalize about their cultural experience, and especially that there are proper occupational and social roles for them. As with other racisms, racialization and othering of Hispanics/Latinos often entails identifying the bodies of these people and the spaces they occupy as contaminated or dangerous. Hispanics who are dark-skinned, who appear to be of African or Native American descent, are most liable to racist stereotyping and discrimination; indeed, they may even suffer this from other Hispanics/Latinos. But most people who identify or are identified as Hispanic/Latino are liable to be on the receiving end of racism some of the time. Anti-Hispanic racism is structural and institutionalized, moreover, insofar as it is written into the social division of labor, the archetypes of television and movies, and the practices of landlords, mortgage lenders, school districts, and dozens of other institutions.

Not every person associated with the group Hispanics/Latinos experiences all of the disadvantages or otherings to which relations of belonging, linguistic privilege, and racism make them liable. All are positioned by these structures, however, and these complex structures often have far-reaching material consequences for their quality of life and freedom to pursue their chosen goals. These conditions too often affect the educational and employment opportunities of Hispanics/Latinos, their relation to state agencies and authorities, their residential situation, and their ability to access services.

As I consider Hispanic/Latino political claims, I find that they largely arise from a protest against the ways these structures tend to operate together to limit choices and opportunities at the same time that they may privilege others. These three aspects of the structural positioning of Hispanics/Latinos frequently work together to reinforce significant material constraint and deprivation. Employers restrict those who are or are perceived to be foreigners to low-wage, menial labor others don't want; in this work their language skills do not improve. Their income and perceived racial and cultural difference seriously limit their housing options; they thus end up living far from other possible employment, learning, and training opportunities, and so on. Some Hispanics/Latinos are able to learn and work their way out of these structural constraints on material opportunity, and the lives of others have not been so directly affected by them. The combination of cultural connection with those whose lives are constrained in this way and the experience of being positioned as Hispanic/Latino in some ways, however, make most Hispanics/Latinos more sensitive to issues of citizenship, language, prejudice, and exclusion than are many Anglos. This awareness serves as a basis of political mobilization.

Conclusion: What Is and Is Not Identity Politics

I have argued in this essay that it is misleading to label as identity politics many of the claims of justice that Hispanics/Latinos have made in recent decades in the context of U.S. society. These claims are indeed a politics of *difference*, calling for politics and policy to attend to the particular socially differentiated situations of Hispanics/Latinos and even to compensate for the inequalities these situations often produce. This social differentiation is primarily a consequence of structural relations, however, which may rely on cultural identities but cannot be reduced to them. The reinforcing structural constraints and enablements arising from being positioned as Hispanic/

Latino have consequences at least as much to do with economic, social, and political opportunity to achieve well-being as they have to do with the expression of personal or cultural identity. The primary political claims expressed by Hispanic/Latino social movements, then, do not constitute claims of the assertion of cultural identity as opposed to other identities.

The label "identity politics" for Hispanic/Latino social movements is not entirely misplaced, however. I will conclude by briefly discussing some further aspects of this politics of difference for which this label makes sense.

In the face of marginalization and discrimination in American society, some Hispanics/Latinos in the last thirty years have engaged in a solidarity-forming and difference-asserting identity politics. They have organized fora, discourses, and cultural expression aimed at reversing the stereotypes and deprecations by which the dominant society has positioned them. These have often had the purpose of celebrating Hispanic/Latino history, language, art, forms of community, and particular cultural practices. Such solidarity-producing cultural politics does consist in the assertion of specificity and difference toward a wider public, from which the movement expects respect and recognition of its agency and values.

Another kind of movement activity often brought under the label "identity politics," however, I find more ambiguous. The project of revaluation and reclaiming identity often involves individual collective exploration of the meaning of Hispanic/Latino cultures and histories. Many people devote significant energy to documenting these meanings and adding to their creative expression in music, visual images, and written and visual narratives. With Charles Taylor and other liberal nationalist theorists, I agree that cultural membership is an important source of self for most people. For this reason, exploring the expressive and documentary possibilities of cultural meaning is an intrinsically valuable human enterprise, and one that contributes to the reproduction of social groups. In themselves and apart from conflicts and problems of political and economic privilege or civil freedom, however, these are not *political* enterprises. To the extent that such activity is mistaken for politics or displaces politics, critics of identity politics may have some grounds for their complaints.

Projects of the exploration and expression of cultural meaning easily become political, however, under at least the following circumstances: (1) those engaged in these projects are denied the liberty to express their cultural identity or engage in their chosen practices; (2) educational practices and curriculum content come under dispute because several groups wish to reproduce their cultural meanings in their children; (3) groups fail to gain access to media, institutions, and resources they need to further their projects of exploring and creating cultural meaning. These three circumstances constitute the primary context of what has come to be called multicultural politics. While often important and contentious, however, such issues of multicultural politics constitute only a portion of the political issues that arise in a politics of difference for Hispanics/Latinos.

I have argued that the primary concern of such politics of difference, among Hispanics/Latinos as well as among a number of other social groups, is with the consequences of social structures that tend to privilege some people in some respects at the same time that they tend to disadvantage others. Some recent depictions of Hispanic/Latino politics trivialize these concerns by narrowing them to a concern with identity and culture. Persons who are called or who call themselves Hispanic or Latino do not share a single identity or set of attributes, but they are similarly positioned in social structures that make them liable to discrimination, stereotyping, and exclusion. A politics of difference as enacted by this structural group, then, ought to mobilize people to press for substantive equal opportunity in the context of respect for cultural specificity.

Notes

1. Jorge J. E. Gracia, *Hispanic/Latino Identity: A Philosophical Perspective* (Oxford: Blackwell, 1999).
2. For a more extended account, see my essay "Difference as a Resource in Democratic Communication," in James Bohman and William Rehg, eds., *Deliberative Democracy* (Cambridge, Mass.: MIT Press, 1997).
3. Jean Bethke Elshtain, *Democracy on Trial* (New York: Basic Books, 1995), especially ch. 3.
4. David Miller, *On Nationality* (Oxford: Oxford University Press, 1995), ch. 5.
5. Todd Gitlin, *Twilight of Common Dreams* (New York: Metropolitan Books, 1995); David Harvey, *Justice, Nature and the Geography of Difference* (Oxford: Blackwell, 1996), especially ch. 12. Nancy Fraser makes similar claims that a politics of difference deflects concern with class inequality, though she claims to value "recognition" as much as "redistribution." See her "From Redistribution to Recognition? Dilemmas of Justice in a 'Postsocialist' Age," in *Justice Interruptus: Cultural Reflections on the "Postsocialist" Condition* (New York: Routledge, 1997), 11–39.
6. Compare Anne Phillips, *The Politics of Presence* (Oxford: Oxford University Press, 1995), 220.
7. Elizabeth Spelman, *Inessential Woman* (Boston: Beacon Press, 1988).
8. María Lugones, "Purity, Impurity and Separation," *Signs: A Journal of Women in Culture and Society* 19, 2 (1994): 458–79.
9. For an account of social groups as constituted relationally, see Larry May, *The Morality of Groups* (Chicago: University of Chicago Press, 1987); and *Sharing Responsibility* (Chicago: University of Chicago Press, 1993).
10. Martha Minow proposes a relational understanding of group difference; see *Making All the Difference* (Ithaca: Cornell University Press, 1990), part II. I have referred to a relational analysis of group difference in *Justice and the Politics of*

Difference (Princeton: Princeton University Press, 1990), ch. 2. For relational understandings of group difference, see also William Connolly, *Identity/Difference* (Ithaca: Cornell University Press, 1993), and Chantal Mouffe, "Democracy, Power and the 'Political,'" in Seyla Benhabib, ed., *Democracy and Difference* (Princeton: Princeton University Press, 1996), 245–56.

11. Jorge J. E. Gracia, "The Nature of Ethnicity with Special Reference to Hispanic/Latino Identity," *Public Affairs Quarterly* 13, 1 (1999): 25–42, and *Hispanic/Latino Identity.*
12. See, for example, William Julius Wilson, *When Work Disappears* (New York: Knopf, 1997); see also Jean Hampton, *Political Philosophy* (Boulder: Westview Press, 1997), 189–90.
13. Marilyn Frye, "Oppression," *The Politics of Reality* (Trumansburg, N.Y.: Crossing Press, 1983).
14. Susan Moller Okin, *Justice, Gender, and the Family* (New York: Basic Books, 1989).
15. Peter Blau, *Inequality and Heterogeneity* (New York: Free Press, 1977), 4.
16. Anthony Giddens, *The Constitution of Society* (Berkeley: University of California Press, 1986), 16–28.
17. Jean-Paul Sartre, *Critique of Dialectical Reason*, ed. Jonathan Ree, trans. Alan Sheridan-Smith (Atlantic Highlands, N.J.: Humanities Press, 1976).
18. Sartre calls such effects "counter-finalities."
19. See Jorge Gracia, "Affirmative Action for Hispanics? Yes and No," in this volume.
20. See *Boston Review* issue on immigration, October-November 1998.

8 Universalism, Particularism, and Group Rights

The Case of Hispanics

Leonardo Zaibert and Elizabeth Millán-Zaibert

Should members of the group "Hispanics" have any special rights, based upon their group membership alone?[1] There are two general strategies used to answer this question affirmatively. The first one is to claim that members of the group have been wronged—and wronged insofar as they are Hispanics—and so deserve special rights that would compensate for or rectify past injustices. Call this the restitutive strategy. The second strategy is based on the view that Hispanics as a group represent a unique set of experiences and perspectives that render their collective voice a subject of special protection or even nurturing. Call this the representational strategy.

It surely is insensitive not to right previous wrongs. Whether or not the victims of these wrongs have been individuals or groups hardly alters the force of this intuition. Whether or not this intuition is universally or even generally accepted is not important for our purposes—we are taking it as a given. And though we wholeheartedly accept it, we shall argue against the restitutive strategy as being a justification for conferring special rights on Hispanics.

We shall also argue against the representational strategy. Its mere formulation begs a crucial question: Why should political institutions nurture, or even protect, unique perspectives? Members of the Ku Klux Klan, as a group, have a set of unique experiences and perspectives that, to say the least, should not be protected or nurtured by our political institutions. Of course, cogent arguments explaining why some groups' sets of experiences and perspectives ought to be protected while others should even be outlawed can be articulated. But the problem with the representational strategy in the case of Hispanics is further complicated by the heterogeneity of the group.

We shall argue against the ascription of group rights in general and to "Hispanics" in particular. Our aim is to ensure that all human beings—including Hispanics and members of other minorities—are treated in a just manner, and we shall suggest that universalism has a better prospect for success than particularism does. The main stages of our argument are as follows. First, we shall explore the fertile relationship between group rights and nationalism. Second, we shall argue that questions centering around who should have this or that right are of limited theoretical value. Finally, we shall show that the group "Hispanics" is extremely difficult to handle in rigorous, philosophical ways, and that this difficulty casts doubt upon the success of the two strategies used to answer our initial question affirmatively.

Group Rights and Nationalism

In *Multicultural Citizenship*, Will Kymlicka briefly touches upon the relationship between group rights and national rights.[2] An important aspect of Kymlicka's project is to show that the emphasis upon minorities and group-differentiated rights is not, as many would suspect, opposed to classical liberalism.[3] He wants to defend group rights from a liberal perspective. Within this context he writes:

> Most liberal theorists accept without question that the world is, and will remain, composed of separate states, each of which is assumed to have the right to determine who can enter its borders and acquire citizenship. I believe that this assumption can only be justified in terms of the same sorts of values which ground group-differentiated rights. I believe that the orthodox liberal view about the right of states to determine who has citizenship rests on the same principles which justify group-differentiated citizenship within states, and that accepting the former leads logically to the latter.[4]

We think that Kymlicka is right in this (merely) formal point. Jacques has rights simply because he belongs to the group of those born in Paris, which Ngo, born in Mogadishu to Somali parents, does not have, and of course vice versa. Dieter, just for belonging to the group of those born to German parents, has rights that Hugo, born in La Paz to Bolivian parents, does not have, and vice versa. That this is the way things are is undeniable. Furthermore, and as Kymlicka correctly points out, accepting that some people be endowed with special rights solely on the basis of their nationality while rejecting special rights on the basis of belonging to non-national ethnic groups is an uphill battle.

If we move beyond the formal level, however, the relationship between national membership and other forms of group membership actually undermines Kymlicka's project and the talk of group rights in general. Otiose as it might be to accept, having this or that nationality can, and usually does, entail important differences in the number and sorts of rights one has. When one's nationality is not chosen, one has to suffer the disadvantages and enjoy the advantages of the nationality that one has, wholly as a matter of luck. And although it is true that liberals who oppose group rights while accepting national rights are guilty of inconsistency along the lines Kymlicka has sketched, the crucial question is equally sidestepped by Kymlicka and by those he attacks, namely, membership into which group justifies having (which) rights?

When working out a full-fledged answer to this momentous question, a goal worth pursuing is to reduce the influence of luck in the distribution of rights and duties, or benefits and burdens.[5] Under this light, limiting the influence of luck in distributing political benefits and burdens is at least a prima facie sign of progress in political philosophy. The Universal Declaration of Human Rights seeks to limit the role that luck plays in shaping the lives of human beings, guaranteeing *some* rights to every human being, independently of membership in any cultural, ethnic, lifestyle, or national group. To emphasize the specificity of group membership in order to grant special rights is, formally speaking, a step in the opposite direction to that of the Universal Declaration of Human Rights.[6] Instead of focusing on what is common to all human beings, group rights theorists emphasize what is specific to some human beings. But the Universal Declaration was, to a great extent, a reaction to the atrocious consequences that racism, sexism, nationalism, chauvinism, and so on had on oppressed minorities. Moreover, the Universal Declaration, in spite of its infelicities, has been the most successful means of protecting human beings from illegitimate harm, and it has done so without instituting any group rights whatsoever.[7]

Instead of merely pointing out that accepting national rights logically entails accepting other forms of group rights (which other forms?), as Kymlicka correctly does, we suggest that a more interesting angle to this issue is revealed when we ask: As political philosophy progresses, should rights based on nationality be given more or less importance? It would be perfectly good logic to question the ascription of group rights to minorities and to nations alike.[8] And since belonging to an ethnic group or to a nation seems to be equally affected by luck, perhaps their importance should be equally diminished.

Part of the suspicion that the talk of group rights elicits in classical liberals might have to do with its particularism, even if this particularism is merely instrumental (and even if this instrumental character is aimed at the attainment of admirable ends). Ernest Gellner's definition of nationalism can help to illustrate some of the dangers that the talk of minority rights could inherit from the talk of nationalism. Gellner defines nationalism in the following way: "Nationalism is primarily a political principle, which holds that the political and the national unit should be congruent."[9] In the sought-after conflation of the nation with the state, and given that the term *national* has been typically (and perhaps inescapably) defined in particularist terms, we find the methodological root of many of the dangers nationalism engenders. Nationalism not only contradicts basic moral intuitions regarding the worth of each and every human life, but it has also given rise to some of the greatest atrocities in history.

It turns out that distributing rights to particular racial or ethnic groups has something in common with nationalism. Nationalistic regimes seek to promote a homogeneous population, whereas proponents of group rights based on ethnicity want to promote precisely the opposite: they want heterogeneous populations and they want to respect and nurture this heterogeneity. But both nationalists and defenders of group rights for ethnic groups want the political to correspond to the national; both want the political outlook of a nation to be shaped by the ethnic outlook of the population.

We do not wish to suggest that these two clearly different political phenomena are analogous; there is much of substance that distinguishes them. The formal similarity between these two phenomena, however, is worth noticing. Group rights theorists who define groups in ethnic or racial terms determine the ascription of rights in ethnic terms such as "Hispanics"; hence the beneficiaries of these rights are defined in terms of their ethnicity rather than in terms of their humanity. Nationalists, too, tend not to treat people as human beings *tout court*, as they treat some (the nationals) differently from others (the foreigners). By showing a similarity between group rights based on ethnicity and nationalism, we merely hope to point out some potential dangers inherent to the talk of group rights based on ethnicity. The best way to avoid the pitfalls of nationalism, we submit, is to sever the connection between the political and the national altogether. A rational, effective political system should be advantageous for any and every human being.

Ad Hoc Theorizing and the Distribution of Rights

For all its partisanship and incendiary overtones, Karl Popper's *The Open Society and Its Enemies* contains a great lesson, which we shall bring to bear upon our topic. In a lucid paragraph that contains the kernel of the central thesis of the book, Popper writes:

> It is clear that once the question "Who should rule?" is asked, it is hard to avoid some such reply as "the best" or "the wisest" or "the born ruler" or "he who masters the art of ruling" (or, perhaps, "The General Will" or "The Master Race" or "The Industrial Workers" or "The People"). But such a reply, convincing as it may sound—for who would advocate the rule of "the worst" or "the greatest fool" or "the born slave"?—is, as I shall try to show, quite useless. [10]

Popper urges us to replace the "Who should rule?" question with the question "How can we so organize political institutions that bad or incompetent rulers can be prevented from doing too much harm?"[11] The rationale for abandoning the "who" approach of the first question in favor of the "how" approach of the second question is simple: by doing this we can develop rational, principled ways of protecting and improving society.

This maneuver can be reproduced within the confines of our discussion in the following way. Instead of asking, "Who should be the recipient of a right?" we should ask, "How can we construct a system of rights which better prevents members of society from being treated unfairly?" Given our discussion in the previous section, it is reasonable to wish that our political system of rights distribution would restrict the influence of luck in this distribution. Thus, such a political system would treat all human beings as human beings, avoiding distinctions based on contingencies such as skin color, national origin, language, and the like.

Of course, endorsing the sort of approach that we recommend over the "who" approach does not preclude "who" questions, yet our favored approach would render these questions derivative. For example, just as Popper would have no trouble answering the question of "Who should rule?" along the lines of "Whoever gets more votes in legitimate elections," we have no trouble answering the question of "Who should have rights?" by saying something like "Whoever has been wronged" or "Whoever needs these rights in order to protect equality of opportunity that has been illegitimately taken away." The problem lies not in the presence of the word *who,* but in the way in which the answer is justified. Our favored approach would allow questions related to who should have this or that right, but it would always also attempt to base the answers on a reasonable system that would seek to minimize luck's influence.

We do not disagree with the claim that if Hispanics have suffered injustices they are therefore entitled to certain rights. Our reluctance comes with the further move of insisting that these rights derive from some sort of shared *Hispanidad* alone, since we see that this step is fraught with difficulties and can be counterproductive to the laudable cause of protecting minorities from oppression and discrimination.

Whoever has been wronged as a result of belonging to a group—be this individual Hispanic, African-American, Irish, or a member of any other ethnic group should be entitled to reparation. A wrong is a wrong is a wrong. So it might be that *some* Hispanics are entitled to some rights to which some non-Hispanics (and some other Hispanics) are not entitled, but these rights are in no way special, nor do they arise from the fact that their bearers are Hispanics. Anyone harmed in a similar way would be entitled to similar reparation. If the general principle were implemented, there would arise no need for special principles.

It is important to take careful notice of the asymmetry. It might be that José is the victim of some harm, and this harm is inflicted upon him solely in virtue of his being Hispanic; yet, when we correct this wrong, we should not do it because José is Hispanic, but because he is a human being and thus subject to the general restitutive principle. We should avoid the uncritical move to preserve symmetries just for their own sake. Darlene Johnson makes this flawed but common move in her claim that "the prevalence of collective wrongs such as apartheid and genocide demonstrates the need for collective rights."[12] Not only does the existence of collective wrongs fail to *demonstrate* anything about collective rights, but collective wrongs do not even *recommend* the need for collective rights. Collective wrongs can be alleviated without instituting collective rights.[13]

In his *Group Rights and Ethnicity*, Thomas Pogge criticizes the view that ethnic groups should receive special consideration. Pogge claims that there is no nonchauvinistic basis to give ethnic groups a more important standing than other groups. He defends the following thesis: "It is irrelevant to the moral assessment of a claim to legal group rights whether the group for which the rights are claimed is or is not (part of) an ethnic group."[14] We agree with Pogge's view and wish to extend it. Just as we should avoid chauvinism between groups, our political institutions should not be chauvinistic between individuals and groups. Pogge's arguments also support the following thesis: It is irrelevant to the moral assessment of a claim to a legal right whether or not the beneficiary for whom the rights are claimed claims these rights as a result of belonging to a group or as an individual.[15] What is relevant in assessing the moral assessment of a claim to a legal right is its justifiability within a reasonable system of rights distribution.

Our view could be objected to along the following lines. It can be argued that we are oblivious to the effects of discrimination, in that José, because he is a Hispanic, would have difficulty making his voice heard, and that group rights precisely seek to guarantee that voices such as José's are heard. Our response is to reiterate that we have nothing against guaranteeing equal access to judicial, political, and administrative mechanisms to *all* human beings, including José. It would surely be an unfair state of affairs if José's voice could not be heard, and we, of course, would want to correct it, but by appealing to José's humanity, rather than to the fact that he is Hispanic. Yet our very appeal to humanity to remedy such an unjust state of affairs has become suspect. Iris Marion Young expresses this suspicion eloquently:

> The politics of difference arose from a frustration with exhortations that everyone should just be thought of as a unique individual person, that group ascriptions are arbitrary and accidental, that liberal politics should transcend such petty affiliations and create a public world of equal citizenship where no particularist differences matter to the allocations of benefits and opportunities. Oppressed groups found that this humanist ideology resulted in ignoring rather than transcending the real material consequences of social group difference, often forcing some people to devalue their own particular cultural styles and forms of life because they did not fit the allegedly neutral mainstream.[16]

It is perhaps a result of this confessed "frustration" with an appeal to something as general as humanity that a sort of optimism regarding the success of appeals to group rights has been welcomed with open arms, and some problems associated with such appeals have been overlooked. First, it is not at all clear if the frustration to which Young alluded was justified, since, to repeat, the Universal Declaration, with its protection of the value and dignity of *every* human being, has helped oppressed groups more than any other legal or political instrument in history. Second, it is not at all clear whether the shortcomings of the "humanist ideology" are inherent to it, or rather the result of problems with its implementation. That is, it is not clearly the case that the "humanist ideology" is beyond repair, or that it involves a hopelessly unattainable "neutral mainstream" in order to take root. Finally, it is not at all clear whether focusing on particularized group membership will necessarily improve conditions for oppressed human beings. Our contention is that insofar as membership in ethnic groups is a matter of luck, this strategy does not do justice to moral intuitions, nor is it likely to yield rational, principled results. Moreover, focusing on the particular promotes the creation of stereotypes, which ultimately harm members of the group and render unfair results. And it is to this problem that we now turn.

Who Is a Hispanic?

This difficult question truly exacerbates the problems already discussed in the previous sections. Whatever the connotation of *Hispanic* might turn out to be, the denotation of the term is so helplessly vague and broad that the ascription of rights to such a fuzzy group is bound to yield erratic, inconsistent, and at times morally outrageous results. The boundaries of many ethnic and lifestyle groups are not sharp. These problematic boundaries are quite complicated in the case of Hispanics, as Latin American philosophy amply reveals. One of the burning issues for Latin American philosophers is cultural identity: Who are we? What are our defining characteristics? How do we differ from other cultures? Who is a *mestizo*? These are questions that have shaped an entire tradition of Latin American philosophy, and they are far from settled.[17] It is only from the bureaucratic perspective of the U.S. government that deciding whether or not someone is a Hispanic is expected to be as easy as checking boxes in meaningless, Orwellian forms. However irritating the governmental banalization of the meaning of the term *Hispanic* is, such oversimplifications are to be expected in the bureaucratic realm, but they should not be welcomed into the philosophical arena.

The group of Hispanics is not homogeneous. Differences amongst various subgroups of Hispanics can be traced back to colonial times.[18] With the establishment of independent states in America, and with the solidification of unique patterns of immigration in each state, the differences have become more pronounced. For example, people from Africa constitute an important element in the process of *mestizaje* in the Caribbean, coastal Venezuela, Colombia, and Panama, but this African migration is by and large absent in Chile, Argentina, and Mexico. The love for soccer commonly referred to as, inter alia, a uniting element amongst Hispanics, for example, is largely absent in Cuba, Puerto Rico, the Dominican Republic, and the rest of the Hispanic Caribbean (where love for baseball is rampant). The indigenous population in Mexico and Central America is very different from the Andean one. Yet the Aztecs and Mayans, on one hand, and the Incas, on the other, were all highly developed cultures and helped to forge national identities in Mexico and Peru in much more important ways than the Caribes or Yanomami in Venezuela and Brazil, or the Guaraní in Paraguay.

The label "Hispanic" encompasses, moreover, not only people with different nationalities within Latin America, but also people belonging to many different races and religions, with very different sexual preferences, and so on, and this heterogeneity (also true of many other groups) renders it (them) difficult to manage. Thomas Pogge, in "Group Rights and Ethnicity," uses Hispanics as a possible example of an ethnic group (or a collection of ethnic groups) on the same page where he denies that they are an ethnic group. He tells us that commonality of descent "is necessary to distinguish ethnic groups from mainly religious and from mainly linguistic groups, such as the Mormons or Hispanics."[19] A few lines later Pogge tells us that "we might . . . view Native Americans, Asian Americans, and perhaps even Hispanics, as ethnic groups."[20] Of course, this is just grist for Pogge's mill, since, like us, he is interested in showing that some of the labels which are imposed on some groups, and which are necessary for the talk of group rights to be articulated at all, are hopelessly vague.

Moreover, aware of the difficulties with establishing precise criteria for membership in the group of Hispanics, many authors have abandoned the so-called essentialist approach, that is, the approach that provides a set of necessary and sufficient conditions for someone to be Hispanic. Instead, they appeal to a relational approach, according to which Hispanics are defined in terms of various relations, both historical and personal. But this move does not help to solve the problems that we present here and which are inherent to the view that Hispanics should have special group rights or benefits. For as the relational strategy abandons the aim of producing a set of necessary and sufficient conditions for someone to be a member of a group, it abandons all hope of establishing precise boundaries for the group.

But if a group is a group by virtue of "the relation in which it stands to others,"[21] if being a Hispanic is a matter of degree,[22] if ethnic groups are "historical families, open and in a constant process of change,"[23] if, in short, the boundary between Hispanics and non-Hispanics is fuzzy, then granting rights or benefits to members of such a group becomes problematic. For as the constitutive relations change, as the familial ties change, so, arguably, change the recipients and the nature of the rights, or, since being a member of the group is a matter of degree, then one has only a certain set of rights, or one has some rights to a certain degree. The principled distribution of rights and benefits requires a sort of specificity and accuracy that the relational strategy is incapable of providing.

The label "Hispanic" as used by group rights advocates imposes as many clichés and stereotypes as it imposes when it is used by bigots or by racists. Of course, these are different clichés, but still clichés. And though perhaps the relational strategy renders these clichés more dynamic, it is hard to see how it could get rid of them altogether. Being labeled is irritating, even if the label can be modified, and even if it is for a "good" cause. These clichés, in addition to clumping Hispanics of different backgrounds, nationalities, religions, and so on under one heading, obscure important differences that are morally relevant.[24] Not all Hispanics have suffered injustice as a result of being members of the group "Hispanic." While Mexicans or Puerto Ricans, viewed as groups, might have suffered discrimination in the United States in the past, Argentinians, Bolivians, Chileans, Colombians, Paraguayans, Uruguayans, and Venezuelans are excellent examples of groups that have not been discriminated against in the United States in the past. But since the relevant differences between all subgroups of Hispanics are obliterated by the coarse label, we witness nationals of some of these nations, who have never suffered any discrimination whatsoever based on their *Hispanidad,* and who came to this country voluntarily, becoming the beneficiaries of, say, affirmative action policies.

In academia, for example, which is the area we know best, our experience is that those Hispanics who have been the recipients of advantages arising from affirmative action policies belong, in their native countries, to the upper socioeconomic classes. They are generally well educated and well-to-do, they came to the United States to pursue advanced academic degrees, and they have never been denied opportunities as a result of their nationality and background. It is hard to see in which way benefiting them corrects wrongs inflicted upon, say, destitute Hispanic agricultural workers in the United States.

Appealing to the representational strategy in order to avoid this difficulty will not do either. After all, the difficulties in establishing who is a Hispanic affect the representational strategy and the restitutive strategy in like manner. For just as it is hard to prove that by benefiting a Chilean corporate lawyer, we are correcting the wrongs inflicted upon Mexican fruit pickers, it is hard to see how this Chilean lawyer represents the perspectives and experiences of the Mexican fruit picker.

An additional problem with focusing exclusively upon representation is that then the vagaries of what constitutes an underrepresented group become an issue. When is a group underrepresented? The most promising answers to this question should include, in one way or another, the fact that the group is underrepresented because its members have been discriminated against. But this fact must by default be ignored when appealing to the representational strategy alone. If the argument is that the proportion of, say, Hispanic professors is lower than their proportion in society at large because Hispanics have been systematically discriminated against in academia, then it is not the representational strategy *alone* that would justify the measure of increasing their numbers in academia, but the representational and the restitutive strategies jointly, or perhaps the restitutive strategy alone.

If Hispanics constitute, say, 10 percent of the population in the United States, yet they constitute only 0.1 percent of university professors, are they *eo ipso* an underrepresented group? Does this fact *alone* justify any measure tending to augment the number of Hispanic professors? We think not. It is, after all, *possible* that Hispanics do not find careers in academia appealing, and thus the purely representational strategy would violate personal autonomy. What should be ensured is that if someone, whether Hispanic, homosexual, African-American, or Irish, wishes to pursue a career in academia, she will have the same opportunities as anyone else.

But if there can be underrepresented groups in this crude and bare sense, there can be overrepresented groups as well. Consider, for example, the facts made public in the well-known study by the Carnegie Commission on Higher Education: in 1969 Jews were around 3 percent of the American population, yet (and in spite of well-documented discrimination) were about 9 percent of university professors.[25] Are Jews overrepresented in academia? Similar questions could be asked about many other groups, such as Asians, Catholics, Germans, Quakers, and even subgroups amongst Hispanics. Should we limit the number of Jews, or any other "overrepresented" group, in academia? Defenders of the purely representational strategy might have a hard time answering these questions negatively.

Conclusion

The reciprocal acceptance of groups with different ethnic backgrounds, lifestyles, and cultures should be encouraged and protected. Some attempts to protect this diversity, however, can be counterproductive. Hispanics should have as many, but just as many, rights as non-Hispanics, and this holds also for members of other groups. Diversity should be protected, but by a comprehensive political system whose goal is to diminish the influence of luck, and there is good evidence that the best such system is one that transcends group differences and focuses on our shared humanity, however passé this may sound. The difficulty with determining who should count as a Hispanic, the inadequacy within political philosophy of asking "who" questions, and the connections between group rights for Hispanics and ethnic chauvinism and nationalism point, in our opinion, to negating the provision of special rights to Hispanics solely on the basis of their *Hispanidad*. And to negate the provision of special rights to Hispanics in no way entails insensitivity to the plight some Hispanics have endured or continue to endure. Our suggestion is that some of the dangers inherent to the particularist approach, which is the approach of group rights advocates, might be avoided by taking a closer look at the Enlightenment's ideal of universality before this ideal is abandoned.

Notes

1. We shall use *Hispanics* and *Latinos/Latinas* as synonyms.
2. Will Kymlicka, *Multicultural Citizenship: A Liberal Theory of Minority Rights* (Oxford: Clarendon Press, 1995), 124–26.
3. Opposed, that is, to the sort of "close to axiomatic," "egalitarian individualism," to use Ronald Dworkin's phrase, which is central to most forms of liberalism. Ronald Dworkin, *A Matter of Principle* (Cambridge, Mass.: Harvard University Press, 1985), 4.
4. Kymlicka, *Multicultural Citizenship*, 124.

5. We take the value of attempts to diminish the influence that luck has in a political system as close to a "primitive" as one could get in political philosophy, in no need of special justification.
6. Though obviously vox populi, it might do to quote from the Universal Declaration. The first sentence of the first article is "All human beings are born free and equal in dignity and rights," and the first sentence of the second article is "Everyone is entitled to all rights and freedoms set forth in this declaration, without distinction of any kind, such as race, color, sex, language, religion, political or other opinion, national or other origin, property, birth *or other status*" (emphasis added).
7. See Johannes Morsink, *The Universal Declaration of Human Rights: Origins, Drafting and Intent* (Philadelphia: University of Pennsylvania Press, 1999), and Paul Gordon Lauren, *The Evolution of International Human Rights: Visions Seen* (Philadelphia: University of Pennsylvania Press, 1998).
8. We assume that membership in a group such as "Hispanic," in standard cases, is not chosen, just as in standard cases, membership in nations is not chosen. In any event, if membership in right-spawning groups were a voluntary matter, the problem would be how to keep people from capriciously claiming membership in such groups.
9. Ernest Gellner, *Nations and Nationalism* (Ithaca: Cornell University Press, 1983), 1.
10. Karl R. Popper, *The Open Society and Its Enemies*, 5th ed. (Princeton: Princeton University Press, 1966), I: 120.
11. Popper, *The Open Society*, I: 121.
12. Darlene Johnson, "Native Rights as Collective Rights: A Question of Self-Preservation," *Canadian Journal of Law and Jurisprudence* 2 (1989): 19–34.
13. As the effects of the Universal Declaration of Human Rights, for example, illustrate.
14. Thomas W. Pogge, "Group Rights and Ethnicity," in Ian Shapiro and Will Kymlicka, eds., *Ethnicity and Group Rights*, Nomos no. 39 (New York and London: New York University Press, 1997), 215
15. Being a human being can also be seen as belonging to a group, so even human rights can be said to be a form of group rights. But this truism does not obscure the obvious difference between rights given to all human beings, in virtue of their membership in a "group" of which they cannot fail to be members, and rights given to some human beings in virtue of their membership in exclusive groups.
16. Iris Marion Young, "Difference as a Resource for Democratic Communication," in James Bohman and William R. Rehg, eds., *Deliberative Democracy* (Cambridge, Mass.: MIT Press, 1997), 386.
17. See Jorge J. E. Gracia, ed., "Latin American Philosophy," special issue of *The Philosophical Forum* 20, 1–2 (Fall-Winter 1988–89), and Ofelia Schutte, *Cultural Identity and Social Liberation in Latin American Thought* (Albany: State University of New York Press, 1993).
18. See Alexander von Humboldt and Aimé Bonpland, *Voyage aux régions équinoxiales du Nouveau Continent* (Stuttgart: F. A. Brockhaus, 1970).
19. Pogge, "Group Rights," 194.
20. Ibid.
21. Young, "Difference as a Resource," 389.

22. Angelo Corlett's thesis in his contribution to this volume.
23. Jorge J. E. Gracia, "The Nature of Ethnicity with Special Reference to Hispanic/ Latino Identity," *Public Affairs Quarterly* 13, no. 1 (1999): 40.
24. An eloquent and convincing criticism of the bureaucratization of identity is found in K. Anthony Appiah, "Identity, Authenticity, Survival: Multicultural Societies and Social Reproduction" in Amy Gutmann, ed., *Multiculturalism* (Princeton: Princeton University Press, 1994), 149–65, especially 162–63.
25. Stephen Steinberg, *The Academic Melting Pot: Catholics and Jews in Higher Education* (New York: McGraw-Hill, 1974).

9 Accommodation Rights for Hispanics in the United States

Thomas W. Pogge

English is the predominant language in the United States. However, Spanish is the native language of some thirty-five million U.S. citizens and residents, whom, for purposes of this essay, I will refer to as "Hispanics."[1] Many of them do not speak English well. Clearly, the fact that English is the predominant language in the U.S. brings a number of significant advantages to native speakers of English ("Anglos") and correlatively a number of significant disadvantages to at least those Hispanics who do not speak English well. This suggests the question whether justice might require special measures designed to protect and/or support Hispanics and the Spanish language within the United States and, if so, what specific measures might be appropriate. I refer to such special measures as "accommodation rights"—an expression Will Kymlicka now prefers to his earlier talk of "minority rights" as well as to the widely used "recognition rights."[2] My discussion of the moral plausibility of such accommodation rights for Hispanics in the United States will be informed by the more general theoretical framework I have outlined in an earlier essay.[3]

One might think that the answer to these questions depends heavily on historical facts. Opponents of accommodation rights can argue that the United States has been an English-speaking country pretty much from its beginning some two hundred years ago. People who come to the United States or choose to stay here certainly have had fair warning of this fact. If they have nevertheless not learned to speak English well, or have not ensured that their children will be fluent speakers of English, then the responsibility for any resulting disadvantages is surely their own. Conversely, supporters of accommodation rights can argue that many current native speakers of Spanish are descendants of persons who were incorporated into the United States without their consent with Spain's ceding of Florida to Great Britain in 1763 or later, in the 1830s and 1840s, when the lands of Texas, California, Nevada, Arizona, Utah, and New Mexico were ceded to the United States by Mexico under circumstances that were rather less than ideal from a moral point of view.

I do not believe that such historical arguments have much weight one way or the other. Our question concerns the plausibility of accommodations among members of the present generation, and it is unclear why the two historical arguments I have sketched should have much relevance to this question. Most of the persons presently disadvantaged by the predominance of the English language have not chosen to incorporate themselves into an English-speaking society—they were simply born here, into Spanish-speaking households and neighborhoods. And none of those currently advantaged by the predominance of English have had anything to do with the ceding of Florida or the annexation of Texas and the Southwest (though they might perhaps be said to benefit disproportionately from the effects of these events).

My downplaying of historical arguments puts me in sharp contrast to Kymlicka, who attaches great moral significance to the distinction between *national* groups or minorities, "groups whose homeland has been incorporated through conquest, colonization, or federation," and *ethnic* groups or minorities, which formed on the present state's territory as a result of immigration.[4] The great significance Kymlicka assigns to this distinction strikes me as morally implausible, especially within the liberal outlook Kymlicka professes to share. Consider two persons, both age eighteen, say, who were born in the United States into Spanish-speaking households and who are disadvantaged by their poor English. Carmen is a member of a national minority, descended from Chicanos who were involuntarily incorporated into the United States in 1848; Letitia is a member of an ethnic minority, descended from more recent Latino immigrants. Other things being equal, can this disparity really make a major difference to the claims these two persons (and their respective groups) have on us? Kymlicka thinks so.[5] But, as we shall see, he also takes it to be part of the very essence of the liberalism he endorses that persons should not be disadvantaged by unchosen inequalities. However, our two women, like all current members of the groups they symbolize, had no choice whatsoever about whether they belong to a national minority or to an ethnic minority in Kymlicka's sense. On this point, Kymlicka's position is then not only implausible but downright self-contradictory.

Let me expand upon this contradiction in a little more detail. One might characterize the disadvantage suffered specifically by national minorities in Nozickean diachronic terms: Members of national minorities—unlike members of ethnic ones—continue to be deprived of something that was once taken from their ancestors by force or fraud. But Kymlicka, as a good liberal, does not do this. Rather, he characterizes this disadvantage in entirely synchronic terms: Members of national minorities—unlike members of ethnic ones—now suffer inferior access to a social primary good that others enjoy in abundance, namely, the good of cultural membership.

But why, then, bring in the past at all? Why not simply look at each member of society today to find who does and who does not have access to cultural membership? In a sense, this is precisely what Kymlicka does. He explicates the relevant good as follows:

> Cultural membership is not a means used in the pursuit of one's ends. It is rather the context within which we choose our ends, and come to see their value, and this is the precondition of self-respect, of the sense that one's ends are worth pursuing. . . . When we take cultural identity seriously, we'll understand that asking someone to trade off her cultural identity for some amount of money is like expecting someone to trade off her self-respect for some amount of money. Having money for the pursuit of one's ends is of little help if the price involves giving up the context within which those ends are worth pursuing.[6]

As minority cultures become marginalized and finally cease to be viable, their members will be forced to give up their cultural identity and context, and to adjust to the cultural identity and context of the majority (Anglo) culture. Do persons to whom this happens count as lacking access to the good of cultural membership; or can we just tell them that they *do* have plenty of access to the majority culture?

That depends, Kymlicka answers. If they are members of a national minority, then they suffer a loss of cultural membership, which the society ought to have prevented. If they are members of an ethnic minority, on the other hand, they suffer no loss of cultural membership, because such groups once immigrated voluntarily, knowing that they would be "expected to become members of the national societies which already exist in their new country."[7] Unlike national minorities, ethnic groups traded off their right to their own native cultural identity when they immigrated. It would be unreasonable for them to expect society to protect their culture—for example, it would be unreasonable for U.S. immigrants to Sweden to demand special efforts from the Swedes toward protecting their Anglophone minority culture.[8] But what about the *descendants* of immigrants? Even if it is true that Letitia's grandparents knew when they immigrated, or should have known, that they would be expected to assimilate, how can this be held against Letitia? Why should Letitia's culture, her cultural membership and identity, not be deserving of protection while Carmen's is? Kymlicka addresses this problem in a footnote: "Of course, the children of immigrants do not consent, and it is not clear that parents should be able to waive their children's rights. For this reason, it is important that governments should strive to make the children of immigrants feel 'at home' in the mainstream culture."[9] But this will not do at all. With respect to members of national minorities, Kymlicka holds that we must not without their consent allow them to be deprived of access to the culture in which they were raised—no matter how much we may strive to make them feel at home in our majority culture. If members of national minorities have this claim on us, how can Kymlicka deny that members of ethnic minorities have it as well? Conversely, if it is permissible to allow descendants of immigrants, who have consented to nothing and whose ancestors could not have consented for them, to be deprived of access to the culture in which they were raised provided we welcome them into the majority culture, then why isn't the same permissible with regard to the members of national minorities?

To conclude this digression: The great moral weight Kymlicka places on the distinction between national and ethnic minorities is implausible and also contradicted by Kymlicka's own liberal commitment. This conclusion could be buttressed by further, more empirical arguments specific to the case of Hispanics, showing that Kymlicka's distinction is not drawn, and could not be drawn, in the real world. Most important, it is not drawn by Hispanics themselves (see note 5), who increasingly see themselves as *one* group united by (inter alia) their language, Catholicism, work ethic, and love of soccer as well as by their own music and media (including the television networks Univisión and Telemundo, the daily *La Opiníon*, and the magazine *Hispanic*). And it could not be drawn, because there are just too many Hispanics with mixed ancestry and too many intermediate cases of other sorts.[10]

If the historical arguments are largely irrelevant, then settling the issue before us would seem to turn centrally on the value of equality or, more specifically, of equal citizenship; this is in fact the value Kymlicka primarily invokes in his discussion of the pros and cons of various kinds of accommodation rights.[11] An appeal to equality, too, can be made by both sides. Kymlicka sketches the egalitarian position *against* accommodation rights as follows: "Ethnocultural groups, like religious groups, should be protected from discrimination, but the maintenance and reproduction of these groups should be left to the free choices of individuals in the private sphere, neither helped nor hindered by the state."[12] (One might rather substitute "equally helped or hindered by the state.") Here the basic idea is that if the state were to help or hinder such groups differentially, it would thereby implicitly express a judgment on the relative worth of these groups—a judgment of precisely the kind that a liberal theory and a liberal state should scrupulously avoid. But if this is the main idea behind this egalitarian argument, then Kymlicka is wrong to associate its conclusion (opposing accommodation rights for minorities in favor of "benign neglect") with the claim that "if a societal culture is worth saving . . . the members of the culture will sustain it through their own choices. If a culture is decaying, it must be because some people no longer find it worthy of their allegiance."[13] A good liberal will avoid making any judgments about the relative value of different cultures and hence, a fortiori, will make no judgments about how the value of a culture correlates with the willingness of its members to sustain it through their choices.

Kymlicka argues that liberalism, so understood, delivers a kind of formal equality, but one that in fact amounts to substantive *in*equality. An early version of this argument involves a modification of a thought experiment initially introduced by Ronald Dworkin.[14] This thought experiment involves an island about to be settled by newcomers. Since no newcomer has a better claim to the island's natural resources than any other, Dworkin suggests an original auction in which the newcomers, each equipped with an equal number of clamshells, can enter bids for particular island resources. These bids may be indefinitely revised in light of the bids entered by others until at long last a stable distribution of resources emerges. In this final distribution, each item goes to the highest bidder, who pays at least as much for it as any other person was prepared to bid. Because this is so, Dworkin reasons, the emerging personal bundles of resources necessarily pass a no-envy test: Immediately after the auction is completed, none of the newcomers will prefer any other newcomer's bundle to his or her own.[15]

Kymlicka's modification involves the assumption that the newcomers arrive simultaneously on two vessels of very different sizes, on which different languages are spoken. We may stipulate that the vast majority of the newcomers, arriving on the larger vessel, speak English, while the remaining newcomers, arriving on the smaller vessel, speak Spanish. If this fact is known, the Hispanics are likely to want to live near one another and their bids will reflect this preference. Kymlicka concludes:

> In order to ensure that they can also live and work in their own culture, the minority members may decide, prior to the rerun of the auction, to

> buy resources in one area of the island, which would involve outbidding the present majority owners for resources which *qua* resources are less useful to their chosen way of life. They must incur this additional cost in order to secure the existence of their cultural community. This is a cost which the members of the majority culture do not incur, but which in no way reflects different choices about the good life (or about the importance of cultural membership within it).[16]

This argument does not go through. Suppose that, in early runs of the auction, the northern part of the island happens to receive a disproportionate number of Hispanic bids. This fact may indeed incline other Hispanics to shift their bids toward the north. But any resulting increase in the price of northern resources would be negated by Anglos shifting their bids southward. Anglos have no reason to pay a premium for northern real estate (on the contrary, many of them may prefer to avoid the more heavily Hispanic north). As the auction is run over and over again, the geographical preference may well strengthen, so that Hispanics will in the end be prepared to pay a considerable premium for northern resources over southern ones, even if the latter are, qua resources, no less useful to their chosen way of life. But no such premium will actually emerge, so long as the Anglos don't share the same preference. To see this clearly, consider an analogous scenario in which phone numbers are auctioned off in a large city. One-tenth of available numbers begin with a 6, and a superstitious 10 percent of the city's population are prepared to pay a fat premium for such a "lucky" number while the remaining 90 percent don't care about the first digit. In this scenario, the superstitious would get their "lucky" numbers for free, because the slightest premium would induce those who do not care about the first digit to switch their bids to a number that does not begin with a 6.[17]

The point Kymlicka seeks to establish through his thought experiment is not borne out in the real world either. Resources located in predominantly Hispanic areas are actually cheaper than intrinsically similar resources located in predominantly Anglo areas. This is no doubt due in part to the fact that Anglos are, on the whole, more affluent than Hispanics. Still, this inequality in affluence is to some extent mitigated by the fact that Hispanics find it cheaper than Anglos do to live among their own.

Even if it is no more expensive for Hispanics to avoid living in Anglo areas than it is for Anglos to avoid living in Hispanic areas, it is still undeniable that, ordinarily, "the members of minority cultures [do] not have the same ability to live and work in their own language and culture that the members of majority cultures take for granted." Kymlicka can then argue that if the distribution of resources is fair in abstraction from this "morally arbitrary disadvantage," then it is unfair when this disadvantage is taken into account.[18] And from this he can conclude that in order to rectify this situation, in order to ensure a fair distribution all things considered, Hispanics must receive some accommodation that evens out their disadvantage.

The problem with this reasoning is that if fully generalized, it proves much too much. The problem is neatly shown through a famous argument that John Roemer has presented against Dworkin's original proposal of an equality-of-resources view.[19] Roemer demonstrates how this proposal is in danger of collapsing into its main competitor, an equality-of-welfare view, as follows: Suppose two persons have equal resources, as assessed by the criterion Dworkin proposes. And suppose they nevertheless have unequal welfare. Then there must be some difference between the two persons that explains the divergence. Roemer assumes, without loss of generality, that the persons differ in their capacity to generate welfare out of resources—that the person with greater welfare has more endorphins, which, Roemer stipulates, facilitate the "conversion" of resources into welfare. Once we become aware of this differential endorphin endowment, it seems only fair to take endorphins into account as yet another resource. This has the consequence that equality of resources now favors an equal distribution of resources broadly conceived (endorphins included), which presumably entails that the distribution of extrapersonal resources should be *un*equal and negatively correlated with the natural distribution of endorphins so as to approximate equal welfare.

Kymlicka himself rejects such an equality-of-welfare position, specifically exempting inequalities that are due to persons' own free choices. Still, he does emphasize again and again throughout his work "the importance of rectifying unchosen inequalities"—always appealing to Rawls and Dworkin in support of this view.[20] In his earlier book we find the same distinction, albeit expressed as a distinction between differential choices and unequal circumstances. Kymlicka writes there:

> No one chooses to be born into a disadvantaged social group, or with natural disabilities, and so no one should have to pay for the costs imposed by those disadvantageous circumstances. Hence liberals favour compensating people who suffer from disadvantages in social environment or natural endowment.... Someone who cultivates a taste for expensive wine has no legitimate claim to special public subsidy, since she is responsible for the cost of her choice. Someone who needs expensive medicine due to a natural disability has a legitimate claim to special public subsidy, since she is not responsible for the costs of her disadvantageous circumstances.[21]

The distinction between chosen and unchosen inequalities Kymlicka invokes does prevent his view from collapsing into an equality-of-welfare position, but it nevertheless entails many of the same counterintuitive results. Do we really believe that unchosen natural differentials—in looks, height, talents, or cheerfulness, for example—ought to be "rectified" through state compensation? This is certainly not a position widely endorsed among liberals, not even among the two Kymlicka cites so frequently. Through his device of a hypothetical insurance market, Dworkin does provide a general approach for dealing with this issue: If persons would, if they could, buy insurance prior to birth against homely looks or a melancholy temperament, then he would want the state to mandate compensatory side payments in the amount of the hypothetical insurance premiums and benefits.[22] Rawls, on the other hand, explicitly rejects any such compensation, insisting that "the natural distribution is neither just nor unjust" and that social positions should thus be defined in terms of social primary goods alone, without regard to the distribution of natural primary goods (such as "health and vigor, intelligence and imagination"): "A hypothetical initial arrangement in which all the social primary goods are equally distributed . . . provides a benchmark for judging improvements."[23] Note also that Rawls's difference principle *permits* (unchosen) inequalities in income and wealth due to differential talents, insofar as they raise the lowest socioeconomic position. Rawls specifically allows then that the more demanding leadership positions be better paid even though they will typically also require special talents and thus be closed to those who, through no choice of their own, lack these gifts. He specifically allows, that is, unchosen inequalities.

The discussion has shown, I believe, that Kymlicka's strategy of defending accommodation rights for Hispanics as one instance under a general principle of rectifying unchosen inequalities is not promising. The latter principle does support the desired conclusion, but it supports a lot of other demands as well—demands that for most of his readers (liberals and nonliberals alike) constitute a reductio ad absurdum of the principle.[24]

In his new book, Kymlicka also presents a quite different, far more plausible argument in favor of rectification (though he does not distinguish the two arguments clearly from each other). This argument turns not on the contingent distribution of language skills (and cultural affiliations) in the society, but on the way its government—funded by and responsible to all citizens—treats various linguistic groups:

> Many liberals say that just as the state should not recognize, endorse, or support any particular church, so it should not recognize, endorse, or sup-

> port any particular cultural group or identity. . . . But the analogy does not work. It is quite possible for a state not to have an established church. But the state cannot help but give at least partial establishment to a culture when it decides which language is to be used in public schooling, or in the provision of state services. The state can (and should) replace religious oaths in courts with secular oaths, but it cannot replace the use of English in courts with no language.[25]
>
> Government decisions on languages, internal boundaries, public holidays, and state symbols unavoidably involve recognizing, accommodating, and supporting the needs and identities of particular ethnic and national groups. The state unavoidably promotes certain cultural identities, and thereby disadvantages others.[26]

At least the state cannot help doing so, one should say more precisely, in certain particular respects. If this is so, and if the state ought to treat all of its citizens with their diverse cultural identities equally, then it is incumbent upon it to rectify the unequal treatment it unavoidably metes out in some respects through inversely unequal treatment in others. If the state gives preference to the Anglos by maintaining English as the official public language, then it must somehow make it up to those of its citizens who are native speakers of any other language.

This line of argument is far more convincing than its predecessor, and has been invoked in many other contexts, often to widespread acclaim. Thus it has been argued that it is unjust for the state to subsidize some kinds of art (opera) but not others (rock and roll), to recognize some kinds of domestic partnership but not others, to construct public facilities without compensating those who cannot use them (for example, because of handicap, obesity, or claustrophobia), and so forth.

Before we can determine which arguments of this sort work, and what rectificatory measures they might then justify, we must first distinguish two different ways in which a government might support cultural groups. First, a government might merely act as a facilitator, allowing any subset of the citizenry to agree to finance some jointly desired good on mutually acceptable terms. Here the government's task is that of finding a distribution of the good's cost that can find unanimous approval: each citizen either contributes nothing or else is willing to contribute his or her assigned share for the sake of securing the good in question.[27] This idea is, of course, vulnerable to free-rider problems, as persons may have an incentive to understate what a particular good is worth to them in order to reduce the contribution assigned to them. Still, this problem can generally be solved for "excludable" goods:

when the cost of a music hall is covered through ticket sales or the cost of a highway through road tolls, potential users have no incentive to dissimulate. In these cases, the government ideally incurs no cost at all, as it can, for instance, issue construction bonds and then finance its interest outlays out of project revenues. The government may nevertheless play an indispensable catalyst role if the project is too large, too risky, or too long-term to be undertaken by the corporate sector. And the government may then rightly be accused of injustice when it is willing to play this facilitating role for some groups and projects but not for others.

Second, a government may, with the support of a mere majority (if that), impose itself on all citizens by subjecting them to rules and procedures, and by forcing them to contribute to projects, irrespective of their individual consent. Government measures of this sort must pass a stringent dual test: they must promote justice or another important good, and the burdens they require must be shared equitably.[28] These two requirements—purpose and equity—may conflict with each other, in which case a plausible balance may have to be found. An example of such balancing occurs when a society is defending itself from an armed attack. Here the purpose (effective defense) would suggest that combat roles be concentrated among citizens likely to do well in them, while equity would suggest that the risk of death in combat be shared equally by all.

These considerations are perhaps best brought to life through the discussion of a concrete issue concerning language rights with regard to public schools. The government finances a public school system, and it also requires that children attend school—either a public school free of charge or else a private school. I assume that there is a plausible justification for requiring all children to attend school and for requiring all taxpayers to contribute to the public school system: the maintenance of just institutions operated by equal citizens requires that all have a basic education, that all can, at minimum, read and write as well as understand the history and structure of the institutional scheme in whose operation they are to participate. Moreover, an educated workforce is necessary for the operation of a modern economy, from which all citizens benefit in a nonexcludable way. Taking all this for granted, the difficult question is what the language(s) of instruction ought to be.

Let us, once more, start out with Kymlicka:

> In a society where the members of minority cultures (e.g. Indians, francophones) could get their fair share of resources within their own cultural community, it's not clear what would justify denying people access to publicly funded education in English. If some of the members of a minor-

> ity culture choose to learn in that language, the notion of protecting the cultural context provides no ground for denying them that opportunity. On the other hand it's not clear why there should be rights to publicly funded education in any given language other than that of the community. Why should the members of minority cultures have a right to a public education in English, but not, say, in Greek? They should of course be free to run a school system in whatever language they choose at their own expense, but why a right to it at public expense?[29]

This passage is not entirely transparent, so let me highlight the main points Kymlicka is making, as I see them. One quite radical claim is not made explicit, but only suggested in the first two sentences of the passage:

> *Claim 1:* In a society where the members of a minority culture cannot get their fair share of resources within their own cultural community, denying the members of this community access to publicly funded education in English is justifiable by the purpose of protecting the cultural context of this community.

I cannot be sure that Kymlicka would in fact endorse claim 1. In any case, it would be a very surprising one for an avowed liberal to make. Claim 1 denies minority families—and only them—the right to avail themselves of an opportunity for their children on the grounds that this restriction on their liberty helps protect an endangered minority culture. It allows the state coercively to press minority children into the service of perpetuating a cultural community irrespective of whether this benefits the children concerned and irrespective also of whether the children themselves, or their parents, support this purpose.[30] This is a clear violation of Kymlicka's own liberal principle, because it would introduce an unchosen inequality (Anglo children are offered public schooling in English, minority children are not). It is precisely for this egalitarian reason that the U.S. Supreme Court unanimously declared the San Francisco School District to be in violation of Title VI of the Civil Rights Act for failing to make available a public education in English to students of Chinese ancestry who do not speak English.[31] One might respond here with a separate-but-equal argument: Anglos and Chinese *were* treated equally, as both received a public education in their respective native language. But this argument holds little promise. A public education in a minority language—and one that, by assumption, is endangered in the United States—is not equal, because it does not give children the same opportunities to participate in the social, economic, and political life of this country.

Another radical claim, again not clearly endorsed in the passage, is put forward in its third and fourth sentences:

> *Claim 2:* There is no more reason to entitle the members of a minority culture to a public education in English than there is to entitle them to a public education in any other (for them) foreign language, such as Greek.

This claim, too, is highly problematic. Hispanic or Chinese or Navajo children derive very much more benefit from receiving an education in English than they would derive from an (otherwise equivalent) education in Greek. Does Kymlicka propose to count the greater benefit to these children as no reason at all? Moreover, offering Navajos a (less useful) public education in Greek and Anglos a (more useful) public education in English would discriminate against the former on the basis of their national origin. Offering both Navajos and Anglos a public education in English would at least greatly reduce, if not eliminate, this unchosen inequality.[32]

I conclude that claims 1 and 2 must be rejected. They give entirely unacceptable reasons for denying members of minority cultures access to a publicly funded education in English on a par with the education available to members of the dominant Anglo culture. More acceptable reasons for such a denial will be considered below.

A less radical claim, which Kymlicka is clearly endorsing, is this:

> *Claim 3:* Members of minority cultures should have the right to send their children to a public school where their instruction is entirely in the minority language.

Kymlicka does little to support this claim, simply writing that "people should have, as part of the respect owed them as members of a cultural community, the opportunity to have a public education in the language of their community."[33] But this appeal to respect is somewhat problematic. It is certainly desirable to show persons respect by allowing them to make decisions about their own lives. But in the case at hand, we would be showing parents respect by allowing them to make decisions about how *their children* will be educated at public expense. In this case, there is a countervailing reason—a reason against allowing parents to make decisions that would be worse for their children.[34] To see whether and how this countervailing reason might come into play, let us examine claim 3 against its most prominent alternative, the thesis that it is permissible for a government in the United States to run its public education system in English. (California voters, by passing Proposition 227 with a 61 to 39 percent margin, have recently obliged their government to do just that.) How might we settle the conflict between such an English-language public education system and a multilingual one in which parents are entitled to choose the language in which their children will be instructed?

I propose that we resolve this conflict in three steps. First, Kymlicka is right to stress that a government has a fundamental duty of equal treatment. Within a liberal outlook, this duty is understood, however, as a government's duty to its individual citizens and residents, rather than as a duty to various groups and cultures. Thus it is by reference to the interests of individual citizens and residents that the conflict is to be resolved.

Second, among the individual interests bearing on the question of how to design a public education system for our children, the interests *of these children* are to be of paramount importance. Many other individual interests may bear on the question: the interest of adult minority members that their language should continue to be spoken in the United States (or perhaps even, in the case of Spanish, that their language should one day become coequal with English in the United States); the interest of adult minority members to communicate easily with their children and grandchildren; the interest of some corporations and government agencies in prospective employees with native foreign-language skills; and so forth. I am not suggesting that all these interests are minor and should be ignored—only that they should not be allowed to outweigh the best interests of the children. The other interests can be brought in, then, only insofar as the interests of the children themselves do not clearly settle the matter.

Summarizing after two steps: I have proposed a fundamental principle of public education, holding, roughly, that the best education for each child is the education that is best for this child. Of course, our public education system does not have the resources to provide each child with the best possible education for him or her. But it should spend whatever resources it has on providing our children with whatever education is best for them. My hope is that if this fundamental principle can be agreed upon, the remaining differences will be much less divisive and probably resolvable through empirical research on whose design experts now in conflict can agree in advance.

Given the principle I have proposed, the fundamental duty of a just public education system is to promote the best interests of each and every child and to do so equally. This duty must trump any desire to increase or decrease the prominence of this or that language or culture in the United States.[35] It is in light of this duty that the legislature must decide whether (a) to mandate that minority children be offered a public education in their native language only, (b) to mandate that all children be offered a public education only in English, or (c) to make available an education in various languages from among which parents can choose for their children.

This brings us to the third and most difficult step, which consists of deciding which of these options is, under given empirical circumstances, favored by the test I have proposed. My discussion of this step is meant to be illustrative only, because much depends on complex empirical assessments with regard to which I can claim no expertise. We should also keep in mind that these empirical assessments may well turn out differently in different contexts (California versus Florida) and differently also for different languages in the same context (Navajo versus Spanish in New Mexico). My objective here is not, then, to propose any particular settlement, but merely to sketch what the debate leading up to such a settlement might look like.

Given the constraints I have imposed, each option would have to be defended by appeal to the best interests of the children whom the public education system in question is supposed to educate. Thus one might argue for option B (California's Proposition 227), for example, by claiming that it best serves the goal of enabling all students to participate fully in U.S. society—socially, economically, and politically. Here is a straightforward way of filling in this kind of argument: One postulates a principle of English first: *The most important linguistic competence for children now growing up in the United States is the ability to communicate in English, and the language of instruction in public schools in the United States should therefore be chosen by reference to the goal of effectively helping pupils develop fluency in English.* One tries then to support the empirical claim that choosing English as the universal language of instruction is part of the most effective method for helping students develop fluency in English.

Let us consider two ways in which this argument could be attacked.[36] One line of attack would deny the empirical claim, asserting that option B does not provide the most effective method for helping students develop fluency in English, that minority students will reach higher levels of English proficiency if they are first helped to develop full literacy in their native language. This line of attack is exemplified by Kymlicka when he writes that "people learn English best when they view it as supplementing, rather than displacing, their mother tongue."[37] If this line of attack were fully successful, it might provide an acceptable argument for option A (in contrast to the unacceptable arguments suggested by claims 1 and 2, discussed above). The other line of attack would appeal to goals other than that of effectively helping pupils develop fluency in English, arguing that once their bearing on the question before us is considered, option B will not come out ahead.

Though formally distinct, both lines of attack are likely to appeal to similar empirical considerations. They would seek to show that being abruptly exposed to a foreign-language environment for several hours per day would constitute a significant shock for many young children—a shock that would make it difficult for them to relate well to their teachers and fellow pupils,[38] and (partly for this reason) difficult also to progress well in English as well as in other subjects.

Now, one might argue in response that these problems, however real, do not alter the fact that children's important long-term interest in being fully literate in English is best served by early immersion and that this interest is stronger than the interest in avoiding those temporary problems. But one might also think of various ways in which option B might be revised to accommodate the stated concerns. Thus one might support programs that make it easier for minority parents to afford preschool exposure to English for their children, and programs that would make it easier for such parents to achieve fluency in English themselves. One might further support the availability of special foreign-language tutors to whom pupils could turn outside regular hours if they find it difficult to follow lessons in English during their first few school years. In addition, one might also support the early introduction (in elementary school) of sufficiently prominent minority languages as academic subjects in order to give students the opportunity to develop full literacy also in their native language and in order to give them a manifest indication that their native language is valued rather than viewed as dispensable and to be displaced. Instruction should be continued through all grades so that native speakers of Spanish, as well as other students after they have learned basic Spanish in more elementary courses, have an opportunity to study the literature and culture of the Spanish-speaking world and to perfect their competence in this language. Such course offerings would make clear that the public school system is endeavoring not merely to give every student full competence in English, but also to give students the opportunity to develop an equally full competence in the native languages of any minorities that (locally) are numerically significant.[39]

Enriched by complementary programs of these four kinds, option B may well become widely accepted among those willing to put the interests of the children before all else. To be sure, acceptance of the English-first principle would tend to reduce the prominence of other languages in the United States below what it would be if they were also used, alongside English, as languages of school instruction. In this sense, the English-first principle privileges English at the expense of these other languages. But this unfairness toward the various languages does not here reflect an unfairness toward the various speakers of different languages.[40] The choice of English as the universal language of instruction is justified by reference to the best interests of children with other native languages, for whom speaking good English (in addition to their native language) will be an enormous advantage in their future social and professional lives. As supplemented, an English-first approach could not then, I believe, be charged with disadvantaging children who are native speakers of other languages vis-à-vis Anglo children. Such children are, in a sense, initially disadvantaged by getting a somewhat later start toward English competence (though they also have a significant and permanent advantage through the head start they enjoy in their native language). But this disadvantage exists before these children enter the public education system, and it is one that this system is designed to erase.

Let me end my illustrative discussion of the third step by emphasizing that the English-first principle I have canvassed is not of a piece with the English-only initiatives that have been cropping up in the last twenty years in Congress and many state legislatures. Endorsement of the English-first principle is fully consistent with the view that it is highly desirable for Spanish and other minority languages to survive as native languages in the United States.[41] This goal is well served by giving native speakers of Spanish, and other children as well, the opportunity to develop full competence in Spanish through the public school system.

While I share the commitment to this goal, I have argued that its pursuit must be constrained by an overriding commitment to the interests of the children our schools are supposed to educate—an overriding commitment to the principle that the best education for each child is the education that is best for this child. It is this fundamental principle of public education (which emerged from the second step and whose application my discussion of the third step was intended to illustrate) that deserves our most basic allegiance, or so I believe. This principle has the potential to bring together all those who genuinely care about the children whose lives our education system will shape so profoundly, guiding them toward a shared assessment of the English-first principle as well as the more specific institutional options that have been in dispute.

I am well aware that this essay is a disappointment to many readers in the United States who are proud of their Hispanic heritage and inclined to favor more extensive accommodation rights than could be supported by the general ideas and principles I have here proposed and defended.[42]

Let me emphasize once more that my rather cautious stance is motivated by a concern for the moral costs of accommodation rights. Moral costs we should be mindful of include, in particular, "liberal" costs in terms of freedom and equality, which arise when individuals are used to promote some group interest. We should be especially alert to such costs when they would be incurred by children, who have so very little influence on the social environment that will shape them so profoundly. An important example of this kind was claim 1, discussed above, which asserted that access to publicly funded education in English may be withheld from minority children if this helps to protect the cultural context of their community whose other members cannot get their fair share of resources within it. Other moral costs we should be attentive to include the costs to other ethnic, linguistic, religious, or lifestyle groups. These costs are especially obvious in the case of language: Even if we agree that residents of the United States should speak more languages than they now do, the number of languages each of us might speak fluently is quite limited. And the promotion of one language through the public education system will thus inevitably come at the expense of other languages, some of whom may then not survive at all (at least in the United States). To be sensitive to such potential costs, those who demand accommodation rights for some group(s) should take care to base these demands on principles by which they would be prepared to judge the demands of any other groups as well.

What I have written is not meant as the last word, not even as *my* last word, on these issues. If future discussions of them will pay somewhat more attention to the concerns I have stressed, this essay will have been worthwhile.

Notes

1. *Latinos* is also frequently used. I prefer *Hispanics* because of its etymological connection to the Spanish language, which will be a main theme of this essay.
2. See Will Kymlicka, "Do We Need a Liberal Theory of Minority Rights?" *Constellations* 4, 1 (1997): 72–87, esp. 73 with endnote 3.
3. Thomas W. Pogge, "Group Rights and Ethnicity," in Will Kymlicka and Ian Shapiro, eds., *Ethnicity and Group Rights,* Nomos no. 39 (New York: New York University Press, 1997), 187–221.
4. Will Kymlicka, *Multicultural Citizenship: A Liberal Theory of Minority Rights* (Oxford: Oxford University Press, 1995), 79. His distinction is most fully explicated in ch. 2, §1.
5. Witness how he conceives of Hispanics as a loose assortment of different groups (*Multicultural Citizenship*, 16) and recognizes Puerto Ricans (16, 167) and Chicanos whose ancestors fell to the United States together with the Southwest territory (16, 116) as two "Spanish-speaking national minorities" (16). But these categorizations are mere constructs of Kymlicka's theory. In the real world, there are Tejanos (Texans with Mexican ancestry), Chicanos (other U.S. residents with Mexican ancestry), Hispanos (New Mexicans with [pretensions to] Spanish ancestry), and so on, but (as far as I know) no distinction is made by Hispanics themselves between Tejanos who did and did not have ancestors in Texas before 1836, or between Chicanos who did and did not have ancestors in the Southwest before 1848.
6. Will Kymlicka, *Liberalism, Community, and Culture* (Oxford: Clarendon Press, 1989), 192f.
7. Kymlicka, *Multicultural Citizenship*, 114. He does recognize that some "immigrants" came involuntarily, as slaves or refugees, and he exempts them in this context.

8. Ibid., 96.
9. Ibid., 215f., n. 19.
10. Such as Puerto Ricans within the fifty states, who might count as members of a national minority insofar as ancestors of theirs were incorporated into the United States together with their homeland and who might also count as members of an ethnic minority insofar as ancestors of theirs voluntarily left Puerto Rico.
11. He considers various additional and complementary arguments for accommodation rights in *Multicultural Citizenship*, ch. 6.
12. Kymlicka, "Do We Need a Liberal Theory of Minority Rights?" 72.
13. Kymlicka, *Multicultural Citizenship*, 107f.
14. Ronald Dworkin, "What Is Equality? Part I: Equality of Welfare," *Philosophy and Public Affairs* 10, 3 (1981): 185–246; Ronald Dworkin, "What Is Equality? Part II: Equality of Resources," *Philosophy and Public Affairs* 10, 4 (1981): 283–345. See also Bruce Ackerman, *Social Justice and the Liberal State* (New Haven: Yale University Press, 1980), which features the denizens of a spacecraft about to touch down upon a virgin planet.
15. If any newcomer did prefer another's bundle to her own, she would rationally have asked for another round of bidding in which she would then have bid for some or all of the resources in the other bundle. Some complication is required to cope with ties (two or more exactly equal bids for the same item).
16. Kymlicka, *Liberalism, Community, and Culture*, 188f.
17. All this is not to say that Kymlicka's modification of Dworkin's thought experiment will make no difference to individuals. Clearly, some Hispanics will be hurt by their linguistic preference in conjunction with their other preferences. A hilltop lover may face a hard choice between living in the north, where hilltops are scarce or highly coveted and therefore expensive, and living among Anglos in the south, where hilltops are more plentiful or less coveted and therefore cheaper. But then, individual Anglos may face similar hard choices, e.g., between a cheaper beachfront site among Hispanics and a more expensive one in the south. Moreover, the prevailing linguistic preferences may also *benefit* individuals: If hilltops are coveted mainly by Hispanics, Anglo hilltop lovers will benefit from Hispanic bids shifting north. And if beachfront is coveted mainly by Anglos, Hispanic beachfront lovers will benefit from Anglo bids shifting south.
18. Kymlicka, *Multicultural Citizenship*, 107f.
19. John Roemer, "Equality of Resources Implies Equality of Welfare," *Quarterly Journal of Economics* 101 (1986): 751–84.
20. Kymlicka, *Multicultural Citizenship*, 109.
21. Kymlicka, *Liberalism, Community, and Culture*, 186.
22. Cf. Dworkin, "What Is Equality? Part II," 297–99.
23. John Rawls, *A Theory of Justice* (Cambridge, Mass.: Harvard University Press, 1971), 102, 62, 62. See also Thomas Pogge, *Realizing Rawls* (Ithaca: Cornell University Press, 1989), esp. §§ 3.5, 4.4, 10.4, where I argue at some length that Rawls's criterion of justice does not take account of natural inequalities and is therefore a "semiconsequentialist" criterion. Kymlicka overlooks this important departure by Rawls from the more Dworkinian liberalism he himself takes for granted.
24. Is there perhaps an even narrower principle that would be more plausible and still entail Kymlicka's desired conclusion? One may think that what entitles those disadvantaged by an inequality to compensation (or "rectification") is not the mere fact that their disadvantage is due to no choice of their own, but rather this fact in conjunction with the further fact that this disadvantage *is* due

to the choices of others: it is unchosen *social* inequalities that call for compen sation, whereas unchosen *natural* inequalities do not. This proposal runs into two difficulties. First, the boundary between these two inequalities is often unclear, as when both natural and social factors are necessary to explain why someone has a melancholy temperament or is considered homely. Second, the proposal does not fully capture common intuitions, as it is generally believed that serious natural handicaps (such as blindness) should be compensated and that certain social disadvantages (unpopularity) should not be. Kymlicka's view is, basically, that Hispanics should be compensated for the bad luck they encounter with regard to the distribution of language skills in the society into which they were born. It is unfortunate for them that their native language is spoken only by a minority while almost everyone speaks English. But life is full of bad luck of this kind. I have unchosen talents whose market value greatly depends on what capacities are in demand in my society—for example, on the kind of music, sports, and other entertainment cherished by my compatriots. I have unchosen desires for things whose market price depends heavily on how strongly they are desired by others. And I have unchosen desires for social activities whose possibility depends importantly on whether others have similar or complementary interests and preferences. I may find myself strongly drawn to a certain research topic, for example, only to discover that this topic is of interest to barely a dozen people. In all these cases, demands for compensation or rectification would be laughed out of public debate. So why should we take seriously the demand, so justified, to compensate native speakers of minority languages?

25. Kymlicka, *Multicultural Citizenship*, 111. For extensive discussion and refinement of this argument, see also Eerik Lagerspetz, "On Language Rights," *Ethical Theory and Moral Practice* 2, 1 (1998): 181–99.
26. Kymlicka, *Multicultural Citizenship*, 108.
27. Rawls suggests the idea of a branch of government, the exchange branch, which is devoted to all and only projects of this sort. See Rawls, *A Theory of Justice*, 282–84. He borrows the general idea from Knut Wicksell, "A New Principle of Just Taxation," in R. A. Musgrave and A. T. Peacock, eds., *Classics in the Theory of Public Finance* (London: Macmillan, 1958).
28. My formulation of the two requirements is intentionally left somewhat vague as there is some disagreement about how they should be specified exactly.
29. Kymlicka, *Liberalism, Community, and Culture*, 194 f.
30. The word *coercively* is not out of place. Most minority families cannot legally avoid sending their children to public school. Only the affluent families can, by enrolling their children in private school—an option Kymlicka graciously concedes in the final sentence of the passage quoted.
31. *Lau v. Nichols*, 414 U.S. 563 (1974).
32. I use *Navajo* here as a stand-in for all minorities. I do so because I am not sure how broadly Kymlicka intends his term "minority culture" here. We can be sure, however, that this term covers the *national*-minority Navajo culture, so I use this culture to illustrate how claim 2 is untenable.
33. Kymlicka, *Liberalism, Community, and Culture*, 195.
34. This reason is recognized in many other contexts: Parents' choices are constrained by child labor laws, for example, and parents are required to send their children to school up to a certain age and are forbidden to withhold modern medical care from their children. In all these cases, we do not allow parents to make certain choices for their children—even when we recognize that such

choices would be conscientiously based on deeply held (e.g., religious) values that deserve recognition and respect.

35. It is frustratingly unclear whether Kymlicka agrees on this point, or whether he would think it permissible, under certain circumstances, to sacrifice the best interests of children to the political goal of preserving an existing culture for the benefit of those for whom it provides their context of choice.
36. I will not consider a third kind of attack, which would deny that the ability to communicate in English is the most important linguistic competence for children now growing up in the United States. This denial can be made plausible by emphasizing that what matters here is the importance of English proficiency in the future, for which our public education system is supposed to prepare the children in its care. But then the *future* importance of English and Spanish proficiencies cannot straightforwardly inform the design of the present education system, because it also depends on this very design: the more children now receive their education in Spanish, the more important Spanish proficiency will be during their adult lives (Linda Alcoff forcefully made this point in discussion). And yet it remains true nevertheless, under any foreseeable realistic scenario, that during the lifespan of the children we raise today, English proficiency will continue to be more important than Spanish proficiency for almost all residents of the United States (some Puerto Ricans excepted).
37. Kymlicka, *Multicultural Citizenship*, 97.
38. And even to their parents, who, if they have little command of the universal language of public education, may come to be seen by their own children as existing at the margin of society.
39. I would like to express this point as a demand for (the availability of) "bilingual education." But this expression is now often used not for an education system under which students can become bilingual, but rather for one under which some students are taught in one language and others in another.
40. Unfairness toward some languages cannot be completely avoided in any case, assuming we reject the goal of making all languages equally prominent in the United States and lack the resources to provide even the sole Kazakh child in Putnam County with a public education in her native language.
41. As far as Spanish is concerned, there is little doubt that it will survive and even thrive as a native language. Through high birth rates as well as legal and illegal immigration, Hispanics are the fastest-growing group in the United States, expected to reach a hundred million around the year 2015. It is not inconceivable that the Spanish language will in fact one day become coequal with English in the United States. There are many obvious reasons to welcome such a development, but also reasons to regret it. If it were as important for persons living in the United States to know both Spanish and English as it now is to know English, then it would most likely become even harder for other languages to survive in this country.
42. Such readers may also view the accommodation rights I *have* supported (in connection with options B and C) as entrenching, rather than overcoming, the current dominance of the English language, and may thus be distinctly unenthusiastic about programs that make it easier for minority parents to afford preschool exposure to English for their children, programs that would make it easier for such parents to achieve fluency in English themselves, availability of special foreign-language tutors for minority pupils, and early introduction of prominent minority languages as academic subjects.

10 Affirmative Action for Hispanics? Yes and No

Jorge J. E. Gracia

I begin with some anecdotes that should be sufficient to call attention to the confusion and problems posed by affirmative action for Hispanics.[1] They are all based on firsthand experience.

When I was about to graduate from the University of Toronto with a Ph.D., I put myself in the market for a position in philosophy. The time was 1970. Affirmative action was already a reality in American society, but conditions were quite different then. The United States had just gone through the stormy sixties, with the rebellion by large numbers of young people against the status quo and the bitter protests against Vietnam. The Vietnam War was still being waged, but the late President Nixon was firmly in control and had an unquestionable mandate. Philosophy jobs had become scarce. The rapid expansion of graduate programs in philosophy in the sixties had already produced the glut of Ph.D.'s that has become endemic in the American philosophical scene.

I interviewed with the State University of New York at Buffalo and the Department of Philosophy voted to recommend to the dean that I be appointed as assistant professor. There was already some pressure in the university to hire minorities. At the time, the department had an African American and two Asian Americans but no Hispanics, so my appointment was presented as a minority one to the dean, partly as a strategic move in order to ensure quick and favorable action.

A few days after the department chair, the late William Parry, had phoned to give me the good news about the department vote, I got another phone call from him explaining that the university affirmative action committee had problems with the appointment, for I did not look anything like a member of a minority group. The reasons given were that I did not come from a disadvantaged background and that, although I had at one time resided in the United States, I was at the time living in Canada. The question of citizenship did not come up, but I imagine it was hovering in the background. Bill asked me whether I considered myself Hispanic and then requested some ammunition he could use with the committee.[2]

I did not hear back from Bill until he called me to say that the letter offering me the job was in the mail, although the affirmative action committee had refused to classify me as a minority. He explained that the dean had gone ahead all the same, and that as far as the university was concerned, I did not qualify as Hispanic. My question to him, then, was: So, what am I? If I am not Hispanic, what should I consider myself? I was miffed! Of course, Bill could not answer, and he openly sympathized with my chagrin, but he also suggested that one should not expect much from university administrators. Bill was quite a cynic; he had been an academic for many years and had suffered under the McCarthy witch-hunts of the fifties. Nothing surprised him when it came to academic politics.

Compare my case with the following. A few years later, the Department of Philosophy at Buffalo was in the market to replace some of the faculty members we had lost through retirements. The dean said that, considering university policy, the size and composition of our department, and the scarcity of resources at his disposal, he could approve only a minority appointment. In the pool of candidates who had applied for the job, there were one Latin American and one African. Neither of them had permanent residency in this country, nor was either disadvantaged in any sense of the word. Yet the affirmative action committee had no reservations about approving an offer to either one of them.

Question: What cogent reason could be given for the committee's decisions with respect to these two cases and mine? The only one I can think of is that the criteria of qualification being used were different because the composition of the committee was different. But this is not very helpful.

The case of a young man who was a high-school classmate of one of my daughters is also instructive. We were fond of this young man, for he was a mature, pleasant fellow, although he was not particularly bright, a fact reflected by his grades in school. All of us were worried about his prospects for college. But he had the good fortune of having had a Mexican-American great-grandfather. He had no other connection to the Hispanic community. His father's last name was English, as was his mother's. His other great-grandparents were of English or German descent and he had never met his Mexican-American great-grandfather—he died long before the young man was born. Neither he nor his family had ever taken an interest in anything vaguely related to the Hispanic culture or community in this country or in any other. Indeed, the only connection he had to anything Hispanic was through his friendship with my daughter. Moreover, he was the son of a full professor in one of the science departments at the University, and his mother was well established in her own career. When it came time to apply for college, however, this young man applied as a Hispanic minority and was accepted at one of the nation's premier universities. Given his desultory record in high school and his mediocre scores on the SATs, it is clear the reason he was accepted was his status as a Hispanic minority. I know from experience that academics can be hypocrites and can manipulate the system when they wish to do so, but this case gave me a shock nonetheless.

Another contemporary of my daughter's was also applying to college at the time. She had gone to one of Buffalo's most expensive private schools. Her parents could well afford it because her father was a prominent physician with a substantial income. The high-school record of this girl was weak, and her subsequent record in college confirmed her generally limited talents. Nevertheless, this student was given a scholarship at a well-known university and kept it for the four years she attended on the basis of her minority status as a Hispanic.

I am sure most Americans are acquainted with cases similar to the ones I have mentioned. Some of these cases are so outrageous that they get into the newspapers and popular media. Recently I read in the *Buffalo News* that there was evidence that some applicants had been allowed to qualify as Hispanic minorities for positions in the police department on the basis of having taken Spanish in high school.[3] On the other hand, no Hispanics other than Mexican Americans or mainland Puerto Ricans qualify as minorities for medical school applications.

These examples should illustrate the extraordinary confusion that prevails in this country concerning affirmative action for Hispanics. The confusion centers, I believe, on the who, what, and why of affirmative action: The who concerns the identity of the group in question: Who counts as Hispanic? The what concerns the aims of affirmative action: What are the goals of affirmative action? Finally, the why concerns the rationale for affirmative action in the case of Hispanics: Why do we need affirmative action for Hispanics?

The discussion in this paper is divided into four parts. The first three provide answers to the three questions just raised, and the fourth presents the situation of Hispanics in American philosophy as a paradigm of the situation of Hispanics in the United States. I argue that: first, although Hispanics do not have a property or set of properties that unites us at all times and places, with our unity instead resembling a family throughout history, nonetheless Hispanics are recognizable as a group and distinguishable from other groups at particular times and places; second, affirmative action aims to ensure equal opportunity to members of groups who have suffered discrimination on the basis of gender, race, or ethnicity, to provide reparation for past wrongs to members of these groups, and to promote the participation of members of these groups in the political and cultural life of the nation; third, affirmative action for Hispanics considered as a group is justified on the basis of participation in the life of the nation, rather than on the basis of equal opportunity or reparation; and finally, affirmative action for Hispanics is needed in American philosophy.

Who Counts as Hispanic?

Who counts as hispanic is by no means easy to determine. I discuss this issue in considerable detail elsewhere, so I cover it only briefly here.[4] The difficulty with determining who counts as Hispanic is that Hispanics do not appear to share any properties in common. Linguistic, racial, religious, political, territorial, cultural, economic, educational, social class, and genetic criteria fail to identify Hispanics in all places and times because not all Hispanics speak the same language, are of the same race, hold the same religious beliefs, belong to the same political unit, live in the same territory, display the same cultural traits, enjoy the same economic status, have the same degree of education, share the same social class, or come from the same genetic line. It is not just that there is not a metaphysical essence to Hispanics, but that there are not even epistemic criteria that can be used for all times and places to establish who is Hispanic. In response to this problem, some argue either that there is no such distinguishable group or that there is such a group but it consists of an arbitrary collection without identity. Of course, if this is so, then to speak about affirmative action for Hispanics is absurd.

My response is that, although Hispanics have no essence and share no common properties at all times and places that can serve to distinguish us, we are nonetheless united by a web of historical relations that also separates us from other groups in the way a family is separated from other families. Wittgenstein made a similar point with respect to such things as games, for example. Games do not share common properties, but are rather like families in which each member is similar in terms of some property or properties common to one or more other members of the group, but not to all of them.[5] A child might resemble her maternal grandfather in the color of her eyes but be different from all other members of the family in that respect, whereas she resembles her mother in the shape of the eyes and no other member of the family does. Games are like families, according to Wittgenstein; no game is like all other games even in one respect, but every game is like some other game in some respect.

The unity of Hispanics should be understood in this sense, except that in this case, the family is historical and transcends national, territorial, linguistic, cultural, genetic, and other similar boundaries. At any particular time and place, there are familial relations that Hispanics share and which both distinguish us from non-Hispanics and are the source of properties that in turn can be used to distinguish us from non-Hispanics. Genetic linkages, physical characteristics, cultural traits, language, and so on can serve to distinguish Hispanics in certain contexts, although they cannot function as criteria of distinction and identification everywhere and at all times. In a place where all and only Hispanics speak Spanish, for example, the language can function as a sufficient criterion of Hispanic identification even if in other places it does not. Likewise, in a society or region where all and only Hispanics have a certain skin color, or a certain religion, and so on, these properties can be used to pick out Hispanics, even if elsewhere there are Hispanics who do not share these properties. Even though Hispanics do not constitute a homogeneous group, then, particular properties can be used to determine who counts as Hispanic in particular contexts.[6] Hispanic identity does not entail a set of common properties that constitutes an essence, but this does not stand in the way of identification. We can determine who counts as Hispanic in context. Just as we generally and easily can tell a game from something that is not a game, we can tell a Hispanic from a non-Hispanic in most instances. But, as with games, there will be borderline cases and cases that overlap. Still, for our purposes, this is sufficient insofar as it makes affirmative action possible.

In the case of Hispanics in the United States in particular, there are added reasons that facilitate an answer to the question of who counts as Hispanic. Two of these may be considered. First, we are treated as a homogeneous group by European Americans and African Americans; and second, even though Hispanics do not in fact constitute a homogeneous group, we are easily contrasted with European Americans and African Americans because we do not share many of the features commonly associated with these groups. Our identification in the United States, then, should be possible, although it certainly will not always be unproblematic.[7]

What Are the Goals of Affirmative Action?

The second area of confusion regarding affirmative action for Hispanics concerns its general aims. One or more of three aims are often identified: first, to ensure equal opportunity for those who, because of their gender, racial, or ethnic background in particular, have not had equal access to opportunities open to members of different gender, racial, or ethnic backgrounds; second, to make reparation for past wrongs that are the result of discrimination against groups on the basis of gender, race, or ethnicity;[8] and third, to promote the participation of underrepresented gender, race, and ethnic groups in the life of the nation.[9]

These three general aims also entail more specific ones. Here are several examples that are frequently mentioned: removal of structural obstacles in society for the development of the target groups, such as rules that exclude African Americans from certain jobs merely in virtue of the fact that they are African Americans; elimination of prejudices that in certain situations can give an unfair advantage to some members of society over others, such as the prejudice that Hispanics are procrastinators (the *mañana* philosophy), which can eliminate them from consideration for jobs where punctuality is of the essence; special education and training of members of target groups who have been deprived of certain social advantages because of their status, so as to prepare them to compete effectively with other members of society, such as special efforts to provide education for women in situations in which they have been deprived of education because of their gender; adoption of laws and regulations that ensure the equitable distribution of goods and services among all members of American society, such as laws that prescribe equitable salaries for women; compensation for past wrongs that resulted in harm to the groups against which discrimination has been exercised, or that precluded these groups from having certain opportunities for advancement available to members of society who are not members of the groups in question, as, for example, granting land and money to Native Americans to compensate them for past abuses; and appointment of members of underrepresented gender, racial, and ethnic groups to positions of leadership in the life of the nation, so that they can function as role models for other members of the group and voice the concerns of their groups in places where otherwise they would not be voiced.

Unfortunately, these aims are not always what the public at large, or even the government, understands as aims of affirmative action. Affirmative action is frequently taken to involve the arbitrary imposition of artificial quotas, the preferential treatment of women and minorities, and the placement of unqualified women and minorities in positions for which qualified nonminority males are available. Affirmative action is also often, and mistakenly, taken to involve group rights. As a result, many of the criticisms leveled against it are misdirected.

Why Do We Need Affirmative Action for Hispanics?

To answer the question of why we need affirmative action for Hispanics, we have to go back to the three general aims of affirmative action: equal opportunity, reparation for past wrongs, and participation in the life of the nation. The justification for these is usually made in one of two ways, in terms of justice or in terms of utility. I will not try to adjudicate between these, for to do so would require more space than I can give to this matter in this context. The first justification argues that justice requires affirmative action with respect to certain gender, racial, and ethnic groups. The second argues for the same based on utility. For equal opportunity and reparation, the justification in terms of justice is based on the principle that no one should suffer discrimination and unfair treatment because of gender, race, or ethnicity, and those who do should be compensated for the harm that such discriminatory treatment causes them. The utilitarian justification is based on the principle that to maintain conditions of discrimination based on gender, race, or ethnicity and not to compensate those who have suffered it is counterproductive to the well-being of society as a whole and to its members.

The justification on the basis of justice for the third general aim of affirmative action, participation in the life of the nation, is based on the principle that in a democratic nation every member of society should be given the opportunity to participate in the life of the nation and every reasonable effort should be made to facilitate and encourage such participation. The justification on the basis of utility is based on the principle that it is socially counterproductive, in utilitarian terms, to accept a situation in which not all members of society are given the opportunity and encouraged to participate in the life of the nation, and therefore to neglect making every reasonable effort to facilitate and encourage such participation.

None of what has been said is unproblematic. For example, no solution has been offered to the conflicts that equal opportunity or reparation may create between groups and individuals or among groups themselves. After all, any diversion of resources from some individuals or groups to others, even when those groups have suffered discrimination, seems to violate the very principle on which the action is based.[10] Likewise, nothing has been said concerning the fact that compensation for past wrongs often goes to those who have not actually suffered the wrongs. Consider, for example, that reparation today for slavery would have to go to persons who have never been slaves. Nor have I made an attempt to distinguish between conquered groups (for example, Mexican Americans who lived in the Southwest before the Mexican-American War) and immigrant groups (for example, Cubans who immigrated to the United States after the 1959 revolution), although the argument has been made that these groups deserve to be treated differently.[11] Naturally, there are moves one can make to deal with these and similar problems raised by the justification of affirmative action I have mentioned, but this is not the place to do it, because I am going to argue that affirmative action is not justified for Hispanics considered as a whole on the bases of equal opportunity or reparation. Let us, then, move to the particular question that pertains to us here, namely: Is affirmative action, understood as the implementation of measures that aim at equal opportunity, reparation, and participation, justified in the case of Hispanics?

Equal Opportunity and Reparation

The first part of the answer is that affirmative action for Hispanics considered as a whole, and understood as aiming at equal opportunity and reparation, is not justified. One reason is that although some Hispanics suffer or have suffered unequal treatment, and they are harmed or have been harmed by such treatment, this is not the case for all, or even a majority, of us. Moreover, for those who have, it is very difficult to demonstrate that they have done so because they are Hispanic. Perhaps a comparison with the situation of African Americans and women will help clarify this point.

Consider the case of African Americans first. One fundamental justification of affirmative action for them is reparation for past wrongs committed against the group. The salient fact in the history of African Americans is slavery. Slavery is probably one of the most, if not the most, dehumanizing state that can be imposed on a group of people. The atrocities that African Americans had to endure as consequences of slavery have been eloquently recorded elsewhere, so I need not repeat them here. It is sufficient to note that they were deprived of their culture, language, religion, freedom, basic human rights, education, and dignity. Moreover, a strong case can be made that the effects of slavery extend to all African Americans to this day. There is, therefore, much in the way of reparation that is justified for African Americans. Moreover, there is the fact that African Americans are not always treated as equal to other members of American society even today. When certain social choices become available, it seems that unless affirmative action is brought to bear, European Americans are still frequently favored over African Americans in many cases. This indicates that African Americans do not enjoy equal opportunity. Finally, and most important, the discrimination and abuse African Americans suffer and have suffered have been a result of their race. Being black is the fundamental reason for their mistreatment in American society.

The case for women also involves reparation and equal opportunity. It is a fact of human history that women have generally been relegated to a secondary, subservient role. With few exceptions, power has always been concentrated in masculine hands, and even on the few occasions when women have been able to wrest power away from males, they did so for very short times, and it seldom led to the permanent improvement of women's lot in society. To this day in many countries, women do not have the same rights as men, and in many cases have few rights of their own to speak of. Often whatever power they have is only vicarious, because males have granted it to them. Indeed, many personal and social gains made by women have been the result of masculine needs or wants. Consider the fact that women such as Cleopatra and Madame de Pompadour derived their power from the weakness of males who needed or wanted them. Consider also the reason women in the United States were asked to join the workforce during World War II: the need to fill spaces vacated by men. And why does a large proportion of married women work in the United States today? Surely one reason is that the salaries their husbands make are not enough to fulfill the needs of the home. In short, most women suffer, or have suffered, some form of discrimination and the adverse effects of discrimination, and they suffer, or have suffered them, because they are women. This can be used to justify affirmative action in terms of equal opportunity and reparation for them.

In contrast with African Americans and women, the argument based on reparation does not seem to work for Hispanics for three reasons: (1) not all, not even most, Hispanics have suffered discrimination, (2) the degree of discrimination and abuse some have suffered never reached the levels suffered by African Americans or women, and (3) it is difficult to prove that the reason some Hispanics have suffered discrimination and abuse in the United States is because they are Hispanics. Hispanics have not been subjected to the kind of abuse to which African Americans and women have been subjected. Hispanics have never been slaves; we were not brought into this country against our will to work for others and be subservient to their whims; we were not deprived of our culture, language, religion, freedom, basic human rights, education, or dignity; and, unlike women, we have not, as a whole, played a secondary role in American society. Under these circumstances, reparation does not seem justified. There is nothing, or not much, that must be given back to Hispanics as a group because it was taken away from us. And there is no harm done to us as a group that cries out for repair.

Matters, however, are not so clear. One could very well point out, for example, that there have been serious wrongs committed against some Hispanics in some places, such as Mexican Americans and Puerto Ricans, even if such wrongs have not been committed against all Hispanics. Consider the case of Mexican Americans. The conquest of 45 percent of the Mexican territory by the United States during the last century, the subsequent annexation of the territory, and the imposition of American culture, political structure, and law on the inhabitants of the territory are certainly a wrong. Here are some people who, prior to the conquest, were living in the country of their choice, in their own lands, and in the midst of their own culture. Yet, as a result of American military conquest, they found themselves in a different country, under a different government and different laws, and they were forced to adapt to a different culture, which was imposed on them.

The case of Puerto Ricans is somewhat similar. After the United States won the Spanish-American War, Puerto Rico became an appendage to this country. This resulted in some changes that were certainly unwelcome by Puerto Ricans and that have adversely affected the population of the island. One of these was the attempt to impose English as the official language. This was very damaging to Puerto Rican society and culture. It left many Puerto Ricans in a linguistic limbo. The result is that some of them lost some of the language proficiency they had in Spanish without gaining the fluency in English that was required for integration into American society. The consequences of this are still quite evident today among some Puerto Ricans: confinement to ghettos, failure in school performance, undereducation, social alienation, and so on. So here, again, a case could be made for restitution and reparation.

All the same, the situation of Mexican Americans and of Puerto Ricans is not quite like that of African Americans. What the United States did to African Americans appears to be in a class of its own, and for this reason Hispanics should not have the same claims to reparation that African Americans have. Moreover, the situation of women appears idiosyncratic as well. But even if a case for affirmative action could be made on the basis of reparation for Mexican Americans and Puerto Ricans, as it can for African Americans and women, it certainly cannot be made for Hispanics as a whole, since many Hispanics, both individuals (I certainly do not deserve it) and groups (think of Cubans and Argentinians), have not suffered what Mexican Americans and Puerto Ricans have suffered. So much, then, for the argument based on reparation.

The argument for affirmative action based on equal opportunity, used for African Americans and women, does not seem to apply to Hispanics, either. For reasons similar to the three given in the case of reparation, it does not appear that Hispanics as a whole are subjected to the same kind of discrimination to which African Americans and women are subjected, or that Hispanics are subjected to any kind of discrimination because we are Hispanic. One reason for this may be that many Hispanics do not look very different from the many Americans of Mediterranean ancestry. It is often difficult to tell Hispanics apart from Italians, Greeks, or Israelis. And even those Hispanics who are more easily identifiable do not stand out as starkly as most African Americans and all women do. Naturally, this makes it more difficult for those who wish to discriminate against us to do so. Not even the greatest bigots go around asking for the ethnic identification of persons who look like them. In short, Hispanics as a whole encounter less discrimination than African Americans and women, and the discrimination to which we have been and are subjected is less pronounced or nefarious, even if some Hispanic individuals and groups have encountered strong and destructive discrimination.

To say this, however, does not mean that affirmative action for Hispanics is not needed. As long as there are some acts of discrimination against Hispanics, there is a need for rectifying the situation that leads to these acts.[12] But there is another problem: it is difficult to demonstrate that those Hispanics who have been or are subjected to discrimination have been or are so subjected because they are Hispanic and not for some other reasons. For example, some Mexican Americans may experience discrimination because of their facial features, rather than because they are Hispanic; some Cuban Americans may experience discrimination because of their skin color, rather than because they are Hispanic; some recent arrivals from Central America may experience discrimination because they do not speak English well, and not because they are Hispanic; some Dominican Americans may experience discrimination because they are poor, and not because they are Hispanic; and so on. Whereas African Americans generally suffer discrimination because of their race and women suffer discrimination because of their gender, it is not at all clear that those Hispanics who suffer discrimination do so because they are Hispanic. And this means that even if Hispanics suffer discrimination because they are Hispanic, without proper knowledge of it society cannot justify anti-discriminatory actions toward Hispanics on the basis of their ethnic identity.

In sum, the case for affirmative action for Hispanics, when this is understood as equal opportunity and reparation, is difficult to make even though some Hispanics may have legitimate claims of this sort. Note that I am not saying that it cannot be made. It is possible that it could, and if so, then affirmative action on the basis of equal opportunity and reparation would be in order. My point is that the pertinent empirical evidence—and surely the argument would have to rest on empirical evidence—is conflicting. In any case, the burden of proof is on those who wish to defend affirmative action for Hispanics on these bases, and proof must go beyond belief, contrary to what Angelo Corlett appears to argue in this volume. Because I find the empirical evidence unclear, I argue for affirmative action for Hispanics on other grounds: participation in the life of the nation.

Participation in the Life of the Nation

The justification for affirmative action in terms of participation in the life of the nation also may, in principle, take two forms: one based on justice and one based on utility. And again I will refrain from adjudicating between these at this time. The first is based on the principle that in a democratic nation, justice requires that every member of society be given the opportunity to participate in the life of the nation and that every reasonable effort be made to facilitate and encourage such participation. If some members of society are not given such opportunities and no reasonable efforts are made to facilitate and encourage participation of certain gender, racial, and ethnic groups, the situation needs correction. The utilitarian justification runs along the same lines, except that it is based on the principle of utility: a nation in which all members of society are given the opportunity and encouraged to participate in the life of the nation achieves better results than one in which some members are not given the opportunity or encouraged to participate and not every reasonable effort is made to facilitate and encourage the participation of everyone.

In order for the argument based on participation to be clear, we must answer at least three questions: (1) Who is to participate and be encouraged to participate? (2) What degree of participation is required? (3) With regard to what is the participation to take place? In principle, the answers to these questions would appear to be quite straightforward: Everyone should participate and be encouraged to participate, as far as possible, and with respect to every aspect of the life of the nation. When one looks more carefully at these answers, however, it is clear that they are unsatisfactory. First, it is questionable whether "everyone" should extend to such persons as illegal immigrants, tourists, terrorist infiltrators, and so on. Second, the degree of participation must necessarily be limited by practical considerations. For example, in a very small democratic community, it is possible for all the citizens to get together and agree on a certain course of action, but in a large nation, political participation has to be vicarious, through some form of indirect representation. Finally, it makes no sense to say that everyone must participate in every aspect of the life of the nation. Not everyone should teach mathematics, work as a physician, or be a member of the legislature. Clearly the answers to these questions need considerable elaboration. For our purposes, however, we do not need to provide a full story about them. It suffices to show that in at least some aspects of the life of the nation, participation by Hispanics is desirable in terms of justice or utility, although the degree of participation will depend also on the aspect in question. In order to simplify matters I shall point to two areas where it seems that participation is important in the case of Hispanics. The first is political participation and the second is cultural participation.

I understand political participation to involve being engaged in the process whereby decisions that affect the life of the polity are arrived at. Being engaged implies that those who participate in the process are consulted either directly, by being asked what they think, or indirectly, by having their representatives asked. In principle, the justification for political participation can be made in terms of both justice and utility.[13] In terms of justice, the argument is that it is unfair to arrive at decisions and adopt laws affecting persons who have not been allowed to voice their opinions and have not been given the opportunity to do what they can within the democratic process to prevent such decisions from being taken and such laws from being adopted. The argument in terms of utility is, mutatis mutandis, similar.

With respect to cultural participation the situation is less clear. It appears that cultural participation entails at least the freedom to engage in cultural practices, such as religious observances, speaking the language of one's choice, listening and playing the music one likes, and so on. One can argue, however, that freedom here needs to be understood more strongly than as just being allowed to do certain things. Freedom needs to be understood as providing the means to allow for freedom in the first sense to take place. It is one thing is to be free to eat in the sense of being allowed to do it; it is another is to be free to eat in the sense that we are provided with the means to do it. Similarly, cultural participation means not just being allowed to engage in cultural practices and activities of one's choice, but also being given the resources that make it possible to do.

This understanding of freedom to participate is too strong, however. It entails, for example, that society provide resources to different religious groups, groups with different musical preferences, and so on, and this is clearly unacceptable. A weaker version of this view argues that what is involved here is both the removal of obstacles that stand in the way of cultural practices and also an open, respectful, and accepting attitude toward the cultural practices of others. It is not enough not to stand in the way; there must be a will and a way to accept the cultural preferences of all members of society.

Of course, even this modified position encounters a difficulty, namely, that not all cultural practices are benign and, therefore, acceptable. Consider, for example, such practices as female circumcision, opposition to certain medical treatments known to be beneficial, and so on. Clearly there are limits to the cultural freedom that can be allowed: cultural practices that adversely affect others or the polity as a whole should not enjoy the open, respectful, and accepting attitude about which we are speaking. Participation in the cultural life of the nation must be understood within these parameters.

Now, the particular question that concerns us here is whether affirmative action, understood as measures aimed at increasing participation in the two areas mentioned, namely, politics and culture, is justified for Hispanics. Justification in these cases requires two conditions to be satisfied: (1) Hispanics are identifiable, and (2) Hispanics do not participate at all, or participate insufficiently, in the political and cultural life of the nation.

Satisfying the first condition should not be an insurmountable problem if we take seriously what was said earlier concerning who counts as Hispanic. Although Hispanics are not homogeneous and have no common properties at all times and places, we are generally identifiable in context, and certainly we are, with some exceptions, identifiable in contemporary American society. Satisfying the second condition involves showing that in fact Hispanics participate less in the political and cultural life of the nation than our numbers would seem to warrant.

Someone might want to object that the justification of affirmative action in terms of participation in the life of the nation is not different from the justification based on equal opportunity. After all, can we not frame the former as affirmative action intended to ensure equal opportunity to participate in the life of the nation? My response is that if one construes participation in the life of the nation as a kind of opportunity, then obviously justification of affirmative action on the basis of the first is not different from that on the basis of the second. But I do not think participation in the political and cultural life of the nation can be construed as an opportunity. I wish to maintain, then, that there is a difference between these two kinds of justification for affirmative action. Equal opportunity generally refers to the distribution of goods and services in society—such things as jobs, salaries, health services—and it is stretching things quite a bit to think of participation in the political and cultural life of the nation as a good or service in this sense.

I cannot engage here in an overall justification of affirmative action based on the participation of Hispanics in the political and cultural life of the nation. Statistics confirm that there are fewer Hispanics in government and that fewer of us vote in elections than our numbers would seem to warrant. Moreover, it seems quite evident that many cultural traits generally associated with Hispanics today seem to be relegated to a secondary and marginal role. Indeed, when we consider expressions of so-called high culture, such as art, literature, and philosophy, anything associated with Hispanics is ignored, dismissed, or squeezed out to make room for something else. Moreover, there is relatively little openness, respect, and acceptance of cultural traits associated with Hispanics. And, indeed, in some cases, as with language, there is open hostility in certain quarters.[14]

Because I know more about my own field of specialization than about other areas of culture, I will use the condition of Hispanics in American philosophy to illustrate this situation, although obviously what I say cannot be applied without qualification to other cultural expressions. This example will allow me to argue for affirmative action in terms of cultural participation. The case for affirmative action based on political participation will have to wait for another time.

The Case of Hispanics in American Philosophy

First, let us be clear as to the insufficient participation of Hispanics in philosophy.[15] The results of a 1992 questionnaire sent by the American Philosophical Association's Committee for Hispanics in Philosophy to 850 philosophy departments at four-year and graduate institutions provide evidence of the small number of Hispanics in philosophy and, more specifically, of a dramatic drop in the number of philosophy undergraduate majors who continue graduate work in philosophy. Of the 316 departments responding to the survey, only 31 percent (99 schools) reported that there were any Hispanics among their faculty, graduate students, or undergraduate majors. In these departments, there was a total of 277 Hispanic undergraduate philosophy majors, 66 Hispanic graduate students, and 55 Hispanic faculty members (part- and full-time).[16] Even three years later, when I stepped down as chair of the Committee for Hispanics in Philosophy, there were still only 68 faculty and 59 graduate students registered with the committee.

Because there are roughly 12,000 philosophers teaching in the United States today, these figures mean that the percentage of Hispanic faculty is around one-half of 1 percent. This is a much lower percentage than that of Hispanics in the population at large, which is around 10.3 percent.[17] Indeed, even if one counts only philosophers who are members of the American Philosophical Association, roughly 9,000, and triples the number of Hispanic faculty registered with the committee to account for many who may not have registered, still the percentage of Hispanics in philosophy comes out very low: 2.26 percent.

Particularly alarming is the low number of Hispanic graduate students in philosophy. The total graduate-student population in philosophy in this country is about 1,700. So if the numbers reported earlier are accurate, the percentage of Hispanic graduate students in philosophy is 3.8 percent. This means that unless a dramatic shift in interest occurs among Hispanic undergraduates, the number of teaching Hispanic philosophers will not increase sufficiently to match the proportion in the Hispanic population.

Other statistics confirm the low number of Hispanics in philosophy. Indeed, the number of Ph.D.'s in philosophy awarded to persons of Hispanic descent each year since 1974 appears to be the lowest of any discipline except for English.[18] In a 1987 report on a survey of the profession by the American Philosophical Association's Committee on the Status and Future of the Profession, the number of Hispanic philosophers falls below even the extraordinarily low figures for the humanities in general.[19]

A more recent survey of philosophy in the United States carried out in 1994 by the American Philosophical Association Committee on the Status and Future of the Profession does not show any significant amelioration of the situation.[20] And the situation with graduate and undergraduate students is not significantly different.[21]

So much for numbers and percentages. Consider an equally discouraging fact: Currently there are only half a dozen Hispanics who have become established philosophers in the United States and Canada, and all of them are foreign-born. By "established" I mean philosophers who have full rank in philosophy Ph.D. programs and who are known in the profession for their work in some subfield of philosophy: Mario Bunge was born in Argentina in 1919; Ignacio Angelelli was born in Italy in 1933 but considers himself Argentinian; Alfonso Gómez-Lobo was born in Chile in 1940; and Ernesto Sosa (1940), Ofelia Schutte (1943), and I (1942) were born in Cuba. There is no other Hispanic in the over-fifty age group who is established in his or her field, although there are a few younger members of the profession who are fast developing a profile.

There is also another fact that needs to be taken into account. Many African-American philosophers who have achieved prominence have done so by working precisely in areas that are intrinsically related to African or African-American philosophy, the African-American experience, and the condition of African Americans in this country. And the same goes for many women. Many of the best-known women in the profession are known for work related to the condition of women in society and the philosophical thought of other women. The work of African Americans and women in these areas has earned them high praise, and they have secured appointments at full rank in graduate philosophy programs or elite undergraduate colleges.[22] In contrast, only one of the aforementioned Hispanic philosophers, Ofelia Schutte, has as a primary field the study of the Hispanic condition or Hispanic thought. Two others, Angelelli and I, have done some work in areas related to Hispanic philosophy, but have as primary fields of research other areas of philosophy and are known for work in the latter rather than in the former. All of the others have had little or nothing to say about Hispanic issues, and some of them in fact have publicly criticized those Hispanic philosophers who have.[23]

Perhaps even as significant, the philosophy curriculum in this country generally ignores Hispanic philosophy, even though there is no dearth of Hispanic philosophers in both Latin America and the Iberian peninsula. From the sixteenth century until today, there has been a steady production of philosophical work of high caliber among Hispanics.[24] Moreover, both the quantity and quality of this work measures well when compared with that of other philosophical traditions that receive considerable attention in the college curriculum in this country. There may be as few as a dozen universities and colleges that offer courses in Hispanic (either Iberian or Latin American) philosophy. The 1994 American Philosophical Association report cited earlier does not mention Hispanic, Latin American, Latino, Spanish, or any other kind of philosophy particularly associated with Hispanics. It does mention, however, the percentages of departments that offer courses at least every two years in Eastern/Asian (33 percent), Eastern/Indian (21 percent), Arabic/Islamic (5 percent), and African (27 percent) philosophy.[25] This leads one to conclude that either Hispanic philosophy is simply not part of the philosophy curriculum in this country or those who carried out the survey were not sensitive to it. I believe it is the former, but even the latter would be a clear indication of little regard for Hispanic philosophy among American philosophers.

But, of course, one should not be surprised, for among the many historical and systematic fields for which the American Philosophical Association has advisory committees to the Program Committee, none is included that has to do with Latin American, Spanish, Hispanic, or Latino philosophy. Yet there are committees for all sorts of other fields, including Eastern and African philosophy.

Add to these facts that the American Philosophical Association did not have a committee devoted to Hispanic issues until 1991, when Robert Turnbull, chair of the Board of Officers, single-handedly decided it was time for the association to take us into account. By contrast, the Committee for Blacks in Philosophy has been in existence since the late 1960s. Incidentally, when I contacted the national office of the American Philosophical Association in the summer of 1997 to ask for information about Hispanics in the association, I was told that the national office could not help me because it had no information at all on this matter. I believe this response indicates quite clearly how invisible, and unimportant, Hispanics still are in the American philosophical establishment.

This neglect, surely, has contributed to making philosophy an uninviting area of study, not to mention career choice, for most Hispanic undergraduates. Political science, sociology, literature, modern languages, and religious studies appear—at least to students in introductory courses—to be more immediately and effectively relevant and welcoming to Hispanic undergraduate students.

There is a society devoted to Hispanic philosophy, the Society for Iberian and Latin American Thought (SILAT), founded in 1976 by a group of scholars concerned with the lack of attention given to Hispanic thought in this country. But its history does not show many successes.[26] Indeed, although the society is now more than twenty years old and regularly organizes sessions at the meetings of the American Philosophical Association's Eastern Division, it has been a struggle to keep it alive, and the number of active members is not larger than a dozen.

In short, then, there is insufficient participation of Hispanics in American philosophy in three ways: (1) Hispanics are grossly underrepresented in the ranks of American philosophers, (2) Hispanic issues and concerns are seldom given attention by the philosophical community, and (3) Hispanic philosophy is generally absent from both the philosophy curriculum and professional philosophical discussions. By Hispanic philosophy I mean the history of the thought of Hispanic philosophers. I do not claim that there is anything necessarily peculiar to the way Hispanics do philosophy, but only that there is a corpus of philosophical thought produced by Hispanics that is both substantial and different from the corpus of philosophical thought produced by non-Hispanic philosophers.

Many reasons can be given for the lack of participation of Hispanics in philosophy, but I need not dwell on them here.[27] For the present argument it is sufficient to show that Hispanics do not participate sufficiently in the philosophical life of the United States in the mentioned ways, when in principle it would appear both just and better that we do. Active measures need to be taken, then, to make room for Hispanics in American philosophy, and reasonable efforts should be made to facilitate and encourage Hispanic participation in philosophy. These should include recruitment of Hispanics in philosophy, discussion of Hispanic issues among philosophers, and the inclusion of Hispanic philosophy in the curriculum and in professional philosophical discussions. I hope it is clear that I have argued for a broad notion of participation in terms of affirmative action. Not only should the American philosophical community make efforts to recruit Hispanics, it should also open the doors to the discussion of Hispanic issues and Hispanic philosophy. The last two, I believe, will encourage Hispanics to enter the field.

Conclusion

The answer to the question in the title of this essay, "Affirmative Action for Hispanics?" is given by the subtitle: "Yes and No." Yes, to the extent that affirmative action makes sense for Hispanics, because although we are part of American society, we constitute a distinguishable ethnic group that must be given the opportunity and encouragement, to participate in the life of the nation, for reasons of justice or utility. No, to the extent that affirmative action is not always justified for Hispanics. Only secondarily and in specific cases can a case be made for affirmative action based on equal opportunity and reparation.

As a last word, let me go back to the anecdotal cases presented at the beginning to illustrate how my view helps us deal with practical affirmative action decisions. Was the university affirmative action committee right in rejecting me as a Hispanic minority? No, it was wrong insofar as I am identifiably Hispanic and Hispanics were, at the time, underrepresented in the Department of Philosophy (and are still underrepresented in philosophy in general). Was the later committee right in accepting the foreign candidates as minorities? Yes, for the same reason given in my case. Was the elite college that accepted as Hispanic the friend of my daughter with the Mexican-American great-grandfather, right? No, for this young man could not in any meaningful sense of the term qualify as a member of the Hispanic community. Was the elite college that gave a scholarship to the daughter of our prominent Hispanic friend because she was Hispanic right? No, because the purpose of a scholarship is to make it possible for someone disadvantaged to go to school, or to compensate someone for past harms based on discrimination. But as we saw earlier, neither justification applies to Hispanics considered as a whole.[28]

Notes

1. For present purposes the use of *Hispanics* or *Latinos* is immaterial. I choose *Hispanics* for reasons that I explain in Jorge J. E. Gracia, *Hispanic/Latino Identity: A Philosophical Perspective* (Oxford: Blackwell, 2000), ch. 3.
2. Although the official adoption of *Hispanic* for purposes of affirmative action at the federal level seems to have taken place in the mid-seventies, the term was in circulation long before then to refer to the people, speech, or culture of Spain, Portugal, and Latin America. See *Hispanic* in *Webster's Third New International Dictionary* (Chicago: Encyclopaedia Britannica, Inc., 1966). Something similar can be said for the use of *hispánico/a* in the Iberian peninsula and Latin America. See, for example, Miguel de Unamuno, "Hispanidad," in *Obras completas* (Madrid: Exelsior, 1968 [1927]), 4: 1081.
3. Luo Michel, "Group Claims Some Police Officers Posed as Hispanics in Order to Gain Employment," *Buffalo News*, January 20, 1998, B1, B10.
4. Gracia, *Hispanic/Latino Identity*.
5. Ludwig Wittgenstein, *Philosophical Investigations* (New York: Macmillan, 1965), § 75.
6. Jorge J. E. Gracia, "The Nature of Ethnicity: With Particular Reference to the Case of Hispanic/Latino Identity," *Public Affairs Quarterly* 13, 1 (1999): 25–42.
7. This is the thrust of Corlett's and of Zaibert and Millán-Zaibert's criticisms of my position in this volume. According to Corlett in particular, my theory does not provide effective criteria to distinguish Hispanics for legal purposes. But, of course, what I have said here is not intended to do this. I am merely establishing logical possibility and a correct metaphysical conception of Hispanics as an ethnic group. Nor do I have space here to deal with the problem of identification criteria *in concreto*. This will have to wait for another occasion.
8. More narrow, legal definitions of affirmative action, however, imply the exclusion of reparation. See Corlett's article in this volume. Including reparation in affirmative action here does not affect my argument because I do not make reparation the basis for affirmative action for Hispanics.
9. I speak mainly of gender, race, and ethnic groups here, but some of what I say

also applies to other groups in which age, handicap, and the like are involved. What I say is not intended to apply, however, to groups whose members freely choose to belong to them, such as religious communities, for their situation is more complicated.

10. For some of these difficulties, see Thomas W. Pogge, "Group Rights and Ethnicity," in Will Kymlicka and Ian Shapiro, eds., *Ethnicity and Group Rights*, Nomos no. 39 (New York: New York University Press, 1997), 187–221, and Nathan Glazer, "Individual Rights against Group Rights," in Will Kymlicka, ed., *The Rights of Minority Cultures* (Oxford: Oxford University Press, 1995), 123–38.
11. See Will Kymlicka, *Multicultural Citizenship: A Liberal Theory of Minority Rights* (Oxford: Oxford University Press, 1995), 11–26, although his terminology is slightly different.
12. These acts of discrimination are well documented in the pertinent literature. See, for example, Suzanne Oboler, *Ethnic Labels/Latino Lives* (Minneapolis: University of Minnesota Press, 1995).
13. See, for example, Iris Marion Young, "Together in Difference Transforming the Logic of Group Political Conflict," in Will Kymlicka, ed., *The Rights of Minority Cultures* (Oxford: Oxford University Press, 1995), 155–76.
14. One measure of the marginalization of Hispanics is that even affirmative action measures, such as providing government funds for Hispanic art, have often been counterproductive to the extent that they have created a kind of cultural ghetto for Hispanics who, as a result, have a place separate and distant from the place of "mainstream" culture. See John David Skrentny, *The Ironies of Affirmative Action: Politics, Culture, and Justice in America* (Chicago: University of Chicago Press, 1996).
15. The following has been taken largely from Jorge J. E. Gracia, "Hispanics, Philosophy, and the Curriculum," *Teaching Philosophy* 23, 3 (1999): 214–18. I present an extended discussion of the situation of Hispanics in American philosophy in Gracia, *Hispanic/Latino Identity*, ch. 7.
16. *Proceedings and Addresses of the American Philosophical Association* 66, 5 (1993): 45–46.
17. U.S. Bureau of the Census, *Statistical Abstract of the United States, 1996*, 116th edition (Washington, D.C.: U.S. Government Printing Office, 1996), chart 13. By the year 2025, it is expected that Hispanics will constitute 17.6 percent of the population, whereas non-Hispanic whites will constitute 78.3 percent and non-Hispanic blacks 14.2 percent.
18. National Research Council, *Summary Report: Doctorate Recipients from the United States Universities*, appendix C (Washington, D.C.: National Academy Press, 1987), 66–71.
19. *Proceedings and Addresses of the American Philosophical Association* 61, 2 (1987): 359–60.
20. "Philosophy in America in 1994," *Proceedings and Addresses of the American Philosophical Association* 70, 2 (1996): pp. 135–137.
21. Ibid., 149.
22. Here are some examples of African Americans: Leonard Harris (Purdue), Howard McGary (Rutgers), and Lucius Outlaw (Haverford). Among established women philosophers known for their work in feminist issues are Kathryn P. Addelson (Smith), Louise Antony (North Carolina at Chapel Hill), Susan Bordo (Kentucky), Lorraine Code (York, Ontario), Nancy Frankenbury (Dartmouth),

Alison Jaggar (Colorado at Boulder), Carolyn Korsmeyer (Buffalo), Elizabeth Spelman (Smith), and Nancy Tuana (Oregon).

23. Mario Bunge, for example, has expressed impatience with those who work on the history of Latin American philosophy and is on record as noting that there is not much philosophy even in Argentina, which is certainly one of the most philosophically sophisticated countries in Latin America. "Testimonio de Mario Bunge," in Ana Baron, Mario del Carril, and Albino Gómez, eds., *¿Porqué se fueron? Testimonios de argentinos en el exterior* (Buenos Aires: EMECE, 1995), 60.
24. See Jorge J. E. Gracia, *Filosofía hispánica: Concepto, origen y foco historiográfico* (Pamplona: Universidad de Navarra, 1998).
25. *Proceedings and Addresses of the American Philosophical Association* 70, 2 (1996): 153.
26. For a short history of SILAT, see Antón Donoso, "The Society for Iberian and Latin American Thought (SILAT): An Interdisciplinary Project," *Los Ensayistas: Boletín Informativo* 1–2 (1976): 38–42.
27. I have discussed some of these in "Hispanics, Philosophy, and the Curriculum," and *Hispanic /Latino Identity*, ch. 7.
28. My gratitude goes to James Brady, Leonardo Zaibert, Thomas Pogge, Angelo Corlett, Pablo De Greiff, Elizabeth Millán-Zaibert, Suzanne Oboler, and Heron Simmonds for their useful comments and criticisms.

Latino Identity and Affirmative Action 11

J. Angelo Corlett

After decades in which United States citizens have lived with affirmative action programs, there is increasing doubt among many as to the justifiability of the very policies on which such programs are based. As philosophers continue the discussion of the moral status of affirmative action programs, arguments lead rather naturally to questions of ethnic group membership.[1] Several would argue that if affirmative action programs are morally justified, then public policy ought to be enacted so that such programs are instituted and sustained in viable and fair ways. However, in order for affirmative action programs to be instituted with a minimum of unfair play, it is imperative that they function according to a sound and workable notion of ethnic group membership concerning the groups targeted for affirmative action. Latinos constitute one such group.[2] And so it is crucial that affirmative action programs operate according to a plausible and workable idea of Latino identity. Thus there is a vital conceptual connection between Latino identity and affirmative action.[3]

Certainly one position to argue about Latino identity and affirmative action is that not only is there no fixed (essentialist) conception of Latino identity that reaches across time and circumstance universally, but that even if there were such a view of Latino identity, affirmative action policies ought not to extend to Latinos for reasons of either equal opportunity or reparations. Jorge J. E. Gracia analyzes the concept of Hispanic identity, and among other things argues that affirmative action is *not* due Latinos for reasons of equal opportunity or reparation because Latinos have not been treated in the harsh ways in which African Americans and women have been treated in U.S. society.[4] Instead, affirmative action for Latinos is justified on grounds that it is vital for them to be able to participate in the life of the United States. Another position would be that there *is* an analysis of Latino identity and that Latinos *should* qualify for programs of affirmative action for reasons of, say, past injustices against them. Indeed, there are other such views about Latino identity and affirmative action. But I shall confine myself to a discussion of these particular viewpoints within the context of the U.S. legal system.

In this paper, I shall discuss critically the nature of Latino identity, using as my conceptual backdrop some of Gracia's remarks about it. In so doing, I will develop the philosophical foundations of a plausible theory of Latino identity. More specifically, I will provide some desiderata for an adequate theory of Latino identity, and suggest the foundations of a philosophical analysis of Latino identity. Following this, I shall argue that if affirmative action itself is morally justified, then Latinos *are* deserving of affirmative action for backward-looking reasons.

Latino Identity

Prior to discussing the nature of Latino identity, it is important to delineate some essential elements of a theory or analysis of Latino identity. First, a theory of Latino identity should be able to distinguish members of the group (or cluster of groups) "Latino" from other ethnic groups with as little ambiguity as possible. Second, a theory of Latino identity ought to identify Latinos according to standards that are used generally for the identification of members of other ethnic groups. In other words, what makes someone a Latino should not differ markedly, insofar as basic conditions of categorization are concerned, from what makes one, say, an African American, a Native American, and so on. The reason for these first two desiderata is that it is a good thing to seek to minimize arbitrariness in the categorization of us as members of ethnic groups.

Third, a theory of Latino identity should separate the question of the nature of Latinos from any moral evaluation of Latinos. This precaution guards against the use of identifying ethnic group membership for racist reasons, as has been done in the past (and is being done so now, for that matter) on various occasions. Fourth, a theory of Latino identity ought not to provide criteria that would politicize the conditions of what counts as being a Latino. This element seeks to separate the question of the nature of a Latino from the question of a Latino's particular standpoint on politics. It assumes, among other things, that the nature of ethnicity is not wholly a social construction. Fifth, a theory of Latino identity should reflect an in-group perspective of what counts as being a Latino. Such a theory ought not to be developed by out-group members, no matter how well-meaning they may be. Part of the project of defining or identifying who and what we are as Latinos is the ethnic pride that comes with naming and celebrating who and what we are, ethnically speaking. And identifying who and what we are as Latinos is, among other things, a process of self-empowerment. The act of identification, especially self-identification, empowers the self, and this self-empowerment can be either individual or collective. Sixth, a theory of Latino identity should be sensitive to the ways in which history has continued, does continue, and will continue to shape what counts as a Latino from one generation to the next. This ought to give pause to those who believe that they are able to provide a decisive and complete account of who is or who is not a Latino.

Having articulated some desiderata of a theory of Latino identity, I think it is important to consider one of the leading theories of what counts as a Latino. Gracia has devoted significant philosophical energy to the task of identifying us Latinos. Concerning Latino identity, he writes that there is no property or group of properties that characterizes all Hispanics at all times and in all places; rather, there are relations that link them. Gracia goes on to argue that

> at any particular time and place, there are familial relations that Hispanics share and which both distinguish us from non-Hispanics and are the source of properties that in turn can be used to distinguish us from non-Hispanics. Genetic linkages, physical characteristics, cultural traits, language, and so on can serve to distinguish Hispanics in certain contexts, although they cannot function as criteria of distinction and identification everywhere and at all times.

This view of Latino identity is a nonessentialist one. It serves as a bold recognition of the Herculean task one faces in trying to define "Latino" in terms of, say, necessary and sufficient conditions. I concur with the admonition that it is problematic, if not absurd, to discuss the plausibility of affirmative action for Latinos if the concept of Latino identity is defined arbitrarily.[5] Thus defining the boundaries of who counts as a Latino is important at least for purposes of public policy.

Consider another of Gracia's statements:

> Even though Hispanics do not constitute a homogeneous group, then, particular properties can be used to determine who counts as Hispanic in particular contexts. Hispanic identity does not entail a set of common properties that constitutes an essence, but this does not stand in the way of identification. We can determine who counts as Hispanic in context.[6]

It seems difficult to reconcile this view with the notion that Latino identity should not be unacceptably arbitrary and can be useful for purposes of public policy administration, for the same arguments that are leveled against Latino identity essentialism globally count also against any attempt to delineate Latinos more locally, say, in the United States, or in a state, or in a certain city. Thus contextualizing Latino identity, as Gracia argues that we can do, does not allow him to escape the full force of his own antiessentialist arguments.[7]

Not only are there conceptual problems with the contextualization of Latino identity, this conception of Latino identity will not suffice for purposes of determining wronged parties in cases of racist harms, nor will it make public policy administration likely to succeed in, say, awarding affirmative action benefits to Latinos. For example, precisely how would a governing body determine who counts as a Latino in terms of criteria such as Latino culture, physical characteristics, language, and so on? Exactly which physical characteristics would count as being adequately Latino? Just which cultural traits would count? And what level of competency in which Latino language or dialect would count for such purposes of public policy administration? It is dubious whether these and related questions can be answered in a nonarbitrary way. Yet the plausibility of any analysis of Latino identity is contingent on its being as nonarbitrary as possible.

It would appear, then, that a significantly more workable conception of Latino identity would be one that seeks to define the boundaries of Latinohood in some property or cluster of properties that current U.S. law (or the laws of any other legal system, for that matter) can, in principle and in practice, verify or falsify empirically, for example, genealogical ties. On such a conception, one is a Latino to the extent that he has a genealogical bond to those who are Latinos. This anchors Latino ethnicity in Latino genealogical lineage. Yet it hardly ignores the importance of Latino culture,[8] language, names, and other factors in determining the extent to which one is a Latino.[9] This kind of view of Latino identity makes easier public policy decisions concerning ethnic groups such as Latinos. It also evades certain difficulties faced by competing conceptions. First, it would appear that on some views, it would make sense to say of an Angla child who was adopted and raised in a Latino context that she is a Latina. Yet this seems just as counterintuitive as it would be to argue that I am an African American to the extent that I was raised around African Americans, yet had no genealogical tie to them.[10] Perhaps such a person is, say, a Latina in some cultural sense of her living as a voluntary and intentional participant in a Latina context. But recall that the analysis of Latinohood at issue here is one that, among other things, is workable in terms of public policy administration. Thus a "cultural Latino," if I may coin a term, should not count as a Latino for purposes of public policy, for there seems to be no adequate method by which "cultural Latinos" can be readily verified, empirically speaking. A genealogically based analysis of Latinohood, on the other hand, provides the law with a way of supporting public policies seeking to uphold distributive and corrective justice for Latinos.[11]

Second, some conceptions of Latino identity appear to make room for the possibility that the offspring of two Latino parents, having been adopted by Anglo parents and raised apart from Latino culture, would no longer be a Latino. Yet this too is counterintuitive. As I have argued elsewhere, though ethnicity is not a natural kind, it is not completely a matter of social convention either.[12] One cannot lose entirely that to which one is genealogically bound. Insofar as one's ethnicity is contingent on one's genealogy, one cannot lose one's ethnicity entirely.

It might be insisted, even in light of the aforementioned considerations, that a cultural understanding of Latinohood is superior to a genealogical one, even for public policy administration. But how would a government (U.S. or not) effectively remedy or rectify harm done to Latinos through anti-Latino racism?[13] As we have seen, without a clear and unambiguous idea of the nature of Latinohood, public policies aimed at distributive or corrective justice for Latinos become unacceptably arbitrary. A purely cultural definition of "Latino" is insufficiently precise to distinguish us Latinos from those who are not. On the other hand, a conception of Latino identity anchored in Latino genealogical bonds, along with Latino cultural, linguistic, and other factors, seems to be a more promising foundation for the identification of us Latinos for purposes of administering public policy. Moreover, the genealogically based moderate essentialist conception of Latino identity need not and ought not to be determined by out-group members, for ethnic identity requires a group's self-identity in order for it to exercise self-empowerment.[14]

Thus a moderate (genealogical) essentialist conception of Latino identity better serves the interests of public policy in identifying individuals belonging to an ethnic group deserving of instruments of distributive or corrective justice within the current U.S. legal system. This implies that the moderate (genealogically based) conception of Latino identity best enables government agencies in identifying those Latinos who qualify for affirmative action programs.

Affirmative Action for Latinos?

However, even if it could be shown that there is a way to identify Latinos for public policy purposes, Gracia argues, Latinos hardly qualify as plausible candidates for such policy administration, at least for reasons of equal opportunity or reparation. While African Americans and women have been treated very badly and deserve reparations, he argues, Latinos have not and do not:

> Affirmative action for Hispanics considered as a whole, and understood as aiming at equal opportunity and reparation, is not justified. The reason is that although some Hispanics suffer or have suffered unequal treatment, and they are harmed or have been harmed by such treatment, this is not the case for all, or even a majority, of us. Moreover, for those who have, it is very difficult to demonstrate that they have done so because they are Hispanic.[15]
>
> In contrast with African Americans and women, the argument based on reparation does not seem to work for Hispanics for three reasons: (1) not all, or even most, Hispanics have suffered discrimination, (2) the degree of discrimination and abuse some have suffered never reached the levels suffered by African Americans or women, and (3) it is difficult to prove that the reason some Hispanics have suffered discrimination and abuse in the United States is because they are Hispanics. Hispanics have not been subjected to the kind of abuse to which African Americans and women have been subjected. Hispanics have never been slaves; we were not brought into this country against our will to work for others and be subservient to their whims; we were not deprived of our culture, language, religion, freedom, basic human rights, education, or dignity; and, unlike women, we have not, as a whole, played a secondary role in American society. Under these circumstances, reparation does not seem justified. There is nothing, or not much, that must be given back to Hispanics as a group because it was taken away from us. And there is no harm done to us as a group that cries out for repair.[16]

Is affirmative action justified for reasons of reparative justice? If so, is such affirmative action to Latinos justified? It is helpful to clarify the nature of reparation, especially in light of Gracia's implication that affirmative action can be a kind of reparation.

However, whether or not affirmative action is justified for Latinos for backward-looking reasons, it is a category mistake to construe affirmative action as a means of reparation.[17] For as indicated by the definitions of "reparations" and "affirmative action" (in *Black's Law Dictionary*), reparation is a matter of a group's being compensated for harms experienced unjustly, and reparation is *un*earned. However, affirmative action programs typically involve hiring or promoting someone to perform a task or fill a position for which she will perform and *earn* compensation. Furthermore, affirmative action, unlike reparation, need not be grounded in backward-looking reasons. Thus it is misleading to construe affirmative action programs as forms of reparation.

Nonetheless, even though affirmative action is not in fact a legitimate mode of reparation, it might be seen as being justified for other reasons, for example, as a means of achieving distributive justice.[18] The basic idea here is that Latinos should be beneficiaries of affirmative action programs because this would allow Latinos a more equal opportunity in education and employment. Such affirmative action is based not on backward-looking reparative considerations, but rather on present realities of anti-Latino racism and the significant inequalities they produce in U.S. society.

Gracia's statement of the various reasons in favor of affirmative action is rather insightful. However, one might take issue with him on the issue of whether or not Latinos are, on average and as a class, deserving of affirmative action and on what grounds.

Gracia implies that Latinos do *not* deserve reparations in the form of affirmative action because "not all, or even most, Hispanics have suffered discrimination." Of course, this is an empirical claim, and it is crucial that it enjoy sufficient support by way of empirical evidence if we are to accept it as being true. Surely the majority of us Latinos (as well as numerous others) believe that we as a people, or cluster of peoples, have experienced and continue to experience significant ethnic discrimination here in the United States. Perhaps this serves as prima facie evidence of anti-Latino discrimination. If so, then we need reasons why most of us are indeed *not* discriminated against in order to defeat the considered judgments of those millions of us who believe that we *are* in some significant measure treated poorly. Nonetheless, this prima facie evidence of in-group members' widespread perception of anti-Latino racism in the United States is insufficient to defeat the claim that Latinos as a whole have been and are discriminated against so as to warrant their being recipients of affirmative action programs based on reparative justice considerations.

But if the experimental social psychology of racism is reasonably accurate, then racism is much more widespread than most folks think it is. Indeed, ethnic prejudice is virtually universal in scope, and discrimination is much more universal in practice than most understand it to be. There is a variety of kinds of and motivations for racism, and racism need not be limited to specific ethnic groups. Moreover, a target of racism need not know or believe she is a victim of racism in order to be its victim.[19] The nature and functions of racism make it inductively plausible to believe that most, if not all, Latinos *have* suffered some significant form of ethnic discrimination in the United States, whether or not they are conscious of the discrimination.

Gracia argues that it is "very difficult to demonstrate" that most of us Latinos are discriminated against because we are Latinos. In reply to this point, it might be argued that whether or not Latinos deserve either affirmative action or reparation is not contingent on the difficulty of proving that they have been discriminated against because they are Latinos. Rather, it is contingent on nothing other than whether they have in fact been discriminated against because they are Latinos. For they can indeed deserve what a court of law finds itself unable to award in damages, given certain rules of evidence and due process. Yet this would hardly demonstrate that Latinos do not *deserve* such settlements.

But even if it is a condition of Latinos deserving affirmative action or reparations that it be shown that Latinos are discriminated against because they are Latinos, then, it might be argued, this criterion might count against *any* ethnic group's receiving affirmative action benefits. It is often, if not always, just as difficult (especially in a court of law) to show that, for example, African Americans are discriminated against *because* they are African Americans. Yet would we deny that at least most African Americans deserve affirmative action benefits, whether on grounds of distributive justice or otherwise?

Nonetheless, the history of Latinos in the United States is transparent on the matter of anti-Latino discrimination, whether it concerns the discriminatory practices against us in the U.S. military, the social relations that led to the zoot suit riots in East Los Angeles, current and long-standing negative attitudes of Anglos toward us, or any of numerous other examples. Whether in the form of ethnocentrically based anti-Latino cultural imperialism, institutional racism, or noninstitutional racism, evidence that we are discriminated against because we have been and are Latinos is plain. Anti-Latino racism is in principle no more difficult to demonstrate than it is to show that certain other ethnic groups have been discriminated against because of what they are, ethnically speaking. And this fact holds despite the unforgivable levels and kinds of harms committed against Native Americans and African Americans by the U.S. government and many of its citizens, making racism against these groups even more easily identifiable than anti-Latino racism.[20] Thus not only have a majority of Latinos been discriminated against, they have been discriminated against *because* they are Latinos. Throughout the history of the United States, anti-Latino attitudes have often given rise to anti-Latino discrimination based on such attitudes.

Furthermore, simply because Latinos have not been enslaved in U.S. society and have not been treated as harshly as Native Americans and African Americans in no way means that Latinos are not deserving of reparation, or even of affirmative action for backward-looking reasons. For there are degrees of racist harm inflicted on us Latinos, and corresponding degrees of reparation and affirmative action that might be awarded by a court and/or legislative policy. For instance, while a court might award, upon due consideration of the facts of each case, Native Americans and African Americans rather substantial amounts of reparation and forms of affirmative action for, say, considerations of distributive justice, it might award Latinos less substantial amounts of reparation for reasons of corrective justice and lesser forms of affirmative action for reasons of distributive justice.[21] Latinos most certainly *have* been treated unjustly in U.S. society when it comes to basic human rights, including educational rights and rights to human dignity.[22]

Even if it is true that Latinos have been and are discriminated against because we are Latinos, is it true that "the degree of discrimination and abuse some have suffered never reached the levels suffered by African Americans or women"? It is obvious that African Americans have suffered significantly more than Latinos. But is it true that anti-Latino discrimination has never reached the levels of discrimination against women?

Gracia intimates that Latinos (presumably on average and as a group) have not been treated as poorly as women (on average and as a group) in the United States. In reply to this position, it might be argued that although women (and men) of color[23] have been treated rather poorly in the United States, even by Anglas such as Susan B. Anthony and Louisa May Alcott,[24] it is dubious to claim or imply that Anglas were, on average and as a group, treated more poorly than Latinos. Whatever role Anglas have played in U.S. society, Latinos have played an even *more* secondary role. In fact, Anglas in the United States were, and remain, among our more ardent oppressors, for many such women (as a class) were, and remain, members of a ruling class of Anglos that serves as an incessant source of racism.[25] It seems naive to think that such racism among Anglos would not extend in significant measure to us Latinos. Basic everyday practices confirm this point. It is true that many women are raped and abused by men. But then again, so are many Latinas. It is true that many women do not receive a fair wage for their labor, but this is even truer of Latinos (especially Latinas) as a group. It is true that in general women are disrespected in U.S. society, though in some ways they are placed on pedestals when it comes to standards of physical beauty. But the dominant society has never thought that brown is beautiful, unless, of course, the brown person in question has various Angla physical features that make her "acceptable" to Anglo eyes. Although Anglas suffer from psychological issues regarding their physical selves, this is typically based on the shape of their bodies. But Latinas suffer even more, for they suffer not only from being judged according to the shape of their bodies, but also from perceptions of themselves and others regarding the *color* of their bodies. This is a kind and degree of discrimination that Anglas have not experienced in U.S. society. In fact, this latter kind of suffering is experienced by Latino males as well. It goes without saying that perception of skin color is one way in which we as cognizers tend to categorize one another, sometimes for racist purposes. Anglas hardly suffered from racism to the extent that we Latinos did. To suggest otherwise would do violence to a reading of U.S. history.

Moreover, for the most part Anglas participated in a system of racial segregation in the United States that prohibited Latinos from living in "whites-only" neighborhoods, thereby effecting school segregation, which in turn meant that Latino children were not accorded an equal opportunity in education. In light of this, the claim that the discrimination and abuse *some* Latinos have suffered never reached the levels experienced by women becomes a profoundly surprising assertion. For if the right to vote in a relatively democratic society counts as a significant possession, we must bear in mind that women were guaranteed the right to vote by the Nineteenth Amendment to the U.S. Constitution (1920). Yet it was almost half a century later that Latinos and other people of color in the United States were actually permitted to vote, subsequent to generations of harshly imposed segregation laws and practices throughout the land. Thus Anglas enjoyed a significant democratic right to vote much earlier than did Latinos. Anglas could in principle and often in reality attend any school they could afford to attend far sooner than Latinos could, whereas segregation and racist mores kept Latinos out of Anglo schools until (even) *after* the passage of the Civil Rights Act. The fact that relatively few Anglas stood up for Latino rights is significant evidence that Anglas as a whole were content, like the rather bad Samaritans they were, to sit alongside their Anglo counterparts in some of the higher seats of power that effected anti-Latino discrimination. So not only is it false to claim that the degree of discrimination and abuse some of us Latinos have suffered never reached the levels suffered by women, but Anglas themselves were perpetrators of much of the anti-Latino racism.

Thus the argument for Hispanic affirmative action based on reparative justice is significantly stronger than some would admit. Anti-Latino racism in the United States was and is sufficiently significant and harmful to Latinos that backward-looking reasons would ground claims to affirmative action for Latinos based on (not only distributive justice, but) corrective justice.[26]

Thus it would seem that not only are Latinos deserving of reparations due to harms that they have experienced in U.S. society (due to backward-looking reasons), but Latinos are perhaps even justified in remaining beneficiaries of affirmative action programs due to, perhaps, considerations of *distributive* justice.

Summary and Conclusion

After having set forth some desiderata of a theory of Latino identity, I proffered some of the defining features of Latinohood. Following this, I discussed the moral status of affirmative action programs for Latinos residing in the United States. Not only do we have a workable notion of Latinohood for purposes of public policy, but there is good reason to think that Latinos deserve affirmative action based on considerations of *distributive* justice. Aside from this, Latinos might well deserve some form of compensatory reparations based on historic anti-Latino racism in the United States.[27]

Notes

1. Some important philosophical discussions of affirmative action include William T. Blackstone and Robert D. Heslep, eds., *Social Justice and Preferential Treatment* (Athens: University of Georgia Press, 1977); Bernard Boxill, *Blacks and Social Justice* (Totowa: Rowman & Littlefield, 1984); Marshall Cohen, Thomas Nagel, and Thomas Scanlan, eds., , *Equality and Preferential Treatment* (Princeton: Princeton University Press, 1977); Robert K. Fullinwider, *The Reverse Discrimination Controversy* (Totowa: Rowman & Littlefield, 1980); Alan H. Goldman, *Justice and Reverse Discrimination* (Princeton: Princeton University Press, 1979); Kent Greenawalt, *Discrimination and Reverse Discrimination* (New York: Alfred A. Knopf, 1983); Barry R. Gross, ed., *Reverse Discrimination* (Buffalo: Prometheus Books, 1977); Thomas E. Hill Jr., "The Message of Affirmative Action," *Social Philosophy and Policy* 8 (1991): 108–29; Thomas Nagel, "Equal Treatment and Compensatory Discrimination," *Philosophy and Public Affairs* 2 (1973): 348–63; Richard Wasserstrom, "Preferential Treatment," in Richard Wasserstrom, ed., *Philosophy and Social Issues* (Notre Dame: University of Notre Dame Press, 1980).
2. Throughout this paper, I use "Latino" and its cognates synonymously with "Hispanic" and its cognates. I also use these terms gender-inclusively.
3. This connection is recognized in Richard Delgado and Vicky Palacios, "Mexican Americans as a Legally Cognizable Class," in Richard Delgado and Jean Stefancic, eds., *The Latino/a Condition: A Critical Reader* (New York: New York University Press, 1998), 284–90, where it is deemed important for legal and public policy purposes to legally define "Mexican American" and "Chicano."
4. In "Affirmative Action for Hispanics? Yes and No," in this volume. Gracia's view of "Hispanic identity" is more fully articulated in his book *Hispanic/Latino Identity: A Philosophical Perspective* (Oxford: Blackwell, 2000).
5. This point is made independently in J. Angelo Corlett, "Latino Identity," *Public Affairs Quarterly* 13 (1999), 273–95.
6. In Gracia, "Affirmative Action for Hispanics? Yes and No."
7. Such antiessentialist arguments are found in Gracia, *Hispanic/Latino Identity.*
8. The significance of Latino culture for Latino identity is emphasized in Delgado and Palacios, "Mexican Americans," 286.
9. This analysis of Latino identity is set forth and defended in Corlett, "Latino Identity." Similar conditions of Latino identity are recognized in Delgado and Palacios, "Mexican Americans," 284.
10. This point is echoed in Delgado and Palacios, "Mexican Americans," 285.

11. Thus a child of Italian immigrants to, say, Brazil who is being brought up as a Brazilian would be a "cultural Latino" (perhaps even a Latino in a linguistic sense). However, for purposes of public policy administration, this sense of being a Latino is insufficient for her to qualify as a Latino.
12. See Corlett, "Latino Identity."
13. Assumed here is the plausibility of the notion of collective rights, as articulated and defended in J. Angelo Corlett, "The Problem of Collective Moral Rights," *Canadian Journal of Law and Jurisprudence* 7 (1994): 237–59.
14. For a more complete articulation and defense of the moderate conception of Latino identity, see Corlett, "Latino Identity."
15. Gracia, "Affirmative Action for Hispanics? Yes and No," 201 in this volume.
16. Gracia, "Affirmative Action for Hispanics? Yes and No," 201 in this volume.
17. J. Angelo Corlett, "Reparations to Native Americans?" in Aleksandar Jokic, ed., *War Crimes and Collective Wrongdoing* (London: Blackwell, forthcoming).
18. Gracia makes room for this reason for affirmative action. Other philosophers have sought to ground affirmative action in matters of distributive justice. See, e.g., Nagel, "Equal Treatment and Compensatory Discrimination."
19. See J. Angelo Corlett, "Analyzing Racism," *Public Affairs Quarterly* 12 (1998): 23–50.
20. For a philosophical discussion of racist harms against Native Americans and African Americans, see J. Angelo Corlett, "Surviving Evil: Jewish, African and Native Americans," *Journal of Social Philosophy* 31 (2000).
21. For a philosophical discussion of this problem, see Corlett, "Reparations to Native Americans?"
22. Rudolf Acuna, *Occupied America*, 3rd ed. (New York: HarperCollins, 1988); T. Almaguer, "Historical Notes on Chicano Oppression," *Aztlan*, 1974; James Diego Vigil, *From Indians to Chicanos* (Prospect Heights: Waveland Press, 1980), 173–84.
23. Mary Romero, *Maid in the U.S.A.* (London: Routledge, 1992).
24. Angela Y. Davis, *Women, Race, and Class* (New York: Random House, 1981), chs. 3, 4, 7, 9.
25. bell hooks, *Ain't I a Woman: Black Women in Feminism* (Boston: South End Press, 1981); *Talking Back: Thinking Feminist, Thinking Black* (Boston: South End Press, 1989); *Yearning: Race, Gender, and Cultural Politics* (Boston: South End Press, 1990).
26. For an analysis of the concept of racism, see Corlett, "Analyzing Racism."
27. A version of this paper was presented at the conference "Ethnic Identity, Culture, and Group Rights," State University of New York at Buffalo, October 3, 1998, organized by Jorge J. E. Gracia and Pablo De Greiff. I am grateful to those at the conference for incisive discussion of these issues.

Deliberation and Hispanic Representation 12

Pablo De Greiff

The changing demographic composition of most contemporary societies provides a powerful incentive to examine questions associated with the political representation of the diverse groups that constitute ever more plural nation-states. These groups, whose political representation different societies may want to guarantee, need not be minority groups.[1] They are groups that have suffered forms of marginalization. In the United States, however, most discussions about political representation refer to the representation of minority groups. This chapter concentrates on this issue, with special attention to the political representation of Hispanics.

Among political philosophers, deliberative conceptions of democracy are receiving significant attention. Here I will examine whether deliberative conceptions of democracy offer a grounding for a defense of guaranteed group representation. Some theorists of minority representation have found these conceptions useful in justifying such guarantees, but there is no agreement concerning the relationship between deliberative democracy and minority representation. For some, a conception of democratic politics that emphasizes deliberation is inimical to group representation.[2] Others, such as Iris M. Young and Cass Sunstein, argue that deliberative democracy requires group representation.[3] In this paper I will concentrate my attention on Habermas's discourse-theoretic version of deliberative democracy. This is a version with whose basic premises Sunstein and Young, among others, are in sympathy. Habermas, who has arguably articulated one of the most developed theories of deliberative democracy thus far, is almost entirely silent on the question of minority political representation,[4] and some have taken this silence as a result not simply of oversight but of an intrinsic tension between group representation and deliberation.[5] Surprisingly, there is as yet no full discussion of this issue in relation to his work. This paper is intended to fill that gap.

The problem of minority underrepresentation, which guarantees of political representation seek to solve, can be described as follows: although liberal democracy has, at least of late, committed itself to the idea of an equal right to vote—a commitment that might be justified in various ways, for example, by appealing to the ideals of autonomy, justice, rationality, stability, and so forth—members of minority groups might be locked into a position in which their numerical disadvantage means that they have at best a slim chance of electing representatives of their choice. Their status as minorities leads to the dilution of their votes. This is particularly true in places such as the United States, where there is a strong tendency toward and a long history of racial bloc voting, and where almost without exception, elections take place in single-member districts and are of the winner-take-all kind.[6]

From the standpoint of one of the traditional ways of understanding liberal democracy, namely, as a procedure of preference aggregation (with some side constraints), there is no clear way of making sense of this problem. If with interest-group or pluralist or market-driven liberalism we think of legitimacy as a function of majority decisions, it seems that as long as the opportunity to vote is guaranteed, marginalized groups do not have a valid claim against the results of democratic elections, even if they are permanently locked out of representative positions. This is the problem that different policies promoting group representation seek to address. (There are, of course, different ways of guaranteeing representation. These include proportional representation schemes which save legislative seats for members of specific groups, or special districting arrangements and so on, but neither their specific shape nor their effectiveness will be the focus of my attention. In the realm of political practice, the United States has favored redistricting measures in order to save some positions for minority candidates. European and Latin American countries have, by contrast, experimented with different systems of proportional representation.)[7]

Some democrats have argued that within the very framework of democratic theory resources can be found not merely to make sense of the problem of minority underrepresentation, but also to address it. Prominent among the critics of the interest-group understanding of liberalism are deliberative democrats. In a nutshell, the contrast between aggregative liberalism and deliberative democracy lies in the latter's idea that the legitimacy of law depends not merely on whether a law has accurately represented a given balance of interests, but rather on the rational acceptability of a law to *all* who are affected by it, where the rational acceptability can be established only under conditions of free and open deliberation.

Deliberative democracy, then, takes persuasion and participation to be at the core of politics. Whereas aggregative liberalism sees politics as a mechanism of compromise formation among parties whose interests conflict, deliberative democrats see politics as a means of rational conflict resolution. Politics is understood differently both in terms of procedure and aim. Aggregative liberalism sees politics in terms of bargaining, deliberative democracy in terms of argumentation. The former sees the end of politics in terms of equilibrium among competing forces, the latter in terms of mutual agreement.[8] Each position focuses on a different moment of the political process: whereas aggregative liberalism focuses on the electoral mechanism as the critical moment and understands it mainly as an ex post facto check on power, deliberative democracy focuses on the longer term processes of political opinion and will formation, and in the exchanges between formal parliamentary arenas and the informal public sphere. This of course, leads to very different ideas concerning participation: whereas aggregative liberalism thinks of participation in weak terms, both because participation is important infrequently at best (i.e., during elections), and for limited purposes (i.e., in order to assert interests), deliberative democracy defends a more robust notion of participation, one that requires a high level of engagement, and whose purposes are ultimately to make the exercise of power rational.[9]

How useful is this understanding of democracy for justifying group representation? Discourse theory offers an attractive starting point for arguments in defense of minority representation, not just because of its insistence on the importance of participation, but primarily because of its insistence on conditions of openness and symmetry. I would like to argue, however, that discourse theory supports only a certain range of arguments in defense of group representation, and that while it supports mechanisms of group representation intended as corrections to distorted communication, it does not support such measures simply for the sake of increasing diversity. While this limitation seems to me to be legitimate and at the same time to leave sufficient room to address most of the urgent political problems indicated by the supporters of minority representation, it might be a disappointment to those who have a more ambitious reformist political agenda. Of course, these remarks do not address the desirability or defensibility of that broader agenda—other than to say that this more ambitious plan needs to go beyond discourse theory for support.

The argument that I want to examine is the following: given that for a deliberative democrat the legitimacy of the law is a function of its rational acceptability to all those who are affected by it, an interest in the legitimacy of the law justifies an interest in guaranteeing that the diverse social groups that are affected by legislation are adequately represented in it.[10] The transition between the premise's interest in individual representation and the conclusion's defense of group representation is usually mediated not only by the familiar sorts of considerations that move us generally from direct to representative democracy, but, more specifically, by arguments concerning the de facto relevance of group labels. I will return to these intermediary steps later in the paper.

The grounds of this defense of group representation are the same as those that in the sphere of morality led to the distinctive discourse theoretical insistence on the importance of participation. The mark of discourse ethics is not merely its adoption of a test of universalizability or generalizability which makes the validity of norms dependent on their rational acceptability, but, specifically, its insistence on a dialogical application of any such test.[11] It is important to recognize why this insistence is justified. Part, but only part, of the rationale is epistemic. For a broad range of matters discourse ethics endorses the view that each person has a defeasible epistemic privilege concerning what is good for him or her.[12] While it is crucial to keep firmly in mind the defeasibility of this privilege whatever doubts one may have about this position, that it contains a kernel of truth is particularly clear when given a negative formulation; its basic insight is that others are in an even worse position than each of us is to know what is best for us—again, as individuals.

The same considerations apply in the domain of politics. It seems true, generally speaking, that allowing those who are affected by a norm to participate in the discussions in which its validity is determined might increase the possibility that the decision will be reached on the basis of accurate and relevant information. Since discourse theory places great stock in the difference between rational consensus and de facto agreement, and hence reaffirms the importance of conditions of discursive symmetry and openness, the epistemic rationale for participation appears particularly compelling: it seems reasonable to think that as long as people are allowed to express their own positions freely, and assuming that everyone is sufficiently reflexive to open up his or her claims to discursive examination, the norms that are agreed to under such circumstances would be norms that are reasonably in the interest of all. Here again, the point is particularly persuasive in its negative formulation: if the only way of securing support for a norm is by excluding from consideration some of those affected by it, then we have reason to question the legitimacy of such a norm.[13]

Long before Habermas worked out his discourse theory of democracy and law in *Between Facts and Norms*, Young had already extended discourse ethics into the realm of politics in just this way. Putting in a new context the argument about the importance of real dialogue allowed Young and others to construct a persuasive argument in favor of minority representation. It is only in retrospect that the argument seems of obvious significance, just as it is only in retrospect that the principle of dialogue is obviously preferable to the categorical imperative. In any case, the communicative argument in favor of minority representation, then, is that given that legitimacy is a function of discursive acceptability, it is crucial for the legitimacy of law to guarantee that all those who are affected by the law participate in its formulation. So, Habermas's argument that the best way to know whether a norm is universalizable is to secure its universalizability in a free and open dialogue becomes the basis of an argument to defend the possibility of having the views of one's social group represented in the political sphere.

However, the critic will claim, correctly, that a certain distance separates the abstract account of what makes a norm valid from the much more concrete argument about group representation. This might be counted as the first hurdle that any attempt to use discourse theory as a premise for group representation might have to overcome. The issue is a very general one. It has to do with the possibility of deriving concrete political obligations—such as one in favor of guaranteed political representation—from broad moral principles. Even if one is willing to accept the general account of moral validity embodied in discourse ethics, I have the suspicion that we might be making life too easy for ourselves by thinking that this account, on its own, provides sufficient support for mechanisms of guaranteed representation. Habermas, for one, warns against the direct application of the discourse principle to politics, and has urged us to avoid the sort of naïveté that, according to him, plagues normative political philosophy when it ignores the institutional complexity of modern societies.[14] To share the discourse-theoretical conviction that the validity of norms of action depends upon their acceptability to *all* who are affected by those norms still leaves open the question of how we should think about this *all* in the context of a modern, complex democracy. A commitment to a discursive account of validity is obviously a promising starting point for an argument in favor of minority participation in politics, but this commitment clearly underdetermines questions of concrete institutional setup. In a complex society participation in politics will always require some sort of mediation, and the mediation might break the smooth inference between the account of validity and the defense of group representation. After all, the discourse-theoretic premises of the argument were articulated with individuals rather than groups in mind. Once again, some intermediary steps would have to be taken in order to go from the original support for individual participation to the desired goal of justifying group representation. These steps, needless to say, are the crucial ones for this discussion.

Habermas's own writings constitute a telling example of how the commitment to a discursive account of legitimacy underdetermines the question of minority politics. In his latest works, he reiterates the importance of the representativeness of members of legislative assemblies, and of the need to involve all those whose interests will be affected in the articulation and implementation of programs.[15] Moreover, the whole thrust of his position points in the direction of greater overall citizen involvement: according to his discourse theory of rights, there is an internal relationship between liberalism and democracy such that the only way of securing even basic liberal rights is by exercising democratic, political rights (and the only way of exercising political rights is under the protection of liberal, "subjective" rights).[16] The account of politics that supplements this theory of rights similarly emphasizes the importance of widespread participation and intense engagement with political issues in the public sphere. Nevertheless, this (two-track) account of politics is more concerned with fleshing out the conditions of discursive acceptability in terms of the openness of the specialized discussions in legislative chambers to the more chaotic, informal, and inclusive discussions in the public sphere than with specifying mechanisms for redressing imbalances within legislative assemblies. Habermas's general point is that the sort of deliberation on which the legitimacy of law rests goes beyond parliamentary deliberation, and includes concern for the quality of the debates that take place in the periphery of state institutions, and for the porosity of the latter to the influences of the former.[17]

In response, one can of course grant that Habermas's reservations about the traditional focus of political theory on state actors are well grounded. But, conceding that the state is just one among many social actors does not force us to concede that the significance of the state is just that of any other actor. To recognize the continued special significance of the state—and therefore of minority representation in its institutions—need not amount to objectionable state-centric political theorizing. Similarly, it is possible to grant that to democratize and increase the openness and accessibility of the public sphere—which in turn would require facilitating access to the means of gathering and distributing news and to the instruments of cultural production such as the entertainment and publishing industries—would have far-reaching consequences in terms of the legitimacy of our laws, in comparison to which legislative diversity pales. Clearly, neither Habermas nor the critic should take this as an either/or choice. Most likely, there will be interesting relationships between the projects of increasing diversity in legislatures and that of democratizing the public sphere despite the disparity of their magnitude.

But let me go back to the communicative argument in favor of minority representation in order to examine in some detail what it is in the argument that does the brunt of the work, and to ask then how far the position can be extended. While I think that it is possible to construct on the basis of discourse theory an important argument in favor of guaranteed representation as a form of prevention of and redress for discrimination, I do not think that it is possible to construct on the same basis an argument for representation as a mechanism to foster diversity. Ultimately, I will argue that these are two different political aims, and that it is important to keep them apart. There are, of course, other reasons why one might be interested in minority representation beyond the two that I examine in this paper, namely, the prevention and redress of discrimination, on the one hand, and fostering diversity, on the other. Charles Beitz provides a more complete catalog of reasons in his *Political Equality*, and Thomas Pogge has recently offered a challenging defense of group representation on the basis of fuller political participation. I cannot examine all possible arguments for minority representation here. The two rationales on which this paper concentrates are the primary ones in recent debates, and the analysis that follows covers the cases that on Pogge's own criteria are most pressing, namely, the representation of those groups—ethnic or not—that have been systematically excluded.[18]

One way of putting the argument in favor of securing minority representation is that this is a way to guarantee a voice or some degree of power to those who would be excluded otherwise.[19] In a society torn by racism, sexism, classism, and other forms of discrimination, unless we provide this guarantee, we can be sure that some groups will be systematically excluded. There is nothing distinctly discourse-theoretic about this (absolutely defensible) argument. Still, discourse theory explains why it would be so important to extend the guarantees in question: to the extent that we aspire to live under legitimate laws, we must ensure that all those who are affected by the laws have a say in their articulation. But this formulation is still too general, and hence will not be particularly helpful in answering the difficult questions that are bound to arise in real political discussion. In particular, this formulation of the argument will not help determine which groups ought to have their presence guaranteed in legislative assemblies.

Minority representation can be and is often defended in terms of the contribution that we (minorities) make to political deliberation. In other words, and to be very positive, one might say that the defense hinges on a certain epistemic advantage that minorities enjoy, which explains why it is so important to include us. But there are two accounts of this epistemic advantage, and from my perspective only the first one is defensible. The first version of the argument is that it is crucial to secure the participation of minorities, for our representatives will be able to reveal aspects of institutional life in our country that the majority would otherwise ignore. That is to say, the argument is that it is important to guarantee minority representation in politics, even if this requires setting aside legislative seats for purposes of proportional representation, because minority representatives will contribute to political discussion the characteristic experiences of those whose identities are recognized only as a result of a struggle. The contribution that we make consists of reminders of the many ways in which the majority might mistakenly think that its norms are fair. Here one can say that minorities have a special perspective and a distinct experience, and that our inclusion guarantees to everyone, not just to us, the benefits of this perspective. We can reveal the underbelly of the beast, as it were: the large and small indignities suffered by those who have been excluded, the costs of being minorities, costs that are reflected in all sorts of quality-of-life indicators such as housing, education, income, mortality, and so on.[20] Two important points are being made: first, that guaranteed representation is necessary in order to unblock the participation of groups who would otherwise remain on the fringes of the political system, and second, that their inclusion will make a difference, for their representatives bring to the table an instructive perspective on the costs of institutional life. Young, for example, makes both points in her argument for minority group representation. She argues that group representation is justified under conditions of oppression, for, first, in an oppressive society, it is only this mechanism that allows minorities to gain representation: "group representation provides the opportunity for some to express their needs or interests who would not likely be heard without that representation." Second, once representation has been achieved, it will then work because it "exposes in public the specificity of the assumptions and the experience of the privileged. For unless confronted with different perspectives on social relations and events, different values and language, most people tend to assert their own perspective as universal." Or, in an even more concise formulation, "group representation is the best antidote to self-deceiving self-interest masked as an impartial or general interest."[21] Although the second claim, that being confronted with difference leads to important realizations, depends on the self-reflectivity of the parties and to that extent is heavily contextual, both points are defensible.

Having in the background the success of this claim to an important epistemic contribution, one might want to generalize it. This is the beginning of the second account of the epistemic advantage that, some argue, justifies guaranteeing minority group participation in politics. The claim would now be not that it is important to secure the political participation of minorities who are discriminated against, for otherwise everybody would be deprived of the benefit of our distinct and uncontroversially relevant contribution—namely, our experience of the way our legal system (mal)dis tributes benefits and burdens—but that it is important to guarantee the representation of minorities in general, because again, in general, we might have a distinct contribution to make, *not on account of our experience of the unequal distribution of benefits and burdens that our institutions establish and engender, but on account of the fact that we as minorities have, broadly speaking, a different perspective.*[22] In this version of the argument, what justifies mechanisms of minority representation is not our experiences of the structural constraints often faced by minorities, that is, what I will call our political difference, but all those features that go into defining our group identity, namely, our cultural difference. The argument involves, then, a judgment about the *cultural* distinctness of minority groups as a rationale for their *political* inclusion, and it claims that the participation of minorities must be secured because we can contribute something of value to political discussions *on account of our different cultural perspective.*

It is easy to run these two versions of the argument together, for both hinge on an appeal to an epistemic privilege which minorities are said to have, that allows them to make a distinct contribution to political deliberation. But the arguments are quite different. One focuses on the epistemic privileges that results from having had certain experiences related to occupying or having occupied a certain social position in an institutional setup whose continued existence requires deliberate choices; the other focuses on a very different epistemic privilege, and hence, also on a very different set of contributions that can be made as a result of factors that are more difficult to specify, and that go beyond the experiences just mentioned. Iris Young seems to me to be fundamentally correct when she writes that

> group representation unravels the false consensus that cultural imperialism may have produced, and reveals group bias in norms, standards, styles, and perspectives that have been assumed as universal or of highest value. By giving voice to formerly silenced or devalued needs and experiences, group representation forces participants in discussion to take a reflective distance on their assumptions and think beyond their own interests. When confronted with interests, needs, and opinions that derive from very different social positions and experience, persons sometimes come to understand the limitations of their own experience and perspective for reaching a conclusion about the best policy for everyone.[23]

But we inch toward the second position already if we take this argument in its full generality as the relevant reason to establish group political rights. It seems patently true that different social groups have different experiences, and that those experiences affect the way people think about political issues.

It is also true, although this requires some optimism, that confronting difference, in general, fosters reflective detachment and a new understanding of the limitations of one's position. But surely neither point, by itself or jointly, is sufficient to establish group rights. Granted, one can say that a distinct contribution might otherwise be missed. But that is beside the point. From the standpoint of the discourse-theoretic premises of the argument, what carried justificatory force in this defense of securing some legislative positions for minorities was both that they would otherwise be excluded and that they had something important to reveal to us about the legal system under which we all live, and whose currency we choose to prolong.

Perhaps shifting angles here might help both to clarify further the distinction I am trying to draw between the two rationales for securing group representation and to explain why I think that discourse theory will not support the second one, which centers on diversity alone. Although a discursive theoretic account of legal legitimacy need not be procedural in the sense of eschewing all appeal to moral values,[24] this account offers no room for securing anyone's participation on the basis of the substance of what participants might say in deliberation. That would require establishing some sort of criterion to select significant contributions that deserve special protection, where discourse theory "merely" wants deliberation to be free and open. On what grounds could we then make efforts to secure the presence of some people? Surely not on the assumption that they will make a specific type of contribution, that is, a "culturally distinct" one. This would amount to a dubious argument in favor of something like "political folklorism." The only available discourse-theoretic grounds for securing the representation of certain classes of people is that unless we do so, they will be structurally barred from entering the conversation, and that what would be thereby excluded is relevant knowledge about the costs of living under a system of law we are collectively responsible for maintaining.

Some clarifications (and even some reiterations) are appropriate here. First, and (I hope) needless to say, I have no interest in disputing the distinctness of the experience of different ethnic, cultural, national, or social groups. I am querying whether this distinctness alone should be taken as a sufficient reason for securing political representation. Nor is my position based on a negative evaluation of the significance of the contribution that could be made about our institutional life from a different cultural perspective. My argument hinges in part on the difficulties that would be involved in making judgments about sufficient cultural distinctness *for purposes of deciding which groups should have their representation in legislatures guaranteed through the saving of seats implied by different mechanisms of proportional representation.* A proceduralist understanding of democracy simply offers no instruments with which to make substantive judgments of this sort.

Perhaps I should be even more specific on this point. In thinking about the case for Hispanic political representation from the perspective of the diversity defense, I would have the following general concern: I would not like the case for increased Hispanic representation in politics to hinge on whether we can make a sufficiently distinct contribution to politics on account of our cultural difference. My worry in this case goes beyond, but also includes, familiar concerns about essentialism: who gets to say what the authentic Hispanic contribution might be and how we should account for shifts in the composition of the group and in its interests—including the trend toward the apparent indistinctness of our political preferences—are questions whose significance has received recognition lately, but which still give rise to many puzzles. In any case, proceduralists should mistrust judgments of cultural distinctness. My position is that a history of social discrimination and political marginalization provides the only sort of epistemic advantage that counts for the specific purpose at hand, namely, a knowledge of the nooks and crannies of our political system that is endogenous to its structural framework, and whose relevance therefore cannot be denied. Not only is this sort of privileged perspective undeniably relevant (having as its object our very own social structure) and to some extent assessable (definite social indicators can be used as proxies to determine whose views have been traditionally and are likely to be marginalized) but also, given that the perspective is internally related to an institutional structure that is willfully maintained, it is connected with a claim for redress. None of these things can be said of the differences that arise from cultural diversity alone.

In a final reiteration before moving on, my point thus far is not that a political system that takes diversity as a sufficient rationale for extending guarantees of representation is indefensible. Rather, my point is a more modest one: it is not clear that such a system could be grounded on a (Habermasian) conception of deliberative democracy alone. A further argument would be required, but that is rarely offered.

Some critics may still want a broader defense of guaranteed political representation than the one just offered. Although the following argument will not go as far as some of them might want, I hope it will assuage at least some of their discontent.

In my construction of the discourse-theoretic argument above, I said that part of the reason for its insistence on dialogicity was epistemic, namely, the premise that in general, the best way to guarantee that people's perspectives are represented is to allow them to represent those perspectives themselves. But this cannot be the whole reason in favor of dialogicity; the correct representation of one's views is not the only value served by participation.

If it were, the argument in favor of participation would be undermined by recalling the opacity of our own impressions of what is best for us, especially concerning long-term interests and issues that require complex coordination with others.[25] The other part of the discourse-theoretic defense of participation is more explicitly normative in spirit, and it corresponds to the conception of human worth of modernity, still revealed in our context by Rawls's description of individuals as "self-originating sources of valid claims."[26] So the first, more epistemic part of the discourse-theoretic defense of participation captures the intuition that moral validity is not divorced from correctness (and that universalizability is the relevant standard of correctness here). The second and more normative part of the defense captures the intuition that in morality it matters not only that norms be correct (or valid), but also that they be our own. Similarly, in the domain of politics, at least of democratic politics, it matters a whole lot not only that we live under sound laws, that is, under laws that promote our interests, as each group sees those interests from its own perspective, but also that we live under laws we can consider ourselves to have authored.

As a matter of fact, regardless of how we theorize about this issue, this is a society in which group membership is politically relevant. The relevance of such membership cannot be cashed in uniformly. In some cases membership is accompanied by privileges, in others by huge burdens. Nor is the nature of such groups of a kind. Some groupings are more arbitrary than others. Nevertheless, people act as if groups matter, and that alone makes them behaviorally relevant, as is well known particularly by those who suffer the burdens of inequitable social systems. The aim of democratic politics cannot be simply policies that reduce inequity in the distribution of benefits and burdens. Enlightened despotism, no matter how enlightened, will never succeed in passing as democracy. Democratic politics are committed to the ideal of the self-authorship of laws. In a context in which groups are politically relevant, this entails a commitment to the creation of conditions in which groups have good reasons to think that we are full members of society, and that the fullness of our membership is revealed as well in our shared participation in the making of our laws.

Since, as I said above, neither the groups, nor the costs of belonging or being ascribed to them are of a kind, there is no workable system of representation that could aspire to give presence to all the various groups into which populations are divided and divide themselves. I have argued here, on the basis of a discursive account of legitimacy, in favor of the continued relevance of experiences of marginalization—over considerations of diversity—as a criterion for guaranteeing political representation. To the extent that Hispanics/Latinos have arguably suffered marginalization, the argument would defend extending such guarantees to the group. Notice, however, that this criterion is situationally sensitive: it may be the case that our situation, at some point, will no longer be that of a group that carries undue social burdens. At that time, guarantees will no longer be justified. Until then, however, the best way of securing the legitimacy of the laws that all of us—Hispanics and not Hispanics—have to live by, is to make sure that we have a voice in the formulation of those laws.

Notes

Jorge Gracia, Thomas McCarthy, Thomas Pogge, and Iris Marion Young gave me useful suggestions for this paper. A conversation with Rodolfo de la Garza helped me clarify my general position. Walter Mignolo, Suzanne Oboler, and Peter Hare responded to a presentation of a short version of this draft. James Fishkin, David Braybrook, and Benjamin Gregg offered exciting suggestions after I presented a version of the paper at the Department of Government, University of Texas at Austin, in April 1999. My gratitude to all of them. An earlier version of this paper will appear in *Social Theory and Practice* 26 (2000).

1. So, for instance, different European countries try to secure the political representation of women. In South America, Colombia is debating a program that would save 30 percent of political appointments within a bureaucratic range, for women.
2. See for example, Cynthia V. Ward, "The Limits of 'Liberal Republicanism': Why Group-based Remedies and Republican Citizenship Don't Mix," *Columbia Law Review* 91 (1991): 581–607.
3. See Cass Sunstein, "Beyond the Republican Revival," *Yale Law Journal* 97 (1988): 1549–90, and "Democracy and Shifting Preferences," in A. Hamlin and Phillip Pettit, eds., *The Good Polity: Normative Analysis of the State* (Oxford: Polity Press, 1989), 196–230. Iris M. Young, "Polity and Group Difference: A Critique of the Ideal of Universal Citizenship," *Ethics* 99 (1989): 250–74, and "Justice and Communicative Democracy," in Roger Gottlieb, ed., *Radical Philosophy: Tradition, Counter-Tradition, Politics* (Philadelphia: Temple University Press, 1993), 123–43.
4. Jürgen Habermas, *Between Facts and Norms*, trans. W. Rehg (Cambridge, Mass.: MIT Press, 1993). The "almost" is due to the fact that he does not neglect the question of representation entirely. Habermas writes that "representation can only mean that the selection of members of parliament should provide for the broadest possible spectrum of interpretive perspectives, including the views and voices of marginal groups. . . . The political balancing of interests requires the election of delegates who are charged with the task of compromise formation; the mode of election must provide for fair representation and aggregation of the given interests and preferences. Achieving collective self-understanding and moral justification demands the election of competent participants in representative discourses (instead of spokespersons for group interests); the mode of election must ensure, via choice of personnel, that all relevant voices are included" (183). I return to Habermas's positions below.

5. This is Anne Phillips's position in *The Politics of Presence* (Oxford: Oxford University Press, 1996), 154–55.
6. See Lani Guinier, *The Tyranny of the Majority: Fundamental Fairness in Representative Democracy* (New York: Free Press, 1994).
7. See, for example, Giovanni Sartori, *Comparative Constitutional Engineering: An Inquiry into Structure, Incentives, and Outcomes* (New York: New York University Press, 1994).
8. Deliberative democracy needs, and expresses, a vision of the transformative effects of deliberation. Unlike interest-group democrats, deliberative democrats argue that preferences ought not to be taken as given, that they are subject to transformation, and that deliberation is one of the means to effect such transformation. Without this transformative possibility, it is not clear that deliberative democracy could overcome the stalemate that would almost certainly follow the mere expression of conflicting views without collapsing, under the pressure of the need to arrive at timely decisions, into another form of aggregative politics. See Sunstein, "Democracy and Shilling Preferences," and Robert Goodin, "Laundering Preferences," in *Foundations of Social Choice Theory*, ed. Jon Elster and Aanund Hylland, (Cambridge: Cambridge University Press, 1986), pp. 75–101. In his recent work James Fishkin provides empirical evidence of the transformative effects of deliberation. See *The Voice of the People. Public Opinion and Democracy* (New Haven: Yale University Press, 1995).
9. See Habermas, BFN chs. 7 and 8, and Amy Gutmann and Dennis Thompson, *Democracy and Disagreement* (Cambridge: Harvard University Press, 1996).
10. Young and Sunstein, among many others, can be said to endorse and articulate this sort of position. The discourse-theoretic understanding of legitimacy in terms of rational acceptability to all affected parties becomes particularly controversial if it is further accompanied by the requirement that all the parties converge on the *same* reasons. One can weaken this requirement, however, and discourse theory will still provide an attractive starting point for argument in favor of minority representation. Legitimacy will now be understood in terms of the assumption made by citizens that given the conditions of deliberation, democratic decisions "allow an ongoing cooperation with others of different minds that is at least not unreasonable." But what warrants this assumption is that the conditions of deliberation be such as to satisfy conditions that involve inclusiveness, for unless minority groups can reasonably expect that they will be able to influence future outcomes, they will have no reason to continue cooperating. Hence, this weaker version of the discourse account of legitimacy will serve the same justificatory purpose as its strong counterpart. The strong version of democratic legitimacy is defended by Habermas in *Between Facts and Norms*, for which he has been criticized even by sympathetic commentators. See Thomas McCarthy, "Practical Discourse: On the Relation of Morality to Politics," in *Ideals and Illusions: On Reconstruction and Deconstruction in Contemporary Critical Theory* (Cambridge, Mass.: MIT Press, 1991), 181–99; and Thomas McCarthy, "Legitimacy and Diversity: Dialectical Reflections on Analytic Distinctions," *Cardozo Law Review* 17 (1995): 1083–125; James Bohman, "Public Reason and Cultural Pluralism: Political Liberalism and the Problem of Moral Conflict," *Political Theory* 23 (1995): 253–79: James Bohman, *Public Deliberation: Pluralism, Complexity, and Democracy* (Cambridge, Mass.: MIT

Press, 1996); James Bohman and William Rehg, "Discourse and Democracy: The Formal and Informal Bases of Legitimacy in Habermas's *Faktizität und Geltung*," *Journal of Political Philosophy* 4 (1996): 79–99. For the sake of clarity I will continue to refer to Habermas's formulation of legitimacy. I had a useful discussion of this topic with Iris M. Young.

11. As is well known, Habermas criticizes Kant's monological application of the principle of validity. Habermas adopts McCarthy's formulation of the point: "Rather than ascribing as valid to all others any maxim that I can will to be a universal law, I must submit my maxim to all others for purposes of discursively testing its claim to universality. The emphasis shifts from what each can will without contradiction to be a general law, to what all can will in agreement to be a universal law."

    Of course, this merely expresses that participation is a better procedure than solitary reflection, without explaining why. The explanation offered is the following: "For one thing nothing better prevents others from perspectivally distorting one's own interests than actual participation. It is in this pragmatic sense that the individual is the last court of appeal for judging what is in his best interest." Habermas, "Discourse Ethics: Notes on a Program of Philosophical Justification," in *Moral Consciousness and Communicative Action*, Christian Lenhardt and Shierry Weber Nicholsen, trans., (Cambridge, Mass.: MIT Press, 1990), p. 67. The quotation from Thomas McCarthy is from his *The Critical Theory of Jürgen Habermas* (Cambridge: MIT Press, 1978), p. 326.
12. This view of the individual's epistemic privilege was famously advanced by J. S. Mill in *On Liberty* (Indianapolis: Hackett, 1978 [1860]).
13. I have deliberately framed the discourse-theoretic argument in favor of participation on the basis of an epistemic consideration, namely, the quality of information, rather than in terms of moral considerations such as fairness. One could construct a discourse-theoretic defense of group representation according to which fairness requires guaranteeing the representation of groups that have suffered discrimination, for this would help to make sure that laws are fair. This argument would not be unsound, but it is a shortcut. It begs the question concerning the connection between fairness and inclusion. My approach seeks to be faithful to the epistemic dimension of discourse theory, although, as will be clear later, discourse theory does not justify participation on epistemic grounds *alone*. Discussions with Tom McCarthy were useful on this point.
14. As Habermas puts it, "the logic of discourse must not be too quickly identified with constitutional procedures. An *unmediated* application of discourse ethics (or an unclarified concept of discourse) to the democratic process leads to muddled analyses; these then offer skeptics pretexts for discrediting the project of a discourse theory of law and politics at its inception." Habermas, *Between Facts and Norms*, 158. On the institutional näiveté of normative political philosophy, see ch. 1. Against the direct application of the discourse principle to politics, see chs. 3 and 4.
15. Ibid., ch. 9.
16. Ibid., chs. 3 and 4, and Jürgen Habermas, "On the Internal Relationship between Democracy and the Rule of Law," in *The Inclusion of the Other: Studies in Political Theory*, ed. Ciaran Cronin and Pablo De Greiff (Cambridge, Mass.: MIT Press, 1998), 253–64.

17. Habermas, *Between Facts and Norms*, chs. 7 and 8. No doubt the relative homogeneity of the German polity must have played a role in Habermas's lack of attention to the issue of minority representation. Now that *Gastarbeiter* are likely to be granted citizenship under the auspices of the new Social Democratic government, the issue will become more pressing. Habermas had already expressed support for minority set-asides in other domains, for example, labor. In a recent interview Habermas links his position on preferential hiring with his political views as follows:

    > Struggles for recognition in the democratic constitutional state possess legitimate strength only to the extent that all groups find access to the political sphere, that they all speak up, that they are all able to articulate their needs, and that no one is marginalized or excluded. From the viewpoint of representation and "qualification for citizenship," it is already important to secure the factual preconditions for equal opportunity to exercise formally equal rights. This is true not only of political participation, but also for social participation and for private rights to freedom, since no one can act in a politically autonomous fashion unless the conditions for private autonomy are guaranteed. In this connection I support quotas: for example, I support a policy of "preferred hiring" in all sectors of education and employment where that is the only way to secure the "fair value" of equal rights for historically and structurally disadvantaged groups. These measures are supposed to have "a remedial effect" and are therefore only temporary in nature.

    "A Conversation about Questions of Political Theory," in *A Berlin Republic: Writings on Germany*, trans. Steven Rendall (Lincoln: University of Nebraska Press, 1997), 150.
18. Charles Beitz, *Political Equality* (Princeton: Princeton University Press, 1989), esp. ch. 6; Thomas Pogge, "Group Rights and Ethnicity," in Will Kymlicka and Ian Shapiro, eds., *Ethnicity and Groups Rights,* Nomos no. 39 (New York: New York University Press, 1997), 187–221.
19. Of course, guaranteeing voice is not the same as guaranteeing power, although it is a first step. The guarantees of minority representation might be such that they ensure only that minorities elect a sufficient number of representatives so that their voice is heard, regardless of whether their proposals will be outvoted nevertheless. Guaranteeing power requires ensuring sufficient clout—even if this is attained through coalition building—to have proposals carry the day. I thank Thomas Pogge for discussions about this point.
20. See Rodolfo O. de la Garza et al., eds., *Latino Voices: Mexican, Puerto Rican, and Cuban Perspectives on American Politics* (Boulder: Westview Press, 1992).
21. Iris M. Young, "Polity and Group Difference," 262, 263.
22. I borrow the vocabulary of established and engendered effects of an institutional scheme from Thomas Pogge, who uses the term *established* to refer to those phenomena that are directly called for in the written or unwritten rules of a social system, and the term *engendered* to refer to phenomena that, although not directly called for by the relevant rules and procedures of an institutional scheme, foreseeably come about through them. See his *Realizing Rawls* (Ithaca: Cornell University Press, 1989), 38.
23. Iris M. Young, "Justice and Communicative Democracy," 136.
24. For a useful examination of the sense in which Habermas's account of democ-

racy is 'proceduralist,' see Keneth Baynes, "Democracy and the Rechtsstaat: Habermas's *Fakitizität und Geltung*," in *The Cambridge Companion to Habermas*, Stephen K. White, ed., (Cambridge: Cambridge University Press, 1995), pp. 201–232, especially pp. 214–15.

25. See, for example, Gerald Dworkin, "Paternalism," in Richard Wasserstrom, ed., *Morality and the Law* (Belmont, Calif.: Wadsworth, 1971), 107–26, and Richard Arneson, "Paternalism, Utility and Fairness," *Revue Internationale de Philosophie* 170 (1989): 409–23.
26. John Rawls, "Kantian Constructivism and Moral Theory," *Journal of Philosophy* 67 (1980): 543.

Bibliography

Ackerman, Bruce. 1980. *Social Justice and the Liberal State.* New Haven: Yale University Press.

Acuña, Rudolfo. 1988. *Occupied America,* 3rd ed. New York: HarperCollins.

Alarcón, Norma. 1994. "Traddutora, Traditora: A Paradigmatic Figure of Chicana Feminism." In Inderpal Grewal and Caren Kaplan, eds., *Scattered Hegemonies.* Minneapolis: University of Minnesota Press, 110–33.

Alcoff, Linda Martîn. 1997. "The Politics of Postmodern Feminism, Revisited." *Cultural Critique* 36 (Spring): 5–27.

———. 1999. "Latina/o Identity Politics." D. Bastone and E. Mendieta, eds., *The Good Citizen.* New York: Routledge, 93–112.

———. 1999. "The Phenomenology of Racial Embodiment." *Radical Philosophy* 95 (May-June): 15–26.

Allen, Anita. 1994. "Recent Racial Constructions in the U.S. Census," paper presented at the conference "Race: Its Meaning and Significance," Rutgers University, November.

Allen, Theodore W. 1994. *The Invention of the White Race,* vol. 1*: Racial Oppression and Social Control.* London: Verso.

———. 1997. *The Invention of the White Race,* vol. 2: *The Origin of Racial Oppression in Anglo-America.* London: Verso.

Anderson, Benedict. 1983. *Imagined Communities: Reflections on the Origin and Spread of Nationalism.* New York: Verso.

Anderson, Walter Truett. 1997. "'Denizens' to Become the New Citizens of the World." *Philadelphia Tribune,* April 29, 6A.

Anzaldúa, Gloria. 1987. *Borderlands/La Frontera.* San Francisco: Aunt Lute.

Apel, Karl-Otto. 1980. *Towards the Transformation of Philosophy.* Trans. Glyn Adley and David Frisby. London: Routledge and Kegan Paul.

Appiah, K. Anthony. 1992. *In My Father's House: Africa in the Philosophy of Culture.* New York: Oxford University Press.

———. 1994. "Identity, Authenticity, Survival: Multicultural Societies and Social Reproduction." In Amy Gutmann, ed., *Multiculturalism.* Princeton: Princeton University Press, 149–65.

———. 1997. "The Multicultural Misunderstanding." *New York Review of Books* 44, 15: 30–36.

Apple, R. W. Jr. 1998. "What's Next? Don't Guess after This Year." *New York Times,* December 20.

Arciniegas, Germán. 1975. *Latin America: A Cultural History.* New York: Alfred A. Knopf.

Arendt, Hannah. (1976 [1948]). *The Origins of Totalitarianism.* New York: Harcourt Brace and Company.

Arneson, Richard. 1989. "Paternalism, Utility and Fairness." *Revue Internationale de Philosophie* 170: 409–23.

Associated Press. 1998. "IRS Overhaul Bill Glides through House." *Star Tribune* (Minneapolis), June 26, 9A.

Balibar, Etienne. 1991. "Is There a Neo-Racism?" In Etienne Balibar and Immanuel Wallerstein, *Race, Nation, Class: Ambiguous Identities.* New York and London: Verso, 17–28.

Banton, Michael. 1987. *Racial Theories.* Cambridge: Cambridge University Press.

Barber, Benjamin. 1984. *Strong Democracy.* Berkeley: University of California Press.

Baubock, Rainer, Agnes Heller, and Aristide R. Zolberg, eds. 1996. *The Challenge of Diversity: Integration and Pluralism in Societies of Immigration* Avebury: Ashgate.

Behar, Ruth, ed. 1995. *Bridges to Cuba/Puentes a Cuba.* Ann Arbor: University of Michigan Press.

Beinart, Haim. 1983. *Los conversos ante el tribunal de la Inquisición.* San Juan: Río Piedras Ediciones.

Beiner, Ronald, ed. 1995. *Theorizing Citizenship.* Albany: State University of New York Press.

Beitz, Charles. 1989. *Political Equality.* Princeton: Princeton University Press.

Berger, Mark T. 1995. *Under Northern Eyes: Latin American Studies and U.S. Hegemony in the Americas, 1898–1990.* Bloomington: Indiana University Press.

Berry, Wendy. 1999. "America's Wealth Pyramid." *Washington Post,* January 6, A24

Bickel, Alexander. 1975. *The Morality of Consent.* New Haven: Yale University Press.

Blackstone, William T., and Robert D. Heslep, eds. 1977. *Social Justice and Preferential Treatment.* Athens: University of Georgia Press.

Blau, Peter. 1977. *Inequality and Heterogeneity.* New York: The Free Press.

Bohman, James. 1995. "Public Reason and Cultural Pluralism: Political Liberalism and the Problem of Moral Conflict." *Political Theory* 23: 253–79.

———. 1996. *Public Deliberation: Pluralism, Complexity, and Democracy.* Cambridge, Mass.: MIT Press.

Bohman, James and William Rehg. 1996. "Discourse and Democracy: The Formal and Informal Bases of Legitimacy in Habermas's *Faktizität und Geltung.*" *Journal of Political Philosophy* 4: 79–99.

Bolton, Herbert E. 1921. *The Spanish Borderlands: A Chronicle of Old Florida and the Southwest.* Albuquerque: University of New Mexico Press.

Bonilla, Frank. 1998. "Rethinking Latino/Latin American Interdependence: New Knowing, New Practice." In F. Bonilla et al., eds., *Borderless Borders: U.S. Latinos, Latin Americans, and the Paradox of Interdependence.* Philadelphia: Temple University Press, 217–30.

Bonilla, Frank, Edwin Meléndez, Rebecca Morales, and María de los Angeles Torres. 1998. *Borderless Borders: U.S. Latinos, Latin Americans and the Paradox of Interdependence.* Philadelphia: Temple University Press.

Boxill, Bernard. 1984. *Blacks and Social Justice.* Totowa: Rowman and Littlefield.

Bunge, Mario. 1995. "Testimonio de Mario Bunge." In Ana Barron et al., eds., *¿Porqué se fueron? Testimonios de argentinos en el exterior.* Buenos Aires: EMECE.

Bunis, Dena and Heather Macdonald. 1998. "Equity Goes South in Border-Check Plan: Immigration Proposals Call for Stricter Enforcement at the Mexican Border than at the Canadian Line, and Would Split the INS." *Orange County Register*, October 10, A17.

Cabán, Pedro. 1994. "The New Synthesis: Latin American and Latino Studies: Refurbishing or Challenging Hegemony in the Academy." Paper prepared for the Inter-University Program for Latino Research conference "The Global Society and the Latino Community," Bellagio, Italy, December, 12–16 (mimeo).

———. 1998. "The New Synthesis of Latin American and Latino Studies." In F. Bonilla et al., eds., *Borderless Borders: U.S. Latinos, Latin Americans and the Paradox of Interdependence.* Philadelphia: Temple University Press, 195–215.

Cardoso, Fernando Enrique. 1977. "The Consumption of Dependency Theory in the United States." *Latin American Research Review* 12, 3. Reprinted in Portuguese in *As Ideias e seu lugar.* Petropolis: Editora Vozes, 1993.

Carr, Raymond. 1984. *Puerto Rico: A Colonial Experiment.* New York: New York University Press.

Carter, Stephen. 1991. *Reflections of an Affirmative Action Baby.* New York: Basic Books.

Casteñeda, Jorge. 1995. *The Mexican Shock.* New York: New Press.

Chafe, William H. 1986. "The End of One Struggle, The Beginning of Another." In Charles W. Eagles, ed. *The Civil Rights Movement in America.* Jackson: University Press of Mississippi, 127–48.

Chavez, Leo. 1997. "Immigration Reform and Nativism: The Nationalist Response to the Transnationalist Challenge." In Juan F. Perea, ed., *Immigrants Out! The New Nativism and the Anti-Immigrant Impulse in the United States.* New York: New York University Press, 61–77.

Chávez, Linda. 1991. *Out of the Barrio: Toward a New Politics of Hispanic Assimilation.* New York: Basic Books.

Chronicle of Higher Education. 1998. "Disparities Grow in SAT Scores of Ethnic and Racial Groups." September 11, A42.

Cline, Howard F. 1966. "The Latin American Studies Association: A Summary Survey with Appendix." *Latin American Research Review* 2, 1: 57–79.

Cohen, Joshua. 1989. "Deliberation and Democratic Legitimacy." In A. Hamlin and Phillip Pettit, eds., *The Good Polity: Normative Analysis of the State.* Oxford: Polity Press, 17–34.

Cohen, Marshall, Thomas Nagel, and Thomas Scanlon, eds. 1977. *Equality and Preferential Treatment.* Princeton: Princeton University Press.

Connolly, William. 1993. *Identity/Difference.* Ithaca: Cornell University Press.

Corlett, J. Angelo. 1994. "The Problem of Collective Moral Rights." *Canadian Journal of Law and Jurisprudence* 7: 237–59.

———. 1998. "Analyzing Racism." *Public Affairs Quarterly* 12: 23–50.

———. 1999. "Latino Identity." *Public Affairs Quarterly* 13, 273–95.

———. 2000. "Surviving Evil: Jewish, African and Native Americans." *Journal of Social Philosophy* 31.

———. 2000. "Reparations to Native Americans?" In Aleksander Jokic, ed. *War Crimes and Collective Wrongdoing.* London: Blackwell.

Coronil, Fernando. 1996. "Beyond Occidentalism: Toward Nonimperial Geohistorical Categories." *Cultural Anthropology* 11, 1: 52–87.

Crenshaw, Kimberlé W. 1997. "Color Blindness, History and the Law." In Wahneema Lubiano, ed., *The House That Race Built: Black Americans, U.S. Terrain.* New York: Pantheon, 280–88.

Curry, George, ed. 1997. *The Affirmative Action Debate.* Reading, Mass.: Addison-Wesley.

Davila, Arlene. 2000. "Advertising and Latino Cultural Fictions." In Arlene Davila and Agustín Lao-Montes, eds., *Mambo Montaje: The Latinization of New York.* New York: Columbia University Press.

Davis, Angela Y. 1981. *Women, Race, and Class.* New York: Random House.

———. 1997. "Race and Criminalization: Black Americans and the Punishment Industry." In Wahneema Lubiano, ed., *The House That Race Built: Black Americans, U.S. Terrain.* New York: Pantheon, 264–79.

De Greiff, Pablo. 1998. "International Courts and Transitions to Democracy." *Public Affairs Quarterly* 12, 1: 79–99.

de la Cadena, Marisol. 1997. "Silent Racism and Intellectual Superiority in Peru." *Bulletin of Latin American Research,* May: 143–64.

de la Garza, Rodolfo O., et al., eds. 1992. *Latino Voices: Mexican, Puerto Rican, and Cuban Perspectives on American Politics.* Boulder: Westview Press.

Degler, Carl N. 1971. *Neither Black nor White: Slavery and Race Relations in Brazil and the United States.* New York: Macmillan.

Delgado, Richard. 1997. "Citizenship." In Juan F. Perea, ed., *Immigrants Out! The New Nativism and the Anti-Immigrant Impulse in the United States.* New York: New York University Press, 318–23.

———. 1998. "The Black/White Binary: How Does It Work?" In Richard Delgado and Jean Stefancic, eds., *The Latino/a Condition: A Critical Reader.* New York and London: New York University Press, 369–75.

Delgado, Richard, and Vicky Palacios. 1998. "Mexican Americans as a Legally Cognizable Class." In Richard Delgado and Jean Stefancic, eds., *The Latino/a Condition: A Critical Reader.* New York: New York University Press, 284–90.

Dietz, James L. *Economic History of Puerto Rico: Institutional Change and Capitalist Development.* Princeton: Princeton University Press.

Domínguez, Virginia. 1998. "Editor's Foreword: The Dialectics of Race and Culture, " *Identities: Global Studies in Culture and Power* 1, 4: 297–300.

Donoso, Antón. 1976. "The Society for Iberian and Latin American Thought (SILAT): An Interdisciplinary Project." *Los ensayistas: Boletín informativo* 1–2: 38–42.

Duany, Jorge. 1998. "Reconstructing Racial Identity: Ethnicity, Color, and Class among Dominicans in the United States and Puerto Rico." In Helen Safa, ed., "Race and National Identity in the Americas," special issue of *Latin American Perspectives* 25, 3: 147–72.

Dworkin, Gerald. 1971. "Paternalism." In Richard Wasserstrom, ed., *Morality and the Law.* Belmont, Calif.: Wadsworth, 107–26.

Dworkin, Ronald. 1981. "What Is Equality? Part I: Equality of Welfare." *Philosophy and Public Affairs* 10, 3: 185–246.

———. 1981. "What Is Equality? Part II: Equality of Resources." *Philosophy and Public Affairs* 10, 4: 283–345.
———. 1985. *A Matter of Principle.* Cambridge: Harvard University Press.
Elshtain, Jean Bethke. 1995. *Democracy on Trial.* New York: Basic Books.
Elster, Jon. 1986. "The Market and the Forum: Three Varieties of Political Theory." In Jon Elster and Aanund Hylland, eds., *Foundations of Social Choice Theory.* Cambridge: Cambridge University Press, 103–32.
Fanon, Franz. 1967. *Black Skin, White Masks.* New York: Grove.
Finkelman, Paul, ed. 1997. *Slavery and the Law.* Madison: Madison House.
Fishkin, James. 1995. *The Voice of the People: Public Opinion and Democracy.* New Haven: Yale University Press.
Flores, Juan. 1993. "'Qué assimilated, brother, yo soy asimilao': The Structuring of Puerto Rican Identity in the U.S." In *Divided Borders: Essays on Puerto Rican Identity.* Houston: Arte Publico Press.
———. 1997. "Latino Studies: New Contexts, New Concepts." *Harvard Educational Review* 67, 2: 208–21.
Flores, Juan, and George Yudice. 1990. "Buscando América: Languages of Latino Self-Formation." *Social Text* 24: 57–84.
Flores, William, and Rina Benmayor, eds., 1997. *Latino Cultural Citizenship: Claiming Identity, Space, and Rights.* Boston: Beacon Press.
Foner, Eric, and Olivia Mahoney. 1995. *America's Reconstruction: People and Politics after the Civil War.* New York: HarperCollins.
Forbes, Jack. 1992. "The Hispanic Spin: Party Politics and Governmental Manipulation of Ethnic Identity." *Latin American Perspectives* 19, 4: 59–78.
Foucault, Michel. 1970. *The Order of Things: An Archaeology of the Human Sciences.* New York: Random House.
Franklin, John Hope, et al. 1998. *One America in the Twenty-first Century: Forging a New Future: The Advisory Board's Report to the President.* Washington, D.C., September.
Fraser, Nancy. 1997. "From Redistribution to Recognition? Dilemmas of Justice in a 'Postsocialist' Age." In *Justice Interruptus: Cultural Reflections on the "Postsocialist" Condition.* New York: Routledge, 11–39.
Fredrickson, George M. 1999. "The Strange Death of Segregation." *New York Review of Books* 46, 8: 36–38.
Frye, Marilyn. 1983. "Oppression." In Marilyn Frye, *The Politics of Reality.* Trumansburg, N.Y.: The Crossing Press, 1–16.
Fuenzalida, Edmundo F. 1983. "The Reception of 'Scientific Sociology' in Chile." *Latin American Research Review* 18, 2: 95–113.
Fullinwider, Robert K. 1980. *The Reverse Discrimination Controversy.* Totowa: Rowman and Littlefield.
Furnefold, M. S. 1976 [1898]. "For the Restoration of White Supremacy in North Carolina." *Annals of America, 1895–1904.* Chicago: Encyclopaedia Britannica, 12:229–31.
García, John. 1997. "Latino Studies and Political Science: Politics and Power Perspectives for Latino Communities and Its Impact on the Discipline." Occasional paper no. 34, Julien Samora Research Institute, Michigan State University.
Gellner, Ernest. 1983. *Nations and Nationalism.* Ithaca: Cornell University Press.

Gerbi, Antonello. 1982 [1955]. *La disputa del Nuevo Mundo. Historia de una polémica, 1750–1900.* Trans. Antonio Alatorre. México: Fondo de Cultura Económica.

Giddens, Anthony. 1986. *The Constitution of Society.* Berkeley: University of California Press.

Gilroy, Paul. 1993. *The Black Atlantic: Modernity and Double Consciousness.* Cambridge: Harvard University Press.

Giménez, Martha. 1988. "Minorities and the World-System: Theoretical and Political Implications of the Internationalization of Minorities." In Joan Smith et al., eds., *Racism, Sexism and the World-System.* Westport, Conn.: Greenwood Press, 39–56.

Gitlin, Todd. 1995. *Twilight of Common Dreams: Why America Is Wracked by Culture Wars.* New York: Henry Holt.

Glazer, Nathan. 1983. *Ethnic Dilemmas: 1964–1982.* Cambridge: Harvard University Press.

———. 1995. "Individual Rights against Groups Rights." In Will Kymlicka, ed., *The Rights of Minority Cultures.* Oxford: Oxford University Press, 123–38.

———. 1997. *We Are All Multiculturalists Now.* Cambridge: Harvard University Press.

Goldberg, Carey. 1997. "Hispanic Households Struggle amid Broad Decline in Income." *New York Times,* January 30, 1, 16

Goldman, Alan H. 1979. *Justice and Reverse Discrimination.* Princeton: Princeton University Press.

Goodin, Robert. 1986. "Laundering Preferences." In Jon Elster and Aanund Hylland, eds., *Foundations of Social Choice Theory.* Cambridge: Cambridge University Press, 75–101.

Gooding-Williams, Robert. 1998. "Race, Multiculturalism, and Justice." *Constellations* 5, 1: 18–41.

Gordon, Lewis. 1995. *Bad Faith and Antiblack Racism.* Atlantic Highlands, N.J.: Humanities Press.

Gracia, Jorge J. E. 1998. *Filosofía hispánica: Concepto, origen y foco historiográfico.* Pamplona: Universidad de Navarra.

———. 1999. "The Nature of Ethnicity: With Special Reference to Hispanic/Latino Identity." *Public Affairs Quarterly* 13, 1: 25–42.

———. 1999. "Hispanics, Philosophy, and the Curriculum." *Teaching Philosophy* 23, 3: 241–8.

———. 2000. *Hispanic/Latino Identity: A Philosophical Perspective.* Oxford: Blackwell.

———, ed. 1988–89. "Latin America Philosophy. " *The Philosophical Forum* 20: 4–32.

Graham, Richard, ed. 1990. *The Idea of Race in Latin America, 1870–1940.* Austin: University of Texas.

Greenawalt, Kent. 1983. *Discrimination and Reverse Discrimination.* New York: Alfred A. Knopf.

Griswold del Castillo, Richard. 1997. "History from the Margins: Chicana/o History in the 1990s." Occasional paper no. 28, Julian Samora Research Institute, Michigan State University.

Grosfoguel, Ramón. 1997. "The Divorce of Nationalist Discourses from the Puerto Rican People: A Sociohistorical Perspective." In F. Negron-Muntaner and R. Grosfoguel, eds., *Puerto Rican Jam: Essays on Culture and Politics.* Minneapolis: University of Minnesota Press, 57–76.

Grosfoguel, Ramón, and Chloé S. Georas. 1996. "The Racialization of Latino Caribbean Migrants in the New York Metropolitan Area." *CENTRO Journal of the Center for Puerto Rican Studies* 8, 1–2.

———. 2000. "'Coloniality of Power' and Racial Dynamics: Notes towards a Reinterpretation of Latino Caribbeans in New York City," in *Identities.*

Gross, Barry R., ed. 1977. *Reverse Discrimination.* Buffalo: Prometheus Books.

Guinier, Lani. 1994. *The Tyranny of the Majority: Fundamental Fairness in Representative Democracy.* New York: Free Press.

Gutmann, Amy. 1983. "Communitarian Critics of Liberalism." *Philosophy and Public Affairs* 14: 308–22.

Habermas, Jürgen. 1990. *Moral Consciousness and Communicative Action.* Trans. Christian Lenhardt and Shierry Weber Nicholsen. Cambridge, Mass.: MIT Press.

———. 1993. *Between Facts and Norms.* Trans. W. Rehg. Cambridge, Mass.: MIT Press.

———. 1997. "A Conversation about Questions of Political Theory." In *A Berlin Republic: Writings on Germany.* Trans. Steven Rendall. Lincoln: University of Nebraska Press, 131–58.

———. 1998. "On the Internal Relationship between Democracy and the Rule of Law." *The Inclusion of the Other: Studies in Political Theory.* Ed. P. De Greiff and C. Cronin. Cambridge, Mass.: MIT Press, 253–64.

———. 1998. "Three Models of Democracy." *The Inclusion of the Other: Studies in Political Theory.* Ed. P. De Greiff and C. Cronin. Cambridge, Mass.: MIT Press, 203–36.

Hall, Stuart, and David Held. 1990. "Citizens and Citizenship." In Stuart Hall and Martin Jacques, eds., *New Times: The Changing Face of Politics in the 1990s.* New York: Verso, 173–90.

Hampton, Jean. 1997. *Political Philosophy.* Boulder: Westview Press.

Hannaford, Ivan. 1996. *Race: The History of an Idea in the West.* Baltimore: Johns Hopkins University Press.

Harris, Marvin. 1964. *Patterns of Race in the Americas.* New York: Walker and Company.

Harvey, David. 1996. *Justice, Nature and the Geography of Difference.* Oxford: Blackwell.

Hathaway, James C. 1995. "New Directions to Avoid Hard Problems: The Distortion of the Palliative Role of Refugee Protection." *Journal of Refugee Studies* 8, 3: 288–94.

Heginbotham, J. Stanley. 1994. "Rethinking International Scholarship." *Items* [Social Sciences Research Council] 48, 2–3: 33–40.

Henry, William A. III 1990. "Beyond the Melting Pot." *Time,* April 9, 28 ff.

Henze, Brent. 2000. "Who Says Who Says?: The Epistemological Grounds for Agency in Liberatory Political Projects." In Paula M. L. Moya and Michael R. Hames-García, eds., *Reclaiming Identity: Realist Theory and the Predicament of Postmodernism.* Berkeley: University of California Press.

Hernández, Tanya K. 1998. "Multiracial" Discourse: Racial Classifications in an Era of Color-Blind Jurisprudence, " *Maryland Law Review* 57, 1: 97–173.

Hill, Thomas E. Jr. 1991. "The Message of Affirmative Action." *Social Philosophy and Policy* 8: 108–29.

Hochschild, Jennifer. *Facing Up to the American Dream.* Princeton: Princeton University Press, 1996.

Hollinger, D. A. 1995. *Postethnic America: Beyond Multiculturalism.* New York: Basic Books.

———. 1997. "The Will to Descent: Culture, Color, and Genealogy." Lecture delivered at the National Humanities Center, Durham, N.C. (mimeo).

Holmes, Stephen. 1988. "Gag Rules or the Politics of Omission." In Jon Elster and Rune Slagstad, eds., *Constitutionalism and Democracy.* Cambridge: Cambridge University Press, 19–58.

Holmes, Steven A. 1998. "Clinton Panel on Race Urges Variety of Modest Measures." *New York Times,* September 17, A1.

hooks, bell. 1981. *Ain't I a Woman: Black Women in Feminism.* Boston: South End Press.

———. 1989. *Talking Back: Thinking Feminist, Thinking Black.* Boston: South End Press.

———. 1990. *Yearning: Race, Gender, and Cultural Politics.* Boston: South End Press.

Horsman, Reginald. 1981. *Race and Manifest Destiny: The Origins of American Racial Anglo-Saxonism.* Cambridge, Mass.: Harvard University Press.

Hulme, Peter. 1992. *Colonial Encounters: Europe and the Native Caribbean, 1492–1797.* London: Routledge.

Jackson, David, and Paul de la Garza. 1996. "Rep. Gutiérrez Uncommon Target of a Too Common Slur." *Chicago Tribune,* April 18, 1.

Jaggar, Alison. 1983. *Feminist Politics and Human Nature.* Totowa, N.J.: Rowman and Littlefield.

Johannsen, Robert W. 1985. *The Halls of the Montezumas: The American War in the American Imagination.* New York: Oxford University Press.

Johnson, Darlene. 1989. "Native Rights as Collective Rights: A Question of Self-Preservation." *Canadian Journal of Law and Jurisprudence* 2: 19–34.

Johnson, Kevin R. 1998. "Citizens as Foreigners." In Richard Delgado and Jean Stefancic, eds., *The Latino Condition: A Critical Reader.* New York: New York University Press, 198–201.

Johnson, Lyndon B. 1997. "To Fulfill These Rights." In George Curry, ed., *The Affirmative Action Debates.* Reading, Mass.: Addison-Wesley.

Jonas, Susanne. 1999. "Rethinking Immigration Policy and Citizenship in the Americas: A Regional Framework." In Susanne Jonas and Suzie Dod Thomas, eds., *Immigration: A Civil Rights Issue for the Americas.* Wilmington, Del.: Scholarly Resources, 99–118.

Kant, Immanuel. 1978 [1792]. *Anthropology from a Pragmatic Point of View.* Trans. V. L. Dowdell. Rev. and ed. H. H. Rudnick. Carbondale: Southern Illinois University Press.

Klor de Alva, Jorge, Earl Shorris, and Cornel West. 1998. "Our Next Race Question: The Uneasiness between Black and Latinos." In Antonia Darder and Rodolfo D.

Torres, eds., *The Latino Studies Reader: Culture, Economy and Society.* Oxford: Blackwell.

Knight, Alan. 1990. "Racism, Revolution, and *Indigenismo*: Mexico, 1910–1940." In Richard Graham, ed., *The Idea of Race in Latin America: 1870–1940.* Austin: University of Texas Press, 71–113.

Kymlicka, Will. 1989. *Liberalism, Community, and Culture.* Oxford: Oxford University Press.

———. 1995. *Multicultural Citizenship: A Liberal Theory of Minority Rights.* Oxford: Oxford University Press.

———. 1997. "Do We Need a Liberal Theory of Minority Rights?" *Constellations* 4, 1: 72–87.

Lagerspetz, Eerik. 1998. "On Language Rights." *Ethical Theory and Moral Practice* 2, 1: 181–99.

Laguerre, Michel S. 1998. *Diasporic Citizenship: Haitian Americans in Transnational America.* New York: St. Martin's Press.

Lange-Churión, Pedro. 1998. "Una hispanidad dialógical y conflictiva," in Quimera, 58–64.

Lao-Montes, Agustín. 1997. "Islands at the Crossroads: Puerto Ricaness Traveling between the Translocal Nation and the Global City." In F. Negro-Muntaner and R. Grosfogel, eds., *Puerto Rican Jam. Essays on Culture and Politics.* Minneapolis: University of Minnesota Press, 169–88.

———. 2000. "Introduction." In *Mambo Montaje: The Latinization of New York.*

Lauren, Paul Gordon. 1998. *The Evolution of International Human Rights: Visions Seen.* Philadelphia: University of Pennsylvania Press.

Lewis, Bernard. 1995. *Cultures in Conflict: Christians, Muslims, and Jews in the Age of Discovery.* Oxford: Oxford University Press.

Lodge, Henry Cabot. 1976[1895]. "For Intervention in Cuba." *Annals of America.* Chicago: Encyclopaedia Britannica, 12: 85–87.

Loewen, James W. 1996. *Lies My Teacher Told Me: Everything Your American History Textbook Got Wrong.* New York: Simon and Schuster.

López, Ian F. Haney. 1996. *White by Law: The Legal Construction of Race.* New York: New York University Press.

López Torregrosa, Luisita. 1998. "Latino Culture Whirls onto Center Stage." *New York Times,* March 26, E1, E6.

Lugones, María. 1987. "Playfulness, 'World-Travelling,' and Loving Perception." *Hypatia: A Journal of Feminist Philosophy* 2, 2: 3–19.

———. 1994. "Purity, Impurity and Separation." *Signs: Journal of Women in Culture and Society* 19, 2: 458–79.

Lugones, María, and Elizabeth V. Spelman. 1983. "Have We Got a Theory for You! Feminist Theory, Cultural Imperialism and the Demand for 'the Woman's Voice.'" *Women's Studies International Forum* 6, 6: 573–81.

Manning, Patrick. 1990. *Slavery and African Life: Occidental, Oriental and African Slave Trades.* Cambridge: Cambridge University Press.

Marshall, Ineke Haen. 1977. "Minorities, Crime and Criminal Justice in the United States." In I. H. Marshall, ed., *Minorities, Migrants and Crime: Diversity and Similarity across Europe and the United States.* Thousand Oaks, Calif.: Sage Publications, 1–35.

Martí, José. 1979. *Política de Nuestra América*. Ed. José Aricó. México: Siglo XXI.

Martínez, Elizabeth. 1998. *De Colores Means All of Us: Latina Views for a Multi-Colored Century*. Boston: South End Press.

Marx, Anthony W. 1998. *Making Race and Nation: A Comparison of South Africa, the United States, and Brazil*. Cambridge: Cambridge University Press.

Marx, Karl. 1978 [1843]. "On the Jewish Question." In *The Marx-Engels Reader*. Ed. Robert Tucker. New York: Norton, 26–52.

Mason, Peter. 1990. *Deconstructing America: Representations of the Other*. London: Routledge.

Mato, Daniel. 1997. "Problems in the Making of Representations of All-Encompassing U.S. Latina/o—'Latin' American Transitional Identities." *The Latino Review of Books* 3, 1–2: 2–7.

May, Larry. 1987. *The Morality of Groups*. Notre Dame: University of Notre Dame Press.

———. 1993. *Sharing Responsibility*. Chicago: University of Chicago Press.

McCarthy, Thomas. 1991. "Practical Discourse: On the Relation of Morality to Politics." In *Ideals and Illusions: On Reconstruction and Deconstruction in Contemporary Critical Theory*. Cambridge, Mass.: MIT Press, 181–99.

———. 1995. "Legitimacy and Diversity: Dialectical Reflections on Analytic Distinctions." *Cardozo Law Review* 17: 1083–125.

Mendel-Reyes, Meta. 1995. *Reclaiming Democracy: The Sixties in Politics and Memory*. New York: Routledge.

Merkx, Gilbert W. 1995. "Foreign Area Studies Back to the Future?" *LASA Forum* 26, 2: 5–8.

Michel, Luo. 1998. "Group Claims Some Police Officers Posed as Hispanics in Order to Gain Employment." *Buffalo News*, January 20, B1, B10.

Mignolo, Walter D. 1993. "Colonial and Postcolonial Discourse: Cultural Critique or Academic Colonialism?" *Latin American Research Review* 28, 3: 120–31.

———. 1996. "Postoccidentalismo: Las epistemologias fronterizas y el dilema de los estudios (latinoamericanos) de areas." *Revista Iberoamericana* 62, 176–77: 679–96.

———. 1998. "Globalization, Civilization Processes and the Relocation of Languages and Cultures." In F. Jameson and M. Miyoshi, eds., *The Cultures of Globalization*. Durham: Duke Unversity Press, 33–53.

———. 1999. "Colonialidad del poder y diferencia colonial." *Anuario Mariateguiano*. Lima.

———. 2000. *Local Histories/Global Designs: Coloniality, Subaltern Knowledges and Border Thinking*. Princeton: Princeton University Press.

Mill, John Stuart. 1978 [1859]. *On Liberty*. Indianapolis: Hackett.

Miller, David. 1995. *On Nationality*. Oxford: Oxford University Press.

Miller, Richard B. 1996. *Casuistry and Modern Ethics*. Chicago: University of Chicago Press.

Minority Rights Group. 1995. *No Longer Invisible: Afro-Latin Americans Today*. London: Minority Rights Group.

Minow, Martha. 1990. *Making All the Difference*. Ithaca: Cornell University Press.

Mitchell, Christopher. 1992. "Introduction." In Christopher Mitchell, ed. *Western*

Hemisphere Immigration and United States Foreign Policy. University Park: Pennsylvania State University Press.

Mohanty, Satya. 1997. *Literary Theory and the Claims of History: Postmodernism, Objectivity, Multicultural Politics*. Ithaca: Cornell University Press.

Moody-Adams, Michele. 1997. "Excitable Speech: A Politics of the Performative." *Women's Review of Books* 15,1 (October): 13–14.

Moore, Joan. 1997. "Latino/a Studies: The Continuing Need for New Paradigms." Occasional paper no. 29, Julian Samora Research Institute, Michigan State University.

Mörner, Magnus, ed. 1965. *Race and Class in Latin America*. New York: Columbia University Press.

Morsink, Johannes. 1999. *The Universal Declaration of Human Rights: Origins, Drafting and Intent*. Philadelphia: University of Pennsylvania Press.

Mouffe, Chantal. 1996. "Democracy, Power and the Political." In Seyla Benhabib, ed. *Democracy and Difference*. Princeton: Princeton University Press, 245–56.

Moya, Paula. 1997. "Postmodernism, 'Realism,' and the Politics of Identity: Cherríe Moraga and Chicana Feminism." In M. Jacqui Alexander and Chandra Talpade Mohanty, eds., *Feminist Genealogies, Colonial Legacies, Democratic Futures*. New York: Routledge.

Moya, Paula, and Michael Hames-García, eds. 2000. *Reclaiming Identity: Realist Theory and the Predicament of Postmodernism*. Berkeley: University of California Press.

Nagel, Thomas. 1973. "Equal Treatment and Compensatory Discrimination." *Philosophy and Public Affairs* 2: 348–63.

National Council of La Raza. 1998. *NCLR Joins Poverty Dialogue Project*. May 1.

National Research Council. 1987. *Summary Report: Doctorate Recipients from the United States Universities*. Washington, D.C.: National Academy Press.

Netanyahu, Benzion. 1992. *The Origins of the Inquisition in Fifteenth Century Spain*. New York: Random House.

Oboler, Suzanne. 1995. *Ethnic Labels/Latino Lives: Identity and the Politics of (Re)presentation in the United States*. Minneapolis: University of Minnesota Press.

———. 1999. "Anecdotes of Citizen's Dishonor in the Age of Cultural Racism: Toward a (Trans)national Approach to Latino Studies." *Discourses* 21, 3.

Okin, Susan Moller. 1989. *Justice, Gender, and the Family*. New York: Basic Books.

Omi, Michael, and Howard Winant. 1986. *Racial Formation in the United States: From the 1960s to the 1980s*. New York: Routledge.

Oquendo, Angel R. 1998. "Re-imagining the Latino/a Race." In Richard Delgado and Jean Stefancic, eds., *The Latino/a Condition: A Critical Reader*. New York: New York University Press, 60–71.

Pagden, Anthony. 1993. *European Encounters with the New World*. New Haven: London: Yale University Press.

———. 1995. *Lords of All the World: Ideologies of Empire in Spain, Britain and France c. 1500–1800*. New Haven: Yale University Press.

Pederson, Rena. 1995. "Diversity and Assimilation." *Dallas Morning News*, April 4, 21.

Perea, Juan F. 1998. "The Black/White Paradigm of Race." In Richard Delgado and Jean Stefancic, eds., *The Latino/a Condition: A Critical Reader*. New York: New York University Press, 359–68.

Perlez, Jane. 1998. "A Wall Not Yet Built Casts the Shadow of Racism." *New York Times*, July, A4.

Phillips, Anne. 1995. *The Politics of Presence*. Oxford: Oxford University Press.

———. 1996. "Dealing with Difference: A Politics of Ideas, or a Politics of Presence." In Seyla Benhabib, ed., *Democracy and Difference*. Princeton: Princeton University Press, 139–52.

Pletsch, Carl E. 1981. "The Three Worlds, or the Division of Social Scientific Labor, circa 1950–75." *Comparative Studies in Society and History* 23, 4: 565–90.

Pogge, Thomas. 1989. *Realizing Rawls*. Ithaca: Cornell University Press.

———. 1997. "Group Rights and Ethnicity." In Will Kymlicka and Ian Shapiro, eds., *Ethnicity and Groups Rights*, Nomos no. 39. New York: New York University Press, 187–221.

Popper, Karl R. 1966. *The Open Society and Its Enemies*. 5th ed. Princeton: Princeton University Press.

Postrel, Virginia, and Nick Gillespie. 1995. "On Borders and Belonging: A Conversation with Richard Rodriguez." *Utne Reader*, March–April, 76–79.

Proceedings and Addresses of the American Philosophical Association 61, 2 (1987); 66, 5 (1993); 70, 2 (1996).

Quijano, Aníbal. 1997. "Colonialidad del poder, cultura y conocimiento en América Latina." *Anuario Mariateguiano* 9, 9: 113–21.

———. 1998. "The Colonial Nature of Power and Latin America's Cultural Experience." In R. Briceño-León and H. R. Sonntag, eds., *Sociology in Latin America*, proceedings of the ISA Regional Conference for Latin America, Venezuela, July 7–9, 1997. International Sociological Association, 27–38.

Quijano, Aníbal, and I. Wallerstein. 1992. "Americanity as a Concept, or the Americas in the Modern World-System." *ISSA* 1, 134: 549–54.

Rawls, John. 1971. *A Theory of Justice*. Cambridge: Harvard University Press.

———. 1980. "Kantian Constructivism and Moral Theory." *Journal of Philosophy* 67: 515–72.

Rhea, Joseph Tilden. 1997. *Race Pride and the American Identity*. Cambridge, Mass.: Harvard University Press.

Ribeiro, Darcy. 1972. *The Americas and Civilization*. New York: E. P. Dutton.

Rivera-Cusicanqui, Silvia. 1993. "Mestizaje colonial andino: una hipótesis de trabajo." In X. Albo, ed., *Violencias encubiertas en Bolivia*. Vol. 1: *Cultura y Política*. La Paz: CIPCA, 55–96.

Rodríguez, Clara E. 1989. *Puerto Ricans Born in the U.S.A.* Boston: Unwin Hyman.

Rodríguez, Nestor. 1999. "The Battle for the Borders: Autonomous Migration, Transnational Communities and the State." In Susanne Jonas and Suzie Dod Thomas, eds., *Immigration: A Civil Rights Issue for the Americas*. Wilmington, Del.: Scholarly Resources, 131–44.

Rodríguez, Richard. 1983. *Hunger of Memory: The Education of Richard Rodriguez*. New York: Bantam Books.

———. 1992. *Days of Obligation: An Argument with My Mexican Father*. New York: Penguin.

Roemer, John. 1986. "Equality of Resources Implies Equality of Welfare." *Quarterly Journal of Economics* 101: 751–84.

Romero, Mary. 1992. *Maid in the U.S.A.* London: Routledge.

Romero, Mary, Pierre Hondagneu-Sotelo, and Vilma Ortíz, eds. 1997. *Challenging Fronteras: Structuring Latina and Latino Lives in the U.S.* New York: Routledge.

Root, Maria P. P., ed. 1996. *The Multiracial Experience: Racial Borders as the New Frontier.* Thousand Oaks, Calif.: Sage Publications.

Rosaldo, Renato. 1989. *Culture and Truth: The Remaking of Social Analysis.* Boston: Beacon Press.

Rout, Leslie. 1976. *The African Experience in Spanish America.* New York: Cambridge University Press.

Rufino dos Santos, José. 1996. "O Negro Como Lugar." In Marcos Chor Maio and Ricardo Ventura Santos, eds., *Raça, ciência e sociedade.* Rio de Janeiro: Editora Fiocruz, 219–24.

Ruiz, Ramón Eduardo, ed. 1963. *The Mexican War: Was It Manifest Destiny?* Hinsdale, Ill.: Dryden Press.

Sachs, Lowell. 1999. "Recent Changes in U.S. Immigration Policy and Attitudes." In Susanne Jonas and Suzie Dod Thomas, eds., *Immigration: A Civil Rights Issue for the Americas.* Wilmington, Del.: Scholarly Resources, 145–56.

Safa, Helen I. 1998 . "Introduction." Special issue of *Latin American Perspectives,* 25, 3: 3–20.

———, ed. 1998. "Race and National Identity in the Americas." Special issue of *Latin American Perspectives* 25, 3.

Said, Edward. 1978. *Orientalism.* New York: Vintage Books.

Saldívar, José. 1992. *The Dialectics of Our America: Genealogy, Cultural Critique and Literary History.* Durham: Duke University Press.

Sánchez Korrol, Virginia. 1983. *From Colonia to Community: The History of Puerto Ricans in New York City.* Berkeley: University of California Press.

Sartori, Giovanni. 1994. *Comparative Constitutional Engineering: An Inquiry into Structure, Incentives, and Outcomes.* New York: New York University Press.

Sartre, Jean-Paul. 1976. *Critique of Dialectical Reason.* Ed. Jonathan Ree, trans. Alan Sheridan-Smith. Atlantic Highlands, N.J. : Humanities Press.

Sassen, Saskia. 1996. *Losing Control? Sovereignty in an Age of Globalization.* New York: Columbia University Press.

Schlesinger, Arthur Jr. 1992. *The Disuniting of America: Reflections on a Multicultural Society.* New York: W. W. Norton and Co.

Schmickle, Sharon. 1998. "Dispute over Canada Border Restrictions Heats Up in Congress." *Star Tribune* (Minneapolis), July 31, 16A.

Schutte, Ofelia. 1993. *Cultural Identity and Social Liberation in Latin American Thought.* Albany: State University of New York Press.

Shafer, Gershon. 1998. *The Citizenship Debates: A Reader.* Minneapolis: University of Minnesota Press.

Shklar, Judith. 1991. *American Citizenship: The Quest for Inclusion.* Cambridge: Harvard University Press.

Shorris, Earl. 1994. *Latinos: Biography of the People.* New York: Avon.

Sicroff, Albert A. 1960. *Les controverses des statuts de "pureté de sang" en Espagne du XVème au XVIIème siècle.* Paris: Didier.

Sitkoff, Harvard. 1993. "The Struggle for Black Equality: 1954–1992." New York: Hill and Wang.

Skidmore, Thomas. 1972. "Toward a Comparative Analysis of Race Relations since Abolition in Brazil and the United States." *Journal of Latin American Studies* 4, 1: 1–28.

———. 1993. "Bi-racial U.S.A. vs. Multi-Racial Brazil: Is the Contrast Still Valid?" *Journal of Latin American Studies* 25: 373–86.

Smith, Rogers. 1997. *Civic Ideals: Conflicting Visions of Citizenship in U.S. History.* New Haven, Conn.: Yale University Press.

Spelman, Elizabeth. 1988. *Inessential Woman.* Boston: Beacon Press.

Steele, Shelby. 1990. *The Content of Our Character: A New Vision of Race in America.* New York: St. Martin's Press.

Steinberg, Stephen. 1974. *The Academic Melting Pot: Catholics and Jews in Higher Education.* New York: McGraw-Hill.

Stepan, Nancy Leys. 1996. *"The Hour of Eugenics": Race, Gender and Nation in Latin America.* Ithaca: Cornell University Press.

Stephanson, Anders. 1995. *Manifest Destiny. American Expansion and the Empire of Right.* New York: Hill and Wang.

Stolke, Verena. 1994. "Is Sex to Gender as Race Is to Ethnicity?" In Teresa del Valle, ed., *Gendered Anthropology.* New York: Routledge.

Subirats, Eduardo. 1994. *El Continente Vacio.* Mexico: Siglo XXI Editores.

Sunstein, Cass. 1988. "Beyond the Republican Revival." *Yale Law Journal* 97: 1549–90.

———. 1989. "Democracy and Shifting Preferences." In A. Hamlin and Phillip Pettit, eds., *The Good Polity: Normative Analysis of the State.* Oxford: Polity, 196–230.

Suro, Robert. 1998. *Strangers among Us: How Latino Immigration Is Transforming America.* New York: Alfred A. Knopf.

Tabucci, Antonio. 1998. "En busca de un tribunal." *El Pais Semanal.* Special edition: "50 Aniversario de la Declaración de Derechos Humanos." *Diario El País.* December 6. (http//www.elpais.es/p/d/especial/derechos/princi.htm).

Takagi, Dana Y. 1998. *The Retreat from Race: Asian-American Admissions and Racial Politics.* New Brunswick: Rutgers University Press.

Takaki, Ronald T. 1993. *A Different Mirror: A History of Multicultural America.* Boston: Little, Brown.

Tannenbaum, Frank. 1946. *Slave and Citizen: The Negro in the Americas.* New York: Vintage Books.

Taylor, Charles. 1984. "Hegel: History and Politics." In Michael Sandel, ed., *Liberalism and Its Critics.* New York: New York University Press, 177–99.

———. 1985. "Atomism." In *Philosophy and the Human Sciences: Collected Papers.* Cambridge: Cambridge University Press, 2: 187–210.

———. 1994. "The Politics of Recognition." In Amy Gutmann, ed., *Multiculturalism: Examining the Politics of Recognition*, 2nd ed. Princeton: Princeton University Press, 25–73.

Toranzo Roca, Carlos F., ed. 1992. *Diversidad Etnica y Cultural.* La Paz: Instituto Latinoamericano de Investigaciones Sociales.

———, ed. 1993. *Lo pluri-multi o el reino de la diversidad.* La Paz: Instituto Latinoamericano de Investigaciones Sociales.

Toro, Luis Angel. 1998. "Race, Identity, and 'Box Checking': *The Hispanic Classification in OMB Directive No. 15.*" In Richard Delgado and Jean Stefancic, eds., *The*

Latino/a Condition: A Critical Reader. New York: New York University Press, 52–59.

Travis, Alan. 1998. "Fortress Europe's Four Circles of Purgatory." *The Guardian* (London), October 20, 19.

Trouillot, Michel-Rolph. 1995. *Silencing the Past: Power and the Production of History*. Boston: Beacon Press.

U.S. Bureau of the Census. 1966. *Statistical Abstract of the United States, 1966*, 116th ed. Washington, D.C.: U.S. Government Printing Office.

U. S. Bureau of the Census, Population Division. 1988. *Development of the Race and Ethnic Items for the 1990 Census*. New Orleans: Population Association of America, April.

Unamuno, Miguel de. 1966. "Hispanidad." In *Obras completas*. Madrid: Exelsior, 4: 1081–4.

Uslar Petri, Arturo. 1997. "The Other America." In Ilan Stavans, ed., *The Oxford Book of Latin American Essays*. New York: Oxford University Press, 207–15.

Varese, Stefano. 1996. "Parroquialismo y globalización. Las etnicidades indígenas ante el tercer milenio." In S. Varese, ed., *Pueblos indios, soberanía y globalismo*. Quito: Abya-Yala, 15–30.

Vigil, James Diego. 1980. *From Indians to Chicanos*. Prospect Heights: Waveland Press.

von Humboldt, Alexander, and Aimé Bonpland. 1970. *Voyage aux régions équinoxiales du Nouveau Continent*. Stuttgart: F. A. Brockhaus.

Wachtel, Nathan. 1984. "The Indian and the Spanish Conquest." In Leslie Bethell, ed., *The Cambridge History of Latin America*. Vol. 1: *Colonial Latin America*. Cambridge: Cambridge University Press, 207–48.

Wade, Peter. 1997. *Race and Ethnicity in Latin America* . London: Pluto Press.

Wallerstein, Immanuel. 1974. *The Modern World-System: Capitalist Agriculture and the Origins of the European World-Economy in the Sixteenth Century*. New York: Academic Press.

———. 1987. "World-System Analysis." In A. Giddens and J. H. Turner, eds., *Social Theory Today*. Cambridge: Polity, 309–24.

———. 1991. *Geopolitics and Geoculture. Essays on the Changing World-System*. Cambridge: Cambridge University Press.

———. 1995 "The Insurmountable Contradictions of Liberalism: Human Rights and the Rights of Peoples in the Geoculture of the Modern World-System." In *After Liberalism*. New York: New Press, 145–61.

Wallerstein, Immanuel, C. Juma, E. Fox Keller, J. Kocka, D. Lecourt, V. Y. Mudimbe, K. Mushakoji, I. Prigogine, P. J. Taylor, and M-R. Trouillot. 1996. *Open the Social Sciences*. Report of the Gulbenkian Commission on the Restructuring of the Social Sciences. Stanford: Stanford University Press.

Walzer, Michael. 1997. *On Toleration*. New Haven, Conn.: Yale University Press.

Ward, Cynthia V. 1991. "The Limits of 'Liberal Republicanism': Why Group-Based Remedies and Republican Citizenship Don't Mix." *Columbia Law Review* 91: 581–607.

Wasserstrom, Richard. 1980. "Preferential Treatment." In Richard Wasserstrom, ed. *Philosophy and Social Issues*. Notre Dame: University of Notre Dame Press.

Weber, David. 1988. "Turner, the Boltonians and the Borderland." In *Myth and the*

History of the Hispanic Southwest. Albuquerque: University of New Mexico Press, 33–54.

———. 1991. "The Idea of the Spanish Borderland." In David Thomas, ed., *Columbian Consequences: The Spanish Borderlands in Pan-American Perspective.* Washington, D.C.: Smithsonian Institution Press, 3, 3–20.

Webster's Third New International Dictionary. Chicago: Encyclopaedia Britannica Inc., 1966.

Wicksell, Knut. 1958. "A New Principle of Just Taxation." In R. A. Musgrave and A. T. Peacock, eds., *Classics in the Theory of Public Finance.* London: Macmillan.

Williams, Patricia. 1997. *Seeing a Color Blind Future: The Paradox of Race.* New York: Farrar, Straus, and Giroux.

Williamson, Edwin. 1992. *The Penguin History of Latin America.* New York: Penguin Books.

Wilson, William J. 1978. *The Declining Significance of Race: Blacks and Changing American Institutions.* Chicago: University of Chicago Press.

———. 1997. *When Work Disappears: The World of the New Urban Poor.* New York: Knopf.

Winant, Howard. 1994. *Racial Conditions: Politics, Theory, Comparisons.* Minneapolis: University of Minnesota Press.

Winn, Peter. 1993. *Americas: The Changing Face of Latin America and the Caribbean.* New York: Pantheon Books.

Wittgenstein, Ludwig. 1965. *Philosophical Investigations.* New York: Macmillan.

Young, Iris M. 1989. "Polity and Group Difference: A Critique of the Ideal of Universal Citizenship." *Ethics* 99: 250–74.

———. 1990. *Justice and the Politics of Difference.* Princeton: Princeton University Press.

———. 1993. "Justice and Communicative Democracy." In Roger Gottlieb, ed., *Radical Philosophy. Tradition, Counter-Tradition, Politics.* Philadelphia: Temple University Press, 123–43

———. 1995. "Together in Difference Transforming the Logic of Group Political Conflict." In Will Kymlicka, ed., *The Rights of Minority Cultures.* Oxford: Oxford University Press, 155–76.

———. 1997. "Difference as a Resource in Democratic Communication." In James Bohman and William Rehg, eds., *Deliberative Democracy.* Cambridge: MIT Press, 383–406.

Zack, Naomi. 1993. *Race and Mixed Race.* Philadelphia: Temple University Press.

Contributors

Linda Martín Alcoff is professor of philosophy, political science, and women's studies, and Laura J. and L. Douglas Meredith Professor, at Syracuse University. She works in epistemology, continental philosophy, feminism, and race theory. Among recent publications are *Feminist Epistemologies*, coedited with Elizabeth Potter (1993), *Real Knowing: New Versions of the Coherence Theory* (1996), the edited volume *Epistemology: The Big Questions* (1998), "Philosophy and Racial Identity," in *Radical Philosophy* (1996), "The Problem of Speaking for Others," in *Cultural Critique* (1991–92), and "Cultural Feminism vs. Poststructuralism: The Identity Crisis in Feminist Theory," *Signs* (1988).

J. Angelo Corlett is assistant professor of philosophy at San Diego State University. He works in moral, social, and political philosophy, and in epistemology. He is the founding Editor-in-Chief of *The Journal of Ethics*. Among recent publications are *Analyzing Social Knowledge* (1996), "Secession and Native Americans" in *Peace Review* (forthcoming), "Can Terrorism Be Morally Justified?" in *Public Affairs Quarterly* (1996), "Marx and Rights," in *Dialogue* (1994), "What Is Civil Disobedience?" in *Philosophical Papers* (1997), "Interpreting Plato's Dialogues," in *The Classical Quarterly* (1997), and "Collective Moral Responsibility," in *Journal of Social Philosophy* (forthcoming).

Pablo De Greiff is assistant professor of philosophy at the State University of New York at Buffalo. He works in ethics and social and political philosophy. Among recent publications are the edited volume *Drugs and the Limits of Liberalism* (1999), *The Inclusion of the Other: Studies in Political Theory, by Jürgen Habermas*, coedited with Ciaran Cronin (1998), *Deliberative Democracy and Transnational Politics* coedited with Ciaran Cronin (2000), "International Tribunals and Transitional Democracy," in *Public Affairs Quarterly* (1998), and "Trial and Punishment: Pardon and Oblivion," in *Philosophy and Social Criticism* (1996).

Jorge J. E. Gracia is Samuel P. Capen Chair and SUNY Distinguished Professor of Philosophy at the State University of New York at Buffalo. He works in metaphysics, historiography, theory of interpretation, medieval philosophy, and Hispanic philosophy. Among recent publications are *Hispanic/Latino Identity: A Philosophical Perspective* (2000), *Metaphysics and Its Task: The Search for the Categorial Foundation of Knowledge* (1999), *Texts: Ontological Status, Identity, Author, Audience* (1996), *A Theory of Textuality: The Logic and Epistemology* (1995), and *Philosophy and Its History: Issues in Philosophical Historiography* (1992).

Eduardo Mendieta is assistant professor of philosophy and ethics at the University of San Francisco. Among his recent publications are the edited volumes *Toward a*

Transcendental Semiotics (1994), *Ethics and the Theory of Rationality* (1996), and *The Underside of Modernity* (1996), and the coedited volumes *Liberation Theologies, Postmodernity and the Americas* (1997) and *The Good Citizen* (1999).

Walter D. Mignolo is William H. Wannamaker Professor of Literature and Romance Studies, and professor of literature and cultural anthropology at Duke University. He works on colonial and global issues. Among recent publications are *The Darker Side of the Renaissance: Literacy, Territoriality and Colonization* (1995), *Writing Without Words: Alternative Literacies in Mesoamerica and the Andes*, coedited with Elizabeth Hill Boone (1994), and *Local Histories/Global Designs: Coloniality, Subaltern Knowledges and Border Thinking* (2000).

Elizabeth Millán-Zaibert is assistant professor of philosophy at DePaul University. She works in early-German Romanticism and Latin American and Spanish philosophy. Among recent publications is "The Essay as Literary Form and The Problem of Spain's Identity in Ortega's Philosophy," in *Dissens* (1996); with Jorge Gracia, she is the coauthor of articles on Alejandro Korn, Latin American philosophy, Luis de Molina, José Ortega y Gasset, and Francisco Suárez for the *Oxford Companion to Philosophy* (1995). She has translated M. Beuchot's *Mexican Colonial Philosophy* (1998), and has translated and written an introduction to M. Frank's *The Philosophical Foundations of Early German Romanticism* (1999).

Paula M. L. Moya is assistant professor of English at Stanford University. She works in American literature, Chicana/o and U.S. Latina/o literature, and minority and feminist theoretical perspectives. Among recent publications are "Postmodernism, 'Realism,' and the Politics of Identity: Cherríe Moraga and Chicana Feminism," in M. Jacqui Alexander and Chandra Talpade Mohanty, eds., *Feminist Genealogies, Colonial Legacies, Democratic Futures* (1997), and *Reclaiming Identity: Realist Theory and the Predicament of Postmodernism*, coedited with Michael Hames-García (2000); she is currently working on a book entitled *Learning from Experience: Realist Theory and Chicana/o Identity.*

Suzanne Oboler is associate professor of ethnic studies and American civilization at Brown University. She works in issues related to race and citizenship in the Americas, ethnicity, and Hispanics/Latinos. Among her recent publications are *Ethnic Labels/Latino Lives: Identity and the Politics of (Re)Presentation in the United States* (1995) and "Racializing Latinos in the United States: Toward a New Research Paradigm," in Lilana Goldin, ed., *Identities on the Move: Transnational Processes in North America and the Caribbean Basin* (1999).

Thomas W. Pogge is associate professor at Columbia University. He works in moral and political philosophy, and on Kant. Among recent publications are "Human Flourishing and Universal Justice," in *Social Philosophy and Policy* (1999); "A Global Resource Dividend," in David A. Crocker and Toby Linden, eds., *Ethics of Consumption: The Good Life, Justice, and Global Stewardship* (1998); "The Bounds of Nationalism," in Jocelyn Couture et al., eds., *Rethinking Nationalism: Canadian Journal of Philosophy Supplementary Volume 22* (1998); "Three Problems with Contractarian-Consequentialist Ways of Assessing Social Institutions," in *Social Philosophy and Policy* (1995); "How Should Human Rights Be Conceived?" in *Jahrbuch für Recht und Ethik* (1995); and "Cosmopolitanism and Sovereignty," in *Ethics* (1992).

Ofelia Schutte is professor of women's studies and philosophy at the University of South Florida at Tampa. She works in feminist theory, continental philosophy, Latin American philosophy, and the philosophy of culture. Among her publications are *Cultural Identity and Social Liberation in Latin American Thought* (1993); *Beyond Nihilism: Nietzsche without Masks* (1984); "Cultural Alterity: Cross-Cultural Communication and Feminist Thought in North-South Dialogue," in *Hypatia* (1998); "Latin America," in A. Jaggar and I. M. Young, eds., *A Companion to Feminist Philosophy* (1998); and "A Critique of Normative Heterosexuality: Identity, Embodiment, and Sexual Difference in Beauvoir and Irigaray," in *Hypatia* (1997).

Iris Marion Young is professor of political science at the University of Chicago. She works in feminist theory and political philosophy. She is the author and editor of several books, including *Justice and the Politics of Difference* (1990), *Throwing like a Girl and Other Essays in Feminist Philosophy and Social Theory* (1990), and *Intersecting Voices: Dilemmas of Gender, Political Philosophy and Policy* (1997). The Oxford Series in Political Theory will publish her book *Inclusion and Democracy* in 2000, from which the argument of her chapter in this book is derived.

Leonardo Zaibert is assistant professor of philosophy at Grand Valley State University. He works in the philosophy of law and moral and political philosophy. Among recent publications are "On Deference and the Spirit of the Laws," *Archiv für Rechts- und Sozialphilosophie* (1996), "Intentionality, Voluntariness and Criminal Liability: A Historical-Philosophical Analysis" in *Buffalo Criminal Law Review* (1998), and "Philosophy of Law in Latin America," coauthored with Jorge J. E. Gracia, in Christopher B. Gray, ed., *The Philosophy of Law: An Encyclopedia* (1999). Forthcoming are: "Collective Intentions and Collective Intentionality," *American Journal of Sociology and Economics*, "Philosophical Analysis and the Criminal Law," *Buffalo Criminal Law Review*, and "The Construction of Social Reality," in B. Smith, ed., *John Searle.*

Subject Index

affirmative action, 5, 14–16, 30, 129–132, 176, 223–224; goals of, 205–222, 227–234; pros and cons of, 63–64, 201–222; recipients of, 78–79, 176, 201–204, 206–222, 227–234
asimilao(s), 6, 8; value of being, 77–98 (esp. 89–90)
assimilation (acculturation): alternative of, 46; logic of, 5; as an individual or as a group, 62–66; general vs. critical, 8; neoconservative minorities' ideal of, 83–85; pros and cons of, 62–66, 77–98, 101–103

behavior: political vs. market, 238
biculturality, 66–75

category(-ies): administrative, 4; as convention, 24, 68–75; black, 4; cultural, 1–9; establishment of by location, 104–105; ethnic, 1–9, 36–44, 132–144; history of Hispanic/Latino, 3–4, 15, 45–60, 99–109; insulting, 3; of citizenship and rights, 128–132; racial, 1–9, 28–33, 36–44, 71–75; sub-categories for Hispanics, 51–54, 68–70; white vs. black, 4, 32–33, 36–44, 49–50, 131; "woman of color" as a, 71–72
civil rights: call for new framework for, 46; movement, 62, 126–132
class: as differentia, 1, 9, 46
colonial difference, 99–124
colonialism: history of and relation to Hispanic/Latino identity, 51–59, 99–109
coloniality of power, 7–8, 99–110
communication: importance of cross-cultural, 86–89
community of equals: problems facing a, 126–139
criollos, 52–53 culture(s): of scholarship, 99–124

deliberation: political, 16–17 (*see* discourse theory)
deliberative democracy, 16–17, 19, 235–254
deracialization: 39, 44
dialogicity, 239–248
discourse theory: 16–17, 19, 239–247
discrimination: ethnic vs. racial, 62, 229–230; legacy of, 150; redress for, 2–3, 16–17, 30, 172–173, 227–234 (*see also* restitution); structural, 17, 125–139, 161–162; (*see also* racism)
duty: of a just public education system, 193–200

education: as differentia, 1, 9; minorities in higher, 63–66; debate over bilingual, 78, 181–200; of children (public), 12–14, 94n., 190–200; principal duty of, 12–14, 193–200
epistemic advantage: 16–17, 243–244; of identity politics, 90–94
epistemic difference, 101, 109–124
equality: formal, 185; linguistic, 160–161; of opportunity, 11–12, 14–15, 208–211; political (civil), 236
essentialism: critiques of, 18–20, 28–33, 61–76, 99–124, 151–154, 173–177, 204–205; moderate, 15–16, 18, 223–227

ethnicity: concept of, 24; Hispanics as an, 49; paradigm, 33–36; supposition of, 47 (*see also* identity)
ethno-race, 3–4, 42
exclusion: racial, 45–47

family resemblance: as basis for relational account of identity, 14–15, 18, 204–205

gender: as differentia, 46, 208–211
globalization: its effects on racial formation, 56, 132–144
governmentalization: processes of, 19, 29

hegemony: racial, 56
Hispanic(s)/Latino(s): divisions of (Colombian, Cuban-American, Latino, Mexican American, Puerto Rican, etc.), 5, 24–36, 47–48, 66–75, 99–109, 174–175, 208–211; ethnicity, 1–9; identity, 1–9, 17–20, 23–44, 61–76, 99–124, 125–144, 173–177, 204–205, 222–227; in American academia, 109–124, 177, 201–204, 215–222; population growth in America, 1; racializing, 48–56; rights, 1–2, 9–17, 125–144, 173–180; social practices and institutions, 49
history: of racial categories, 4, 7–8, 45–59, 127–144; relevance for understanding Hispanics/Latinos, 2, 7–9, 18, 39, 45–59, 99–109, 127–144 (in Latin America, 4, 7, 46–59; in U.S., 4, 46–59)

identity: construction of Latino/a, 61–70; essentialist account of, 223–227; group (collective), 2–3, 6, 10–12, 23–44, 61–76; Hispanic concern with, 28–33; hybrid identities, 66–75; individual, 6, 61–76; individual vs. group, 61–66, 77–98, 151–154, 182–186; negotiating novel, 5, 61–75; refusal of racial 78–85; relational vs. essentialistic approaches to, 18–20, 204–205; strategic vs. metaphysical (essentialistic) considerations in regard to, 15–16, 23–33, 36–44; theories of, 28–33; various philosophical approaches to, 18–20, 99–124, 151–154, 173–177, 204–205
ideology(-ies): individualistic, 2–3, 25–28; new ideology of race, 8–9; of race, 35; racist ideologies employed against Native Americans, 55; racial, 125–144
inclusion: democratic, 45–47
inequality (or disadvantages): chosen vs. imposed, 182–193; economic, 46, 130–131, 186; structural, 11–12, 125–144, 154–166
International Monetary Fund, 63

justice: claim for or to, 8–12, 49, 56, 145–166, 205, 211, 218–219; corrective, 232; distributive, 231–233; vs. utility, 206–207, 211–213, 218–219

labels: 3; and the impact of globalization, 134–135; 'Hispanic', 7, 132–144; negotiating racial, 48; official bureaucratic (white, Asian or Pacific Islander, black, American Indian or Alaskan Native, Hispanic), 8, 31, 127, 132
language(s): and language rights, 181–200; as differentia, 1, 6, 9, 14, 18, 87–88, 101, 159–161, 204–205; as means to negotiate identity, 68–69; Ayamara, 101; English, 7, 49, 68, 159, 181–200; French, 7, 49; German, 7; Guaraní, 49; Italian, 7; Latin, 7, 52; Nahuatl, 49, 52; Portuguese, 7, 49; Quechua, 49, 101; Spanish, 7, 68, 74, 101, 159, 181–200; Toltec, 49
language instruction: in English, 11, 12–14, 190–200
latina: the concept of, 5, 68–69
legitimation: processes of, 19
liberal democracy, 236–237
liberal principle, 12–14, 181–200

liberalism: classical, 16–17, 19, 168–170, 182–185, 192–197

marketing and advertisement: as race-determining forces, 18–19, 28–33, 66–67
Melting Pot, 83, 133
mestizos, 52–53
mestiza(je), 7, 52, 56–57, 68–69, 107–108, 131, 174
mulattos, 52–53
multiculturalism: current idiom of, 38; debates about, 101–102, 116–124; defense of, 6–7; realist conception of, 90

narratives: historical, 47–59; legitimizing, 39
nationalism: its relation to arguments concerning group rights, 168–170
negros, 52–53
neoconservative minority critics: 6, 25, 77–98
norms: rational acceptability of, 16–17, 239–247

Office of Budget and Management (U.S.), 8, 35, 132
oppression: descriptions of, 154–162
other groups, in so far as they shed light on the questions concerning Hispanics/Latinos: (as racial, national, cultural, religious, or some combination thereof) African, 52, 54; African American, 4, 7, 25, 35–40, 48, 102, 133, 172, 201, 208–211, 226, 228, 230–231; Afro-Latinos, 102; all of those which affected Hispanics/Latinos, 99–124; Amerindians, 4, 7, 51–56, 101; Anglo-Saxon, 7, 54–55, 102, 186, 227–231; Asian American, 201; Canadians, 73; English, 153; Europeans, 2, 73; European Americans, 26, 38; Frenchmen, 55; German, 48; Indians, 55; Irish, 3, 25, 38–39, 48, 172; Italians, 3, 25, 48; Jews, 3–4, 38–39, 54; Maori, 153; Mexicans, 73; Muslims, 4; Native Americans, 25, 39, 230–231; Pilgrims, 48; Portuguese, 52; Spanish-Christian white, Spaniards, 4, 51–56; women, 208–211, 228, 230–231

participation in the life of the nation, 211–214
particularity: cultural, 77–98; vs. universal humanity, 86–89
philosophy: relevance of this book to, 2; Hispanic, 216–222; Hispanics working in, 15, 201–204, 215–222
philosophical approaches: postmodern vs. traditional, 18–20, 77–98, 99–124
politics: emancipatory, 151; group representation in, 235–247; of Hispanic/Latino concerns, 9; of knowledge, 116–124; of location, 73–74; of recognition, 27, 148
politics of difference: 10–12, 19, 147–166
politics of identity: 10–12, 23–44, 73–74, 90–94, 145–166; critiques of, 149–151
principle(s): difference, 188; liberal, 19, 188, 191
properties of Hispanics/Latinos: 1–9, 14–15 (*see* Hispanics/Latinos, and identity)
public policy: 15–16 (*see* affirmative action)

race: as differentia, 1, 46; assessing the realities of, 36–44; concept of, 24–36; dilemma of, 45–46; Hispanizing, 45, 48–56; history of race in U.S. and Latin America, 45–59 (*see also* identity)
racialization: 3–4, 8–9, 24, 36–44, 46, 48, 81, 139, 161–162
racism: in Latin America, 8–9, 18, 24; directed against individual vs. directed against group, 62–66; persistence of (particularly in U.S.), 8–9, 125–144, 161–162, 229–230, 232–233
racismo, 50, 58

relational accounts of identity, 1, 6, 10–12, 61–76, 204–205
religion: 1, 14, 49, 213
representation: group, 235–247; guaranteed, 16–17; political, 9, 14–15
restitution (or reparation): debate concerning, 12, 14–17, 167–180, 208–211, 227–229, 232–233
rights: accommodation, 9, 12–14, 181–200; as group, 1, 9, 12, 65–66, 125–144, 205–222, 245–246; as individual, 1, 9, 12; claims to, 49, 65–66, 158–166; discourse theory of, 242–247; distribution of, 170–173; Hispanic/Latino, 1; human, 9, 137, 169–170; individual vs. group, 167–180; linguistic, 9, 181–200; of citizenship, 9, 128–144; question of, 132–144; special vs. general, 167–180

SAT, 24, 33, 203
slavery, 56
social ontology, 23–44
society of equals: unlikelyhood of, 8–9; liberal (in classical sense),12–14
Society for Iberian and Latin American Thought (SILAT), 217
solidarity: Latin American, 27–28; negative aspects of, 18; with other racialized people of color, 41
stereotyping, 161–162
strategy: restitutive vs. representational, 167–168, 176
studies: area, 99–124; Hispanic/Latino, 7–8, 63, 99–124; Latin American, 7–8, 99–124; subaltern, 107–108
subalternation of knowledge, 7–8, 107–108

Universal Declaration of Human Rights, 137, 169, 173
universal humanity: a realist approach to, 86–89
universalism: vs. particularism, 167–180
universality: of neoconservative critics, 6, 77–98
University at Buffalo, SUNY, 20, 201–202, 234
Univisión, 30, 184

values: Enlightenment vs. other systems, 77–90; Hispanic/Latino, 1; North vs. South American, 68–75; traditional liberal, 19

war: Civil (U.S.), 106; Cold, 7; Korean, 125; Mexican revolution of 1910, 52; Mexican-American, 207; Spanish-American, 7, 210; Vietnam, 201; World War II, 100, 109, 131, 209
welfare state: crisis of, 50
world-system analysis: 7, 45–59, 99–110; First, Second, Third Worlds, 7, 45–59

Name Index

Ackerman, Bruce, 198
Acuna, Rudolf, 234
Addelson, Kathryn P., 220
Adley, Glyn, 251
Alarcón, Norma, 75
Alatorre, Antonio, 122
Alcoff, Linda, 2–3, 5, 18, 23–44, 59, 200
Alcott, Louisa May, 231
Alexander, M. Jacqui, 97
Allen, Anita, 33, 43
Allen, Theodore W., 59, 122
Almaguer, Tomás, 123, 234
Alva, Jorge Klor de, 34–35, 43, 58
Anderson, Benedict, 143
Anderson, Walter Truett, 136–137, 143
Angelelli, Ignacio, 216
Anthony, Susan B., 231
Antony, Louise, 220
Anzaldúa, Gloria, 5, 68–69, 74
Apel, Karl-Otto, 16, 251
Appiah, Anthony, 35, 43, 119, 124, 179
Arciniegas, Germán, 54, 59
Arendt, Hannah, 105, 122–123, 137, 139, 143
Arneson, Richard, 253

Baez, Anthony, 135
Balibar, Etienne, 133, 141
Banton, Michael, 140
Barber, Benjamin, 249
Baron, Ana, 221
Barragan, 114
Barret, Linton Lomas, 59
Barret, Marie McDavid, 59
Baubock, Rainer, 143
Behar, Ruth, 75
Beinart, Haim, 122
Beiner, Ronald, 143
Beitz, Charles, 243, 252
Belnap, J., 124
Benhabib, Seyla, 165
Benmayor, Pina, 143
Berger, Mark T., 121, 123
Berry, Wendy, 144
Bethell, Leslie, 59
Beveridge, A., 123
Bianchi, Maria Eugenia Matute, 132
Bickel, Alexander, 139
Blackstone, William T., 233
Blau, Peter, 155, 165
Bohman, James, 164, 178, 251
Bolívar, Simón, 27
Bolton, Herbert Eugene, 100, 123
Bonilla, Frank, 111–112, 123–124, 142
Bordo, Susan, 220
Borges, 31
Boxill, Bernard, 233
Briceno-León, R., 120
Brimlow, Peter, 141
Buffon, Leclerc de, 106
Bunge, Mario, 216, 221
Bunis, Dena, 144
Burgess, John William, 122

Cabán, Pedro, 113, 115, 123, 144
Cadena, Marisol de la, 132, 141
Cardoso, Fernando Enrique, 112, 123
Carr, Raymond, 96
Carril, Mario del, 221
Carter, Stephen, 6, 81, 84–85, 88, 94, 96
Casanova, González, 114
Castañeda, Jorge, 138, 144
Castillo, Richard Griswold del, 111, 121, 123

Chafe, William H., 140
Chavez, Leo, 140, 143
Chávez, Linda, 6, 77–78, 81, 85, 94, 96
Cline, Howard F., 121
Code, Lorraine, 221
Cohen, Joshua, 250
Cohen, Marshall, 233
Connolly, William, 165
Conyers, Rep., 140
Cook, Captain, 153
Corlett, Angelo, 9, 15–16, 18, 20, 179, 211, 219, 223–234
Coronil, Fernando, 121
Cortés, 52, 54
Crenshaw, Kimberlé W., 139
Cronin, Ciaran, 250, 252
Curry, George, 140
Cusicanqui, Rivera, 114

Darwin, Charles, 109
Davida, Arlene, 124
Davila, Arlene, 30, 42–43
Davis, Anela Y., 109, 144, 234
Degler, Carl N., 58
De Greiff, Pablo, 9, 16–20, 57, 144
Delgado, Richard, 42–43, 57, 139, 233–234
Dietz, James L., 96
Dominguez, Virginia, 37, 43
Donoso, Antón, 221
Dowdell, V.L., 122
Duany, Jorge, 143
Dussel, 114
Dworkin, Gerald, 253
Dworkin, Ronald, 177, 185, 187, 198

Eagles, Charles W., 140
Elshtain, Jean Bethke, 42, 150, 164
Elster, Jon, 250

Fanon, Franz, 62, 74
Finkelman, Paul, 57
Flores, Juan, 43, 89, 97, 123–124
Flores, William, 143
Foner, Eric, 139
Forbes, Jack, 141
Foucalt, Michael, 19, 29, 43
Frank, Gunther, 112
Frank, Rep. Barney, 140
Frankenbury, Nancy, 221
Franklin, Benjamin, 95
Franklin, John Hope, 140
Fraser, Nancy, 59, 164
Fredrickson, George M., 59
Frisby, David, 251
Frye, Marilyn, 154, 165
Fuenzalida, Edmundo F., 121
Fullinwider, Robert K., 233
Furnefold, M.S., 122

García, John A., 111, 123
Garza, Paul de la, 125, 139
Garza, Rodolfo de la, 253
Gellner, Ernest, 170, 178
Georas, Chloé S., 35, 37, 43, 121
Gerbi, Antonello, 122
Giddens, Anthony, 122, 156, 165
Gillespie, Nick, 94
Gilroy, Paul, 40–41, 44
Giménez, Martha, 142–143
Gitlin, Todd, 26, 42, 150, 164
Glazer, Nathan, 57, 121, 132, 141, 220
Gobineau, Count Arthur de, 105, 108–109
Goldberg, David Theo, 42
Goldman, Alan H., 233
Gómez, Albino, 221
Gómez-Lobo, Alfonso, 216
Gómez, Máximo, 75
Goodin, Robert, 250
Gooding-Williams Robert, 40–41, 44
Gordon, Lewis, 40, 44
Gottlieb, Roger, 249
Gracia, Jorge, 6, 9–10, 14–15, 16, 18, 20, 31–33, 38, 41–43, 49, 57, 59, 140, 145, 153, 164–165, 178–179, 201–222, 223–231, 233–234, 248
Graham, Richard, 59, 141
Grant, Linda, 143
Greenawalt, Kent, 233
Grosfuguel, Ramón, 35, 37, 43, 115, 121, 124
Gross, Barry R., 233
Guevara, Che, 27
Guinier, Lani, 249

Gutiérrez, Luis, 125–126, 134, 139
Gutman, Amy, 96, 121, 179, 249

Habermas, Jürgen, 16, 28, 235, 241–247, 249–252
Hale, Charles R., 141
Hall, David, 139
Hall, Stuart, 139
Hames-García, Michael, 94, 97
Hamlin, A., 249–250
Hampton, Jean, 165
Hankins, Frank Hamilton, 122
Hannaford, Ivan, 59
Harris, Leonard, 220
Harris, Marvin, 58–59
Harvey, David, 150, 164
Hathaway, James, 137, 144
Hegel, G.W.F., 106
Heginbotham, J. Stanley, 121
Heller, Agnes, 143
Henry, William A. III, 141
Henze, Brent, 97
Hernandez, Ezequiel, 135
Hernandez, Tania, 141
Heslep, Robert D., 233
Hill, Thomas E. Jr., 233
Hochschild, Jennifer L., 42
Hollinger, 105, 116–118, 122, 124
Hollingsworth, Stacia, 125
Holmes, Steven A., 140, 250
Hondagneu-Sotelo, Pierre, 57
Honore, Carl, 143
hooks, bell, 40, 234
Horsman, Reginad, 59, 121
Hulme, Peter, 58
Hylland, Aanund, 250

Jackson, Andrew, 95
Jackson, David, 125, 139
Jackson, Jesse, 35
Jacques, Martin, 139
Jaggar Alison, 82, 95, 221
Jameson, F., 121
Jefferson, Thomas, 95
Johannsen, Robert W., 123
Johnson, Darlene, 172, 178
Johnson, Kevin R., 139
Johnson, Lyndon B., 36, 129, 133, 140
Jonas, Susanne, 143
Juma, C., 123

Kant, Immanuel, 86, 104–105, 122
Keller, Fox, 123
Kenyatta, Jomo, 84
King, Rep. Peter, 140
Knight, Alan, 59
Kocka, J., 123
Korrol, Virginia Sánchez, 96
Korsmeyer, Carolyn, 221
Kymlicka, Will, 168–169, 177–178, 181–188, 190–194, 197–200, 220, 249, 252

Lagerspetz, Eerik, 199
Laguerre, Michel, S., 115, 124
Lange-Churión, Pedro, 50, 58
Lao, Augusto, 42
Lao-Montes, Agustín, 115, 124
Lauren, Paul Gorden, 178
Laviera, Tato, 77, 89
Leahy, Sen. Patrick, 144
Lecourt, D., 123
Leguizamo, John, 44
Lenhardt, Christian, 251
Lewis, Bernard, 58
Limón, José, E., 123
Linnaeus, 105
Lodge, Henry Cabot, 122
Loewen, James W., 95
Lubiano, Wahneema, 139, 144
Lugones, María, 75, 152, 164

Macdonald, Heather, 144
MacIntyre, Alasdair, 249
Maclean, Joan, 59
Mahoney, Olivia, 139
Maio, Marcos Chor, 141
Manning, Patrick, 122
Marshall, Ineke Haen, 140, 144
Martí, José, 27, 52, 69, 74–75
Martínez, Elizabeth, 140, 144
Marx, Anthony W., 58
Marx, Karl, 249
Mason, Peter, 58

Mato, Daniel, 30, 42–43
May, Larry, 164
McCarthy, Thomas, 251
McGary, Howard, 220
Meléndez, Edwin, 123, 142
Mendel-Reyes, Meta, 140
Mendieta, Eduardo, 3–5, 18, 45–59
Merkx, Gilbert W., 121
Mignolo, Walter, 7–8, 18–19, 99–124, 248
Mihoshi, M., 121
Mill, John Stuart, 240, 251
Millán-Zaibert, Elizabeth, 9, 12, 19, 167–180, 219
Miller, David, 150, 164
Miller, Richard B., 249
Minnow, Martha, 164
Mitchell, Christopher, 142
Mohanty, Chandra Talpade, 97
Mohanty, Satya, 86–87, 90, 94, 96–97
Montejano, David, 123
Moody-Adams, Michelle, 41, 44
Moore, Joan, 111, 123
Moraga, Cherríe, 97
Morales, Rebecca, 123, 142
Mörner, Magnus, 141
Morsink, Johannes, 178
Mouffe, Chantal, 165
Moya, Paula, 5–8, 10, 18–19, 77–98, 102
Mudimbe, V.Y., 123
Musgrave, R.A., 199
Mushakoji, K., 123
Myrdal, Gunnar, 45

Nagel, Thomas, 233–234
Nandy, Ashis, 125, 139
Negro-Muntaner, F., 124
Netanyahu, B., 58
Nicholsen, Shierry Weber, 251
Nixon, Richard, 201

Oboler, Suzanne, 8–9, 18, 20, 29, 43, 120, 124, 125–144, 220
Okin, Susan, 155, 165
Omi, Michael, 28, 38, 43, 47, 57, 141
Oquendo, Angel R., 24, 33–34, 42–43
Ortiz, Vilma, 57
Outlaw, Lucius, 220

Paggen, Anthony, 58–59
Palacios, Vicky, 233–234
Parry, William, 201–202
Peacock, A.T., 199
Pederson, Rena, 96
Pedraza, Silvia, 123
Perea, Juan F., 57, 140, 143
Perlez, Jane, 143
Pettit, Philip, 249–250
Philips, Anne, 164, 249
Pizarro, 52, 54
Pletsch, Carl, 110, 123
Pogge, Thomas W., 9, 12–14, 18–20, 99, 174–175, 178, 181–200, 220, 243, 248, 252–253
Popper, Karl, 170–171, 173
Postrel, Virginia, 94

Quijano, Anibal, 103–105, 114–115, 120–122

Ramos, Demetria, 122
Rawls, John, 187–188, 198–199, 248, 253
Ree, Jonathan, 165
Rehg, William, 164, 178, 249, 251
Rendall, Steven, 252
Rhea, Joseph Tilden, 57
Ribeiro, Darcy, 59
Rivera-Cusicanqui, Silvia, 121
Roca, Carlos F. Toranzo, 121
Rodó, 52
Rodriguez, Clara, 34, 43
Rodríguez, Nestor, 143
Rodríguez, Richard, 6, 77–85, 88, 94–97, 118
Roemer, John, 187, 198
Romero, Mary, 57, 234
Root, Maria P.P., 141
Rosaldo, Renato, 95
Rout, Leslie, 141
Rudnick, H.H., 122
Ruiz, Ramón Eduardo, 123

Safa, Helen I., 59, 143
Sahagún, Bernardino de, 106
Said, Edward, 121

Saldívar, Jose, 121, 123
Sandel, Michael, 249
Santos, José Rufino dos, 141
Santos, Ricardo Ventura, 141
Sarmiento, Domingo Faustino, 108
Sartori, Giovanni, 250
Sartre, Jean-Paul, 157, 165
Sassen, Saskia, 143–144
Scanlan, Thomas, 233
Schlesinger, Arthur, 26, 42
Schmickle, Sharon, 144
Schutte, Ofelia, 3–6, 18–20, 29, 61–75, 96–97, 178, 216
Shafer, Gershon, 143
Shapiro, Ian, 178, 197, 220, 252
Shklar, Judith N., 57
Shorris, Earl, 58–59
Sicroff, Albert A., 122
Sitkoff, Harvard, 140
Skidmore, Thomas, 58–59
Skrentny, John David, 220
Smith, Alan Sheridan, 165
Smith, Jane, 142
Smith, Rogers, 57
Sonntag, H.R., 121
Sosa, Ernesto, 216
Spelman, Elizabeth V., 75, 152, 164, 221
Stavenhagen, 114
Steele, Shelby, 6, 77–85, 88, 94–97
Stefancic, Jean, 42–43, 57, 139, 233
Steinberg, Stephen, 179
Stepan, Nancy Leys, 141
Stephanson, Anders, 122
Stolke, Verena, 142
Subirats, Eduardo, 55, 59
Sunstein, Cass, 235, 249–250
Suro, Roberto, 46, 57–58

Tabucci, António, 141
Takagi, Dana Y., 58
Takaki, Ronald T., 57
Tannenbaum, Frank, 58
Taylor, Charles, 96, 121, 160, 163, 249
Taylor, J.P., 123
Thomas, David, 121
Thomas, Judge Clarence, 40
Toro, Luis Angel, 35, 43
Torregrosa, Luisita López, 142
Torres, María de los Angeles, 123, 142
Torres, Rodolfo D., 58
Travis, Alan, 143
Trouillot, Michel-Rolph, 120, 123
Tuana, Nancy, 221
Tucker, Robert, 249
Turnbull, Robert, 217
Turner, J.H., 122

Unamuno, Miguel de, 219
Ureña, 52

Vaconcelos, 52
Valle, Teresa del, 142
Varese, Stefano, 121
Vigil, James Diego, 234

Wachtel, Nathan, 59
Wade, Peter, 51, 58–59, 130, 140–141
Wallerstein, Immanuel, 7, 100, 103–104, 120–123, 141
Walzer, Michael, 121
Ward, Cynthia V., 249
Wasserstrom, Richard, 233, 253
Waters, Rep., 140
Weber, David, 121, 123
West, Cornel, 34, 43, 58
Wicksell, Knut, 199
Williams, Patricia, 40, 44
Williamson, Edwin, 59
Wilson, William J., 58, 141, 165
Winant, Howard, 28, 38, 43, 47–48, 57, 140–141
Winn, Peter, 49, 57–58
Wittgenstein, Ludwig, 14–15, 18, 204–205, 219

Young, Iris M., 6, 9–12, 18, 100, 120, 145–166, 173, 178, 220, 235, 241, 244–245, 248–249–251, 253
Yudice, George, 43

Zack, Naomi, 35, 43
Zaibert, Leonardo, 9, 12, 19, 167–180, 219
Zolberg, Aristide R., 143